GREAT CUISINES
OF THE WORLD

GREAT CUISINES OF THE WORLD

CONTENTS

ACKNOWLEDGMENTS

This book is dedicated to the talented chefs of Hyatt International Hotels, whose contributions have made this book possible.

Designed and produced by Liane Sebastian and Kathleen Aiken, Synthesis Concepts Inc. Chicago, U.S.A.

Graphic advice by Alain Chan, Ottawa, Canada.

Section photography by Toni Soluri, Chicago, U.S.A.

Props for section photography taken at the residence of 1420 North Dearborn Parkway, Chicago, U.S.A.

Selected food photography by Studio Tangs, Singapore.

Selected photography by Helmut Horn, Chicago, U.S.A.

Cookbook consultation by Carole Berglie.

Proofreading for British English by Zephyr Cooper.

Proofreading of recipes by Karen Underwood, Lake Forest, U.S.A.

Published by PBC International, Glen Cove, New York, U.S.A.

Printed by Toppan Printing Company (H.K.) Ltd.

Maps for pgs. 10, 11, and the cities of Xian, Surabaya, Guadalajara, Acapulco, Saipan, Auckland, Jakarta, Villahermosa, Adelaide, Tahiti, and Bali, © 1990 Esselte Map Service, Stockholm, Sweden.

Other maps © Instituto Geografico DeAgostini, 1988, from the Illustrated Atlas of the World, published by Rand McNally, Chicago, U.S.A.

Library of Congress Cataloging-in-Publication Data
Great cuisines of the world/by the chefs of Hyatt International Hotels.
    p. 464 cm. 23 x 30.5
  ISBN 0-86636-118-9
  1. Cookery, International. I. Hyatt International, Inc.
TX725.A1G719 1989
641.59—dc20   89-71122
                                    CIP

HOW TO USE THIS BOOK

The recipes in this book include three sets of measurements: Imperial, U.S. customary, and metric. Depending on where you live, you should follow the set of measurements you are accustomed to. Be sure to follow the same measurements throughout the recipe; don't switch from Imperial to metric, for example. Note also that measurement conversions are not precise. They have been rounded off for ease of use.

Most recipes in the book serve 4 persons. However, serving size is a variable concept and your preference may be different. For example, portions in many Asian-style recipes are smaller than in Western dishes. This is because Asian meals often consist of several dishes in combination. Read all recipes through before beginning to cook. Note if sauces or basic recipes should be prepared first, before beginning the last-minute portion of the dish. In particular, check your sequence of steps for more complicated recipes. We have broken down the steps, but you may prefer to space out the procedure differently to avoid too much last-minute preparation.

It is recommended that you read the Glossary and Basics Section prior to cooking any of the recipes.

ABBREVIATIONS

c	cup	**lb**	pound
C	Celsius	**ml**	millilitre
cm	centimetre	**mm**	millimetre
F	Farenheit	**oz**	ounces
fl oz	fluid ounces	**pc**	piece
g	gram	**pt**	pint
gal	gallon	**qt**	quart
kg	kilogram	**tbs**	tablespoon
l	litre	**tsp**	teaspoon

INTRODUCTION

Wider, wilder horizons: it comes with the territory of the New Age Traveller. The world has not shrunk; just the intimidations formerly associated with global wandering.

○

And a zest for international adventure—new countries, different languages, beautiful cultures—also comes with a taste for new flavours. Today's traveller is quick to grab opportunities to sample local and regional cuisines.

○

In the last two decades an increasing number of ethnically diverse foods have taken popular hold in different countries. Key kitchens such as French, Chinese, Japanese, Thai, Indian, Italian and Spanish can be experienced almost universally.

○

The continued diffusion of a variety of foods has resulted in new trends, the so-called "Marriage of Cuisines". The crossing of culinary traditions has combined elements of old and new styles with local and foreign menus to create new recipes, tastes and presentations.

○

Recognising this, Hyatt chefs were encouraged to draw upon a variety of courses to provide the guest with simple and practical cooking instructions to produce authentic flavours of an international range of dishes.

○

Hyatt International's unique food and beverage philosophy dictates that they no longer operate "typical" hotel restaurants. They create restaurants that appeal and cater to the local market. If the local market remains pleased and interested, visitors are certain to be equally impressed.

○

Now is the best time to experience and experiment. Using Great Cuisines of the World, the reader can cook and serve an appetizer from the Philippines, a soup from Mexico, a main dish from Japan, and a dessert from France in his or her own home.

○

Food is an essential and exciting part of experiencing a new country and culture. We invite you to "cook up" many adventures . . . and share them with your friends.

CHINESE CUISINE

No people in the world maintain as high a degree of culinary consciousness as the Chinese. It is said that if you ate a different Chinese dish every day for 20 years you would not exhaust the repertoire. A vast land of great diversity, China offers an infinite variety of foods. Its gastronomic selection is full of such curious delicacies as bear's paw, camel's hump, shark's fin, and fish lips.

To understand the diversity of Chinese cuisine, one must look at its roots, the country's regional cooking styles. China's culinary regions fall under broad categories: Northern—Peking, Shantung and Anhui, Eastern/Coastal—Chekiang, Fukien and Kiangsu, Western/Central—Hunan and Szechuan, and Southern—Cantonese. In Chinese cuisine, different preparation methods range from barbecuing, braising, stewing, sautéing, stir-frying and smoking, to steaming.

Noodles, steamed buns and dumplings are the staples of the northern provinces. The food is light, elegant, and mildly seasoned. Eastern cuisine is characterised by the use of sugar to sweeten dishes, with rice wine providing a pungency to many sauces. The western region is known for its hot, spicy and distinctly seasoned food, while dishes from the south are often cooked with thick but delicate sauces to enhance the tint, taste and

fragrance of the main ingredients.

It has been suggested that China's preoccupation with food was a result of chronic food scarcity. As a result, economy in the use of materials and fuel is a hallmark of Chinese cooking. Meat and fish used in small quantities are eaten with rice or wheat products. Fruits, fish, and roots are dried, smoked, and preserved in the spring and summer for use during the long and frequently harsh winter.

The sophisticated refinement and high aesthetic standards of Chinese cooking are an extension of Chinese cosmic theories and medical practices. Chinese cuisine and eating habits strictly observe seasonality, and the Chinese will not spare effort nor expense to find foods believed to have good medicinal qualities.

Yin represents the female—negative, dark, cold, wet facets of the world and everything in it; Yang represents the contrasting

male—positive, bright, hot, dry qualities.

Every individual is dominated by one of the two elements, and according to the nature of his constitution, a man should eat and drink chiefly those things which will help to retain his normal balance. The cooling Yin foods are bland, thin and low-calorie, while the heating Yang foods are fishy and oily.

Another fundamental concept of Chinese cooking is the difference between *fan* and *tsai*. Fan means grains and other starches and tsai are vegetables and meat dishes. A balanced meal must have an appropriate amount of both fan and tsai. The five flavours: salty, sweet, sour, bitter and hot must be skillfully blended, with no one accent dominating a meal. Rich food must be counterbalanced by bland foods, smooth texture by crunchy, the hot by the cold.

The popularity of Chinese cuisine around the world is ever increasing since it is so diversified and is considered an art.

INDIAN CUISINE

Cooking in India is a very special affair. The cuisine has evolved over 4,000 years and the preparation of food is endowed with an ancient sanctity. What makes Indian cuisine a gastronomic adventure is the diversity of food. Indian cooking embraces several cuisines that represent the nation's geographical regions, cultural heritage and religious beliefs. In the course of the chequered history of India, the country has absorbed many culinary influences. Each style of cooking has innumerable schools, each school more than one style, each style its own "guru."

To the uninitiated, Indian food is either rich or spicy, synonymous to "fatty" and "chilli hot." It is rich and spicy but not necessarily "fatty" and "chilli hot."

Indian cuisine encompasses the exquisite garnishes and fragrances of Moghalai cooking, the fiery curries of the Goans, the mustard-laced seafoods of the Bengalis and the cinnamon perfumed roast chicken with plums of the Anglo-Indians.

India is a land of tradition, where recipes are handed down from generation to generation. The element that unites all these styles of cooking is the extensive use of herbs and spices. Some are used as aromatics, some lend colouring, and others function as souring agents.

North India's traditional clay oven is probably the most versatile piece of kitchen equipment. This so-called tandoor cooking helped to popularise this cuisine worldwide.

The notable feature of South Indian cooking is the liberal use of coconut, curry leaves and tamarind, apart from a few others. Contrary to popular belief, the food of South India is not only vegetarian. The most interesting feature is that yoghurt is a compulsory part of every South Indian meal. Lots of imagination and ingenuity has gone into the preparation of vegetarian dishes.

Indian cooking is uncomplicated, quick, and inexpensive. But the secret to mastering the art of classic Indian cooking lies in knowing how to proportion spices, herbs, and roots with other ingredients to achieve the delicate balance of flavour, taste and visual appeal.

Indonesian cuisine is unquestionably one of the most delicious and most diversified in the world.

Influences came from many different horizons: China, India, the Middle East, Portugal and of course, The Netherlands. The diversification came also from the fact that Indonesia is comprised of more than 13,000 islands, over 4,800 kilometres of sea, a blend of many different races, and of different religions, which in most islands are Muslim; Bali is Hindu. Therefore, an original dish evolved quite differently over time from one island to the other.

The base of any Indonesian meal, regardless of its origin, is rice: boiled, steamed or fried with other ingredients. From there, a large variety of dishes are served to create a complex combination of flavours, colours and textures. For each spicy dish, a mild one will balance it; for each sweet one, a salty or sour one will oppose it.

The basic ingredients are a wide variety of fish and seafoods, poultry, beef, and all kinds of vegetables. Pork is used rarely and veal not at all.

The most important aspect of Indonesian cooking is the extensive use of a vast and exotic array of spices, herbs, roots and even fruits. The traditional cooking methods are boiling, deep-frying in coconut oil and cooking in charcoal.

Cuisines vary from region to region and island to island. Sumatran food has strong Indian and Arab influences, and is generally more spicy (*padang food*). Padang food is available all over Indonesia, as its spices and herbs were used in the past to conserve the food and make it suitable for travelling. The food of Java is more subtle, offering a combination of sweet, sour, and hot flavours. The Javanese have a decided sweet tooth and specialise in a variety of sweetmeats, cakes and candies. One of the popular dishes in West Java is *pepes*. The food is simply cooked and less highly flavoured. Meats and fish are often wrapped in banana leaves, steamed and then grilled.

Whatever else is served, rice is always the foundation of an Indonesian meal. The Indonesian penchant for rice led to the famous but vanishing *rijsttafel*, a "ricetable" surrounded by a variety of dishes. *Rijsttafel* symbolised Indonesian cuisine to epicures the world over. Also considered as a "national dish" is *sate*, delicious, bite-sized bits of skewered meat. These are basted with soy sauce, grilled over charcoal and dipped before eating into a hot sauce made of chillies, spices and peanuts or dipped into *ketchap manis*.

Japanese Cuisine

The uniqueness of Japanese cuisine lies in its spirit and philosophy. Ingredients, no matter how simple and few, should be allowed to reveal their particular beauty and elegance. The exquisite refinement of Japanese cookery is a profound result of that country's 200 years of isolation from foreigners in the 17th century. It has been said that Japanese cuisine should be eaten with the eyes. Flavour and visual appeal play an equal role in creating the perfect Japanese showpiece. These, along with creativity and imagination, are all interlinked for the Japanese chef. Precision and order are demonstrated by the colour and quality of the china used and in the way in which the food is displayed and served. While Chinese culinary influences exist, they remain subtle. For example, the preparation of the specialty, sushi, shows Japanese culinary philosophy at work. Rice that is cooked simply is artfully topped or rolled with almost any available ingredient: such as raw fish, hard omelet, seaweed, or carrots.

Beautifully presented, Japanese food traditions include the fireside or friendship meals, and the dish for these occasions is the *sukiyaki*—a Japanese institution as elegant as the tea ceremony. Sukiyaki ingredients, like beef sirloin and vegetables, are cooked in front of the guest and served with a beaten egg and warm sake. Chopsticks are used for eating. Japanese ingredients are simple: seafood, fish, vegetables (such as daikon—a white radish), soybean and tofu. Cooking techniques include the cutting of raw fish, broiling, steaming, simmering, deep-frying and soup-making. Japanese chefs, as one French chef declared, "have had no higher ambition for some thousand years or more than to protect the flesh of fishes and the herbs of the field from over-cooking."

Teppanyaki and *robatayaki* are not traditional cooking methods in Japan. These techniques are a form of "showcooking" that use Japanese ingredients and are created outside of Japan. They were introduced into the country after the second World War.

Korean Cuisine

Family and home take centre stage in the cuisine of Korea, the land of morning calm. Cooking and most food preparations are for and by the family, involving rituals, traditions and celebrations. For example, family members gather in autumn for the making of *kimchi*, the national pickled vegetable dish Koreans love to eat.

With the similarity of landscape, climate and ingredients, Manchurian and Mongolian cuisine has influenced traditional Korean food preparation. In spite of some similarities from country to country in the East, the end result is quite dissimilar in each of them. Korean cooking is discreetly spicy. Koreans mostly season their dishes with garlic, onion, green onions, ginger, red pepper, sesame oil, soy sauce and sesame seeds. It may be said that subtle seasoning is the key to the unique appeal of Korean food.

Other ingredients have historically been used for superstitious purposes to ward off evil spirits and illnesses, for example, ginger, cinnamon, mugwort, fruit of the maximowiczia, chinensis, Chinese quince, azalea, Chinese bellflower, pomegranates, and ginseng.

Ingredients such as beef, pork, fish, and vegetables such as carrots, turnips and bean sprouts are cut into bite-sized pieces. Grilling, marinating and seasoning with sesame oil and soy sauce is common. Bulgogi is a popular dish of beef tenderloin that is marinated with spices and soy sauce then grilled. Rice and noodles are the equivalent of bread. Koreans, like the Chinese and Japanese, use chopsticks for eating, but are the only Asians to use silver chopsticks at formal celebrations or meals.

Most Korean housewives prepare a large supply of *kimchi* at the onset of the winter period, as soon as the temperature drops below freezing. Large amounts of cabbage and turnips are prepared and stored in large earthenware jars (*kimchi pots*). These are then buried in the ground, and allowed to ferment. The *kimchi* is then used during the months of December, January and February (*winter kimchi*).

A typical Korean family style meal consists of a soup, kimchi, seaweed laver, boiled or steamed meat and fried or boiled fish with vegetables and pepper paste with soy sauce, and, of course, rice.

Macanese Cuisine

The cooking of Macau combines and contrasts the great cuisines of China and Portugal. It is believed that four centuries ago, Macau produced the world's first international cuisine when its chefs and kitchens blended ingredients, borrowed cooking techniques and adapted recipes from Europe, South America, India, Africa and Southeast Asia.

The Portuguese brought to Macau peanuts, sweet potatoes, green beans, lettuce, pineapples, papaya, shrimp paste, coffee, wine, port, brandy and a variety of herbs and spices. The Macanese, in turn, introduced tea, rhubarb, celery, tangerines, ginger, soy and the Cantonese art of fast cooking (to trap and seal the flavours and aromas of food). Macanese cookery celebrates the *Bacalhau*, the Portuguese codfish. Meat is prepared the way Portuguese cuisine dictates: marinated days ahead, boiled before being browned, then added into *migas* or stews and soups.

The Portuguese *caldo verde* is as popular as the *sopa alentejana*, which both carry the flavours of garlic and olive oil. Other popular dishes include African and Goanese chicken, prawns baked or grilled with peppers or chillies and the Brazilian *feijoades* (introduced by the Portuguese into Brazil)—stews of kidney beans, pork, potatoes, cabbage, and spicy sausage. The best continental bread rolls of Asia are baked in Macau, while wines from Portugal, including the sparkling *vinho verde*, port and brandy, lend elegance to a typical Macanese meal.

Polynesian and the Pacific Cuisine

Culinary secrets are waiting to be sampled and savoured in Fiji, French Polynesia and the Marianas, some of the islands comprising what Mark Twain called the "lovely fleet of islands in the Pacific."

Fijian cookery features a love of seafood and fresh fish, the root vegetable called sweet potato, and the flavours of coconut milk, garlic and ginger. The use of curry and other hot spices, as well as the cooking of lentil-based dishes, is a charming influence from Indian cuisine transplanted by immigrants. The national dish is the *kokoda*, a type of salad featuring

Walu (Spanish mackerel) marinated with fresh lime juice then sauced with fresh coconut milk and spiked with chilli. Roasting, grilling, broiling and boiling of fresh seafood are common cooking techniques.

Almost all Pacific islands use an earth oven to prepare for a feast and have their own versions and names for this oven. In Fiji, for example, it is called *lovo*.

In French Polynesia, French and Chinese cuisines and cooking techniques subtly influence the Polynesian palate. Leaf cooking (e.g., with banana and coconut leaves) re-

PHILIPPINE CUISINE

The blending of Spanish, Mexican, Malay, Polynesian and Chinese cuisines in Philippine cookery has produced truly Filipino dishes. Culinary scholars rate Philippine food as Asia's most international.

Rice is the anchor of any meal, simple or festive, while noodles are served either as a snack or comfort food, a side dish or symbolic food during feasts and celebrations. Outside the chopstick belt, Philippine cooking uses Spanish ingredients and cooking techniques while utilising utensils of Chinese origin, chiefly the wok.

Lechon, or roast pig, with its crisp orange-red skin, is the undisputed star of the Philippine fiesta. Its succulent flesh is cut into small pieces, the eater first dunking a morsel into a sweetish sauce of ground liver. The head is sometimes left untouched for *Paksiw na Lechon*, stewed in liver sauce with additional vinegar and spices.

While pork is a favourite meat, fish and seafood belong to everyday dishes. Coconut milk and peanut sauce, fish sauce and shrimp paste are also used for flavouring. Bread is baked and

served for breakfast with chocolate, tea or coffee.

Since it is the only Christian country in Asia, Philippine cookery observes the culinary traditions of the Christian world with a flair for highlighting the season of Christmas with a steady stream of cooking. Roast ham, stuffed chicken, olives, raisins, cheese, sausages, rich egg desserts,

rice cakes, puddings and a wide variety of entrees all belong to the festive Filipino table that unfurls the world's longest Christmas celebration. The richness and abundance of food ingredients and the culinary creativity of Filipino chefs have assured the growth of Philippine cuisine as an adventure where East truly meets West.

mains a popular method to enhance food flavours and heighten aroma. This method of cooking finds its application in the traditional Tahitian underground oven called *imaa*, where suckling pig, chicken, local roots and vegetables are cooked á l'etouffée; in its own steam.

The Filipino *pancit* and *adobo* are mainstays in Saipan cooking. The use of soy sauce, bean curd and the technique of sashimi cooking come from Japanese and Chinese cuisines. Rice and sweet potatoes are the bread of these isles.

THAI CUISINE

Cooking that appeals to the senses is of principal importance in Thai cuisine. Fragrance, colour, taste and texture are integral elements for this cooking tradition that derives from the kitchens of the Kings of Siam.

In Thai dishes the flavours of coriander, lemongrass, mint, basil, garlic, fish sauce, shrimp paste, hot chillies and sugar enhance the taste of skillfully prepared fruits and vegetables.

A Thai meal is not considered a meal without soup. Soup is eaten from dawn to dusk, pavements are crowded with soup stalls, and soup vending boats paddle up and down the canals.

Thailand is one of the world's greatest rice producers. Rice is a part of every Thai meal and is accompanied by an assortment of main dishes such as meat, poultry or vegetables.

Chicken is the most popular sort of poultry. From central Thailand, a popular dish is chicken green curry served with salted egg and yam, a Thai salad. Salads are refreshing in the hot climate and accompany most Thai meals. Common dressings include lemon juice, chillies, fish sauce and shallots. Oil is not used in Thai salads.

Vegetables play an important part in Thai nutrition. The best way to savour them comes from the North; raw or slightly cooked, with *nam phrik ong*, a thick dipping sauce of tomatoes, ground pork, garlic and chilli, seasoned with soy sauce and sugar, and served with streaky pork.

In the South, a whole range of curries has been devised, using all sorts of green, yellow or red curry pastes. Southerners are also fond of fried fish, coated with a mixture of turmeric and various herbs and spices, then deep-fried and served with an aromatic sauce.

Many Thai fruits are truly spectacular in shape and colour. A refreshing way of serving fruit as a dessert is *loi kaeo* or "cool float." Fruits are cut in pieces and served in a syrup with crushed ice scented with rose petals or jasmine flowers. Many fruits are preserved in salt water or syrup.

Colourful desserts include such ingredients as crushed ice, water chestnuts, coconut meat and milk, gelatine strips, scented water, palm sugar and egg yolks. Some sweets, such as *foi thong*, are like golden hair and very sugary.

Mexican Cuisine

Mexico's culinary heritage is a four century evolution of royal Aztec court tradition, Old World Spanish fare, and elements of French and North American influences.

Ancient Mexican cultures gave several valuable food products to future generations: corn, chillies, tomatoes, and chocolate are only a few. Corn is used extensively as an ingredient in syrups, desserts, flour and beer. Corn forms *masa*, the dough for *tortillas*—the unleavened, griddle-baked cakes that are a staple of Mexican meals. Just as indispensable are chillies, of which hundreds of varieties are grown in Mexico.

Cheese, herbs and spices are also basic components of Mexican cookery. Cheese is used for toppings and stuffings. Cilantro (fresh coriander) and epazote are two herbs synonymous with Mexican flavours.

From earliest records, Mexican cooking has been a tapestry of colour, texture and flavour . . . lots of flavour. The diversity springs from the culinary distinctions of its various regions: Central Mexico, Southern-Mexico, West-Central Mexico, the Bajio, the Gulf States, the Yucatan and Northern Mexico.

Central Mexico illustrates the duality of the Spaniard and the Aztec. *Mole*, the rich concoction of spices, nuts, chillies and chocolate, epitomises the gastronomy of this region.

Southern Mexico, particularly Oaxaca, exhibits a vital Indian heritage. Indian cooks mix a remarkable variety of dried peppers into Mexico's most varied sauces and stews.

West-Central Mexico is thoroughly *mestizo*. It is the home of Mariachis and tequila, of fried tacos and red-chilli enchiladas.

The Bajio region is known for its many cactus plantations, the cultiva-

tion of the tunas, a pear fruit from the cactus plant and favourite sweet desserts of this region like *arroz con leche* (rice pudding), *burritos* (fritters) and *cajeta* (milkcaramel). This area of Mexico, where the first colonists settled, has a strong Spanish character in its dishes. A fermented cactus drink, *Pulque*, is widely used not only as a beverage, but also as an ingredient in food recipes.

The Gulf States are known for simple, well-seasoned cooking and an enormous variety of seafood—fish with tomatoes, herbs and olives, spicy crab soup, turnovers, and butter fried plantains.

The Yucatan's regional specialties are among Mexico's most unusual: from pork in banana leaves to egg-stuffed pumpkin seed-sauced *papadzules* (a type of tortilla), to chicken with vinegar and spices.

Northern Mexico, the land of the *rancheros* (cowboys) is known for its excellent beef, spicy beans and *tortillas de harina* (flour tortillas). The food is hearty and unpretentious. Fillet in oregano sauce, and *caldillo* (a beef stew flavoured with onions and tomatoes) are examples of this sturdy fare.

Mexican cookery enjoys increasing popularity worldwide, in particular in the United States of America.

FRENCH CUISINE

The cuisine of France, one of the glories of the civilised world, has become the yardstick by which all others are judged. French cuisine actually consists of several cooking styles. Haute cuisine originated in the French court of Charlemagne, who was reputed to have feasted on peacock complete with plumes and fire breathing from its beak! In any case, haute cuisine is noted for its elaboration—in contrast to the simple soups and roasts of the ordinary French table.

The classic cuisine of 19th and early 20th century France features rich and costly ingredients such as goose liver, caviar, truffles and fancy sauces, as well as careful attention to menu planning and ornate tablescapes.

Nouvelle cuisine, on the other hand, evolved during the late 1970s as people began to favour lighter dishes prepared with fresh ingredients and aesthetic simplicity reminiscent of Asian cooking.

Regional cuisine (rustic cooking) offers a gastronomic panorama of France while the bistro cuisine of Paris and other cities provides solid day-to-day fare.

Among the traditional dishes associated with these cuisines are *pot-au-feu* (boiled beef), lamb stew, *daube de boeuf* (beef stew), mutton stew with white beans, grilled sole, and rabbit with tomato and mushroom sauce.

There are countless French regional specialties. In Brittany, seafood and simple preparation are hallmarks. *Crepes, calvados* (apple brandy), and *Camembert* cheese are native to Brittany and Normandy.

The Champagne region, famous for its sparkling wine, is also known for its *choux farcie* (stuffed cabbage). Touraine and the Loire Valley feature such popular favourites as poached fish, roast game, and pork tenderloin cooked with prunes.

Alsace-Lorraine, due to its geographic proximity, has a notable German influence in its cuisine and combines the quality of French with the quantity of German cooking. Look for Quiche Lorraine, Kugelhopf, onion tarts and *baba au rhum*.

Burgundy is home to *quenelles*, sausages, patés, chocolates, charolais beef, and such popular dishes as *coq au vin and boeuf Bourguignon*. In Provence, the cookery is strong and bold. Its flavours come from seafood stews, *ratatouille, bouillabaisse*, and *tapenade*—a spread made from anchovies, capers and olives, which goes well with crusty local breads. Bread, of course, is the staple of all French meals.

Other famous French ingredients include: Perigord truffles, frog legs, escargots (snails), crayfish, pork, tomatoes, green beans, lobster, veal/pork mixtures, potatoes, and many kinds of cheese. Indeed, France has a different cheese for every day of the year.

French cuisine also features a wealth of pastries and desserts. Most are made with basic pastry dough or *patés briesses*. The pastries are usually baked and filled with creams, fruits, sauces or puddings. Biscuit, dusted with sugar and filled with *creme anglaise*, is the French version of cake. Cookies and wafers such as *madeleines* are also popular. *Soufflés*, chocolate mousse, *profiteroles* (creme puffs), *creme caramel* and strawberry tarts are among popular desserts that provide a refreshing touch to the end of a meal.

Wine enhances any meal, and French wines enjoy a stature and richness beyond compare. The hearty Burgundy and Bordeaux, the light-bodied Beaujolais,the full-bodied red wines of the Cotes du Rhone, Burgundy and Alsace, the light wines of Muscadet and Chablis so enjoyable with seafood, the sweet Sauternes of Bordeaux—one is certain to find the perfect complement to every dining experience.

Italian Cuisine

Italy's cuisine is considered the source—the mother—of all Western cookeries and the first fully developed cuisine in Europe. The Romans, inspired by the culinary wealth of Greece and Asia Minor, polished a simple, peasant cookery into an influential cuisine that has left its mark in France and other parts of the Western world.

Modern Italian cuisine can be identified by its two branches: the northern which uses rice, meat, butter and cheese, and the southern which uses pasta, fish, vegetables and olive oil. Northern Italian cuisine produced the culinary institution of cheesemaking, including soft mascarpone and the hard parmesan.

Classic ingredients of Italian cooking are anchovies, bread crumbs, capers, eggplant, mushrooms, olive oil, olives, onions, *pancetta* (a kind of bacon), *prosciutto ham*, *mortadella sausage*, salami, salt pork, tomato sauce and paste, and a variety of hard cheeses including *parmigiano-reggiano* (parmesan), *provolone* and soft cheeses like *fontina*, *gorgonzola*, *mozzarella* and *ricotta*.

Italy's regional cooking gives the national cuisine its legendary appeal, extraordinary diversity and a cheerful spirit. Simple but hearty dishes make use of readily available ingredients.

Bologna, the home of northern cookery, is famous for its flat, ribbony egg noodles called *tagliatelle Bolognese*, Parma ham, and sausage. Neapolitan cooking, on the other hand, is the heart of southern Italy's cuisine and the branch that has made Italian cuisine famous world over. Its pizzas and desserts, *gelati and granite* (ice cream and ices), have left their

indelible marks on other cuisines. The cooking of Naples arose from humble foods and a people's *joie de vivre*.

Italians have other famous dishes such as *polenta*, a dish of finely ground corn meal brushed lightly with butter; *risotto alla Milanese* (rice cooked with beef marrow, vegetables, saffron, and grated parmesan and butter); and *minestrone*, a hearty soup of vegetables and noodles.

Desserts are loved in Italy but the repertoire of recipes is not as broad as main dishes. Milanese cooks have popularised *panettone*, the tall Lombardy cake that holds a wonderful blending of candied fruit and raisins; *torrone*, an almond-based candy especially made during the Christmas holidays; and the *pere ripiene*, sweet pears stuffed with *gorgonzola* cheese.

Spanish Cuisine

The cuisine of Spain is simple, hearty and flavourful. In the Iberian Peninsula, there is no haute nor classic cuisine that divides the social strata. Dishes are the same on the dinner tables of rich and poor alike.

Spanish cooking, with its diverse influences, is Europe's melting pot.

For example, the use of fish and seafood as staple ingredients, and the preservation of fish as a cooking technique (*cevichet*) came from the Phoenicians. The use of olive oil and grape vine was introduced by the Greeks. Garlic arrived via the Romans, while spices such as cinnamon, cloves, ginger, nutmeg, pepper and cumin were brought by the Arabs. *Gazpacho*, a popular tomato-based soup served cold, also came from the Arab cuisine.

Cocido Madrileno, the national dish, illustrates the abundance and vigor of Spanish cooking. *Cocido* is a slow cooked hearty stew that blends textures and flavours of chicken, beef, pork, chorizo sausage, veal, and a staple ingredient of garbanzos (chick peas). Cabbage, potatoes, carrots, onions and noodles are also added. The stew is served with a variety of sauces and always with fresh, crusty bread.

From *el desayuno* (a light breakfast of coffee, chocolate and rolls) to "la cena" (a versatile meal served between 10 pm and midnight), Spaniards typically eat five small meals a day.

Tapas, served in appetizer-sized portions, are uniquely Spanish and one of the most delightful aspects of Spanish cuisine. They range from very simple fare such as cured ham and simple canapes, to sophisticated dishes that use fresh snails, caviar, frog legs and quail.

Also famous is *paella*, a colourful rice dish with seafood or meats, and various vegetables and saffron.

Desserts include flan—a variety of caramel custards, and the *Andalusian Yemas*, a confection of Moorish origin that uses egg yolks and sugar.

In addition to sherry and fine wines, Spaniards frequently serve *sangria*, a cocktail of red wine, brandy, fresh fruit and soda water.

Middle Eastern Cuisine

Rice and lamb cooked with a variety of spices such as coriander, onion, cinnamon, lemon, garlic, hot pepper and saffron is a national dish of the Arabic world. The cuisines of Saudi Arabia, the United Arab Emirates, Qatar, Bahrain, Kuwait and Oman specialise in presenting variations of this dish. In Saudi Arabia it is called *kabsah*, in Pakistan it is *basmati* and in Abu Dhabi, this colourful dish is *biryani*.

Another popular dish is *mousaka*. Of Greek origin, *mousaka* is made from aubergine (eggplant) and ground meat. Vegetable ingredients used in Middle Eastern cuisine include okra, potatoes, carrots, chick peas, lentils, spinach and onions. Spices and yoghurt, dates, fruit drinks laced with rose water, and coffee made with cardamom seeds, round out a typical meal.

Lebanese cooking serves as an excellent introduction to Middle Eastern cuisine. The traditional *mazzah*, or appetizers, are finger foods ranging from vegetable crudités to ground lamb meat pies (*Sambousak*) to other meat pies garnished with pine kernels. Lebanese cooking is chiefly Arabic, but features French influences, especially in presentation.

Many Lebanese dishes are prepared with *tahina* (crushed sesame seeds) which have a nutty flavour when blended with other foods. *Tahina* mixed with garlic, salt, lemon juice and water creates a versatile, smooth sauce that can be combined with additional ingredients to produce a variety of flavourful dishes.

Sweetmeat and pastry shops abound in Arabic cities. A popular pastry is *baklava*. Mistakenly considered a Greek specialty, it is actually an Arabic culinary delight. *Baklava* is a rich, diamond-shaped pastry filled with chopped nuts baked in layered phyllo dough and glazed with spiced honey or syrup. A traditional candy is halva, made from flour, shortening, syrup and nuts.

MOROCCAN CUISINE

The heady, colourful and elegant cuisine of Morocco is one of the richest and most popular in North Africa. Its culinary roots can be traced to the Berbers, Arabs and the Byzantine empire. France loaned its language and the appreciation of French culture to the Moroccans, but failed to penetrate this venerable and respected cuisine. French cooking, however, is available in Morocco as a separate cuisine.

Couscous, the heart of the durum wheat or semolina which is made into pasta-like grains, is the staple food and ingredient. However, bread is also a traditional staple of the family table. *Khubza*, round and crusty Moroccan yeast bread, is famous internationally.

Couscous is steamed in a *keskas* or the *couscousiere*, a double boiler pot. Couscous is very time-consuming and difficult in its preparation for the everyday house-wife, so it is traditionally eaten by Moroccan families only on Friday. Couscous is a dish in itself and is never eaten with bread.

Moroccan cuisine also boasts of

tajines which are stews made of lamb, *beef kefta*, brain, chicken, fish, calves' feet, pigeon, vegetables, fresh and dried fruits, olives and prunes cooked in a cone-shaped pottery dish also called *tajines*. It is the pottery that gives the name to the dish. Islamic food laws prohibit the cooking and eating of pork and any pork-based food, as well as cooking with wine or any other alcohol. Besides couscous, another national dish is *harira*, or Moroccan soup made of lentils, rice and garbanzo beans, eaten at breakfast, lunch or dinner. Harira is also traditional to break the feast of the day at Iftar.

Meat dishes such as *kebabs* are made of beef, lamb, poultry and fish. Other important dishes include: *pastilla*, a sweet and savoury pie

made of phyllo pastry and stuffed pigeon, cinnamon sugar, almonds, eggs, orange-flower water, parsley and coriander; *mechoui*, a whole lamb cooked on a spit over fire or in an oven. The flavours of Moroccan cooking are ginger, cloves, cinnamon, orange-flower water, coriander, lemon, olive oil, cumin, honey, saffron, onions, chilli, paprika and pepper. Mint tea is a beloved beverage and the Moroccan tea ceremony is impressive and touching.

APPETIZERS

CURRYS RIZZSEL TOLTOTT PAPRIKA NEMZETI SZINEKBEN
STUFFED BELL PEPPERS WITH CURRY SAUCE

ATRIUM HYATT BUDAPEST, HUNGARY
SERVES 4

STUFFED PEPPERS

- 1 ½ lb (3 large) bell peppers (various colours if possible)—halved and pips removed (600 g)
- 7 oz (2 ½ c) cooked rice (200 g)
- ⅔ lb (2 large) tomatoes—diced (300 g)
- ½ lb cocktail prawns—peeled and cubed (225 g)
- 2 oz (4 tbs) butter (55 g)
- 3 fl oz (6 tbs) double (heavy) cream (100 ml)
- 3 fl oz (6 tbs) dry white wine (100 ml)
- salt, pepper and curry powder to taste

Preheat oven to 300° F (150° C).

○

Mix rice, tomatoes and prawns.

○

Sauté this mixture in half the butter, adding salt, pepper and curry powder to taste. Set aside.

○

Braise the pepper halves in remaining butter for 2 minutes.

○

Stuff pepper halves with rice mixture.

○

Bake for 10 minutes.

SAUCE

Heat cream, wine and pinch of curry.

○

Serve warm with stuffed pepper halves.

FRIED FETA
ON ASSORTED LETTUCE WITH MINT VINAIGRETTE

HYATT REGENCY JEDDAH, SAUDI ARABIA

SERVES 4

1 lb feta cheese (450 g)

assorted leaves of mache, curly endive (chicory), lolo rosso (red-leaf lettuce)—washed, dried and chilled

2 eggs—beaten

8 oz (2 c) bread crumbs (225 g)

3 fl oz (6 tbs) olive oil (90 ml)

⅓ fl oz (4 tsp) white wine vinegar (20 ml)

2 tsp fresh mint—chopped (5 g)

flour—for dredging

vegetable oil—for frying

salt and pepper to taste

Cut cheese into 12 sections and dredge in flour.

Dip in egg, then in bread crumbs.

Chill for at least 1 hour, then fry in oil. Keep warm.

Make dressing with olive oil, vinegar, mint leaves, pepper and salt.

Pour dressing on greens and toss gently to coat.

Arrange greens on individual plates and arrange the cheese around.

Water Buffalo Terrine
with Kakadu Plums in Port Wine Glaze

Hyatt Regency Adelaide, Australia
Serves 4

Terrine

Water Buffalo and Marinade

19 ½ oz water buffalo meat (550 g)

12 fl oz (1 ½ c) dry red wine (360 ml)

2 fl oz (4 tbs) Mandarin brandy or Grand Marnier (60 ml)

1 tsp juniper berries (5 g)

3 sprigs oregano

2 bay leaves—crushed

Cut a long strip of meat (⅔ x ⅔-inch x length of mould; 15 x 15-cm x length of mould). This is to be used for the centre of the terrine.

Mix remaining ingredients to make marinade.

Cut the meat into small cubes and marinate for 12 hours, refrigerated.

Forcemeat

17 ½ oz fatback or saltpork (495 g)

2 slices white bread (60 g)

1 ½ fl oz (3 tbs) double (heavy) cream (55 ml)

5 ¼ oz (1 ¼ c) lean boneless pork (150 g)

5 shallots—diced

1 oz (2 tbs) butter (30 g)

7 oz (1 ¾ c) pecans—chopped (200 g)

1 pinch saltpeter (optional)

salt and pepper to taste

Semi-freeze the fatback, then slice one-third into wide, thin slices.

Cut the rest into small cubes.

Sear the buffalo strip in a dry pan until pink and allow to cool, then wrap with a slice of fatback and set aside.

Preheat oven to 350° F (180° C).

Soak the bread in the cream.

Cut the pork into small cubes.

Lightly sauté the shallots in butter. Mix the cubed buffalo, cubed lard, pork, soaked bread and shallots, then grind until fine.

Transfer to a bowl and add nuts and seasoning.

Line mould with some fatback slices (lined crosswise so there is plenty of excess to cover the top later).

Pour in half of the meat mixture, then lay in the strip of buffalo.

Cover with the rest of the mixture, packing tightly.

Cover with remaining sliced lard and cover mould.

Put the mould in a pan half-filled with hot water and bake for 40–50 minutes.

Remove mould from oven, uncover, and let rest for 1 hour.

Place a weight on top of terrine and leave in refrigerator overnight.

Note: Saltpeter is a preservative frequently added to sausages and ground meats. Omit if unavailable.

Kakadu Plums in Port Wine Glaze

2 lb (32 large) Kakadu or prune plums (900 g)

3 fl oz (6 tbs) water (100 ml)

¾ oz (1 tbs) sugar (20 g)

12 fl oz (1 ¼ c) Port wine (350 ml)

Place all ingredients in a saucepan and cook for 15 minutes or until plums are soft.

○

Remove plums and set aside.

○

Place sauce back on heat and reduce until it becomes a syrup.

To Assemble and Serve

5 oz (1 medium) orange—in segments (140 g)

4 sprigs fresh herbs

Remove terrine from mould or cut out individual slices.

○

Place a slice of terrine on centre of each plate.

○

Arrange 8 plums around slice and pour some glaze over top.

○

Garnish with a few orange segments and herb sprig.

Tacos de Camarones
Prawn Tacos

Hyatt Regency Guadalajara, Mexico

Serves 4

⅓ oz (2 tsp) butter (10 g)

1 lb prawns—peeled and deveined (500 g)

1 oz (2 cloves) garlic—minced (30 g)

1 ½ oz (3 tbs) onion—chopped (45 g)

4 oz (1 medium) tomato—peeled, pips removed and diced (115 g)

½ fl oz (1 tbs) chipolte chilli sauce (15 ml)

1 ¾ fl oz (3 ½ tbs) fish stock (50 ml) (see glossary)

salt and pepper to taste

pinch fresh marjoram—chopped

pinch fresh coriander—chopped

8 flour tortillas

1 avocado—halved, stone removed, peeled and sliced

1 lb (4 medium) tomatoes—sliced for garnish (450 g)

5 fl oz (⅔ c) Mexican hot sauce—chilled (150 ml)

Melt butter. Sauté prawns, garlic and onion until golden brown.

Add diced tomato and chipolte sauce. Simmer for 2 minutes.

Add stock, salt and pepper. Cook for 3 minutes more.

Remove from heat and add fresh herbs.

Gently warm tortillas in a non-stick pan or in microwave.

Stuff tortillas with shrimp mixture.

Fold and put 2 tortillas on each plate.

Decorate with avocado and tomato slices.

Serve hot sauce on the side.

SHREDDED ROAST DUCK AND JELLYFISH

HYATT REGENCY SINGAPORE, SINGAPORE

SERVES 4

7 oz **Chinese roast duck—julienned (200 g)**

3 oz (6 tbs) **red bell pepper—pips removed and julienned (85 g)**

3 oz (6 tbs) **green bell pepper—pips removed and julienned (85 g)**

3 oz (6 tbs) **carrots—julienned (85 g)**

3 oz (6 tbs) **cucumbers—julienned (85 g)**

3 oz (6 tbs) **cantaloupe—julienned (85 g)**

8 oz (1 large) **mango—peeled, halved and julienned (225 g)**

7 oz **jellyfish—julienned (200 g)**

⅓ fl oz (2 tsp) **fish sauce (10 ml) (see glossary)**

⅓ fl oz (2 tsp) **light soy sauce (10 ml)**

1 tsp **chilli oil (5 ml)**

⅓ fl oz (2 tsp) **oriental sesame oil (10 ml)**

1 tsp **sesame seeds (7 g)**

¼ oz (1½ tsp) **fresh coriander— chopped (7 g)**

¼ oz (1½ tsp) **red chilli—sliced (7 g)**

1 tsp **fresh hot red chilli—minced (7 g)**

Arrange duck, fruits, vegetables and jellyfish on a platter leaving a space for sauce bowl.

Mix fish sauce, soy sauce, chilli oil and sesame oil.

Put in small bowl on plate and sprinkle with sesame seeds, coriander and chilli.

CAMARONES CON COCO Y CERVEZA BATIDA
COCONUT BEER-BATTER SHRIMP

HYATT CANCUN CARIBE RESORT & VILLAS, MEXICO

SERVES 4

SHRIMP

juice of ½ lime

salt to taste

12 (large) prawns—peeled and deveined

3 oz (6 tbs) coconut—grated (85 g)

Flour—for dredging

Vegetable oil—for deep-frying

Sprinkle lime juice and salt on shrimp.

Lightly coat the shrimp with flour, then dip in beer batter; roll in coconut.

Deep-fry shrimp in oil until golden brown. Season with salt.

SAUCE

1 ½ oz (1 tb) orange marmalade (45 g)

¾ oz (1½ tbs) grainy mustard (20 g)

⅓ oz (2 tsp) horseradish—grated (10 g)

2 fl oz (4 tbs) dry white wine (60 ml)

2 fl oz (4 tbs) orange juice (60 ml)

6 oz (1 large) orange—peeled and sectioned (170 g)

Mix all ingredients (except orange) and warm over low heat.

To serve, spoon sauce onto individual plates, lay shrimp on top and garnish with orange sections.

BEER BATTER

5 fl oz (⅔ c) beer (150 ml)

5 fl oz (⅔ c) milk (150 ml)

½ oz (1 tbs) flour (15 g)

4 eggs — beaten

1 tsp baking powder (5 g)

salt and pepper to taste

Whisk ingredients until smooth.

Strain if lumpy.

SMOKED SALMON AND POTATO TERRINE

U. N. PLAZA HOTEL, A PARK HYATT HOTEL, NEW YORK, U.S.A.

SERVES 4

20 oz (4 large) potatoes (560 g)

6 fl oz (¾ c) olive oil (180 ml)

10 oz smoked salmon—sliced (280 g)

3 shallots—minced

1 oz (1 bunch) chives—minced (30 g)

black peppercorns—finely crushed

2 fl oz (4 tbs) sour cream (60 ml)

4 radicchio leaves

4 mache leaves

4 curly endive (chicory) leaves

Preheat oven to 300° F (150° C).

○

Peel potatoes and slice thinly lengthwise.

○

Lay in bottom of roasting pan and drizzle some olive oil over (be sure potatoes are well-soaked).

○

Bake for 5 minutes. Baste potatoes with oil; this keeps them from browning.

○

Line four 5 oz (½ c ; 120 ml) moulds or ramekins with cling wrap. Be sure some cling wrap extends beyond rim.

○

Place a circle of smoked salmon in the bottom, then make a second layer with some potato slices.

○

Sprinkle with some shallots, chives and crushed peppercorns.

○

Repeat procedure until you fill moulds (a salmon circle should be the last layer).

○

Cover top layer with the overlapping wrap.

○

Place a glass filled with water on top of ramekin to weight it down. Store overnight in refrigerator.

○

Blend sour cream with remaining minced chives and shallots.

○

Arrange the greens on 4 plates.

○

Turn ramekin upside down, remove cling wrap and place mould in centre of each plate.

○

Spoon some sauce onto each plate.

PINOY ENCHILADAS
PORK-STUFFED TORTILLAS

HYATT REGENCY MANILA, PHILIPPINES

SERVES 4

TORTILLAS

6 ½ oz (1¼ c) flour (190 g)

2 ½ oz (5 tbs) lard (70 g)

½ fl oz (2 ½ tsp) lukewarm water (12 ml)

½ tsp salt (2.5 g)

Combine flour and salt in a bowl.

○

Add lard. With fingers, rub flour and fat together until it resembles coarse meal.

○

Pour in water and mix with fingers until dough can be gathered into a ball.

○

Set aside for 15 minutes.

○

Divide dough into 12 equal portions and, on a lightly floured surface, roll out each into a thin round shape.

○

Lightly brown each tortilla in a non-stick pan, and place on a tray covered with a damp cloth until ready for filling.

Note: Flour tortillas are also sold pre-made, available in supermarkets and Mexican groceries.

FILLING

9 oz (2 small) onions—chopped (255 g)

1 fl oz (2 tbs) vegetable oil (30 ml)

2 pt (4 c) chicken stock (1 l) (see glossary)

8 black peppercorns—crushed

3 bay leaves

10 ½ oz boneless pork loin—diced (300 g)

¾ pt (2 c) sour cream (500 ml)

3 oz (¾ c) fresh red chilli—diced (85 g)

3 oz (1 ½ stalks) celery—chopped (85 g)

Lightly sauté 1 onion in half the amount of oil.

○

Add chicken stock, peppercorns, bay leaves and pork.

○

When pork is cooked, remove and set aside.

○

Reduce liquid by half. Add sour cream and simmer until sauce thickens. Set aside.

○

With remaining oil sauté remaining onion, chilli and celery in a pan, then add to sauce.

○

Moisten pork mixture with a small amount of sauce (just enough to bind the filling).

TO ASSEMBLE AND SERVE

2 oz cheddar cheese—grated (50 g)

1 oz (2 tbs) black olive slices (30 g)

1 oz (2 tbs) red bell pepper—pips removes and julienned (30 g)

Lay softened tortilla on flat surface.

○

Spread 2 tbs (30 ml) of filling over lower third of the tortilla.

○

Fold the bottom edge of tortilla up and over the filling to cover almost completely.

○

Starting at the filled edge, roll the tortilla into a tight cylinder.

○

Put the rolled tortilla in a baking dish and cover enchiladas with sauce. Sprinkle on the bell pepper, olive slices and grated cheese.

○

Bake until sauce bubbles and browns.

○

Serve immediately.

PRAWN TABOULET

RABAT HYATT REGENCY, MOROCCO

SERVES 4

PRAWN TABOULET

4 sprigs parsley—stems and stalks discarded

2 sprigs mint—stems and stalks discarded

6 oz prawns—cooked, peeled and chopped (150 g)

1 lb (4 large) tomatoes—peeled, pips removed and cut into cubes (450 g)

6 oz (1 ½ medium) onions—minced (150 g)

salt and pepper to taste

lemon juice and olive oil to taste

Wash and dry parsley and mint leaves.

Shred herbs.

In bowl combine prawns, tomatoes and onions. Season with salt, pepper, lemon juice and olive oil to taste. Chill.

TOMATOES AND SALAD

1 lb (4 large) tomatoes (450 g)

40 small shrimp—cooked, partially shelled (tails left on)

seasoned mixed greens

Cut each tomato into 5 wedges. Remove inner portion of each and mould taboulet onto wedge.

Decorate each tomato "petal" with 2 prawn tails.

Arrange the greens in centre of plate and place stuffed tomato wedges around. Serve cold.

CHICKEN KELAGUIN

HYATT REGENCY SAIPAN, MARIANA ISLANDS

SERVES 4

10 oz (⅔ lb) boneless chicken breast (280 g)

½ pt (1 c) soy sauce (240 ml)

5 oz (½ c + 2 tbs) coconut—shredded (140 g)

2 small fresh hot chillies—finely minced

2 oz (4 tbs) onion—finely minced (60 g)

½ lemon—squeezed

salt and pepper to taste

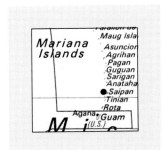

Marinate chicken in soy sauce for 30 minutes. Drain.

Broil or sauté chicken in non-stick pan until tender, about 15 minutes.

Cut into small slices and set aside.

Mix coconut, chillies, onion, lemon juice, salt and pepper in a bowl and add chicken.

Place chicken mixture on Titijas breads and serve.

Note: Titijas bread is a flat bread. Flour tortillas may be substituted.

POISSON CRU A LA TAHITIENNE
MARINATED TUNA TAHITIAN STYLE

HYATT REGENCY TAHITI, FRENCH POLYNESIA
SERVES 4

1 medium coconut

8 oz (½ lb) fresh albacore tuna—cut into ½ inch (1.25 cm) cubes (225 g)

8 oz (1 c) fresh lemon juice (240 ml)

2 oz (1 small) carrot—julienned (55 g)

½ (large) cucumber—julienned (85 g)

2 oz (1 small) onion—diced (55 g)

1 (small) tomato—diced (85 g)

salt and pepper to taste

4 palm leaves—for garnish

Puncture coconut and drain off water. Crack open and scrape out flesh. Grate the flesh.

Put grated flesh in bowl with ¾ pt (1 ½ c; 355 ml) water. Mix well.

Pour mixture through a fine towel and collect liquid in a bowl. This is the coconut milk.

Refrigerate coconut milk and discard flesh.

Marinate tuna in lemon juice for 4-5 minutes.

Drain off marinade and add coconut milk and vegetables to tuna.

Season with salt and pepper. Divide among 4 plates.

Garnish plates with palm leaves.

WARM PACIFIC PRAWN SALAD
WITH AVOCADO, MANGO AND CURRIED DILL SAUCE

HYATT REGENCY HONG KONG, HONG KONG

SERVES 4

1 head curly endive (chicory)

2 leaves red chicory or red-leaf lettuce

4 king or jumbo prawns, steamed and peeled, but tails intact

1 lb (2 medium) mangoes (450 g)

6 oz (1 large) avocado (170 g)

1 oz (2 tbs) red bell pepper—cored and chopped (30 g)

⅓ oz (2 tsp) curry powder (10 g)

pinch fresh dill—chopped

14 fl oz (1 ¾ c) vinaigrette of choice (400 ml)

Rinse and dry endive and chicory. Spread neatly on platter.

○

Slice the prawns down the centre from tail to head ("butterflied") and spread open, but keep attached.

○

Slice mangoes in half; discard stones, then peel.

○

Place vinaigrette and flesh of 1 mango in liquidiser and purée with dill and curry powder.

○

Cut avocado in half, remove stone, then peel. Quarter avocado halves lengthwise to have 8 pieces.

○

Slice mango halves several times to form fans.

○

To serve, arrange prawns and mango and avocado slices over bed of endive and chicory. Drizzle vinaigrette over arrangement and sprinkle with red pepper.

CHICKEN QUENELLES
WITH GIPPSLAND BLUE CHEESE SAUCE

⟨○⟩

THE HOTEL CANBERRA, A PARK HYATT HOTEL, AUSTRALIA

SERVES 6

CHICKEN QUENELLES

1 lb chicken breasts—boned, skinned and diced (500 g)

2 egg whites

1 ¼ pt (2 ¾ c) double (heavy) cream—chilled (650 ml)

salt and pepper to taste

Put diced chicken breast and egg whites in a liquidiser and process to a smooth paste.

○

Press mixture through a fine sieve, into a bowl set over crushed ice.

○

With a wooden spoon, beat chilled cream into mixture, a little at a time. Season with salt and pepper.

○

Bring a large pot of salted water to a boil, reduce heat to simmer.

○

Using 2 dessert spoons, shape the quenelles into small egg-like forms.

○

Poach the quenelles for 5–6 minutes; they are done when they float.

○

Remove with a perforated (slotted) spoon and place on a towel to drain.

BLUE CHEESE SAUCE

3 oz Gippsland (or any other fine) blue cheese—grated (85 g)

1 ¾ oz (2 tbs) onion—chopped (50 g)

½ oz (1 tbs) butter (60 g)

1 ¾ fl oz (3 ½ tbs) dry white wine (50 ml)

8 fl oz (1 c) double (heavy) cream (240 ml)

In a saucepan, sauté onion with butter; do not colour.

○

Add white wine and simmer until reduced by half.

○

Pour in cream and simmer until it thickens.

○

Add cheese and whisk until smooth.

○

Press sauce through a sieve.

TO ASSEMBLE AND SERVE

6 sprigs dill

4 oz (1 medium) red apple—cut into strips (115 g)

2 ¼ oz (½ small) tomato—diced (60 g)

6 slices truffle

Place 3–5 quenelles on each plate.

○

Pour sauce over quenelles. Garnish with dill, apple strips, tomatoes and truffles.

Deep-Fried Squid Balls

Grand Hyatt Taipei, Taiwan

Serves 4

3 ¼ lb squid—washed, cleaned and sliced (1 ½ kg)

1 tsp garlic—finely minced (5 g)

2 tsp pork fat—finely minced (10 g)

1 tsp sugar (5 g)

pinch salt (1.5 g)

1 fl oz (2 tbs) dry white wine (30 ml)

½ oz (2 tsp) cornflour (cornstarch) (10 g)

2 egg whites

2 eggs—beaten

salt and pepper to taste

flour—for coating

bread crumbs—for coating

vegetable oil—for deep-frying

soy sauce

Pass squid through a meat grinder twice.

Transfer ground squid to a bowl.

Add garlic, pork fat, sugar, salt and wine.

Mix well, then add the cornflour and egg whites.

Season with salt and pepper to taste; stir well in one direction.

Form small balls the size of a walnut with hands.

Poach squid balls in simmering salted water for 5 minutes. Drain and cool.

Roll squid balls in flour, beaten egg and bread crumbs.

Deep-fry until golden.

Arrange in dumpling steamer baskets and serve with soy sauce.

SMOKED TASMANIAN SALMON
AND SHIITAKE MUSHROOM SALAD

⬯

HYATT ON COLLINS, MELBOURNE, AUSTRALIA
SERVES 4

12 oz (¾ lb) smoked Tasmanian salmon—sliced (320 g)

6 shiitake mushrooms—quartered or sliced

¾ oz (1 ½ tbs) carrot—julienned (20 g)

¾ oz (1 ½ tbs) leek—julienned (20 g)

¾ oz (1 ½ tbs) celery—julienned (20 g)

¾ oz (1 ½ tbs) red bell pepper—pips removed and julienned (20 g)

⅓ fl oz (2 tsp) soy sauce

2 drops oriental sesame oil

1–1½ fl oz (2–3 tbs) olive oil (30–45 ml)

1–2 tsp rice or white wine vinegar (5–10 ml)

salt and pepper to taste

20 sprigs chervil

On a platter, arrange smoked salmon in a star pattern. Chill.

⬯

Place vegetables in a bowl and blend gently.

⬯

Combine soy sauce, sesame oil, olive oil, vinegar, salt and pepper to taste in a small bowl.

⬯

Pour dressing on vegetables and toss.

⬯

Place salad in centre of salmon and garnish with chervil as shown in photo.

Yabbies in Leek Papillotes

with Mushroom Ravioli

Hyatt On Collins, Melbourne, Australia

Serves 4

12 fresh yabbies—steamed, shelled and tails deveined (225 g)

2 lb (6 large) leeks—well rinsed (900g)

vegetable oil—for deep-frying

salt and pepper to taste

½ lb pasta dough—rolled into 2 thin sheets, each 8 inches (20 cm) square (225 g)

2 eggs—beaten

1 oz (4 tbs) duxelles (30 g) (see glossary)

½ pt (1 c) lemon-butter (240 ml) (see glossary)

¾ oz (6) basil leaves—julienned (20 g)

Note: Yabbies are a South Pacific crustacean. Substitute prawns or langoustines.

Remove large, outer leaves from leek and, with a knife, scrape pulp away from leaves.

Blanch leaves, then drain and dry.

Slice inner leek stalks into julienne, yielding 8 oz (225 g).

Deep-fry leek juliennes in oil until golden brown. Set aside.

Season yabbies with salt and pepper, then wrap in leek leaves, making a uniform package.

Moisten pasta sheets by brushing with beaten egg. Lay 1 sheet on work surface and use a knife to divide into 4 equal squares.

Put 1 tbs of duxelles on each square of the bottom sheet, cover completely with second sheet, then seal ravioli squares, making sure there are no air pockets.

Cut squares with a 3-inch (7-cm) round cookie cutter, then cook ravioli in boiling water until al dente, about 5 minutes. Drain.

Place yabbie packages on plates. Garnish with deep-fried leeks. Mix butter sauce and basil and drizzle over ravioli. Pour lemon-butter sauce over recipe.

Mini Pastilla Bil Halazoun oua Salsat Charmoula
Escargot Wonton with Moroccan Charmoula Sauce

Casablanca Hyatt Regency Morocco
Serves 4

Escargots

24 canned snails—drained

½ oz (1 tbs) butter (15 g)

½ oz (1 tbs) shallot—chopped (15 g)

½ oz (1 clove) garlic—crushed (15 g)

1 tsp chive—chopped (5 g)

1 tsp powdered ginger (5 g)

2 ½ fl oz (5 tbs) dry red wine (80 ml)

salt and pepper to taste

12 round phyllo sheets (5 inches; 12.5 cm in diameter); unwrapped and kept covered to stay moist

1 egg yolk—beaten

vegetable oil—for deep-frying

Sauté snails in butter, shallot, garlic, chive and ginger.

○

Add red wine, salt and pepper. Simmer until reduced by half.

○

Remove snails from liquid and let cool.

○

Spread a phyllo sheet open and place 2 snails in the centre.

○

Brush sheet with beaten yolk and fold securely into a small package. Repeat for remaining sheets and snails.

○

Deep-fry wonton packages until golden.

Note: Snails are available in tins, in most gourmet shops.

Charmoula Sauce

12 oz (3 medium) tomatoes—peeled and chopped (355 g)

1 fl oz (2 tbs) olive oil (30 ml)

2 oz (1 clove) garlic—crushed (55 g)

1 tsp tomato concentrate (paste) (5 g)

½ oz (1 tbs) fresh coriander—chopped (15 g)

½ oz (1 tbs) fresh parsley—chopped (15 g)

1 tsp cumin—ground (5 g)

4 oz (1 medium) green bell pepper— pips removed and finely chopped (115 g)

salt and pepper to taste

dash lemon juice

In a pot, sauté tomatoes in olive oil and garlic and tomato concentrate.

○

Blend in rest of ingredients and simmer for 10 minutes.

○

Pour sauce on centre of plate.

○

Neatly arrange 3 escargot wontons over sauce.

GADO-GADO
VEGETABLE SKEWERS WITH COCONUT AND PEANUT SAUCE

HYATT REGENCY SURABAYA, INDONESIA

SERVES 4

VEGETABLE SKEWERS

1 ½ lb assorted, seasonal vegetables (720 g)

16 bamboo skewers

Select seasonal vegetables, cooked or raw.

Clean well. Cut into bite-size cubes and place alternately on the bamboo skewers.

Serve with sauce (recipe follows).

SAUCE

1 lb raw peanuts—shelled and skinned (250 g)

vegetable oil—for deep-frying

⅔ oz (2 medium) shallots (20 g)

½ oz (1 clove) garlic (10 g)

1 ½ oz (3 tbs) fresh, hot red chilli—minced (40 g)

½ oz (1 tbs) brown sugar (15 g)

⅔ oz (2 tbs) tamarind pulp (20 g)

2 stems lemongrass—crushed

2 kaffir lime leaves

12 oz (1 ½ c) coconut milk—canned or homemade (375 ml) (see glossary)

salt to taste

Deep-fry peanuts until light brown. Drain on paper towels and grind.

Deep-fry shallots, garlic and chilli for several seconds. Drain and grind in a meat grinder or liquidiser. Add peanuts and grind again.

Transfer ingredients to a saucepan; add brown sugar and tamarind pulp, then mix and add lemongrass and lime leaves.

Pour in coconut milk; season with salt.

Bring mixture to a boil, then simmer, stirring constantly, for approximately 10 minutes.

Discard lemongrass and lime leaves, then put sauce back in liquidiser. Blend at medium speed until smooth.

Note: Kaffir lime leaves impart a pronounced flavour and fragrance. Look for them in southeast Asian foodstores. Tamarind pulp is available in tins, or substitute lemon juice. Lemongrass is available dried or fresh in Asian foodstores.

SPATCHCOCK BREAST
WITH SQUASH BLOSSOMS AND MUSTARD SPROUTS

HYATT REGENCY SANCTUARY COVE, QUEENSLAND, AUSTRALIA

SERVES 4

¾ oz black mustard seeds (20 g)

4 (large) squash blossoms

7 oz witloof (Belgian endive)—torn into small pieces

7 oz radishes—sliced into fine strips (200 g)

2 tbs balsamic vinegar (30 ml)

juice of ½ lemon

salt and pepper to taste

4 tbs linseed oil (60 ml)

4 Spatchcock breasts—boned

½ oz (1 tbs) butter (15 g)

Note: Spatchcock breasts are baby (spring) chicken breasts of approximately 350 g.

Spread mustard seeds on a damp cloth. Place on a rack and cover with another cloth. Sprinkle with water. Set aside in a warm place for about 2 days, continuously moistening the cloths, which should never dry out.

Blanch squash blossoms for 3 minutes. Set aside.

Arrange witloof and radishes in a flower pattern on each plate.

In a small bowl, combine balsamic vinegar, lemon juice, salt and pepper and whisk. Add the oil a few drops at time, whisking continuously.

Season the breasts and cook on a grill or fry in a pan with butter until done, about 10 minutes. Keep warm.

Toss the mustard sprouts in butter.

Cut squash blossoms in half and arrange on plates alongside breasts and mustard sprouts. Drizzle on dressing and serve.

MASALA LASSI
HERBED YOGHURT DRINK

HYATT REGENCY DELHI, INDIA

SERVES 4

1 pt (2 ⅓ c) chilled water (550ml)

1 tsp cumin pips—toasted and then ground (5 g)

⅓ oz (2 tsp) fresh coriander—finely chopped (5 g)

1 ½ tsp fresh ginger—finely chopped (4 g)

4 fl oz (½ c) plain yoghurt (120 ml)

salt to taste

4 mint leaves—for garnish

Blend all ingredients except mint leaves for 30 seconds.

Garnish with mint leaves and serve chilled.

Marron in Papaya and Chilli Sauce

Hyatt Regency Perth, Australia
Serves 4

4 marron or similar crayfish—cleaned (1 ¾ kg)

14 oz (2 large) papayas (400 g)

3 oz (6 tbs) butter (85 g)

1½ oz (3 tbs) shallots—chopped (45 g)

½ oz (1 clove) garlic—chopped (15 g)

8 fl oz (1 c) fish stock (240 ml) (see glossary)

4 fl oz (8 tbs) dry white wine (100 ml)

1 fresh red chilli—halved, pips removed and chopped

4 fl oz (8 tbs) double (heavy) cream—lightly whipped (100 ml)

1 tsp fresh coriander and basil leaves—chopped and mixed together (5 g)

salt and pepper to taste

Boil marron in salted water for 5 minutes. Rinse in cold water and place in bowl.

Shell tails and claws and discard heads.

Cut 12 diamonds from the papaya and reserve for garnish

Scoop out rest of papaya and finely chop.

Sauté shallots and garlic in half the butter.

Add chopped papaya, fish stock, white wine and chopped chilli.

Reduce mixture by one-half, then pass through a sieve.

Add cream and season to taste.

Halve the tails of marron, removing the vein. Sauté the tails and claws in remaining butter and heat thoroughly.

Drizzle sauce on 4 plates. Neatly arrange marron on each plate and garnish with papaya diamonds and chopped fresh herbs.

Note: Marron are small crayfish (lobster), about 1 lb (450 g) each. Substitute lobster tails (about 1 lb (450 g) of lobster meat).

Deep-Fried Mushrooms Stuffed with Kosher Seafood
On a Saffron-Basil Sauce

Hyatt Regency Jerusalem, Israel

Serves 4

Stuffed Mushrooms

24 button mushrooms (approximately the same size)—stems removed

8 kosher "shrimp"—chopped

2 oz (½ c) cottage cheese (55 g)

3 oz spinach—blanched, drained and chopped (90 g)

2 eggs

1 ¾ fl oz (3 ½ tbs) milk (50 ml)

2½ oz (½ c) flour (70 g)

4 oz (1 c) bread crumbs (115 g)

vegetable oil—for deep-frying

Note: Kosher "shrimp" is fish seasoned to taste like shrimp. If a kosher meal is not required, substitute peeled, cooked shrimp or prawns. For a kosher meal, substitute sealegs.

Wipe mushrooms clean with a dry paper towel.

Mix "shrimp," cottage cheese and spinach in a bowl.

Using a teaspoon, stuff each mushroom cap and place on a tray.

Refrigerate 20 minutes.

Meanwhile, beat the eggs in a bowl and add milk. Set aside.

Sift flour onto a plate and set aside.

Spread the bread crumbs on a plate and set aside.

Roll stuffed mushrooms in flour, then into the egg mixture and finally roll in the crumbs until well coated.

Deep-fry mushrooms until golden brown.

Saffron-Basil Sauce

4 oz (1 medium) onion—chopped (115 g)

½ oz (1 tbs) butter (15 g)

1 ¾ oz (3 ½ tbs) fresh basil—chopped (50 g)

1 ¾ fl oz (3 ½ tbs) dry white wine (50 ml)

¾ pt (2 c) double (heavy) cream (480 ml)

pinch saffron

Sauté onion in saucepan in butter, cooking over low heat until soft.

Add basil and white wine.

Simmer until reduced by half.

Add cream and saffron and continue simmering until reduced by half again.

Press sauce through a sieve.

To serve, pour sauce onto each plate and arrange 6 mushrooms on top of sauce.

Decorate with a tomato rose and basil leaf in centre, if desired.

SMOKED VENISON IN A PASSION FRUIT VINAIGRETTE
WITH MANDARIN ORANGES AND GRAPES

HYATT AUCKLAND, NEW ZEALAND

SERVES 4

SMOKED VENISON

4 passion fruit

10 oz smoked venison—thinly sliced (300 g)

7 oz (1 small bunch) black grapes—cut in half, pips removed (200 g)

7 oz (1 small bunch) seedless green grapes—cut in half (200 g)

6 oz (2 medium) mandarin oranges— peeled and broken into segments (175 g)

Cut passion fruit in half, scoop out the pulp and set aside for vinaigrette.

Arrange slices of smoked venison on plate. Decorate with passion fruit shell, grapes, mandarin segments and mint leaves.

PASSION FRUIT VINAIGRETTE

passion fruit pulp

1 ½ fl oz (3 tbs) walnut oil (50 ml)

salt and pepper to taste

¾ fl oz (1 ½ tbs) raspberry vinegar (25 ml)

Place all ingredients in a bowl.

Mix well. Drizzle over meat and fruit.

Rillettes aux Deux Saumons
Potted Salmon with Fresh Coriander

The Carlton Tower, A Park Hyatt Hotel, London, United Kingdom

Serves 4

7 fl oz (¾ c) olive oil (200 ml)

½ oz (1 clove) garlic—chopped (15 g)

pinch fresh thyme—chopped

16 oz (1 lb) fresh salmon fillets (450 g)

1 pt (2 ½ c) plain yoghurt (550 ml)

2 egg yolks

1 oz (2 tbs) butter (30 g)

1 oz (1 c) fresh coriander—chopped (30 g)

juice of 2 lemons

salt, pepper and cayenne pepper to taste

4 oz (¼ lb) smoked salmon—julienned (115 g)

melba toast or brown bread

Heat olive oil. Sauté garlic and thyme.

Add salmon fillets and sauté until colour changes, about 8 minutes.

Let cool, then chop and purée in liquidiser.

Add yoghurt, egg yolks and butter. Process again until smooth.

Transfer to a bowl placed over ice and beat until cool, adding lemon juice and seasonings.

Add smoked salmon and coriander. Mix until smooth.

Chill for 4 hours.

To serve, shape salmon paste into "eggs" on each plate and serve with melba toast or brown bread.

Lamb-Stuffed Mushroom Caps
with Wild Rice

Hyatt Regency Sanctuary Cove, Queensland, Australia

Serves 4

4 oz (¼ lb) boneless loin lamb—cubed (120 g)

5 basil leaves

2 eggs

3 fl oz (6 tbs) double (heavy) cream (45 ml)

12 button mushrooms

1 sheet puff pastry—cut into 12 circles same size as mushroom caps

1 egg—lightly beaten

½ oz (1 tbs) poppy seeds (15 g)

6 oz (¾ c) wild rice (180 g)

¾ pt (2 c) chicken stock (450 ml) (see glossary)

1½ fl oz (3 tbs) dry white wine (45 ml)

12 cherry tomatoes—blanched with skins removed (450 g)

salt and cracked white pepper to taste

Preheat oven to 425° F (220 °C).

In a liquidiser, blend lamb cubes, basil, eggs and half the amount of cream. Season mousse to taste.

Remove stems from mushrooms and save. Pipe the lamb mousse into mushroom caps.

Place pastry circles on top of caps. Brush with beaten egg and sprinkle with poppy seeds. Place in a greased baking dish and bake for 10 minutes.

Cook wild rice in chicken stock until tender but firm, approximately 45 minutes. Keep warm.

In a saucepan over high heat, reduce white wine by half; add mushroom stems and remaining cream. Simmer 10 minutes then strain through a sieve. Season with salt and pepper.

On each plate, arrange a mound of wild rice in centre. Arrange 3 stuffed mushrooms around rice; spoon a small amount of sauce around mushrooms, then arrange 3 cherry tomatoes over sauce.

Sweet and Sour Snail Wonton

⌒

Hyatt Regency Singapore, Singapore

Serves 4

Snail Wonton

20 escargots (snails)

¾ fl oz (1½ tbs) olive oil (20 ml)

½ oz (1 tbs) shallots—finely chopped (15 g)

⅓ oz (2 tsp) garlic—finely chopped (10 g)

¼ oz (2 tsp) fresh coriander—chopped (7 g)

1 oz shiitake mushrooms—diced (30 g)

¼ oz (1½ tsp) fresh coriander— chopped (7 g)

salt and pepper to taste

Tabasco sauce to taste

vegetable oil—for deep-frying

Heat olive oil in a non-stick pan.

⌒

Sauté shallots, garlic, ginger, mushrooms and coriander.

⌒

Season to taste with salt, pepper and Tabasco.

⌒

Place a snail in the centre of each wonton wrapper and add a small amount of sautéd mixture.

⌒

Fold up 4 corners toward the middle and shape securely into a small parcel.

⌒

Deep-fry in hot (350° F; 180° C) oil.

¼ pt (½ c) orange juice—freshly squeezed (120 ml)

¼ pt (½ c) tomato juice—freshly squeezed (120 ml)

¼ pt (½ c) chicken stock—(120 ml) (see glossary)

¼ oz (1 ½ tsp) cornflour (cornstarch)— dissolved in 1 tsp water (7 g)

2 oz (4 tsp) butter—chilled and cubed (55 g)

In a small saucepan, mix the juices and chicken stock.

○

Bring to a boil and reduce by half.

○

Add cornflour and simmer until thickened.

○

Remove from heat and whisk in chilled butter cubes.

3 ½ oz bean sprouts (100 g)

1 ¾ oz (⅓ c) red bell pepper cored and julienned (50 g)

1 ¾ oz (⅓ c) leek—julienned (50 g)

7 oz asparagus tips (200 g)

1 ½ tbs oriental sesame oil (20 ml)

1 tsp fresh coriander—chopped (5 g)

1 tsp oyster sauce (5 ml)

pinch fresh red chilli—chopped

Bring 1 pt (4¼ c ; 1 l) water and 1 tbs (15 g) salt to a boil. Blanch vegetables. Strain.

○

Heat a non-stick pan with sesame oil and add vegetables. Sauté lightly.

○

Season with coriander, oyster sauce, chilli, salt and pepper. Arrange as shown in photo.

MARINATED TASMANIAN SALMON

○

HYATT ON COLLINS, MELBOURNE, AUSTRALIA

SERVES 4

⅓ oz (2 tsp) fresh dill—chopped (10 g)

¾ lb Tasmanian or other fine salmon fillet (340 g)

½ oz (1 tbs) sea salt (10 g)

½ oz (1 tbs) brown sugar (7 g)

½ oz (1 tbs) black peppercorns— cracked (15 g)

juice of 2 lemons

4 radicchio leaves

4 curly endive leaves (chicory)

4 butter lettuce leaves or other greens

8 chives

4 sprigs thyme

4 sprigs chervil

4 sprigs rosemary

Press dill into the salmon fillet

○

Combine remaining ingredients and rub generously onto salmon.

○

Cover and marinate for 24 hours in refrigerator.

○

Thinly slice salmon and arrange on plate with herbs and greens.

Carpaccio of Fallow Deer
with Paua

Hyatt Auckland, New Zealand

Serves 4

VENISON

5 oz (⅓ lb) fallow deer (venison fillets)—trimmed (150 g)

½ oz (1 tbs) pink peppercorns (15 g)

1 (small) black truffle—chopped, (with 1½ tbs (20 ml) canning juice reserved) (See note)

¼ oz (2 tsp) fresh chervil—chopped (5 g)

¼ oz (2 tsp) fresh parsley—chopped (5 g)

14 fl oz (1¾ c) olive oil (400 ml)

Note: If juice in truffle tin is not sufficient, add brandy to equal amount needed.

Combine ingedients omitting fallow deer.

Coat fillets with marinade and refrigerate for 24 hours.

Drain and dry fillets. Cut into paper-thin slices and arrange on plate in an overlapping pattern.

PAUA

1 ¾ oz (⅛ lb) paua (abalone) (50 g)

2 fl oz (4 tbs) olive oil (60 ml)

⅓ oz (⅛ medium) red bell pepper—cut into strips (10 g)

salt and pepper to taste

mix greens—for garnish

Thinly slice paua, then marinate in mixture of olive oil, salt and pepper for 1 hour.

Cut red pepper strips into diamond shapes.

Place paua, red pepper and greens on carpaccio and serve.

Ceviche Caracol
Sea Conch Cocktail

Hyatt Regency Cancun, Mexico

Serves 4

12 oz white sea conch—cut into small cubes (320 g)

1 oz (2 tbs) onion—finely minced (30 g)

salt and pepper

1 oz (2 tbs) onion—diced (30 g)

3 oz (1 small) tomato—cubed (85 g)

¾ oz (1 ½ tbs) jalapeno pepper—sliced into fine strips (20 g)

1 oz (2 tbs) fresh coriander—minced (30 g)

⅓ oz (2 tsp) garlic—minced (10 g)

juice of 3 lemons

lime slices—for garnish

Note: Conch is a warm-water gasteropod that has a firm texture. It is available locally in warmer climates. There is no close substitute.

Marinate conch cubes for several hours in lemon juice, minced onion and salt. Keep refrigerated while marinating.

Combine diced onion, tomato, jalapeno, coriander and minced garlic.

Drain conch and mix marinade with tomato mixture. Season to taste.

Serve in glass bowl, decorated with lime slices.

LOBSTER-STUFFED SQUID
ON CARROT SAUCE

HYATT REGENCY MANILA, PHILIPPINES
SERVES 4

STUFFED SQUID

8 oz (medium) squid—heads removed and reserved

¼ oz (½ clove) garlic—chopped (5 g)

½ shallot—chopped (3 g)

1 oz (¼ medium) tomato—peeled, pips removed and chopped (30 g)

1 oz (2 tbs) cooked spinach—chopped (30 g)

1 oz (2 tbs) basil—fresh, chopped (30 g)

1 oz (2 tbs) butter (30 g)

3 ½ oz lobster meat—cubed (100 g)

1 fl oz (2 tbs) Galliano liqueur (30 ml)

4 fl oz (½ c) double (heavy) cream (120 ml)

½ c dry white wine (120 ml)

12 fl oz (1 ¼ c) fish stock (300 ml) (see glossary)

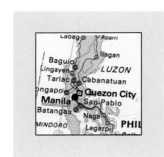

Clean squid thoroughly, keeping tubelike body whole.

◯

Preheat oven to 300° F (150° C).

◯

Sauté garlic, shallot, tomato, spinach and basil in ½ oz (1 tbs) butter.

◯

Add lobster, Galliano and cream.

◯

Simmer 2–3 minutes. Cool.

◯

Fill the squid cavity with the cooled lobster mixture.

◯

Place stuffed squid in pan with the squid heads.

◯

Pour in white wine, fish stock and remaining butter.

◯

Cover pan and bake for 15 minutes.

◯

Remove stuffed squid. Reserve squid heads for garnish.

◯

Strain the remaining stock. Set aside.

CARROT SAUCE

¼ oz (1 tsp) fresh ginger—grated (5 g)

1 ½ oz (3 tbs) onion—chopped (45 g)

½ oz (1 tbs) butter (15 g)

¾ pt (2 c) chicken stock (450 ml) (see glossary)

5 ¼ oz (2 large) carrots—peeled and cubed (150 g)

8 fl oz (1 c) double (heavy) cream (220 ml)

salt and pepper to taste

Sauté ginger and onion in butter until onion is transparent.

◯

Add stock and carrots. Simmer until carrots are very tender.

◯

Cool slightly and purée in liquidiser.

◯

Add cream, salt and pepper to taste.

TO ASSEMBLE AND SERVE

1 ½ oz (3 tbs) tomatoes—peeled, pips removed and diced (45 g)

1 ½ oz (3 tbs) cooked black beans (40 g)

fresh dill sprigs

Glaze each plate with a little carrot sauce.

◯

Slice the stuffed squid diagonally.

◯

Arrange sliced squid on plates, placing squid head in the centre and slices of stuffed squid around it.

◯

Garnish with tomatoes and black beans. Add dill sprigs.

STUFFED CLAM SHELL

CENTURY HYATT TOKYO, JAPAN

SERVES 4

MARINATED SEA BASS WITH CORIANDER

3 oz sea bass or grouper fillet (85 g)

4 fl oz (8 tbs) wine vinegar (100 ml)

½ oz (1 tbs) sugar (15 g)

pinch coriander—ground

salt and pepper to taste

Season fish with salt and pepper, then marinate overnight in a mixture of the vinegar, sugar and coriander.

Slice very thin.

ROLLED COLD ROAST BEEF WITH HORSERADISH CREAM

4 oz (¼ lb) cold roast beef—thinly sliced (120 g)

1 fl oz (2 tbs) double (heavy) cream— whipped (30 ml)

1 oz (2 tbs) horseradish (30 g)

salt and pepper to taste

Season roast beef slices with salt and pepper.

Mix the cream and horseradish.

Spread this mixture on roast beef slices and roll up.

Slice rolls crosswise to be pinwheels.

CRABMEAT IN JELLY

2 oz crabmeat (60 g)

¼ pt (½ c) white wine jelly-warmed until liquid (120 ml)

Mix crabmeat with white wine jelly.

Chill to harden.

Cut into 4 servings.

Note: White or red wine jellies are available in gourmet food stores, especially those carrying English ingredients.

TO ASSEMBLE AND SERVE

12 large clam shell halves—washed and dried

seaweed for garnish

Place 3 clam shells on each plate.

Place a serving of the sea bass slices, roast beef pinwheels and crabmeat in jelly in their own shell.

Decorate plate with seaweed.

SMOKED SALMON EGG ROLLS
ON MIXED GREENS

GRAND HYATT HONG KONG, HONG KONG

SERVES 4

4 eggs

4 (thin slices) smoked salmon

4 leaves curly endive (chicory)—shredded (40 g)

4 leaves red chicory or red-leaf lettuce—shredded

4 fresh asparagus tips—blanched (60 g)

1 oz black olives (30 g)

1 oz (2 tbs) white fungi or cloud ears—sliced (30 g) (see glossary)

3 fl oz (6 tbs) sour cream (90 ml)

¼ oz salmon caviar (7 g)

chives—fresh, snipped for garnish

Lightly beat 1 egg and pour into a non-stick pan. Cook until firm, like a thick crepe.

Remove from heat and lay salmon slice on top.

Roll up the egg like a crepe.

Put on a paper towel, roll up towel with egg roll inside and set aside a few minutes. Repeat for remaining 3 eggs.

Unwrap each roll and slice into 5 slices.

Arrange the greens, asparagus, olives and fungi on each plate.

Place a sliced roll alongside and dress with sour cream. Sprinkle caviar on top and decorate with chives.

STUFFED CHOY SUM
WITH WILD MUSHROOMS AND RICE ON A TOMATO-BASIL COULIS

◯

HYATT REGENCY PERTH, AUSTRALIA
SERVES 4

STUFFED CHOY SUM

½ oz dried morels (10 g)

½ oz dried cepes (10 g)

48 leaves choy sum (Chinese flowering cabbage)

3 ½ oz (1 small) onion—diced (100 g)

½ oz (1 clove) garlic—crushed (15 g)

1 tsp olive oil (5 ml)

3 ½ oz chanterelles—sliced (100 g)

7 oz oyster mushrooms—sliced (200 g)

7 oz button mushrooms—sliced (200 g)

1 tsp mixed dried herbs (chive, thyme, rosemary and basil) (5 g)

salt and pepper to taste

Note: Choy Sum is a light green plant with small yellow flowers. If unavailable, substitute young broccoli rabe.

Soak morels and cepes separately in warm water for 30 minutes; drain and slice.

◯

Briefly blanch the choy sum in boiling water. Refresh in cold water, drain and dry.

◯

Sauté onion and garlic in olive oil.

◯

Add the morels, cepes, button mushrooms, add oyster mushrooms.

◯

Mix, season, then add herbs.

◯

Place mushrooms mixture onto leaves, roll tightly and fold into a tortellini (ringlike) shape. Keep warm.

Rice Timbale

1 ½ oz (2 ½ tbs) each Thai or brown rice, white and wild rice (45 g)

Cook the 3 different types of rice separately, accordingly to their own directions.

○

Brush insides of four 1 c (240 ml) moulds with oil. Press each type of rice separately into cup, creating 3 layers.

Tomato-Basil Coulis

5¼ oz (¾ c) onion—chopped (150 g)
½ oz (1 clove) garlic—chopped (15 g)
½ fl oz (1 tbs) olive oil (15 ml)
1 lb (4 medium) tomatoes—chopped (450 g)
5 basil leaves—chopped
salt and pepper to taste

To Assemble and Serve

Spread each plate with some coulis.

○

Unmould timbales onto plates.

○

Divide tortellini among plates.

○

Sauté onion and garlic in oil.

○

Add tomatoes and basil, then simmer until tomatoes have softened.

○

Purée tomato-basil mixture and press through a fine sieve.

○

Return to heat and reduce until thickened.

○

Season with salt and pepper.

Hummus
Chickpeas with Sesame Seed Paste

○

Hyatt Regency Dubai, United Arab Emirates

Serves 4

8 oz (1 c) chickpeas (garbanzos)— soaked and cooked or canned (drained) (200 g)

1 ½ oz (3 cloves) garlic—coarsely chopped (45 g)

3 oz (6 tbs) tahina (sesame paste) (80 g)

3 oz (6 tbs) lemon juice (80 ml)

½ fl oz (1 tbs) cold water (15 ml)

1 tsp salt (2.5 g)

⅓ fl oz (2 tsp) olive oil (10 ml)

1 tsp parsley—chopped for garnish (5 g)

dash paprika—for garnish

olive oil—for garnish

In a liquidiser, place all ingredients except garnishes until smooth. Check for taste—add more garlic and lemon juice if desired.

○

Spread onto a chilled platter. Using back of spoon, make a slight depression in centre. Chill.

○

To serve, drizzle oil into depression, sprinkle parsley onto remaining surface. Add paprika.

○

Serve with wedges of pita bread for dipping.

SOUPS

Chilled Watercress and Avocado Soup

Hyatt Kingsgate Sydney, Australia

Serves 4

2 oz (4 tbs) butter (55 g)

4 oz (1 large) onion—sliced (115 g)

1 ½ oz (3 cloves) garlic—chopped (45 g)

18 oz (3 large) potatoes—peeled and diced (500 g)

3 ½ oz (¾ c) shallots—chopped (100 g)

½ oz (2) bay leaves (15 g)

2 pt (5 c) chicken stock (1 *l*, 180 ml) (see glossary)

8 oz (2 c) watercress—trimmed and chopped (225 g)

salt and pepper to taste

4 oz (1 medium) avocado—peeled, stones removed and diced (115 g)

¾ fl oz (1 ½ tbs) sour cream (20 ml)

watercress—for garnish

Melt butter in saucepan and sauté onion and garlic until golden brown.

Add potatoes, shallots and bay leaves; sauté 3 minutes longer.

Add chicken stock and boil for 10 minutes or until potatoes are tender.

Add chopped watercress and boil for an additional 2 minutes.

Remove any leaves and process mixture until smooth, adding salt and pepper to taste.

Chill well.

Serve in 4 soup bowls, sprinkled with diced avocado; top each bowl with some sour cream.

Garnish with watercress.

Deritett Gulyasleves
Clear Goulash Soup

Atrium Hyatt Budapest, Hungary

Serves 4

4 oz boneless beef shank or shin (120 g)

1 ¾ pt (4 ¼ c) water (1 _l_)

2 oz (1 stalk) celery—cut into large pieces (55 g)

3 oz (1 medium) red onion—peeled and cubed (85 g)

1 oz (1 clove) garlic—crushed (30 g)

2 oz (1 medium) green bell pepper— pips removed and cubed (55 g)

3 oz (1 large) carrot—peeled and cubed (85 g)

4 oz (1 large) tomato—cubed (115 g)

12 oz (2 large) potatoes—peeled and cubed (340 g)

salt, pepper and caraway seeds to taste

1 ½ oz (1 small) red bell pepper—pips removed and julienned, for garnish (40 g)

In a deep saucepan, place meat and water and bring to a boil, skimming the foam as needed.

Add the vegetables and seasonings and simmer for 2–3 hours, skimming surface to remove foam if necessary.

Strain broth and discard vegetables.

Slice and trim the beef into small cubes and return to the broth.

Heat soup, then serve, garnished with the julienned red pepper.

HOT AND SOUR TOFU SOUP

HYATT REGENCY XIAN, PEOPLE'S REPUBLIC OF CHINA

SERVES 4

3 oz shrimp—peeled and deveined (85 g)

3 oz (¾ c) ham—julienned (85 g)

1 ½ oz (3 tbs) bamboo shoots—julienned (45 g)

1 ½ oz (3 tbs) tofu—julienned (45 g)

⅓ oz (1 ½ tsp) Chinese black mushrooms—soaked in water for 30 minutes, then caps julienned (10 g)

⅓ fl oz (2 tsp) corn oil (10 ml)

8 fl oz (1 c) chicken stock (240 ml) (see glossary)

⅓ oz (1 small) fresh red chilli—julienned (10 g)

½ tsp green onions (scallions) (green part only)—chopped (2 g)

1 ½ oz (5 tbs) cornflour (cornstarch) (45 g)

1 fl oz (2 tbs) water (28 ml)

⅔ fl oz (4 tsp) tomato ketchup (20 ml)

⅔ fl oz (4 tsp) rice vinegar (20 ml)

⅓ tsp oriental sesame oil (1.5 ml)

¼ fl oz (1 ½ tsp) chilli oil (8 ml)

1 egg—beaten

Fill a deep saucepan with plenty of water and bring to a boil.

○

Blanch the shrimp, ham, bamboo shoots, tofu and mushrooms, then drain.

○

Pour corn oil and chicken stock into a large saucepan.

○

Add blanched ingredients along with chilli and green onions, then bring to a boil.

○

Dissolve cornflour in water and stir into soup to thicken.

○

Add ketchup, vinegar, sesame oil and chilli oil to soup.

○

Stir well and bring to a rolling boil.

○

Using a whisk, slowly add beaten egg while beating vigorously. Serve at once.

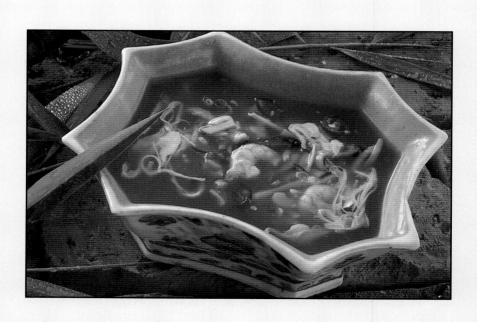

Mushroom Essence
with Pistachio Quenelles

The Hotel Canberra, A Park Hyatt Hotel, Australia
Serves 4

Mushroom Essence

2 oz shiitake mushrooms (50 g)

2 oz porcini mushrooms (50 g)

2 oz oyster mushrooms (50 g)

2 oz pepper mushrooms (50 g)

2 oz dried morels—soaked in warm water for 30 minutes, then drained, stems discarded (50 g)

¾ oz (4 tsp) butter (20 g)

½ tsp chopped shallots (2 g)

1 pinch garlic—chopped

1 ¾ pt (4 ¼ c) cold beef stock (1 *l*) (see glossary)

1 fl oz (2 tbs) cognac (30 ml)

2 egg whites—lightly beaten

Set aside 4 of each wild mushrooms for garnish. Dice the rest.

Melt the butter in a heavy pot and sauté the shallots and garlic. Add the diced mushrooms, including the morels.

Pour stock into pot with mushrooms.

Heat the cognac in a small cup and ignite. Add to the cold stock, then pour in the beaten egg whites to clarify broth. Place pot over moderate heat and heat until it reaches simmering point and egg whites slowly float to the top. Remove from heat and allow to cool until lukewarm.

Strain soup through a cheesecloth, then pour back into pot and place over low heat. Simmer until broth is reduced to the correct strength and flavour. Do not boil.

Note: Depending on which wild mushrooms are available, adjust quantities accordingly but try for a balance between woodsy and wild mushrooms.

Pistachio Quenelles

3 oz (¾ c) chicken breast—ground (85 g)

2 ½ fl oz (5 tbs) double (heavy) cream (80 ml)

1 oz (2 tbs) pistachio nuts—chopped (30 g)

⅓ oz (2 tsp) chives—chopped (10 g)

salt and pepper to taste

Purée the chicken in a liquidiser until very fine. Transfer to a bowl and place bowl over ice.

Mix cream into puréed chicken, then add pistachios and chives. Mix well and season to taste.

Shape small quenelles from the mixture using 2 teaspoons, then poach in salted water for 5–8 minutes. Keep Warm.

How to Serve

chives—fresh, sliced

Place 2 quenelles in each soup bowl and neatly arrange the reserved mushrooms around them. Carefully pour the mushroom essence over and garnish with sliced chives.

FISH DUMPLING SOUP WITH HERBS

○

CENTURY HYATT TOKYO, JAPAN

SERVES 4

7 oz fillet of white fish—cubed (200 g)

1 egg white

¼ oz (1 tbs) cornflour (cornstarch) (8 g)

1 ½ pt (4 c) fish stock (945 ml)
(see glossary)

1 fl oz (2 tbs) sake or medium-dry
sherry (30 ml)

1 oz (2 tbs) chives—chopped (30 g)

½ oz (1 tbs) fresh parsley—chopped
(15 g)

4 oz (1 medium) tomato—sliced
(115 g)

3 oz (6 tbs) courgette (zucchini)—
sliced (85 g)

1 stalk celery—sliced

salt to taste

Add a little salt to cubed fish, then
purée in a liquidiser.

○

Transfer to a bowl and add egg white,
cornflour, 2 tbs of fish stock and sake.
Add chives and parsley. Mix well.

○

Bring a large pot of salted water to a
boil, then reduce heat to a simmer.

○

Drop fish mixture by tablespoonfuls,
one by one, into simmering water and
poach until dumplings rise to surface,
about 3–5 minutes. Remove and keep
warm.

○

Heat remaining fish stock.

○

Put fish dumplings and sliced vegetables into a deep soup tureen, then
gently pour in boiling stock and serve
at once.

Max's Seafood Soup

Hyatt On Collins, Melbourne, Australia

Serves 4

Soup

2 fl oz (4 tbs) olive oil (60 ml)

1 ½ oz (3 tbs) onion—peeled and diced (45 g)

1 ½ oz (3 tbs) celery—peeled and diced (45 g)

1 ½ oz (3 tbs) carrot—peeled and diced (45 g)

2 ½ oz (5 tbs) fennel—diced (70 g)

¼ oz (½ clove) garlic—peeled and diced (7 g)

3 ½ oz (½ large) potato—peeled and diced (100 g)

5 oz (1 very large) tomato—diced (140 g)

½ fl oz (1 tbs) tomato concentrate (paste) (5 ml)

1 pinch saffron

1 sprig tarragon—chopped

1 sprig basil—chopped

1 ¾ pt (4 ¼ c) fish stock (1 *l*) (see glossary)

1 ½ lb lobster, prawn, or crab shells—crushed (650 g)

Preheat oven to 325° F (160° C).

Place half the olive oil in a heavy pot and add onion, celery, carrot, fennel and garlic. Over low heat, cook without browning until soft.

Add the potatoes, tomatoes, tomato concentrate, saffron, tarragon, basil and fish stock. Bring to a boil and then simmer over heat.

In a roasting pan with the remaining olive oil, spread the shells. Roast in oven for 30 minutes, until brightly coloured.

Add roasted shells to the broth and simmer 1 hour.

Strain soup through a fine sieve.

To Garnish and Serve

¾ oz (1 ½ tbs) butter (20 g)

4 oz (¼ lb) seafood (mussels, scallops, prawns or fish)—julienned and lightly poached (115 g)

1 oz (2 tbs) carrots or celery—julienned (30 g)

Bring soup back to a boil, adjust seasonings and add butter, blending with a whisk.

Pour into 4 soup bowls. Garnish with julienned seafood and vegetables.

SEAFOOD CHOWDER SERVED IN A PUMPKIN

GRAND HYATT TAIPEI, TAIWAN

SERVES 4

CHOWDER

1 6-lb (large) pumpkin or 4 , 1 ½ lb (small) pumpkins (2 ¾ kg)

5 ½ oz (1 ½ c) celery, carrot and scallion—diced (160 g)

2 oz (4 tbs) butter (55 g)

14 oz snapper fish fillets—cut in large chunks and soaked in water (400 g)

3 ½ oz mussels in shells—cleaned (100 g)

2 ¾ pt (6 ½ c) cold water (1 ½ *l*)

¼ tsp ground chowder (1g)

¼ tsp black peppercorns (1g)

½ tsp fresh ginger, grated (2 g)

4 water chestnuts—sliced

GARNISH

3 oz (½ c) ham—minced (85 g)

5 ¼ oz Chinese black mushrooms—shredded, soaked and drained (150 g)

4 oysters—shucked

⅓ oz (3 tbs) fresh coriander (10 g)

Wash pumpkin(s). Cut off stem end and discard.

Remove pips and hollow out some of the flesh. Keep pumpkin warm in oven.

Decorate the outside of pumpkin with a nice design.

In a deep pot, sauté the vegetables in butter. Add fish chunks and mussels, and cook 5 minutes.

Add the cold water and bring to a boil.

Add the herbs and spices and simmer 15 minutes. Add water chestnuts and then pour into pumpkin(s).

Garnish soup with ham, mushrooms, oysters and coriander and serve at once.

Soup Buntut
Nutmeg-Flavoured Dark Oxtail Soup

Hyatt Regency Surabaya, Indonesia

Serves 4

Note: Kluwek is a large nut with a smooth reddish-black paste inside. The paste has a mild aroma and gives this soup its characteristic dark colour. There is no substitute for the flavour, but you can reproduce the dark colour by adding a few drops of soy sauce.

Soup

2 ¾ pt (6 ½ c) water (1.5 *l*)

½ oz (1 stalk) lemongrass—crushed (14 g)

1 tsp salt (5 g)

2 ¼ lb oxtail—sliced (500 g)

2 whole nutmegs

6 ¼ oz (1 ⅔ c) carrots—peeled and diced (180 g)

3 ½ oz (¾ c) leeks—coarsely diced (100 g)

2 oz (½ c) shallots—peeled and diced (55 g)

1 kluwek nut—halved and paste scraped out

Place water in a stockpot with lemongrass and salt.

○

Bring to a boil, then add oxtail and cook over low heat for 45 minutes.

○

Add nutmegs, carrots, leeks and shallots.

○

Stir well, then add Kluwek nut paste.

○

Continue simmering soup for another 30 minutes or until oxtail is tender.

○

Remove oxtail from soup and take meat off the bone.

○

Cut meat into cubes and place back in soup.

○

Serve the soup in bowls, garnished as follows or serve garnish accompaniment on a separate plate.

Garnish/Accompaniment

⅓ oz (1 tbs) celery leaves—washed and dried (10 g)

⅔ oz (2 small) shallots—diced and fried (20 g)

1 salted egg—peeled and sliced into wedges

2 ½ oz (4 tbs) bean sprouts (70 g)

4 oz (1 c) fermented tofu—diced (120 g)

3 oz (¾ c) sambal tomat (85 g)

Note: Salted eggs are fresh duck eggs that have been soaked in brine then boiled. If unavailable, substitute hard-boiled eggs sprinkled with salt. Sambal tomat is a spiced Japanese tomato stew; substitute a spicy tomato sauce.

Divide equally among 4 accessory plates and serve with soup.

CHILLED STRAWBERRY AND MANGO SOUP

HYATT REGENCY MANILA, PHILIPPINES

SERVES 4

MANGO SOUP

1 ⅓ lb (3 medium) ripe mangoes
(600 g)

7 fl oz (¾ c) double (heavy) cream
(200 ml)

7 fl oz milk (¾ c) (200 ml)

Slice mangoes in half.

Discard stones.

Scoop out pulp with a spoon.

Place pulp in a liquidiser with cream
and milk. Blend till smooth. Chill.

*Note: If mangoes aren't available,
soup is also delicious made with
equal quantity of ripe peaches.*

STRAWBERRY SOUP

8 oz (1 pt) strawberries—fresh, hulled
(225 g)

6 fl oz (¾ c) milk (150 ml)

8 fl oz (1 c) double (heavy) cream
(240 ml)

1 fl oz (2 tbs) honey (30 ml)

Combine all ingredients in a
liquidiser.

Blend until smooth.

Chill.

*Note: If fresh strawberries aren't
available, substitute 5 oz frozen
berries (150 g).*

TO SERVE

**fresh mango and fresh strawberry
slices—for garnish**

Using 2 pouring cups or jugs, fill each
with one of the soups and hold them
on opposite sides of a large shallow
bowl.

Pour each soup into the bowl at the
same time until the bottom of the
bowl is covered and soups meet in the
middle, moving the ladles forward and
back as you pour, so the soup flows
evenly and together.

Garnish with mango and strawberry
slices.

CHILLED PAPAYA SOUP WITH CRABMEAT

HYATT REGENCY SAIPAN, MARIANA ISLANDS

SERVES 4

2 lb (1 large) papaya (920 g)

½ lb (4 small) papayas (225 g)

2 pt (5 c) chicken stock (1 *l*, 180 ml) (see glossary)

¾ pt (2 c) double (heavy) cream (480 ml)

4 oz crabmeat (100 g)

¾ oz (1 ½ tbs) butter (20 g)

2 green onions—chopped

Cut stem ends off small papayas. Also cut a small sliver off each bottom so papayas can rest evenly on a dish.

With a spoon, dig out pips, wash insides, and set papayas on individual plates.

Peel the large papaya. Half lengthwise; remove pips and reserve.

Cut papaya flesh into cubes and place in liquidiser with stock. Purée until smooth.

Add cream and purée for 20 seconds more.

Pour mixture into the small papayas.

Wash papaya pips, dry well and sprinkle around each papaya on plate.

In a saucepan, briefly sauté crabmeat in butter.

Place crabmeat on top of soup, then sprinkle green onions on top. Serve.

CHORBA BIL KAMH
GROUND WHEAT GERM SOUP

CASABLANCA HYATT REGENCY, MOROCCO

SERVES 4

1 ¾ pt (4 ¼ c) water (1 *l*)

1 lb ground wheat germ—rinsed and strained (500 g)

½ oz (1 tbs) red or green bell pepper—cored and chopped (15 g)

pinch chilli powder

5 ¼ oz fresh navy or lima beans (150 g)

1 oz (2 tbs) fresh coriander, minced (30 g)

salt and pepper to taste

Bring water to a boil in a large pot and add wheat germ, pepper and chilli powder.

Simmer 30 minutes.

Add beans and simmer until tender, about 10 minutes.

Add coriander and salt and pepper and simmer for 2 minutes.

Serve immediately.

PRAWN MEE SOUP

HYATT REGENCY SINGAPORE, SINGAPORE

SERVES 4

PRAWN SOUP

14 oz fresh oriental egg noodles (400 g)

2 ¼ oz kangkong or fresh spinach (60 g)

3 oz bean sprouts (80 g)

1 lb (16 large) prawns—peeled (save shells), cooked and sliced in half lengthwise (450 g)

1 ¾ pt (4 ¼ c) prawn stock (see recipe below) (1 *l*)

½ oz (1 tbs) shallots—sliced, deep-fried (15 g)

½ oz (1 tbs) green onions (scallions)—diced (15 g)

Place noodles, greens and bean sprouts in boiling water for 1 minute.

Drain and place mixture in a deep bowl. Toss in the prawn halves.

Pour in prawn stock and garnish with shallots and scallions.

Note: Kangkong is a long-stemmed green vegetable of Southeast Asia. It is best substituted with fresh spinach.

PRAWN STOCK

1 ¾ fl oz (3 ½ tbs) vegetable oil (50 ml)

3 oz (¾ c) shallots—chopped (85 g)

1 ½ oz (3 tbs) garlic—chopped (45 g)

2 ¼ lb prawn shells (1 kg)

1 ¾ pt (4 ¼ c) chicken stock (1 *l*) (see glossary)

1 ¾ pt (4 ¼ c) water (1 *l*)

¾ fl oz (1 ½ tbs) dark soy sauce (20 ml)

1 ⅓ fl oz (2 ⅔ tbs) light soy sauce (40 ml)

salt and pepper to taste

In a heavy saucepan, heat vegetable oil and fry shallots and garlic lightly without colouring.

Add prawn shells and continue frying until shells turn red.

Add chicken stock and water.

Season with soy sauces and pepper.

Simmer for 2 hours, then strain and adjust seasonings.

Wontons with Salmon Mousse
In a Fennel Chicken Consommé

Grand Hyatt Hong Kong, Hong Kong

Serves 4

Wontons

1 oz fresh salmon fillet (30 g)

1 oz smoked salmon (30 g)

⅓ fl oz (2 tsp) dry white vermouth (10 ml)

⅓ fl oz (2 tsp) dry light vermouth (10 ml)

⅓ fl oz (2 tsp) dry white wine (10 ml)

⅓ fl oz (2 tsp) cognac (10 ml)

salt and pepper to taste

¾ fl oz (4 tsp) double (heavy) cream (20 ml)

20 wonton skins or wrappers

In a liquidiser, liquify the fresh and smoked salmon, vermouth, wine, cognac and salt and pepper.

Using lowest speed, slowly add the cream and process until smooth.

Press salmon mixture through a fine sieve, then chill for at least 10 minutes.

Put a teaspoonful of mousse on center of a wonton wrapper. Wet edges of wonton with water and fold into a triangle. Seal well.

Make remaining wontons, cover and set aside.

Fennel Chicken Consommé

3 oz fresh fennel bulb—chopped and sprigs reserved (85 g)

⅛ oz (2 small sprigs) parsley (5–7 g)

1 lb assorted raw chicken bones (450 g)

⅓ oz (1 ½ tsp) leeks (white part only)— sliced (10 g)

⅓ oz (1 ½ tsp) celery—chopped (10 g)

½ oz (1 tbs) cinnamon stick (15 g)

¾ pt (2 ⅛ c) water (350 ml)

2 egg whites—beaten

3 ½ oz (¾ c) shredded white meat of chicken (100 g)

⅓ oz (1 ½ tsp) shallot—diced (10 g)

⅓ oz (1 ½ tsp) carrot—diced (10 g)

2–3 sprigs dill—for garnish

In a deep pot, place the fennel bulb and sprigs, parsley, chicken bones, leek, celery, cinnamon stick and water.

Bring to a boil, then simmer for 20 minutes, skimming the foam off the top frequently. Strain.

To clarify stock, put the 2 beaten egg whites in a clean pot, then add the chicken meat, shallot and carrot.

Slowly pour in the stock, and bring to a slow boil, stirring continuously.

Lower heat and simmer 5–10 minutes.

Strain consommé through a muslin-lined sieve, then pour consommé back into the pot.

Heat slowly and add the wontons.

Cook for 3–5 minutes.

To serve, garnish with fresh dill sprigs.

Note: Two chicken bouillon cubes can be added to stockpot in place of chicken bones.

Artichoke Cream with Hazelnuts

Hyatt Regency Riyadh, Saudi Arabia

Serves 4

4, 3 oz (medium) artichokes (85 g each)

3 ½ pt (8 ½ c) milk (2 *l*)

1 ½ oz (3 tbs) butter (45 g)

2½ oz (½ c) flour (70 g)

salt and pepper to taste

2 oz (1 c) whipped double (heavy) cream (50 g)

1 ½ oz (⅓ c) hazelnuts (45 g)

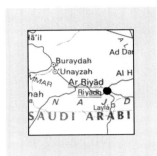

Cut artichokes in half, put them in a stockpot and cover with milk. Simmer artichokes for about 1 hour, then drain, reserving milk.

In a saucepan, melt butter and whisk in flour. Stir to make a roux.

Slowly add the artichoke milk and simmer for 15–20 minutes.

Pass soup through a fine strainer, then season to taste and keep warm.

Roast hazelnuts at 420° F (216°C) for 4–5 minutes, then slip off skins and crush nuts with a meat hammer.

Divide the soup among 4 bowls.

Pipe the whipped cream on top and sprinkle with chopped hazelnuts.

MEE SUP PEDAS
SPICY SEAFOOD MEE SOUP

HYATT KINABALU, MALAYSIA

SERVES 4

SOUP

2 fl oz (4 tbs) sambal ulek (60 ml)

1 (small) red chilli—fresh, crushed

1 fl oz (2 tbs) vegetable oil (30 ml)

8 lemon leaves

3 stalks lemongrass—crushed

3 ½ pt (8 ½ c) chicken stock
(approx. 2 l) (see glossary)

2 fl oz (4 tbs) fish sauce (60 ml)
(see glossary)

juice of 6 limes

salt and pepper to taste

In a heavy pot, sauté sambal ulek and chilli in oil until fragrant.

Add lemon leaves, lemongrass and chicken stock and bring to a boil.

Adjust seasoning with fish sauce, lime juice and additional salt and pepper if necessary. Keep hot.

Note: "Sambal ulek" is an Indonesian hot tomato paste, available in specialty stores. Omit lemon leaves if unavailable.

GARNISH

4 tiger or jumbo prawns

⅓ lb squid—cleaned, sliced and scored rings (150 g)

20 button mushrooms

20 straw mushrooms

8 cherry tomatoes

1 ⅔ lb fresh oriental egg noodles
(750 g)

Add prawns, squid, both mushrooms and tomatoes to boiling soup.

Simmer about 5–8 minutes. Set aside.

Blanch noodles in boiling water for 1 minute. Drain and place in bottom of a soup tureen or bowl.

Pour soup with seafood and mushrooms over noodles and serve hot.

TOM YAM KUNG
PRAWN SOUP

GRAND HYATT ERAWAN BANGKOK, THAILAND

SERVES 4

2.2 lb prawns (1kg)

2 tsp oil (10 ml)

4 ¼ c hot water (1 *l*)

¾ oz coarse salt (20 g)

2 stalks lemongrass

4 lemon leaves

8 (small) green chillies

8 straw mushrooms—sliced

1 tbs nam pla (fish sauce) (15 ml)

2 tsp lemon juice (10 ml)

1 (small) red chilli—pips removed and sliced for garnish

1 tbs fresh coriander leaves—chopped for garnish

3 stalks scallions—sliced for garnish

Shell and devein prawns. Wash prawn heads well. Do not discard.

Heat oil and fry the prawn heads and shells until they turn pink. Add the hot water, salt, lemongrass, lemon leaves and green chillies. Bring to a boil, cover and simmer 20 minutes.

Strain the stock and return it to a bowl. Drop peeled prawns and straw mushrooms and simmer until the prawns are cooked, about 4 minutes.

Add the nam pla and lemon juice to taste. Enough lemon juice should be added to give the soup a traditional acid flavour.

Serve soup in coconut shells or bowls sprinkled with sliced chilli, coriander and scallions.

Sinigang Na Hipon
Filipino Shrimp Soup

⌒

Hyatt Regency Manila, Philippines

Serves 1

¾ pt (2 c) water or fish stock (475 g) (see glossary)

1 ½ oz (3 tbs) onion—sliced (45 g)

4 oz string beans—strings removed (115 g)

4 oz white radish—sliced (115 g)

4 oz (1 medium) banana—chunked (115 g)

2 oz (½ medium) tomato—quartered (55 g)

4 fl oz (½ c) fish sauce (patis) (120 ml)

2 fl oz (4 tbs) lemon juice (60 ml) pepper to taste

1 lb shrimp with heads (455 g)

3 oz (1 c) cooked rice (85 g)

Note: "Patis" is a fermented fish sauce used widely in the Philippines for seasoning foods. Also known as "nouc mam" in Vietnamese and "nampla" in Thai. Available in Asian or specialty food stores, it is a dark, salty liquid, rich in protein.

Place fish stock in a pot with onion and simmer for 2 minutes.

⌒

Add the beans, radish, banana and tomato.

⌒

Simmer for 3 minutes.

⌒

Season with fish sauce, lemon juice and pepper.

⌒

Add shrimp to boiling stock, lower heat and simmer for another minute, then serve in bowls, over rice.

Onion and Herb Soup
with Lamb Shanks

Hyatt Regency Sanctuary Cove, Queensland, Australia

Serves 4

Lamb Shanks and Stock

10 ½ oz lamb shank—sliced into 4 pieces (300 g)

¾ pt (2 ½ c) water (600 ml)

4 ¼ oz (1 c) onion—diced (120 g)

1 bay leaf

1 clove

salt to taste

Place the lamb shank in a heavy pot with water, onion, bay leaf, clove and salt. Bring to a simmer and cook for 35–40 minutes.

Strain stock and set aside for later use.

Trim gristle from shanks and keep meat warm.

Onion and Herb Soup

¾ oz (3 tbs) mixed herbs—chopped (20 g)

9 oz (2 ¼ c) onion—chopped (255 g)

1 oz (2 cloves) garlic—chopped (30 g)

2 oz (4 tbs) butter (55 g)

¾ pt (2 c) chicken stock (500 ml) (see glossary)

¾ pt (2 c) lamb stock (500 ml) (see glossary)

1 fl oz (2 tbs) dry white wine (30 ml)

6 fl oz (¾ c) double (heavy) cream (150 ml)

2 egg yolks

Set aside about 1 tbs (15 g) of the chopped herbs for garnish.

Sauté onions, garlic and herbs in butter until onions are transparent.

Add the stocks and wine. Bring to a boil, then reduce heat and simmer 10 minutes.

Mix the cream with the yolks, then slowly whisk it into soup to thicken.

Arrange shank pieces in soup bowls and pour hot soup over them.

Sprinkle with the reserved chopped herbs and serve.

Note: For mixed herbs, use a combination of tarragon, chervil, thyme, parsley, chives and watercress. If desired, add lemon zest or caraway seeds.

CALDO DE PULPO CON MEZCAL
OCTOPUS SOUP WITH MEXICAN LIQUEUR

─────────── ◯ ───────────

HYATT CANCUN CARIBE RESORT & VILLAS, MEXICO

SERVES 4

½ oz (1 tbs) onion—chopped (7 g)

½ oz (1 tbs) carrot—chopped (7 g)

½ oz (1 tbs) garlic—chopped (7 g)

10 ½ oz cooked octopus—chopped
   into large chunks (300 g)

1 oz (2 tbs) olive oil (30 ml)

½ oz (1 tbs) wine vinegar (15 ml)

1 ¾ pt (4¼ c) fish stock (1 *l*)
   (see glossary)

2 fl oz (4 tbs) Mescal (60 ml)

½ fl oz (1 tbs) Worcestershire sauce
   (15 ml)

juice of 1 lime

salt and pepper to taste

*Note: "Mescal" (Spanish: "Mezcal") is
a distilled alcoholic drink made
from the agave plant. It tastes
vaguely of bitter almonds.
When unavailable, substitute
tequila.*

In a large pot, sauté onion, carrot,
garlic and octopus in olive oil for 5–10
minutes. Remove octopus pieces and
set aside.

◯

Add vinegar to pan and boil vigorously, scraping up any particles from
bottom of pan.

◯

Pour in stock, Mescal, and
Worcestershire. Simmer a few minutes, then add octopus pieces.

◯

Sprinkle on lime juice and season with
salt and pepper. Pour into bowls and
serve.

Spring Vegetable and Coconut Milk Soup
with Frogs' Legs

Hyatt Regency Hong Kong, Hong Kong

Serves 4

5 fl oz (½ c) white vinegar (120 ml)

2 oz frogs' legs—cleaned (60 g)

3 ½ oz (¾ c) carrot—peeled and diced (100 g)

3 ½ oz (¾ c) courgette (zucchini)—diced (100 g)

3 ½ oz (¾ c) yellow crookneck squash—diced (100 g)

3 ½ oz (¾ c) spinach—trimmed, cleaned and shredded (100 g)

2 oz (1 medium) leek—julienned (55 g)

8 oz (4 stalks) asparagus—trimmed and sliced into 3-inch lengths (225 g)

14 fl oz (1 ¾ c) chicken stock (400 ml) (see glossary)

14 fl oz (1 ¾ c) coconut milk (400 ml) (see glossary)

6 fl oz (¾ c) single (light) cream (200 ml)

1 (small) red or yellow pepper—julienned, for garnish

salt and pepper to taste

Bring a large pot of water to a boil with the vinegar and add some pepper for seasoning.

Add frogs' legs and boil for approximately 5 minutes. Drain and cool.

Remove meat from bones of frogs' legs and shred or slice thinly.

In different saucepans, boil each vegetable separately without overcooking. Drain well.

In another saucepan, add chicken stock, coconut milk and cream. Simmer at medium heat until reduced to ⅓ of its original quantity, stirring continuously.

Add the cooked vegetables and frogs' legs meat.

Season to taste.

Garnish with julienned red or yellow bell pepper.

SOPA DE TOMATE E BROCUS CON CHOURICO CHINES
BROCCOLI AND TOMATO SOUP GARNISHED WITH CHINESE SAUSAGE

HYATT REGENCY MACAU, MACAU

SERVES 4

BROCCOLI SOUP

5 oz (1 ¼ c) broccoli flowerettes (150 g)

salt

½ pt (1 ¼ c) double (heavy) cream (280 ml)

Cook broccoli in salted water until soft.

Drain and purée in a liquidiser.

Place broccoli purée in a pot, add cream and heat gently until just boiling.

TOMATO SOUP

1 oz (2 tbs) carrots—diced (30 g)

1 oz (2 tbs) onion—diced (30 g)

1 ½ oz (3 tbs) butter (45 g)

3 ½ oz (1 small) tomato—cut into chunks (100 g)

¾ pt (2 c) chicken stock (480 ml) (see glossary)

1 ¾ oz (3 ½ tbs) tomato concentrate (paste) (50 g)

salt and pepper to taste

4 fl oz (½ c) double (heavy) cream (120 ml)

Sauté carrot and onion in butter.

Add tomato chunks, chicken stock, and tomato concentrate. Cook for 15–20 minutes.

Season with salt and pepper.

Purée mixture in a liquidiser.

Return to pot and add the cream.

Heat through gently, just until boiling.

TO ASSEMBLE AND GARNISH

6 oz (1 ½ c) Chinese sausage—sliced (175 g)

Blanch the sausage in boiling water for 1 minute. Drain and dice.

Combine servings of the 2 soups in one bowl and garnish with Chinese sausage.

Note: Chinese sausage—or lop chong in Cantonese—are hard, red sweet sausages made of pork and pork fat. It is available in Asian or specialty food stores.

Tomato Soup with Coconut

Hyatt Regency Delhi, India

Serves 4

1 fl oz (2 tbs) vegetable oil (30 ml)

3 oz (6 cloves) garlic—crushed (85 g)

1 tsp fresh ginger chopped (5 g)

½ oz bay leaves (14 g)

2 cardamom pods—husked

1 lb ripe tomatoes—chopped (455 g)

1 oz (1) fresh green chilli—chopped (30 g)

2 tsp fresh coriander—chopped, for garnish (10 g)

2 tsp coconut—grated, for garnish (10 g)

Heat oil and sauté garlic, ginger, bay leaves and cardamom until fragrant and golden.

Add tomatoes, stirring occasionally; cook until skins have wrinkled.

Add chilli and salt to taste.

Remove from heat and strain.

Serve hot, garnished with coriander and coconut.

CHILLED MANGO AND CUCUMBER SOUP

○

HYATT REGENCY JEDDAH, SAUDI ARABIA

SERVES 4

6 oz (2 small) cucumbers—sliced in half lengthwise and pips removed (170 g)

2 oz (3 stalks) green onions (scallions)—roughly chopped (55 g)

6 oz (1 ½ c) fresh mango pulp (170 g)

8 oz (1 c) plain yoghurt (225 g)

½ oz (1 clove) garlic—crushed (15 g)

mint sprigs—for garnish

Grate the cucumber. Set aside.

○

Place green onions, mango pulp, yoghurt and garlic in a liquidiser and process until smooth.

○

Add grated cucumber and mix. Chill well.

○

Serve, decorated with mint leaves.

HOT AND SOUR SOUP

○

HYATT TIANJIN, PEOPLE'S REPUBLIC OF CHINA

SERVES 4

1 ½ oz (3 tbs) roast pork—finely shredded (40 g)

½ oz (½ tbs) salt (7 g)

1 fl oz (2 tbs) soy sauce (10 ml)

¼ oz (2 tsp) cornflour (cornstarch) (10 g)

1 ¾ pt (4 ¼ c) chicken stock (1 *l*) (see glossary)

1 ½ oz (3 tbs) cucumber—finely shredded (45 g)

1 ½ oz (3 tbs) bamboo shoots—finely shredded (45 g)

1 ½ oz (3 tbs) Chinese black mushrooms—rehydrated and finely shredded (45 g)

1 ½ oz (3 tbs) ham—finely shredded (45 g)

1 ½ oz (3 tbs) tofu—diced (45 g)

2 eggs

1 fl oz (2 tbs) rice vinegar (10 ml)

½ fl oz (1 tbs) oriental sesame oil (15 ml)

1 tsp black pepper (5 g)

Marinate shredded pork with a pinch of salt, soy sauce, 1 tsp (5 g) cornstarch and 2 tsp (7 ml) water. Set aside for 15 minutes.

○

Bring chicken stock to a boil and add vegetables, ham, pork, and tofu; simmer for 2 minutes.

○

Beat eggs and add remaining cornflour.

○

Pour egg mixture into boiling stock while continuously stirring.

○

Add remaining seasonings.

○

Pour into a soup tureen and serve.

Note: To rehydrate Chinese mushrooms, soak in warm water to cover for 30 minutes. Drain, discard stems and shred the caps.

CHILLED CORN CHOWDER
WITH AVOCADO AND CRABMEAT

U.N. PLAZA HOTEL, A PARK HYATT HOTEL, NEW YORK, U.S.A.

SERVES 4

CORN CHOWDER

2 c fresh corn kernels (reserve a few for decoration)

2 tbs butter (60 g)

3 medium leeks—finely minced (white part only)

1 c clam juice (240 ml)

salt and pepper to taste

In a saucepan, melt butter and sauté the leeks until soft (about 3 minutes).

Add corn kernels and sauté another 10 minutes.

Add clam juice and simmer 10 more minutes.

Cool as quickly as possible.

AVOCADO CRABMEAT SOUP

2–3 avocados, ripe

1 c freshly cooked crabmeat

2 tbs lemon juice (30 ml)

1 ½–2 c sour cream (360–480 ml)

1 onion—grated

few cilantro leaves—chopped

Halve avocado, remove seeds and skin.

Cut avocado meat into cubes and mix with lemon juice, the cooled chowder sour cream, onion, crabmeat and cilantro.

Pour into a blender and purée until soft and creamy. Season to taste.

If consistency is too thick, add more clam juice or chicken stock. If it's too thin, add more avocado meat (consistency depends on size of avocados).

Chill well.

GARNISH AND HOW TO SERVE

½ c crabmeat

2 taco shells—break into small pieces

reserved corn kernels

1 large-size tomato—peeled, seeded and diced

few cilantro leaves—chopped

4 crab claws of stone crab—with the shell removed.

Use four 4-inch (10 cm) deep soup bowls.

Sprinkle crabmeat and broken taco shells.

Pour the soup equally into each bowl.

Sprinkle on top the corn kernels, diced tomato and chopped cilantro.

Place crab claw at centre of each bowl.

Melon Soup
with Pink Shrimp

Hyatt Regency Dubai, United Arab Emirates

Serves 4

1 ½ lb (2 medium) cantaloupe melons
(600 g each)

4 fl oz (½ c) chicken stock (120 ml)
(see glossary)

salt to taste

7 oz (1 c) plain yoghurt (200 g)

juice of 1 lemon

5 oz (12 large) shrimp—peeled and
cooked, with tail intact, for garnish
(150 g)

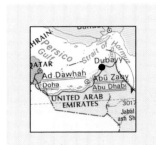

Cut the melons in half crosswise and
discard pips.

Using a small, sharp knife, make a
series of small V-shaped indentations
around the circumference of the
melons (see photo).

Scoop out most of the pulp from the
melon halves.

Place melon pulp in a liquidiser with
the chicken stock, adding salt if you
desire, and purée until smooth.

Blend in yoghurt and lemon juice.

Pour purée into the melon shells add
shrimp and serve.

Cold Green Asparagus Soup

Hyatt Regency Jerusalem, Israel

Serves 4

10 ½ oz (2 ½ c) fresh asparagus (300 g)

1 oz (2 tbs) butter (30 g)

2 shallots—finely chopped

salt and pepper to taste

½ pt (1 ¼ c) chicken stock (300 ml)
(see glossary)

6 oz (¾ c) double (heavy) cream
(150 ml)

½ oz (1 tbs) almonds—flaked,
for garnish (10 g)

Wash asparagus and cut stalks into
1 ½ inch; (3.75 cm) pieces leaving tips
whole.

Blanch tips in salted water till al dente
and save for garnish.

Heat butter in a saucepan. Add
shallots, asparagus stems and salt and
pepper.

Cover and cook over low heat, shaking
pan occasionally for 2–3 minutes.

Stir in chicken stock and simmer
gently for approximately 20 minutes.

Put mixture in a liquidiser and purée,
then strain through a sieve lined with
cheesecloth.

Stir in half the cream and pour soup
into 4 soup plates.

Garnish with remaining cream,
asparagus tips and a few almonds.

Chill thoroughly before serving.

Baby Papaya with Crabmeat

⌒

Hyatt Regency Hong Kong, Hong Kong

Serves 4

4, 12-oz (small) papayas (340 g each)

3 ½ oz crabmeat (100 g)

3 oz (½ c) diced chicken (80 g)

1 ½ oz mushrooms—fresh, diced (40 g)

1 ½ oz (⅓ c) Parma (prosciutto) or Chinese Ham—diced (40 g)

16 fl oz (2 c) fish or chicken stock (500ml) (see glossary)

6 stems fresh chives or sprigs

fresh coriander [chopped for garnish]

Remove the stem ends of the papayas.

⌒

Scoop out and discard pips.

⌒

Place papayas in a heatproof dish to keep them stable.

⌒

Mix remaining ingredients in a small bowl.

⌒

Pour mixture over papaya tops and place in steamer above boiling water. Steam for 20 minutes, or until papaya is soft.

⌒

Garnish tops with chives or coriander.

Sopa de Medula
Marrow Soup

Hyatt Regency Guadalajara, Mexico

Serves 4

1 fl oz (2 tbs) vegetable oil (30 ml)

2 oz (½ c) onion—chopped (55 g)

⅛ oz (1 tsp) garlic—chopped (5 g)

5 ¾ oz (1 ½ medium) tomatoes—peeled and cut into cubes (160 g)

2 bay leaves

1 pinch marjoram—fresh, chopped

2 ¾ pt (6 ½ c) chicken stock (1½ *l*) (see glossary)

3 oz (¾ c) tomato concentrate (paste) (80 g)

12 oz (¾ lb) beef bone marrow—cut into cubes (340 g)

1 oz (2 tbs) chipolte chilli or Mexican hot sauce (30 g)

¾ oz (1 ½ tbs) fresh cilantro—chopped, for garnish (20 g)

In a deep pot, heat the oil and fry onions and garlic until golden brown.

Add tomatoes, bay leaves and marjoram. Mix.

Stir in chicken stock and tomato concentrate, boil for 5 minutes.

Remove bay leaves and place soup in liquidiser. Blend until smooth, then strain.

Pour soup back into pot and place over medium heat, adding bone marrow and chilli sauce.

Serve in bowls or cups garnished with cilantro.

SALADS

Ensalada de Los Chiles Pimiento Morron con Crepas de Elote
Three Pepper Salad with Corn Crepes

Hyatt Regency Acapulco, Mexico

Serves 4

Salad

9 oz (2 medium) red bell peppers (250 g)

9 oz (2 medium) green bell peppers (250 g)

9 oz (2 medium) yellow bell peppers (250 g)

3 ½ oz (¾ c) watercress—washed and dried (100 g)

8 oz (1 c) curly endive (chicory)— leaves separated, washed and dried (225 g)

In a large saucepan of boiling water, briefly blanch the peppers until the skins wrinkle.

Peel the peppers, halve and remove pips.

Cut peppers into 1-inch (2 ½ cm) cubes.

Set out greens for salad.

Vinaigrette

4 tbs wine vinegar (60 ml)

¼ pt (½ c) olive oil (120 ml)

3 ½ oz (¾ c) button mushrooms— sliced (100 g)

2 oz (½ c) onion—minced (50 g)

2 oz (1 c) fresh basil leaves—minced (50 g)

salt and pepper to taste

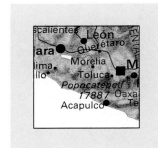

Crepes

2 eggs

1 egg yolk

3 ½ oz (3 ¼ c) flour (100 g)

8 fl oz (1 c) milk (240 ml)

3 fl oz (½ c) water (100 ml)

salt to taste

3 ½ oz (5 tbs) butter—melted (100 g)

melted butter for pan

Whisk together the eggs and egg yolk. Slowly add the flour until batter is smooth.

Whisk in milk, water and salt.

Add melted butter.

Heat a crepe pan and brush lightly with melted butter. Pour 1 tbs of crepe batter into pan and spread on bottom to make thin crepes.

Cook until bubbly, then invert and cook on other side until golden brown.

Repeat for remaining crepes, stacking them between layers of greaseproof paper.

Corn Stuffing

2 oz (5 tbs) butter (50 g)

9 oz (2 ½ c) corn kernels— cooked (255 g)

2 oz (½ c) onion—minced (50 g)

2 oz (½ c) red bell pepper—pips removed and minced (50 g)

2 oz (½ c) green bell pepper—pips removed and minced (50 g)

2 serrano chillies—chopped

¾ oz (¾ c) fresh coriander— coarsely chopped (20 g)

salt and pepper to taste

Melt butter in a saucepan and sauté all ingredients to heat through. Stir well.

To Assemble and Serve

Place a spoonful of corn stuffing on each crepe. Fold in quarters to create a triangle shape.

Place stuffed crepes on individual salad plates and accompany with the salad greens and peppers.

Pour dressing on salad and serve.

Note: Serrano chillies are small, hot peppers (about 2 inches long), with an intense, lasting bite. Any fiery chilli may be substituted.

AVOCADO AND SMOKED SALMON SALAD

HYATT AUCKLAND, NEW ZEALAND

SERVES 4

SALAD

juice of 2 lemons

2 ripe avocadoes—halved, stone removed, peeled and cut in wedges

3 oz button mushrooms—sliced (85 g)

4 leaves red lettuce—washed, dried and torn apart

7 oz smoked salmon—sliced (200 g)

3 oz green beans—blanched in salted water and drained (85 g)

5 oz (1 large) tomato—pips removed and cut into wedges or rings (150 g)

1 oz (2 tbs) shallots—finely minced (30 g)

Sprinkle lemon juice on avocado wedges and mushrooms to prevent discolouration.

On individual salad plates, arrange a lettuce leaf, a few avocado wedges and some smoked salmon.

Mix the beans, mushrooms, tomato and shallots in a bowl. Drizzle on some of the dressing (recipe below) and toss.

DRESSING

2 fl oz (4 tbs) olive oil (60 ml)

1 fl oz (2 tbs) balsamic vinegar (30 ml)

1 tsp Dijon mustard (5 g)

salt and pepper to taste

Cayenne pepper to taste

lemon juice to taste

Blend oil, vinegar and mustard. Add seasonings and lemon juice to taste.

TO SERVE

1 lime, cut in wedges

16 black olives

4 dill sprigs

Drizzle remaining dressing on the avocado, salmon and lettuce.

Arrange the vegetables neatly beside them.

Garnish with lime wedges, black olives and dill sprigs.

Salata Bil Fatayer
Crispy Salad on Pitta Bread

⟨⟩

Casablanca Hyatt Regency, Morocco

Serves 4

Bread and Cheese Spread

½ oz (1 tbs) butter (15 g)

½ oz (1 clove) garlic—minced (15 g)

2 pitta breads—halved crosswise to make 4 round slices

8 fl oz (1 c) plain yoghurt (240 ml)

1 oz fresh goat or feta cheese—crumbled (30 g)

Melt butter over low heat.

○

Lightly sauté the garlic, then pan-fry the bread slices.

○

Cool bread and spread lightly with a mixture of yoghurt and goat cheese. Place each piece of bread on a separate plate.

Topping

4 oz (1 medium) cucumber—peeled (115 g)

5 oz (1 medium) green bell pepper—pips removed (140 g)

5 oz (1 medium) red bell pepper—pips removed (140 g)

8 oz (8 small) radishes—peeled (225 g)

8 oz (2 medium) tomatoes—peeled and pips removed (225 g)

(4 tbs) vegetable oil (60 ml)

2 oz (½ medium) onion—minced (60 g)

2 sprigs mint—coarsely chopped

salt and pepper to taste

Cut cucumber, peppers, radishes and tomatoes into small pieces, then mix with the oil, onion and mint. Season to taste.

○

Place vegetable mixture on the pitta bread slices, mounding it in the centre, and serve.

Note: Pitta bread is a round flat bread of the Middle East that can be split open to form a pocket for a filling.

CRISPY RATATOUILLE IN PHYLLO PASTRY
ON DICED TOMATOES FLAVOURED WITH HERBS

HYATT REGENCY SEOUL, KOREA

SERVES 4

5 oz courgettes (zucchini) (140 g)

5 ½ oz aubergine (eggplant) (155 g)

2 ½ oz (½ medium) red bell pepper (70 g)

2 ½ oz (½ medium) green bell pepper (70 g)

1 ¾ fl oz (3 ½ tbs) olive oil (52 ml)

1 oz (¼ c) onion—chopped (30 g)

10 ½ oz (2 large) green tomatoes—peeled and juice removed; cubed (298 g)

¼ oz (1 tbs) garlic—chopped (7 g)

½ oz (2 tbs) each basil, thyme, oregano—chopped (15 g)

4 sheets phyllo pastry 8x10 inches (20x25 cm)

4 green onions (scallions)—green part only, blanched

Preheat oven to 400° F (200° C).

Dice all vegetables, except the tomatoes, onion and garlic.

Heat a nonstick pan with a little of the oil and briefly stir-fry vegetables (except tomatoes, onion and garlic), keeping them crisp.

Drain vegetables, setting any juice aside.

Briefly sauté the green tomatoes, then add onion and garlic.

Pour in reserved vegetable juices and cook for a few minutes.

Add herbs and remove from heat. Keep warm.

Cut the phyllo sheets in half crosswise.

Put 2 half-sheets of phyllo dough together and place 2 oz (½ c ; 50 g) sautéed vegetables on top. Gather corners in middle to make a bundle. Tie top with green onion.

Make remaining 3 bundles. Place all in greased baking dish. Bake for 15 minutes, or until crisp.

Arrange tomatoes on a large platter. Add phyllo bundles and serve.

Fresh Lobster Salad
with Saffron-Mango Dressing and Stuffed Lychees

Hyatt Regency Hong Kong, Hong Kong

Serves 4

2 small lobsters (approximately 1 ¼ lb (575 g) each)

4 fresh lychees

pinch of saffron

1 ½ fl oz (2 tbs) honey vinegar or any clear vinegar (30 ml)

2 mangoes—halved and flesh scooped into small balls

14 fl oz (¾ c) mayonnaise (400 ml)

1 ¾ fl oz (3 ½ tbs) honey (50 ml)

6 oz (1 small) head curly endive (chicory)—washed and separated into leaves (170 g)

⅔ lb thin green beans—trimmed and cooked (300 g)

Cook lobsters in boiling water for 10 minutes.

Carefully remove tail and claws from shell.

Remove vein and slice tail into 1.3-inch (1 cm) thick medallions.

Keep lobster claw meat intact if possible.

Peel lychees and carefully remove pips.

Mix saffron with honey vinegar and set aside for 15 minutes.

Set 4 mango balls aside and purée the rest.

Add puréed mango, mayonnaise and honey to the saffron vinegar and mix well.

Stuff mango balls into lychees and set aside.

Place endive on individual salad plates. Top with some beans.

Place lychees on salad, drizzle over the dressing and serve.

Note: Lychee is a Chinese fruit that consists of a single pip surrounded by a sweet, edible raisin-like pulp enclosed in a rough brown papery shell. Tinned lychees may be used.

Rojak Betik Muda
Young Papaya Salad

○

Hyatt Saujana, Kuala Lumpur, Malaysia

Serve 4

10 ½ oz (2 large) cucumbers—cubed (300 g)

10 ½ oz (1 small) pineapple—peeled, cored and cubed (300 g)

7 oz (1 large) yam—peeled and cubed (200 g) (see glossary)

1 lb (1 large) young papaya (medium ripe)—peeled and cubed (400 g)

1 lb (1 large) young green mango—peeled and cubed (450 g)

5 mild dried red chillies, or to taste

7 oz belacan (fermented prawn paste) (200 g)

2 fl oz (4 tbs) otak otak (wet prawn paste) (60 ml)

8 fl oz (1 c) tamarind juice (240 ml)

8 oz (1 c) sugar (200 g)

1 lb ground nuts (peanuts)—fried and roughly ground (450 g)

4 fresh coriander leaves—for garnish

Place cucumber, pineapple, yam, papaya and mango in a bowl.

○

Add the chilli, belacan, otak otak, tamarind juice and sugar. Mix well.

○

Sprinkle with peanuts and garnish with coriander.

Note: Belacan, otak otak and tamarind juice are available in Southeast Asian food stores.

Salada de Espinafres, Abacate Azeitonas e Laranja Com Molho de Mel e Gekigibre
Spinach, Avocado, Olives, and Orange Salad, with Honey and Ginger Dressing

Hyatt Regency Macau, Macau

Serves 4

Salad

10 ½ oz spinach—trimmed and cleaned (298 g)

10 oz (2 medium) oranges—peeled, pips removed, pith removed (300 g)

12 oz (2 small) avocadoes—halved, stone removed, peeled and sliced (340 g)

12 black olives

Dressing

6 fl oz (¾ c) honey (180 ml)

3 oz (¾ c) fresh ginger—peeled and grated (85 g)

juice of 2 limes

Blend ingredients in a bowl.

To Assemble and Serve

Place spinach in a bowl and toss with dressing. Place greens on salad plates.

Garnish with orange segments, avocado slices and olives.

GLASS NOODLE SALAD
WITH SEAFOOD AND CRABMEAT

HYATT REGENCY SINGAPORE, SINGAPORE

SERVES 4

NOODLES AND SEAFOOD

1 tsp salt

½ lb glass (cellophane) noodles—soaked in cold water for 30 minutes and drained (240 g)

½ oz (1 tbs) shallots—finely chopped (15 g)

5 ¼ oz crabmeat (150 g)

8 baby octopus—cleaned and cooked

8 medium prawns—peeled, deveined and cooked

2 stalks lemongrass—finely chopped

1 fresh red chilli—pips removed and diced

⅓ oz (2 tsp) fresh ginger—grated (10 g)

⅔ oz (4 tsp) fresh coriander—chopped (20 g)

1 tbs fresh mint—minced (15 g)

1 tsp fresh red chilli—minced (5 g)

Bring ¼ pt (3 ½ c; 1 *l*) water to a boil. Add salt.

Add noodles. Remove and cool.

Drain and rinse noodles under tap water to cool well.

In a deep bowl, combine noodles, shallots, crabmeat, octopus, prawns, lemongrass, chilli, ginger and coriander.

Mix well and set aside.

Make dressing (recipe follows).

Arrange ingredients as shown in photo. Garnish with mint and chilli.

DRESSING

¾ fl oz (5 tsp) lime juice (25 ml)

1 fl oz (2 tbs) fish sauce (30 ml)

¼ oz (1 tsp) sugar (5 g)

¼ oz (1 tsp) fresh coriander—chopped (5 g)

⅓ oz (2 tsp) green onion—sliced (10 g)

Combine ingredients for dressing in small saucepan and bring to a boil, stirring continuously. Remove from heat.

Allow to cool.

Avocado Salad
with Tomato and Egg

Hyatt Regency Dubai, United Arab Emirates

Serves 4

Salad

2 avocadoes—cut in half, peeled and
  stone removed

10 oz (2 large) tomatoes (285 g)

salt and pepper to taste

3 oz bacon—chopped (85 g)

4 eggs

1 pt (2 ½ c) water (600ml)—with 1 tsp
  of vinegar added

8 oz (1 head) iceberg lettuce (225 g)

4 oz (1 medium) onion—sliced into
  rings (115 g)

2 oz (4 tbs) pine kernels (pignoli) (60 g)

Blanch tomatoes briefly in boiling
water 3–5 minutes.

Plunge into ice water, drain and peel.

Remove pips and chop into small
cubes.

Season tomato cubes with salt and
pepper and set aside.

Fry bacon till golden brown. Set aside
and keep warm.

Poach eggs carefully in vinegar-water
3–5 minutes.

Remove with a perforated spoon and
plunge into cold water.

Separate lettuce leaves and arrange on
salad plates.

Place avocado halves on plates. Fill
hollows with tomato cubes.

Drizzle half the amount of dressing
over avocado (recipe follows).

Arrange eggs on top of avocado and
garnish with bacon.

Arrange onion rings alongside avocado
and garnish with pine kernels.

Serve remaining dressing with salad.

Dressing

4 fl oz (4 tbs) corn oil (60 ml)

½ fl oz (1 tbs) sherry or red wine
  vinegar (15 ml)

½ fl oz (1 tbs) beef or chicken stock
  (15 ml) (see glossary)

salt, pepper and sugar to taste.

Mix ingredients well.

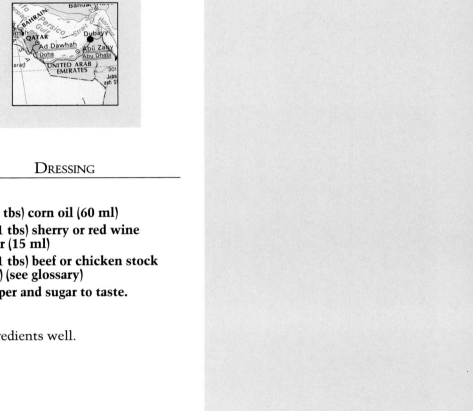

TROPICAL KING PRAWN SALAD

⌒

HYATT REGENCY SANCTUARY COVE, QUEENSLAND, AUSTRALIA

SERVES 4

14 oz king or jumbo prawns—cooked and shelled (400 g)

1 ¼ lb spinach—trimmed, cleaned and chopped (500 g)

3 oz (⅓ c) orange segments (85 g)

1 ½ oz (3 tbs) macadamia nuts—toasted and flaked or chopped (45 g)

1 lb (1 small) pineapple—trimmed, cored and sliced into rings (450 g)

4 ¼ oz cottage cheese (130 g)—formed into balls with a melon baller

Set aside 4 prawns for garnish. Slice the rest into cubes.

○

Mix the spinach with the prawns, orange segments and half the macadamia nuts. Place in centre of a salad platter.

○

Arrange the pineapple rings around spinach mound.

○

Put cottage cheese balls on each pineapple ring.

○

Place 4 prawns between the pineapple rings.

○

Sprinkle with remaining nuts and serve with vinaigrette of choice.

YAM NUA
THAI BEEF SALAD

GRAND HYATT ERAWAN BANGKOK, THAILAND

SERVES 4

BEEF AND MARINADE

4 slices (4 ½ oz) beef tenderloin (120 g)
7 tbs white vinegar (100 ml)
1 ½ oz white sugar (45 g)
1 ½ oz garlic—minced (45 g)
3 tbs Nam Pla (Thai fish sauce) (45 ml)
4 ¼ oz Tau Pan (Chinese chilli paste) (120 g)

Mix the vinegar, sugar, garlic, fish sauce and chilli paste together.

Grill the meat until medium rare.

Slice the meat thinly and marinate for a few minutes.

SALAD AND DRESSING

2 heads Romaine lettuce—cleaned and dried
1 c lime juice—freshly squeezed (240 ml)
⅓ c Thai fish sauce (85 ml)
2 tsp light soy sauce (10 ml)
2 oz fresh coriander—finely chopped (55 g)
2 oz scallions—fresh and finely chopped (55 g)
1 oz garlic—finely chopped (18 g)
1 oz red chilli—finely chopped (28 g)
1 oz green chilli—finely chopped (28 g)
salt and pepper to taste

Neatly arrange the lettuce leaves on centre of plate. Set aside.

Combine all ingredients for the dressing and set aside.

GARNISH

9 oz cabbage—shredded into coarse strips, approximately 2 inches (5 cm) long
fresh cilantro leaves
1 (large) cucumber
1 ripe papaya—peeled and sliced into 2 inch (5 cm) sticks

Cut cucumber lengthwise and remove pips.

Cut again crosswise and further cut into thinner strips.

Marinate the cabbage strips in the same marinade used for the beef.

Place a small amount of marinated cabbage on a strip of cucumber and roll up.

Do the same for the papaya, roll up papaya sticks on cucumber strips.

TO ASSEMBLE AND SERVE

Place sliced, marinated beef on top of lettuce

Surround the salad with 3 cabbage and 3 papaya rolls.

Spoon dressing over the beef, lettuce and rolls.

Generously garnish top of beef with fresh cilantro leaves.

Shredded Carrot and Radish Salad
with Smoked Salmon

Century Hyatt Tokyo, Japan

Serves 4

2 oz (¼ c) carrot—shredded (60 g)

4 oz (1 c) white radishes—shredded (115 g)

1 tbs salt (15 g)

8 dried apricots

8 prunes

5 fl oz (½ c) wine vinegar (120 ml)

1 oz (2 tbs) sugar (30 g)

2 ½ oz smoked salmon—sliced (60 g)

grated lemon zest—for garnish

12 corn salad (mache)—for garnish

Mix the carrots and radishes in a bowl; sprinkle with the salt. Toss and leave for 15 minutes.

Soften the apricots and prunes in cold water. Drain and cut into strips.

Rinse carrot and radishes under running water. Drain well.

Mix vinegar and sugar, then add the carrot, radishes, apricots, prunes and smoked salmon.

Place above mixture on individual plates and garnish with lemon zest (rind) and corn salad.

Ensaladang Talong
Warm Filipino Eggplant Salad

Hyatt Regency Manila, Philippines

Serves 4

24 oz (4 medium) aubergines (eggplant) (680 g)

10 oz (2 ½ medium) onions—peeled and julienned (285 g)

8 oz (2 medium) tomatoes—diced (225 g)

½ oz (1 stalk) green onion (scallion)—diced (15 g)

¼ oz (1 small) fresh hot chilli—thinly sliced (7 g)

1 oz (2 tbs) bagoong (30 g)

slivered fresh hot chilli—for garnish

slivered green onion—for garnish

salt and white pepper to taste

Note: Bagoong is a fermented shrimp paste, available in Asian markets.

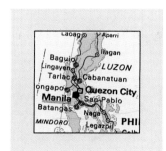

Boil the aubergines till tender—about 5 minutes.

Drain, then slice each open lengthwise and then on both ends so they fold open like a book. Keep warm.

In a bowl, mix onions, tomatoes and green onion.

Blend the bagoong with the chilli, and add to tomato-onion mixture.

Toss gently, then season with salt and white pepper.

Top the aubergine with the mixed salad. Garnish with additional chilli and green onion as shown.

RED EMPEROR FISH ON GARDEN SALAD
WITH A TOASTED PINE-KERNEL VINAIGRETTE

HYATT REGENCY PERTH, AUSTRALIA

SERVES 4

SALAD

1 ¼ lb red emperor fish fillets—cut into 20 strips (575 g)

salt and pepper to taste

pinch coriander pips—crushed

juice of 1 lemon

flour for dusting

1 oz (2 tbs) butter (30 g)

8 leaves butter (bibb) lettuce—washed and dried

8 leaves mignonette lettuce—washed and dried

8 leaves iceberg lettuce—washed and dried

8 leaves trevise lettuce—washed and dried

8 leaves festival (curly endive) lettuce—washed and dried

8 leaves witloof (Belgian endive) lettuce—washed and dried

Season the fish strips with salt and pepper, coriander pips and lemon juice.

Lightly flour the fish and sauté in butter until golden.

Tear the leaves apart with hands and mix in a bowl. Place on individual salad plates.

Place the warm fish strips on salad (5 slices per plate) and toss gently.

Drizzle vinaigrette (recipe follows) over greens and sprinkle with pine-kernels.

PINE-KERNEL VINAIGRETTE

1 ½ oz (3 tbs) pine-kernels (pignoli)—toasted lightly (45 g)

3 fl oz (6 tbs) white wine vinegar (90 ml)

3 fl oz (6 tbs) walnut oil (90 ml)

¾ oz (3 tbs) onion—chopped (20 g)

¾ oz (3 tbs) chive—chopped (20 g)

salt and pepper to taste

Set aside ¼ of pine-kernels for garnish.

Mix the remaining ingredients.

ENSALADA DE NOPALITOS
CACTUS SALAD

HYATT REGENCY CANCUN, MEXICO

SERVES 4

8 oz (2 medium) prickly pear cactus
leaves (225 g)

4 oz (1 medium) lemon—halved (115 g)

3 ¼ oz (1 small) onion—cubed (90 g)

3 ¼ oz (1 small) tomato—cubed (90 g)

1 oz (¼ c) fresh coriander—chopped
(30 g)

1 jalapeno chilli—seeded and chopped

1 ½ fl oz (3 tbs) vinegar (44 ml)

salt and pepper to taste

1 ¾ oz Monterey Jack or other mild
white cheese like mozzarella—
grated (50 g)

5 oz (1 large) onion—sliced into rings
for garnish (150 g)

*Note: Fresh cactus leaves are a
popular ingredient in Mexico,
but extremely difficult to locate
elsewhere. There is no substitute.*

Remove the thorns from cactus leaves,
then cut into ¼-inch (6 cm) cubes.

Rinse cactus cubes under running
water, then drain.

Bring a pot of salted water to a boil,
add the lemon halves and cactus, and
cook until tender but firm.

Drain and cool.

Place cactus in a salad bowl with the
onion, tomato, coriander, jalapeno,
vinegar, salt and pepper. Chill.

When ready to serve, sprinkle the
grated cheese on top of salad and
decorate dish with onion rings.

Tender Scallops Sautéed in Café de Paris Butter
with Chilled Apples and Cheese Salad

◯

The Hotel Canberra, A Park Hyatt Hotel, Australia

Serves 4

Café de Paris Butter

1 lb unsalted butter (450 g)
½ oz anchovy fillets (12 g)
½ oz capers (12 g)
1 oz tomato ketchup (28 g)
½ oz paprika (12 g)
½ oz cayenne pepper (12 g)
½ oz crushed garlic (12 g)
½ oz English mustard (12 g)
1 oz parsley—chopped (28 g)
1 oz chives—chopped (28 g)
2 oz shallots (55 g)
⅓ oz fennel (10 g)
⅓ oz thyme (10 g)
⅓ oz tarragon (10 g)
⅓ oz curry powder (10 g)
3 white peppercorns—chopped
4 tsp Worcestershire sauce (20 ml)
4 drops Tabasco sauce
3 tsp brandy (15 ml)
3 tsp sherry (15 ml)
juice and zest of 1 lemon
juice and zest of 1 orange

Cut butter into cubes and set aside. chill.

◯

Place remaining ingredients in a bowl and marinate overnight.

◯

Next day, force the marinade through a sieve.

◯

Cream the butter with a mixer until smooth.

◯

Gradually add the sieved marinade until well mixed, light and double in bulk.

◯

Set aside in refrigerator.

Salad and Dressing

12 oz assorted lettuce (340 g) (fuzzee, red leaf, chicory, radicchio)
1 (medium) red apple—shred into wedges with skin on
2 tbs bacon—chopped, fry until brown and crispy
2 ½ oz parmesan cheese (70 g)
1 ¾ oz croutons (50 g)
2 oz chives—chopped (55 g)
1 (medium) tomato—diced
3 ½ fl oz (7 tbs) walnut oil (100 ml)
1 ¾ fl oz (3 ½ tbs) white wine vinegar (50 ml)
½ fl oz (1 tbs) sherry (15 ml)
salt and pepper to taste

For the sherry vinaigrette, add oil, vinegar, sherry, salt and pepper in a bowl and mix well.

◯

For the salad, wash and dry the lettuces and tear apart with your hands.

◯

Sprinkle on little of the vinaigrette.

◯

Toss and place salad on centre of 4 serving plates.

◯

Arrange 3–4 slices of apple per plate.

◯

Sprinkle on the bacon, cheese and croutons, then top with chives and diced tomato.

◯

Chill and set aside.

Scallops

24 scallops—cleaned, and shells discarded
Café de Paris butter

In a saucepan, melt down the Café de Paris butter slowly.

◯

Separate 2 spoonfuls of the butter and reheat in a sauté pan.

◯

Quickly sauté the scallops until cooked (2–3 minutes)

To Assemble and Serve

Arrange the warm scallops around the salad and pour the warm Café de Paris butter over.

ROAST QUAIL SALAD
WITH GRILLED COURGETTES AND SPINACH
WITH A BALSAMIC OLIVE-OIL DRESSING

HYATT KINGSGATE SYDNEY, AUSTRALIA

SERVES 4

2 lb (4 large) quail (900 g)

½ fl oz (1 tbs) olive paste or purée (15 ml)

7 fl oz (¾ c) virgin olive oil (180 ml)

1 ½-2 fl oz (3–4 tbs) balsamic vinegar (45-60 ml)

4 oz (1 medium) onion—grated (115 g)

10 oz spinach—stems discarded, washed and leaves shredded (285 g)

15 oz (3 large) tomatoes—peeled (425 g)

12 oz (3 small) courgettes (zucchini) (340 g)

8 small black olives—for garnish

salt and pepper to taste

Season quail with salt and pepper and roast in a hot oven of 450° F (225° C) for 30–40 minutes. Remove breast-bones and keep warm.

Make a dressing by mixing olive paste and oil, vinegar, salt and pepper.

Add a small amount of dressing to grated onion and marinate for 5 minutes.

Add a small amount of dressing to shredded spinach. Toss well.

Cut tomatoes into rounded wedges.

Slice courgettes on an angle crosswise ½-inch (1.25 cm) thick.

Grill courgette slices and place in a bowl. Toss with a small amount of dressing.

Put spinach on each salad plate, placing on top the onion and then the quail in the centre.

Arrange courgette and tomato slices around plate.

Drizzle dressing over top and garnish with olives. Serve.

Spring Salad with Warm Lamb Loin

Hyatt Auckland, New Zealand

Serves 4

Salad

5 oz trimmed, thinly sliced lamb from loin (150 g)

½ fl oz (1 tbs) soybean oil (15 ml)

14 oz assorted spring greens (400 g)

1 ¾ oz bean sprouts (50 g)

8 oz (2 medium) plums—stones removed, then thinly sliced (230 g)

¾ oz (3 tbs) pine kernels (pignoli)—toasted (45 g)

3 red tamarinds (optional) (see glossary)

Briefly sauté the lamb in oil for 2 minutes on each side. Keep warm.

◯

Arrange greens and sprouts in a circle on 4 individual plates.

◯

Place lamb slices on greens with alternating plum slices. Sprinkle with pine kernels and add dressing. If desired, garnish with tamarinds.

Dressing

1 ¾ fl oz (3 ½ tbs) grape-seed or virgin olive oil (50 ml)

1 tsp grainy mustard (5 ml)

1 tsp ginger wine (5 ml)

juice of 2 limes

salt and pepper to taste

Combine all ingredients and mix well.

Note: Ginger wine is available in health food shops or delicatessens; or mix ginger, wine and a little sugar and bring to a boil.

Ensalada de Palmitos con Mejillones Marinados
Avocado-Palm Hearts Salad with Marinated Mussels

◯

Hyatt Cancun Caribe Resort & Villas, Mexico

Serves 4

MUSSELS		MARINADE

½ fl oz (1 tbs) vegetable oil (15 ml)
2 oz (4 tbs) chopped shallots (50 g)
½ oz (1 clove) garlic-chopped (15 g)
5 fl oz (½ c) dry white wine (120 ml)
2 large mussels—cleaned and debearded

Heat a large pan with a little oil and sauté shallots and garlic.

◯

Add white wine, ignite immediately and when flames subside, drop mussels in.

◯

Cover and cook 5 minutes or until shells open.

◯

Discard cooking liquid and shells.

◯

Marinate the mussels for 2 hours (see recipe below), then drain, reserving marinade.

¼ oz (1 tbs) coriander pips—cracked (7 g)
1 tsp fresh coriander—chopped
1 fl oz (2 tbs) olive oil (30 ml)
juice of ½ lime
salt and pepper to taste

Mix.

7 oz hearts of palm (200 g)
3 ½ oz lettuce—torn apart (100 g)
7 oz (1 large) beetroot—trimmed and peeled (200 g)
1 avocado—halved, peeled and stone removed

Mix hearts of palm and lettuce.

Boil beetroot until tender, about 45 minutes.

Slice beetroot into thin "half moons." Slice avocado in the same manner.

Arrange hearts of palm and lettuce on individual salad plates.

Arrange the mussels, beetroot and avocado on greens.

Drizzle the marinade over salad and serve.

LOBSTER AND TROPICAL FRUIT SALAD

HYATT REGENCY TAHITI, FRENCH POLYNESIA

SERVES 4

3 oz (¾ c) carrot—sliced (85 g)
3 ½ oz (1 small) onion—sliced (100 g)
⅓ oz (1 clove) garlic—minced (15 g)
3 fl oz (6 tbs) dry white wine (100 ml)
salt and pepper to taste
3 ¼ lb spiny lobster (1.5 kg)
8 fl oz (1 c) plain yoghurt (200 ml)
⅓ oz (1 tbs) fresh dill—chopped (10 g)
juice of 1 lemon
3 ½ oz (¾ c) papaya—diced (100 g)
3 ½ oz lettuce—washed and dried (100 g)

Bring a large pan of water to a boil and add carrot, onion and garlic.

Add wine, salt and pepper and simmer for 10 minutes.

Add lobster and simmer approximately 15 minutes.

Drain lobster and cool.

Remove lobster shell, then devein and slice the tail into 12 equal pieces crosswise.

Save 4 slices for decoration.

Mix yoghurt with the dill, lemon juice, salt and pepper to taste.

Blend the fruit cubes into half the yoghurt dressing.

Arrange lettuce leaves on individual plates.

Place the fruit yoghurt in the centre and top each plate with 4 slices of lobster.

Serve remaining dressing alongside.

SMOKED LAMB AND GOAT CHEESE SALAD
WITH TOMATO CHUTNEY

HYATT REGENCY COOLUM, QUEENSLAND, AUSTRALIA

SERVES 4

SALAD

8 ½ oz smoked boneless lamb (from loin)—thinly sliced (240 g)

4 ½ oz goat cheese (chevre), cut into quarters (120 g)

4 leaves regency lettuce or other green lettuce

4 leaves radicchio

4 leaves Will and Pieter lettuce or other greens

5 leaves witloof (Belgian endive)

4 oz (1 c) red bell pepper, pips removed and julienned (100 g)

Arrange lamb, cheese, greens and red pepper on individual salad plates.

Serve chutney (recipe follows) on plate or alongside.

CHUTNEY

9 oz (2 medium) tomatoes (250 g)

4 oz (1 c) white onion—diced (125 g)

¼ tsp garlic paste (2 g)

½ fl oz (1 tbs) vegetable oil (15 ml)

1 tbs fresh ginger—finely minced (10 g)

½ bay leaf

⅓ oz (2 tbs) fresh red chilli—finely minced (10 g)

4 oz (1 c) sugar (115 g)

¼ cinnamon stick and 1 whole clove—wrapped in muslin bag

5 fl oz (⅔ c) malt vinegar (150 ml)

Blanch tomatoes in boiling water, cool in ice water and slip off skins.

Remove pips from tomatoes and coarsely chop pulp.

Sauté onions with garlic paste in oil and then add remaining ingredients.

Simmer mixture for 10 minutes, then cool, remove musilin bag and refrigerate with chutney until ready to use.

POULET AU CURRY ET SALADE DE RIZ
CURRIED CHICKEN AND RICE SALAD

HYATT REGENCY TAHITI, FRENCH POLYNESIA

SERVES 4

8 oz (3 c) cooked white rice (225 g)

6 oz boneless and skinless chicken breast—poached and julienned (170 g)

2 oz (½ c) celery—diced (60 g)

1 oz (¼ c) green onion—finely sliced (30 g)

2 oz (½ medium) red or green apple—cored and diced (60 g)

2 oz (½ c) walnuts—coarsely chopped (60 g)

2 ½ fl oz (⅓ c) mayonnaise (85 g)

2 fl oz (4 tbs) red vinegar (60 ml)

1 tsp curry powder (5 g)

juice from 1 lemon

salt and pepper to taste

Combine all ingredients and then mix with rice.

Chill thoroughly and serve.

ENSALADA DE CHAYA Y DURAZNILLOS
CHAYA AND CHANTERELLE SALAD

HYATT REGENCY CANCUN, MEXICO

SERVES 4

6 fl oz (¾ c) hazelnut oil (180 ml)

3 ¼ oz (¾) chanterelles (90 g)

½ oz (1 clove) garlic—minced (15 g)

salt and pepper to taste

3 heads witloof (Belgian endive)—washed, dried and cut into 1-inch (2.5 cm) pieces, except for 12 of best leaves for garnish.

3 ½ oz chaya or spinach—washed and dried (100 g)

6 fl oz (¾ c) raspberry vinegar (180 ml)

½ tsp black peppercorns—crushed (2 g)

Heat a dash of hazelnut oil and sauté chanterelles and garlic until half cooked.

Season with salt and pepper. Allow to cool.

In a bowl, mix the chaya or spinach, endive and chanterelles. Arrange on a large salad plate decorated with the reserved witloof leaves and crushed black peppercorns.

Mix remaining hazelnut oil with the raspberry vinegar and drizzle over salad. Serve.

WARM SALAD OF RABBIT
WITH A MACADAMIA NUT DRESSING

HYATT REGENCY ADELAIDE, AUSTRALIA

SERVES 4

SALAD

8 radicchio leaves
8 red oak-leaf lettuce leaves
16 curly endive (chicory) leaves
16 witloof (Belgian endive) leaves
16 lamb's lettuce leaves
16 misuma lettuce leaves
4 oz (½ c) curly cress (120 g)
2 oz (1 small) tomato—cubed (60 g)
4 oz (2 medium) leek-sliced (115 g)
4 oz (1 medium) green bell pepper
   (115 g)
1 lb rabbit breast fillets (455 g)
salt and pepper to taste
vegetable oil for frying

*Note: Misuma lettuce is a regional
   green. Substitute a local lettuce.*

Wash and dry all greens.

Arrange leaves on individual salad
plates.

Put tomato, leek and green pepper on
the plate.

Season rabbit fillets with salt and
pepper.

Pan-fry for 3–4 minutes over low heat.
Remove pan from heat and keep warm
to finish cooking.

DRESSING

2 egg yolks
1 ¾ fl oz (3 ½ tbs) champagne vinegar
   (50 ml)
4 fl oz (½ c) macadamia nut or walnut
   oil (120 ml)
2 ½ fl oz (5 tbs) double (heavy) cream
   (75 ml)
salt and pepper to taste

Put yolks and vinegar in a liquidiser
and blend until smooth.

Slowly add oil, then cream. Season
with salt and pepper.

TO SERVE

Slice the rabbit into thin strips.

Arrange rabbit strips in a fan shape
over the greens and drizzle on
dressing.

Add garnishes and serve.

Prawn Salad in Chilli-Lime Dressing

Hyatt Regency Singapore, Singapore

Serves 4

Salad

16 large prawns

2 Japanese or regular cucumbers—thinly sliced crosswise

1 ½ oz butter (bibb) lettuce—shredded (45 g)

1 ½ oz red chicory—shredded (45 g)

1 ½ oz romaine lettuce—shredded (45 g)

1 lb (2 large) mangoes—halved, peeled and sliced (450 g)

8 cherry tomatoes—halved

6 quail eggs—hard-boiled and peeled

1 ½ oz enoki mushrooms (45 g)

1 ½ oz alfalfa sprouts (45 g)

Steam prawns for 5 minutes.

Peel, discard shells and devein. Allow to cool.

Arrange greens, mango slices, tomatoes, quail eggs, mushrooms and alfalfa sprouts as illustrated.

Place prawns on top. Serve dressing separately.

Chilli-Lime Dressing

3 ½ fl oz (7 tbs) fish sauce (100 ml) (see glossary)

3 ½ fl oz (7 tbs) lime juice (100 ml)

8 fl oz (1 c) water (240 ml)

1 oz (¼ c) fresh red chilli—minced (30 g)

1 oz (1 tbs) sugar (30 g)

1 oz (¼ c) fresh coriander—chopped (30 g)

salt and pepper to taste

Mix ingredients well and season to taste.

Ensalada de Calamares con Alcachofas y una Vinagreta de Chile Dulce

Calamari and Artichoke Salad with a Sweet Pepper Vinaigrette

Hyatt Regency Acapulco, Mexico

Serves 4

Calamari and Artichokes

4 oz (2 medium) artichokes (225 g)
1 ½ lb calamari (squid)—cleaned, with heads and tentacles discarded (680 g)
juice of 1 lemon
salt to taste
vinaigrette (see recipe following)

Separately fill 2 deep saucepans with water. Add lemon juice and salt, and bring to a boil.

○

Place artichokes in one saucepan and calamari in the other.

○

Simmer both for 45 minutes.

○

Drain both and dip in ice water to refresh.

○

Halve the artichokes and remove the chokes. Set aside.

○

Drain and marinate in 4 fl oz (½ c; 120ml) vinaigrette (see recipe below) for 1 hour.

Salad Greens

7 oz (1 ¾ c) curly endive (chicory)—washed and dried (200 g)
8 basil leaves—washed and dried
3 ½ oz watercress leaves—washed and dried (100 g)

Vinaigrette

4 tbs red wine vinegar (60 ml)
¼ pt (½ c) olive oil (120 ml)
juice of 2 lemons
3 ½ oz (¾ c) red bell pepper—pips removed and diced (100 g)
3 ½ oz (¾ c) green bell pepper—pips removed and diced (100 g)
2 oz (½ c) onion—diced (50 g)
2 ½ oz (5 cloves) garlic—minced (70 g)
1 tbs fresh coriander—chopped (8 g)
salt and pepper to taste

Whisk vinegar and lemon juice with olive oil.

○

Add the peppers, onion, garlic, coriander, salt and pepper. Mix well.

To Assemble and Serve

Arrange salad greens on individual salad plates.

○

Drain calamari and arrange with artichokes on salad plates.

○

Pour remaining vinaigrette over artichokes and serve.

CHAM CHI SALAD WITH GUL SAUCE
RED LEAF LETTUCE AND MARINATED TUNA WITH HONEY DRESSING

HYATT REGENCY CHEJU, KOREA

SERVES 4

TUNA AND MARINADE

2 oz (½ c) salt (55 g)
4 ½ oz (¾ c) sugar (125 g)
1 ¼ oz (7 tsp) fresh dill—chopped (40 g)
¼ oz (2 tbs) juniper berries—minced (7 g)
¼ oz (2 tbs) pine kernels (pignoli)—minced (7 g)
6 fl oz (¾ c) vegetable oil (180 ml)
1 lb fresh tuna fillet (450 g)

Mix salt, sugar, dill, juniper berries, pine kernels and oil. Stir well until salt and sugar are dissolved.

Drizzle some marinade on the bottom of a dish, large enough to hold tuna in one layer.

Place tuna fillet over marinade, then drizzle on rest of marinade.

Cover and marinate for 2 days in refrigerator. Turn 2–3 times.

DRESSING

2 ½ fl oz (5 tbs) wine vinegar (75 ml)
1 egg
⅓ oz (2 tsp) mustard seeds (10 g)
3 fl oz (7 tbs) honey (100 ml)
2 oz (4 tbs) mustard (60 g)
6 fl oz (¾ c) salad oil (180 ml)
salt and pepper to taste

Place vinegar and egg in a liquidiser and blend for a few seconds.

Add next 4 ingredients and mix well.

Season with salt and pepper.

TO ASSEMBLE AND SERVE

10 ½ oz red leaf lettuce—washed, dried and torn into pieces (300 g)
2 oz red bell pepper (60 g)—cored and cut into strips for garnish

Drain and slice tuna into thin pieces.

Place lettuce in the centre of individual salad plates and sprinkle each plate with dressing.

Arrange tuna slices around greens.

Sprinkle red pepper strips on top and serve.

SPINACH SALAD
WITH CHICKEN LIVERS AND RASPBERRY VINAIGRETTE

HYATT TIANJIN, PEOPLE'S REPUBLIC OF CHINA

SERVES 4

SALAD AND DRESSING

14 oz fresh spinach—trimmed, washed
  and dried (395 g)
6 fl oz (¾ c) olive oil (150 ml)
1 ½ fl oz (3 tbs) raspberry vinegar
  (45 ml)
2 dashes lemon juice
¼ fl oz (1 tbs) fresh parsley—chopped
  (5 g)
salt and pepper to taste
2 oz (2 slices) wholemeal (whole
  wheat) bread—crusts removed; cut
  into ½-inch (1.25 cm) cubes (55 g)
vegetable oil for frying
½ oz (1 clove) garlic—chopped (15 g)

Place spinach in a large salad bowl.

Mix oil, vinegar, lemon juice and
parsley. Season with salt and pepper.
Set dressing aside.

Spread the bottom of a pan with oil
and fry the bread cubes and garlic until
golden brown. Drain on absorbent
paper towels; discard the garlic. These
are croutons.

CHICKEN LIVERS

10 ½ oz chicken livers (300 g)
1 tbs vegetable oil (15 ml)
salt and pepper to taste

Cut large chicken livers in half, then
cut all into quarters. Remove any fat.
Rinse and dry well.

Stir-fry livers in hot oil. Season with
salt and pepper. Keep warm.

TO SERVE

Pour dressing on salad, then sprinkle
on the croutons.

Toss until well mixed, then arrange
chicken livers on top and serve.

Fatoush Salad in a Crisp Basket

Hyatt Regency Jerusalem, Israel

Serves 4

Basket

5 oz (1 c) flour (150 g)
3 oz (½ c) yellow cornmeal (85 g)
1 tsp salt (5 g)
½ fl oz (1 tbs) olive oil (15 ml)
4 fl oz (½ c) vegetable oil—for frying (118 ml)
4 fl oz (½ c) water (120 ml)

Mix flour, cornmeal and salt in a bowl.

○

Make a well in the centre and add oil and water.

○

Mix with hands, then knead on a floured board until smooth; roll out very thin.

○

Using an inverted (6-inch, 15 cm) saucer, cut out circles from dough.

○

Shape each dough circle to form "basket."

○

Deep-fry in hot oil until crispy and golden brown.

○

Allow to cool.

SALAD

3 ½ oz romaine lettuce—shredded (100 g)

5 oz (1 medium) red bell pepper—pips removed and cubed (150 g)

5 oz (1 medium) green bell pepper—pips removed and cubed (150 g)

4 oz (1 medium) onion—sliced (115 g)

5 oz (1 medium) cucumber—peeled, pips removed and cubed (150 g)

4 oz (1 medium) tomato—cubed (115 g)

1 tbs sumak (15 ml)

½ fl oz (1 tbs) olive oil (15 ml)

1 fl oz (2 tbs) lemon juice (30 ml)

Mix ingredients in a bowl and toss well.

Note: Sumak is the dried, crushed berry of a species of the sumach tree. It has a sour, lemony taste. Use only commercially packaged sumak. It is available in Middle Eastern groceries as Armenian sumak.

TO SERVE

Place some salad in each basket.

Put each basket on the centre of a plate and garnish with a little red leaf lettuce.

ENSALADA DE ENDIBIAS, AGUACATE, Y ELOTE CON SALSA DE OLIVO
WITLOOF, AVOCADO AND CORN SALAD WITH OLIVE OIL DRESSING

HYATT REGENCY ACAPULCO, MEXICO

SERVES 4

SALAD

4 head witloof (Belgian endive)—separated into leaves, washed and dried

2 avocadoes—halved, peeled, then cut into thin slices

½ lb fresh or frozen corn kernels (250 g)

Arrange witloof, avocado and corn attractively on 4 salad plates and spoon some of dressing on top (recipe follows).

DRESSING

2 egg yolks

dash Worcestershire sauce

juice of ½ lemon

8 fl oz (1 c) olive oil (240 ml)

salt and pepper to taste

Whisk yolks, Worcestershire sauce, lemon juice, salt and pepper until well blended.

Gradually whisk in oil until thick.

Salad of Belgian Endive
with Pears and Roquefort Cheese

Hyatt Continental Montreux, Switzerland

Serves 4

3 ½ oz Roquefort cheese (or other blue
cheese) (100g)

3 fl oz (6 tbs) double (heavy) cream
(100 ml)

1 lb (2 medium) pears—peeled, sliced
in 8 pieces and dipped in lemon
juice (455 g)

4 heads witloof (Belgian endive)—
separated into leaves and julienned

3 fl oz (6 tbs) salad dressing of your
choice (100 ml)

4 sprigs dill—for garnish

Put Roquefort and cream in a
liquidiser and process until smooth.

Season witloof with dressing and
arrange on a salad plate.

Neatly arrange pears alongside witloof
and place a dollop of Roquefort cream
on each slice. Decorate plate with dill
sprigs.

Noodle Salad with Fresh Orange

Hyatt Regency Manila, Philippines

Serves 4

Noodle Salad

14 oz glass noodles (400 g)

¾ oz minced scallions (20 g)

¼ oz chillies–thinly sliced (7g)

1 ½ oz shallots—thinly sliced (40 g)

¼ oz coriander leaves—coarsely chopped (7 g)

¼ oz celery leaves—coarsely chopped (7 g)

5 tsp fish sauce (25 ml)

½ oz sugar (15 g)

2 tbs lime or lemon juice (30 ml)

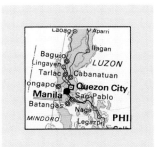

Pour boiling water on the noodles and keep soaking for 2 minutes.

Drain and cool.

Mix sugar, lime or lemon juice and fish sauce until sugar is dissolved.

Add all the ingredients together with the noodles and toss until mixed.

Mound on a plate and sprinkle with fried garlic and garnish with fresh orange sections.

Garnish

4 small-sized oranges—peeled and sectioned

2 tsp minced garlic—fried until golden

POULTRY

Pavo en Mole Poblano
Turkey Breast in Mole Sauce

Hyatt Regency Cancun, Mexico
Serves 4

Turkey Breast

1.6 lb turkey breast—boneless (750 g)

Roast turkey in a preheated 350° F (180° C) oven until cooked, about 1 hour.

Mole Sauce

3 (small) dried pasilla chillies

3 (small) dried mulato chillies

12 fl oz (1 ½ c) boiling water (375 ml)

1 ¾ oz (3 ½ tbs) sesame seeds (50 g)

2 oz (½ c) unblanched almonds (60 g)

2 oz (½ c) raisins (60 g)

3 whole cloves

⅛ oz (1 tsp) coriander pips (2 g)

½ fl oz (1 tbs) vegetable oil (15 ml)

pinch ground cinnamon

4 ¼ oz (1 large) onion—chopped (120 g)

⅓ oz (1 small clove) garlic—chopped (10 g)

¼ oz (1 ½ tsp) anise pips (7 g)

1 ¼ oz (2 ½ tbs) tomato concentrate (paste) (35 g)

2 oz (4 tbs) lard (60 g)

1 ½ oz (3 tbs) Mexican chocolate—chopped (45 g)

8 fl oz (1 c) chicken stock (250 ml) (see glossary)

salt to taste

Note: If Mexican chocolate is unavailable, substitute unsweetened chocolate.

Toast the chillies, then remove pips, devein and rinse.

Soak in boiling water and let stand 1 hour. Drain well. Reserve soaking water.

Toast the sesame seeds in a dry skillet until golden, a few seconds. Set aside.

In same skillet, toast the almonds until light brown, a few seconds.

Add oil and raisins and cook until puffed.

Place the chillies, sesame seeds, almonds, raisins, cloves, cilantro, cinnamon, onion, garlic, anise pips and tomato concentrate in a liquidiser. Blend until smooth.

If mixture looks too thick, add some of the soaking water as needed.

Heat lard in a skillet.

Add chilli mixture and simmer until heated through.

Add chocolate and stir until melted.

Stir in stock a little at a time until sauce is desired consistency. Season with salt.

To Assemble and Serve

8 oz (1 c) white rice—cooked (225 g)

1 oz (¼ c) fresh coriander—chopped (30 g)

½ oz (1 tbs) sesame seeds—toasted (15 g)

4 oz (1 medium) tomato—cut in wedges (115 g)

Place 3 slices of turkey breast on each plate.

Smother with sauce.

Serve with rice and garnishes.

Turkey Medallions with Mango and Choko-Yoghurt Coulis

Hyatt Regency Coolum, Queensland, Australia

Serves 4

14 oz turkey medallions (395 g)

1 ½ fl oz (3 tbs) grape seed oil (45 ml)

2 ½ oz (5 tbs) dry white wine (75 ml)

7 oz (1 small) choko (chayote)—peeled and cubed (200 g)

½ oz (1 tbs) fresh dill—chopped (15 g)

½ tsp celery salt (2 g)

4 fl oz (½ c) plain yoghurt (120 ml)

poppy seeds—for garnish

14 oz (1 large) mango—peeled, stone removed, flesh sliced into wedges (395 g)

chives—minced for garnish

sprig golden oregano—for garnish

Pan-fry the turkey medallions in oil until tender, about 15 minutes.

In a small saucepan, combine wine with dash of water and steam the choko for 3 minutes.

Remove from heat and put in a liquidiser with the dill, celery salt and yoghurt. Blend until smooth.

Spread some yoghurt sauce on each plate. Add the turkey medallions and sprinkle with poppy seeds. Fan out the mango slices. Garnish with chives and oregano.

Soy-Cooked Chicken
with Glass Noodle Salad

Hyatt Regency Jeddah, Saudi Arabia
Serves 4

Chicken Topping

1 pt (2 ½c) soy sauce (600 ml)

6 fl oz (¾ c) water (150 ml)

2 fl oz (4 tbs) dry sherry (60 ml)

3 star anise

1 tsp Szechuan or black peppercorns (5 g)

1 tsp oriental sesame oil (5 ml)

3 ¼ lb chicken (1.5 kg)

In a large pot, place soy sauce, water, sherry, star anise, peppercorns and sesame oil. Bring to a boil.

Reduce heat and place chicken in pot, breast side down.

Cover and simmer for 15 minutes.

Turn chicken in liquid and continue cooking for about 30 minutes, turning occasionally.

Remove from heat and allow chicken to cool in the cooking liquid.

Drain and cut chicken into serving pieces. Keep warm.

Noodle Salad

3 ½ oz (1 c) glass (cellophane) noodles (100 g)

1 ¾ fl oz (3 ½ tbs) rice or white wine vinegar (50 ml)

½ fl oz (1 tbs) oriental sesame oil (15 ml)

½ fl oz (1tbs) soy sauce (15 ml)

salt and pepper to taste

3 oz (¾ c) bean sprouts—washed (80 g)

2 oz (½ bunch) chives—snipped crosswise with scissors into small pieces (55 g)

Soak noodles in very hot water for 5–10 minutes.

Drain and rinse under cold water.

In another bowl, mix vinegar, sesame oil and soy sauce. Season with salt and pepper.

Blanch bean sprouts briefly in boiling water.

Drain and rinse under cold water. Set aside.

Add noodles and chives to dressing. Mix well.

To Assemble and Serve

1 head mache (corn salad) of ½ head curly endive (chicory)—washed, dried and separated.

Twist the noodles around a fork and place a serving on each plate.

Decorate by placing the lettuce around the noodles and garnishing with some bean sprouts.

Neatly arrange chicken pieces and serve.

CHICKEN LEGS IN BASIL AND CHILLI MARINADE

HYATT REGENCY SURABAYA, INDONESIA

SERVES 4

1 fl oz (2 tbs) peanut or vegetable oil (30 ml)

1 ½ oz (5 tbs) shallots—finely diced (45 g)

⅓ oz (1 small clove) garlic—peeled and finely diced (10 g)

3 ½ oz (¾ c) red bell peppers—pips removed and diced (100 g)

¼ oz (1 ½ tsp) fresh ginger—grated (7 g)

16 basil leaves—chopped

1 oz (¼ c) candlenuts—ground (30 g)

4 oz (5 stalks) lemongrass—crushed (115 g)

4 kaffir lime leaves

5 ⅓ oz (1 large) tomato—peeled, pips removed and diced (150 g)

¼ oz (1 ½ tsp) turmeric powder (7 g)

¼ oz (1 ½ tsp) shrimp paste (7 g)

2 fl oz (4 tbs) tamarind juice (60 ml)

salt and pepper to taste

14 oz (8 large) chicken legs—skinned (400 g)

Note: Candlenuts are oily, raw macadamia nuts. There is no substitute. Kaffir lime leaves impart a pronounced tart flavour and fragrance. They are available in Southeast Asian markets.

Heat oil in sauté pan and add shallots, garlic, peppers and ginger.

Sauté for 2–3 minutes without browning.

Add basil leaves, candlenuts, lemongrass and lime leaves.

Sauté for 7 more minutes. Then add tomatoes and turmeric and sauté for another 2 minutes.

Add shrimps paste, tamarind juice and salt. Bring this marinade to a boil.

Add chicken and simmer 4 minutes.

Remove chicken and transfer to a grill.

Reduce marinade over low heat by half.

Discard lemongrass and lime leaves.

Arrange chicken on plate (2 thighs on each plate) and top with a drizzle of marinade.

Serve with rice and shrimp or peanut crackers and raw vegetables.

CHICKEN LEGS STUFFED WITH MUSHROOMS
ON A BED OF CREAMED LETTUCE

HYATT CONTINENTAL MONTREUX, SWITZERLAND
SERVES 4

7 oz (1 ¾ c) button mushrooms—
minced (200 g)

1 ¾ oz (3½ tbs) shallots—minced (50 g)

1 ¾ oz (3½ tbs) butter (50 g)

3 ½ fl oz (7 tbs) dry white wine
(100 ml)

salt and pepper to taste

1 egg—beaten

3 lb (4 large) chicken legs—boned but
skin left on (1 ⅓ kg)

1 head lettuce—cut into strips

½ pt (1 ¼ c) double (heavy) cream
(300 ml)

3 ½ oz (¾ c) red bell pepper—pips
removed, diced for garnish, blanched
and drained (100 g)

Preheat oven to 400° F (200° C).

Sauté mushrooms with half the
shallots in half the butter until
translucent.

Deglaze pan with half the wine and
cook for 5 minutes.

Add salt and pepper to taste.

Allow to cool, then mix in the egg.

Season the chicken legs and stuff with
the mushroom mixture and tie closed.

In a large sauté pan, brown chicken
legs in remaining butter for 7–8
minutes on each side.

Transfer to a baking dish and bake
until done, about 25 minutes.

In same sauté pan, sauté remaining
shallots and deglaze with remaining
wine.

Add lettuce strips, stir and add the
cream.

Transfer chicken legs to sauté pan and
simmer 3 more minutes.

Cut chicken legs into ⅓-inch (8-ml)
slices crosswise.

Put lettuce mixture on dinner plates
and arrange chicken slices alongside.

Garnish with red bell pepper.

Tim Burung Dara Dan Wantan Kangkoung Sauce Bumbu Rijak
Steamed Pigeon Wontons in Sambal Cream Sauce

Hyatt Regency Surabaya, Indonesia

Serves 4

Wontons

½ fl oz (1 tbs) peanut oil (15 ml)

3 ½ oz (¾ c) shallots—chopped (100 g)

1 oz (2 tbs) garlic—chopped (30 g)

4 ½ oz (1 c) fresh red chilli—pips removed and chopped (125 g)

9 oz kangkong or spinach (250 g)

salt and pepper to taste

½ fl oz (1tbs) soy sauce (15 ml)

½ fl oz (1tbs) oriental sesame oil (15 ml)

2.2 lb pigeon (squab) breast—boneless and skinless (1 kg)

24 wonton skins

basil leaves—for garnish

1 fresh red chilli—cut into rings, for garnish

Heat a frying pan or wok with oil and stir-fry the shallots, garlic, chilli and kangkong for 2 minutes.

Season with salt and pepper, soy sauce and sesame oil.

Remove from heat and let cool.

Cut pigeon breast into small chunks and mix into the kangkong. Chill well.

Grind the pigeon-spinach mixture, putting it twice through the grinder or mincer.

Fill each wonton wrapper with about 1 tbs (15 ml) of this mixture and seal with water.

Place on a steamer rack and steam dumplings for 5 minutes.

Place steamed wontons on dinner plates (6 rolls per plate).

Serve with sambal cream sauce (recipe follows). Garnish with whole basil leaves and chilli.

Note: Kangkong is a long-stemmed green, commonly called water spinach or morning glory vine.

Sambal Cream Sauce

2 oz (4 tbs) sambal tomat (60 g) (see glossary)

½ pt (1 ¼ c) double (heavy) cream (300 ml)

juice of 1 lime

Place sambal tomat and cream in a saucepan over high heat and reduce until thick enough to lightly coat the back of a spoon.

Remove from heat and stir in lime juice. Keep warm.

ROSTON SULT CSIRKEMELL GYUMOLCCSEL
GRILLED CHICKEN BREAST WITH FRUIT AND SPINACH PUDDING

ATRIUM HYATT BUDAPEST, HUNGARY
SERVES 4

GRILLED CHICKEN AND FRUIT

1 ½ lb (4 medium) chicken breasts—deboned (680 g)

salt and pepper to taste

5 ¼ oz (1 ½ c) grapes (145 g)

5 oz currants—dried (150 g)

6 oz (1 medium) peach—peeled and cubed (170 g)

6 oz (2 medium) kiwifruits—peeled and sliced crosswise (170 g)

4 oz (1 medium) banana—sliced into 1-inch (2.5 cm) lengths (115 g)

1 ¾ oz (3 ½ tbs) butter (50 g)

1 ¾ oz (3 ½ tbs) sugar (50 g)

pinch ground cinnamon

½ pt (1 ¼ c) dry white wine (300 ml)

Season chicken breasts with salt and pepper. Grill till done.

In a large sauté pan, sauté fruit in butter for approximately 3 minutes.

Add sugar, cinnamon and wine. Simmer 5–10 minutes, then remove from heat.

Serve chicken breast with warm fruit and spinach timbale (recipe follows).

SPINACH PUDDING

5 oz (10 tbs) butter (140 g)

5 oz (1 c) flour (140 g)

½ pt (1 ¼ c) milk (300 ml)

salt and pepper to taste

½ oz (1 clove) garlic—minced (15 g)

7 oz spinach—trimmed, cleaned, cooked and puréed (200 g)

Preheat oven to 350° F (180° C).

In a saucepot, melt butter, add flour and stir for 2 minutes to make a thick roux.

Slowly add milk, garlic and salt and pepper.

Stir continuously until thickened.

Add spinach and pour mixture into buttered and floured 8 fl oz (1 c; 237 ml) moulds or ramekins until two-thirds full. Cover.

Place moulds into pan of hot water and place in oven. Steam for 4 hours, or until firm.

Unmould onto individual plates.

CHILLI-FRIED CHICKEN
WITH PEPPERS

HYATT REGENCY XIAN, PEOPLE'S REPUBLIC OF CHINA

SERVES 4

20 oz chicken breast—boneless, sliced diagonally into 1-inch (1.25-cm) thick fillets (560 g)

1 ½ oz (2 tbs) cornflour (cornstarch) (40 g)

2 tsp light soy sauce (10 ml)

pinch salt

2 fl oz (4 tbs) corn oil (60 ml)

½ oz (1 clove) garlic—minced (15 g)

2 oz (½ c) green bell pepper—pips removed, julienned (60 g)

½ oz (5 tbs) red bell pepper—pips removed, julienned (40 g)

1 ½ oz (5 tbs) dried red chilli—diced (40 g)

2 oz (1 large knob) ginger—fresh, peeled and sliced (60 g)

¾ oz (3 tbs) green onions (scallions)—chopped (20 g)

Rub chicken fillets with a mixture of cornflour, soy sauce and salt.

In a wok, sauté chicken in oil until browned. Remove from wok and set aside.

Using the same wok, stir-fry the garlic, green and red bell peppers, chilli and ginger.

Add chicken fillets to wok and stir-fry until done, about 10 minutes. Sprinkle with green onions and serve.

STIR-FRIED CHICKEN AND PEPPERS
IN A BIRD'S NEST

GRAND HYATT TAIPEI, TAIWAN

SERVES 4

CHICKEN

3 lbs (1 medium) chicken—boned and skinned; cut into ½-inch (1.25 cm) cubes (1 ⅓ kg)

2 fl oz (4 tbs) light soy sauce (60 ml)

3 fl oz (6 tbs) dry white wine (90 ml)

1 ½ fl oz (3 tbs) vegetable oil (45 ml)

2 fl oz (4 tbs) oriental sesame oil (60 ml)

3 oz (¾ c) green onions (scallions)—diced (85 g)

5 oz (1 ¼ c) green bell peppers—diced (140 g)

5 oz bamboo shoots—diced (140 g)

1 ½ oz (3 tbs) ginger—fresh, grated (45 g)

12 button mushrooms—sliced

2 oz (4 tbs) red chilli—fresh, diced (60 g)

¼ tsp cornflour (cornstarch)—dissolved in a little water (2 g)

Marinate the chicken in a mixture of soy sauce and wine for 30 minutes. Drain.

○

Heat vegetable oil in a wok and stir-fry chicken for 2 minutes.

○

Set chicken aside.

○

Heat wok with sesame oil and stir-fry all remaining except cornflour for a few minutes.

Add the chicken cubes, pour in cornflour mixture and stir until sauce is thickened.

○

Spoon chicken mixture into potato nests and serve.

BIRD'S NEST

10 ½ oz (1 ½ large) sweet potatoes—peeled (300 g)

2 ½ oz (½ c) cornflour (cornstarch) (70 g)

salt and pepper to taste

vegetable oil—for deep-frying

Grate the sweet potatoes, using a hand grater or a food processor.

○

Rinse potatoes under cold water and drain very well.

○

Place in a bowl; add cornflour and salt.

○

Using about ¼ of the mixture, put the sweet potato into a 4-inch (10-cm) strainer. Place another strainer (same size) on top to mould.

○

Deep-fry potato basket in hot oil for 4 minutes or until golden brown.

○

Remove strainer and dry the potato basket with a paper towel.

○

Repeat 3 more times, to have 4 baskets, or nests.

Chicken Wrapped in Taro Leaves
Served with Taro Basket and Glazed Shallots

Hyatt Auckland, New Zealand

Serves 4

Chicken

4 small chicken fillets (400 g)

2 oz chicken liver mousse or paté (55 g)

4 large taro leaves—blanched (see glossary)

Spread chicken liver mousse or paté on both sides of each fillet.

Wrap each fillet in a taro leaf.

Lay taro rolls on a steaming dish or rack and steam for 15 minutes.

Let rest for 3 minutes, then slice each roll into 3 diagonal crosswise slices.

Arrange slices on a plate.

Taro Baskets and Carrots

5 ¼ oz baby carrots—peeled (150 g)

½ oz (1 tbs) fresh parsley—minced (15 g)

⅓ oz (2 tsp) butter (10 g)

¾ oz (1 ½ tbs) sugar (20 g)

4 thin slices taro—peeled

vegetable oil for deep-frying

salt and pepper to taste

Sauté the carrots in butter, then sprinkle with sugar. Cook until glazed.

Sprinkle glazed carrots with chopped parsley. Set aside.

Press the taro onto the back of a small ladle to form a basket.

Drop into hot oil and deep-fry until golden brown. Drain and season with salt.

Arrange each taro basket like an open oyster shell on individual plates and fill each with some of the galzed carrots.

Glazed Shallots

5 oz (10 medium)shallots—peeled (150 g)

1 ¾ oz (3 ½ tbs) dry red wine (50 ml)

¼ oz (1 ½ tsp) butter (5–7 g)

¾ oz (1 ½ tbs) sugar (20 g)

Mix the shallots with the remaining ingredients in a small saucepan.

Heat gently and allow sugar to melt. Remove pan from heat once the shallots are glazed.

Use shallots to garnish plates with the chicken roll slices and taro baskets filled with carrots.

CHICKEN KAPSAH

HYATT REGENCY JEDDAH, SAUDI ARABIA
SERVES 4

4 fl oz (½ c) olive oil (120 ml)

8 oz (2 medium) onions—chopped (225 g)

3 ½ lb (1 medium) chicken—cut into serving pieces (1.5 kg)

½ fl oz (1 tbs) tomato concentrate (paste) (15 ml)

8 oz (2 medium) tomatoes—peeled, pips removed and chopped (225 g)

1 ½ oz (3 cloves) garlic—crushed (45 g)

1 ½ pt (4 c) chicken stock (945 ml) (see glossary)

5 cardamom seeds

1 tsp ground cinnamon(5 g)

⅓ oz (2 tsp) cilantro—ground

⅓ oz (2 tsp) salt (10 g)

½ tsp black pepper (2 g)

12 oz (1 ½ c) long-grain rice (340 g)

¾ oz (3 tbs) raisins (20 g)

¾ oz (3 tbs) almonds—cut in half lengthwise and toasted (20 g)

3 eggs—hardboiled and quartered

Heat oil in a deep casserole dish and sauté onions until golden brown.

Add chicken, tomato concentrate, tomatoes and garlic.

Simmer over medium heat for approximately 8 minutes, stirring occasionally.

Add stock, spices and seasonings. Stir.

Cover and cook for 15 minutes.

Add rice and stir.

Cook for another 15 minutes.

Turn off heat but leave cover on to finish cooking for approximately 10 minutes more.

Arrange chicken and rice on plates and garnish with raisins, almond halves and eggs.

GRILLED SQUAB BREAST
WITH RED LENTIL SALAD AND RED CURRANTS

HYATT REGENCY COOLUM, AUSTRALIA
SERVES 4

14 oz (4 medium) squab (pigeon) breasts—skinless (395 g)

celery salt and white pepper to taste

7 oz (1 ¾ c) red lentils—soaked in water overnight (200 g)

1 ½ fl oz (3 tbs) cold pressed almond oil (45 ml)

2 ½ fl oz (5 tbs) raspberry vinegar (75 ml)

3 oz (¾ c) fresh raspberries (85 g)

1 lb (12 medium) green onions (455 g)

1 ¼ lb (4 large) kohlrabi (600 g)

1 ¼ lb (4 small) pattypan squash (600 g)

3 oz (¾ c) red currants (85 g)

Season squab with celery salt and pepper.

Cook in a cast-iron griddle pan until medium-rare, about 25 minutes. Keep warm.

Rinse lentils in fresh water and drain.

Blanch for approximately 1 minute in boiling water.

Drain and mix lentils with almond oil, vinegar, raspberries, celery salt and pepper. Keep warm.

Clean and trim green onions, leaving mostly white part.

Fashion a shovel out of the kohlrabi and blanch.

To form the shell, scoop out most of the centre of the squash with a melon baller.

Blanch in salted water for 1 minute to keep crisp.

Drain, then fill with currants.

Arrange all ingredients on plate as per photo, placing lentil salad in shovel.

Kerabu Taugeh Dan Ayam
Bean Sprout and Chicken Kerabu

Hyatt Kuantan, Malaysia

Serves 4

½ oz (1 tbs) turmeric (15 g) (see glossary)

juice of 2 limes

2 fl oz (4 tbs) vinegar (60 ml)

1 ¾ oz (¼ c) sugar (50 g)

2 fl oz (4 tbs) corn oil (60 ml)

12 ½ oz bean sprouts—blanched and drained (350 g)

14 oz chicken—roasted, julienned (400 g)

2 fresh red chillies—coarsely chopped

3 ½ oz (2 medium) green onions (scallions)—sliced (100 g)

1 oz (2 tbs) sesame seeds (25 g)

1 oz (2 tbs) coconut—grated, toasted (25 g)

Mix the turmeric, lime juice, vinegar, sugar and corn oil in a bowl.

Let it sit for 10 minutes so flavours blend.

Mix bean sprouts and chicken in a large bowl.

Pour in the dressing and toss well.

To serve, sprinkle the red chillies, green onions, sesame seeds and coconut on top.

Ayam Sambal

Baby Chicken in Chilli Sambal

◯

Hyatt Regency Singapore, Singapore
Serves 4

**4 baby chickens or Cornish hens
(1 ⅓ kg)**

**1 fl oz (2 tbs) peanut or vegetable oil
(30 ml)**

**2 oz (¼ c) shallots—finely chopped
(60 g)**

**¾ oz (1 ½ tbs) garlic—finely chopped
(20 g)**

**¾ oz (1 ½ tbs) ginger—freshly grated
(20 g)**

**3 fresh red chilli peppers—pips
removed and chopped**

**1pt (2 ½ c) coconut milk (500ml)
(see glossary)**

⅓ oz (2 tsp) ground coriander (10 g)

⅓ oz (2 tsp) turmeric (10 g)

4 star anise

1 small cinnamon stick

1 oz (1 stalk) lemongrass (30 g)

salt, pepper and tumeric to taste

Preheat oven to 350° F (180° C).

◯

Heat oil in ovenproof baking pan. Add shallots, garlic, ginger and chilli; cover pan and simmer for 2 minutes without browning.

◯

Add coconut milk, corriander, turmeric, star anise, cinnamon and lemongrass.

◯

Bring to a boil and simmer 5 minutes.

◯

Rub chickens with salt, pepper and turmeric powder.

◯

Place chickens in sauce and baste well.

◯

Transfer to oven and bake for 25 minutes, basting 2–3 times.

◯

Increase heat in the last 5 minutes to brown chickens.

◯

Remove chickens, lemongrass and cinnamon from sauce; discard cinnamon stick and lemongrass.

◯

Place sauce in a liquidiser and purée, then pass through a sieve.

◯

If sauce is too thin, pour back in pan and simmer to reduce slightly.

◯

Place chickens on individual plates and serve sauce separately.

Spicy Cantonese Chicken
In Chinese Pumpkin

Hyatt Regency Hong Kong, Hong Kong

Serves 4

4 lb (1 large) Chinese pumpkin or winter squash (1.8 kg)

1 lb chicken breast—boneless, sliced (480 g)

⅓ oz (2 tsp) garlic—chopped (40 g)

⅓ oz (2 tsp) ginger—grated (40 g)

⅓ oz (2 tsp) celery—diced (40 g)

⅓ oz (2 tsp) onion—diced (40 g)

4 fl oz (8 tbs) tomato sauce (120 ml)

1 tsp Tabasco (5 ml)

1 tsp salt

2 tsp sugar

4 tsp cornflour (cornstarch) (20 g)

4 tsp corn oil (20 ml)

12 green onions (scallions) for garnish

Holding pumpkin on its side, cut an opening on top (see photo), preferably using a zig zag motion.

Remove and discard pips.

Place pumpkin in a small baking dish to keep it stable.

Mix remaining except garnish in a bowl.

Fill pumpkin with the mixture and loosely cover top with foil.

Steam or bake pumpkin for 30 minutes.

Garnish with green onions and serve.

Couscous Bil Hammam Oua Tine
Couscous of Aiguillette of Pigeon and Fresh Figs

Casablanca Hyatt Regency, Morocco

Serves 4

Mushroom Mousse

8 fl oz (1 c) water (240 ml)

4 ¼ oz (1 c) powdered milk (125 g)

1 tsp salt (5 g)

pepper and nutmeg to taste

7 oz button mushrooms (200 g)

1 tsp lemon juice (5 ml)

Mix water and powdered milk, then season with salt, pepper and nutmeg.

Put milk in a saucepan and add mushrooms. Simmer for 20 minutes.

Strain the mushrooms and set juice aside.

Put mushrooms in a liquidiser with 6 fl oz (⅔ c; 150 ml) cooking juice and purée until smooth. Add lemon juice and stir.

Sauce and Figs

12 fresh figs

6 fl oz (¾ c) boiling water (150 ml)

6 fl oz (¾ c) dry red wine (150 ml)

⅓ oz (2 tsp) sugar (10 g)

⅓ fl oz (2 tsp) double (heavy) cream (10 ml)

½ oz (1 tbs) mushroom mousse (see recipe) (15 g)

2 ¾ fl oz (5 ½ tbs) mushroom cooking liquid (80 ml)

salt and pepper to taste

Blanch the figs in boiling water for 1 minute. Strain and reserve water.

Poach figs in mixture of red wine and sugar until soft.

Remove the figs and quarter them.

Reduce cooking liquid by ¾. Add the blanching water, cream, mushroom mousse and cooking liquid. Season with salt and pepper. Simmer 7–10 minutes.

Couscous and Pigeon

9 oz (1 c) quick-cooking couscous (250 g) (see glossary)

6 lb (4 medium) pigeons (squab)— boned and skinned; meat thinly sliced lengthwise (2 ¾ kg)

1 oz (2 tbs) butter (30 g)

½ fl oz (1 tbs) vegetable oil (15 ml)

salt and pepper to taste

Melt butter in a pan, then add oil.

Sauté pigeon slices for 8–10 minutes, then season with salt and pepper. Keep warm.

Cook couscous according to directions. Drain.

To Assemble And Serve

Place couscous on a large platter in a mound. Flatten top of mound.

Place pigeon slices on couscous.

Arrange the quartered figs around the pigeon.

Pour on sauce and serve.

Piernas de Pollo con Salsa de Cacahuate
Chicken Legs with Peanut Sauce

Hyatt Regency Acapulco, Mexico

Serves 4

Chicken and Garnish

3 lbs (4 large) chicken legs—boned and skinned (1 ⅓ kg)

salt and pepper to taste

1 ¾ pt (4 ¼ c) chicken stock (1 *l*) (see glossary)

1 lb turnip—peeled and julienned (500 g)

7 oz (1 ¼ c) spinach egg noodles (200 g)

½ fl oz (1 tbs) vegetable oil (15 ml)

Season chicken with salt and pepper. Poach in simmering chicken stock until cooked, about 15 minutes.

Remove chicken and keep warm. Reserve 1pt (2 ½ c ; 500 ml) of stock.

Heat 2 pots with boiling, salted water and cook the turnip and egg noodles separately until noodles are al dente and turnip is tender-crisp.

Drain both.

Add a little oil to the egg noodles and toss well to keep from sticking.

On a serving dish, arrange, turnips and chicken.

Drizzle on sauce (recipe follows) and serve with noodles.

Sauce

½ fl oz (2 tbs) vegetable oil (30 ml)

2 oz (½ c) unsalted peanuts—peeled (55 g)

3 ½ oz (1 small) onion—sliced (100 g)

¾ oz (large clove) garlic—chopped (20 g)

3 ½ oz (1 small) tomato—peeled, pips removed and chopped (100 g)

7 oz (2 large) tomatillos—chopped (200 g)

1 pt (2 ½ c) chicken stock (500 ml) (see glossary)

1 ½ fl oz (3 tbs) honey (40 ml)

In a sauté pan, heat oil and sauté peanuts, onion and garlic until golden brown.

Add the tomato and tomatillos. Fry for several minutes.

Stir in chicken stock and honey; simmer until thickened. Keep warm.

Note: Tomatillos are Mexican green tomatoes. They are available fresh in Mexican groceries and also in tins.

BARBECUED CORNISH HEN

HYATT REGENCY DUBAI, UNITED ARAB EMIRATES
SERVES 4

CORNISH HENS

6 lb (2 large) Cornish hens (2 ¾ kg)

1 tsp prepared mustard (5 ml)

1 oz (2 cloves) garlic—crushed (30 g)

¼ tsp white pepper (1 g)

¼ tsp paprika (1 g)

juice of 2 lemons

2 ½ fl oz (¼ c) plain yoghurt (70 g)

2 fl oz (4 tbs) corn oil (60 ml)

Clean and wash hens; pat dry.

With a sharp knife, make deep incisions in thighs and breasts.

Combine mustard, garlic, pepper, paprika and lemon juice. Rub on the hens and marinate for 3 hours.

Meanwhile, pour yoghurt through a cheesecloth and allow to drip for at least 3 hours so that water drains out.

Mix oil with drained yoghurt and brush this mixture over the hens.

Cook on charcoal grill until done, about 25 minutes.

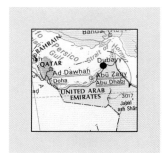

SAUCE

1 ¾ oz (⅓ c) mint leaves—chopped (50 g)

1 oz (¼ c) fresh coriander—chopped (30 g)

3 ½ oz (¾ c) plain yoghurt (100 g)

3 green chillies—fresh, chopped

¼ tsp sugar (1 g)

salt to taste

Put mint, coriander, yoghurt and chilli in a liquidiser or food processor. Blend till fine.

Add sugar and salt a little at a time, blending until well mixed.

Store covered in refrigerator until needed.

TO ASSEMBLE AND SERVE

4 oz (1 medium) tomato—sliced in wedges (115 g)

4 oz (1 medium) onion—sliced (115 g)

6 button mushrooms—sliced

6 oz (2 medium) courgettes (small zucchini)—sliced (175 g)

10 ½ oz (4 c) cooked rice (300 g)

Cut hens in half and place each half on a dish.

Pour sauce over hens and garnish plates with rice, tomato wedges, onion slices, mushrooms and courgettes.

SAM GYOE TANG
SPRING CHICKEN IN GINSENG BROTH

HYATT REGENCY CHEJU, KOREA

SERVES 4

STUFFED CHICKEN

5 ¾ oz fresh ginseng—julienned (160g)

2 oz jujubes (Chinese red dates)—diced (55 g)

5 ¾ oz (¾ c) glutinous rice—washed in cold water and drained (160 g)

1 ½ oz (3 cloves) garlic—chopped (45 g)

4 ½ oz (1 c) chestnuts—peeled and cubed (130 g)

salt and pepper to taste

4 baby chickens or small Cornish hens (300–350 g each)

1 ½ oz (3 tbs) green onions (scallions)—chopped, for garnish

Note: Ginseng is the root of a plant found in mountainous regions of Korea and Manchuria. It can be dried and used as a seasoning in the same way as ginger; its taste is similar to that of fennel.

Mix half the ginseng and dry jujubes with the rice, garlic, chestnuts, salt and pepper.

Clean the chicken cavities very well and stuff with rice mixture. Sew closed or truss.

Place chicken in a large pot.

Add enough water to cover and bring to a boil, then simmer 20 minutes.

Add the remaining ginseng and jujubes, and more salt and pepper.

Cover and simmer for another 20 minutes.

Place chickens in individual bowls along with a little broth, sprinkle with green onions and serve with seasonings.

SEASONINGS

1 ½ oz (¼ c) salt (45 g)

⅛ oz (½ tsp) ground black pepper (2 g)

⅛ oz (1 tsp) sesame seeds (2 g)

Mix ingredients and place in 4 small bowls.

Pollo Costeño Estilo Barra Vieja
Chicken Barra Vieja Style

Hyatt Regency Acapulco, Mexico

Serves 4

Achiote Sauce

3 ½ oz (⅓ c) achiote (100 g)

2 fl oz (4 tbs) orange juice (60 ml)

4 drops vinegar (any type)

1 tsp ground black pepper (7 g)

⅓ oz (2 tsp) ground cumin (10 g)

½ tsp Worcestershire sauce (2 ml)

1 fl oz (2 tbs) vegetable oil (30 ml)

Dissolve achiote in orange juice and vinegar by heating in a saucepan for 5 minutes. Let soak until soft, then grind to a paste in a liquidiser.

○

Add the remaining ingredients and blend until smooth.

Note: Achiote is the seed of the annatto tree. It is sometimes sold in a paste form, but most often only the hard pips are available, usually in Mexican groceries.

Chicken

3 ½ lbs chicken legs (1.6 kg) or 4 small game hens

salt and pepper to taste

7 oz (1 c) butter (200 g)

4 oz (1 large) onion (115 g)

4 oz (1 large) tomato (115 g)

6 oz (1 large) orange—peeled (170 g)

4 banana leaves or sheets of aluminum foil (12 x 8 inches; 30 x 20cm)

Season chicken wih salt and pepper.

○

Melt butter in a pan, then sauté chicken until golden, about 20 minutes.

○

Cut 4 slices each from the onion, tomato and orange.

○

Dip banana leaves in boiling water for 2 minutes; drain and wipe dry.

○

Place the chicken evenly on the banana leaves (or foil) and transfer to a steaming dish.

○

Pour sauce over chicken; add tomato, onion and orange slices.

○

Fold the banana leaves over, making sure sauce stays in.

○

Steam chicken for 15 minutes, then serve in banana leaves.

DUCKLING BREAST
WITH MUSHROOM RAGOUT AND PORT WINE SAUCE

HYATT REGENCY SINGAPORE, SINGAPORE

SERVES 4

DUCK AND MARINADE

2 fl oz (4 tbs) olive oil (60 ml)

1 tsp black peppercorns, crushed (5 g)

1 tsp fresh rosemary—chopped (5 g)

1 tsp fresh thyme—chopped (5 g)

1 ¼ lb duckling breast—trimmed (560 g)

salt to taste

1 fl oz (2 tbs ; 30 ml) oil, peppercorns and herbs

Blend the ingredients and marinate duck for 6 hours in the refrigerator, basting occasionally. Remove duck and season with salt.

○

Preheat oven to 350° F (180° C).

○

Heat a roasting pan with remaining 2 tbs (30 ml) olive oil.

○

Sear duck on both sides to add colour.

○

Roast in oven for 10 minutes, basting and turning duck frequently.

○

Remove from oven and set aside in a warm place.

MUSHROOM RAGOUT

1 oz (2 tbs) butter (30 g)

⅔ oz shallots—finely chopped (20 g)

5 ½ oz fresh chanterelles—cut in half (160 g)

5 ½ oz fresh cepes—sliced (160 g)

1 fl oz (2 tbs) brandy (30 ml)

1 tbs + 1 tsp red port wine (20 ml)

3 fl oz (6 tbs) chicken stock (100 ml) (see glossary)

3 fl oz (6 tbs) double (heavy) cream (100 ml)

Heat butter in a sauté pan and sweat shallots without browning.

○

Add chanterelles and cepes and sauté 2 minutes.

○

Add brandy and ignite. When flames die down, add port wine, stock and cream and reduce over low heat until thickened. Keep warm.

POTATO PANCAKE

9 oz (2 medium) potatoes—peeled and finely shredded or grated (250 g)

1 ½ oz (3 tbs) butter (40 g)

salt and pepper to taste

Put grated potatoes in cheesecloth and squeeze until dry.

○

Heat butter in an 8-inch (20-cm) non-stick pan and add potatoes, shaping them into 8 thin pancakes. Season with salt and pepper and fry both sides until golden brown.

GARNISH

1 oz (2 tbs) butter (30 g)

5 oz shallots (140 g)

4 fl oz (½ c) dry red wine (120 ml)

5 ¼ oz Brussels sprouts (150 g)

5 fl oz (⅔ c) port wine sauce (160 ml) (see glossary)

Melt butter in saucepan and add whole shallots. Sauté until coated with butter.

○

Add wine and stir. Cook over high heat until wine has evaporated and glazed the shallots.

○

Pull Brussels sprouts apart and blanch leaves. Set aside.

TO ASSEMBLE AND SERVE

Place 1 pancake on each plate and cover with a spoon of mushroom ragout.

○

Slice duck breast on the bias and place over mushroom ragout.

○

Cover with a second pancake and pour port wine sauce around.

○

Garnish with glazed shallots and Brussels sprouts leaves as shown in picture.

Frango na Pucara
Chicken Pot

Hyatt Regency Macau, Macau

Serves 4

7 lb (2 medium) chickens—cut into
  8 pieces (3 ¼ kg)

10 oz (2 ½ c) button mushrooms
  (285 g)

1 lb (4 medium) tomatoes—cut into
  chunks (455 g)

6 oz (1 ½ c) bacon—diced (160 g)

8 oz (2 medium) onions—chopped
  (225 g)

1 oz (2 tbs) garlic—chopped (30 g)

¾ pt (2 c) red port wine (480 ml)

4 fl oz (½ c) tomato concentrate (paste)
  (120 ml)

12 oz (2 medium) potatoes—peeled
  and diced (340 g)

3 oz (1 large) carrot—peeled and diced
  (85 g)

salt and pepper to taste

½ fl oz (1 tbs) olive oil (15 ml)

Coarsely dice half the mushrooms.

Purée tomato chunks and diced
mushrooms in a liquidiser. Set aside.

Sauté bacon, onions and garlic in olive
oil. Drain off most of the fat.

Fry chicken pieces in remaining oil till
golden.

Transfer to a deep pot with the bacon,
onions and garlic.

Deglaze pan with half the wine, then
add to pot along with tomato-mush-
room purée.

Stir in tomato concentrate, potatoes
and carrot.

Season with salt and pepper.

Cover pot and simmer 40 minutes or
until chicken is tender.

Keep cooking liquid from thickening
too much by adding remaining wine as
needed.

When chicken is done, add reserved
whole mushrooms and simmer for
another 2–3 minutes.

Serve on individual plates.

Ayam Percik
Grilled Chicken on Bamboo with Coconut Milk

Hyatt Saujana, Kuala Lumpur, Malaysia
Serves 4

2 ¾ lb (1 small) chicken (1 ¼ kg)

2 oz (4 tbs) fresh ginger—grated (60 g)

1 oz (2 tbs) garlic—chopped (30 g)

7 fl oz (1 c) tamarind juice (210 ml)

1 oz (3 tbs) rice flour (20 g)

¾ pt (2 c) coconut milk (480 ml) (see glossary)

⅓ oz (2 tsp) chilli (10 g)

salt and pepper to taste

1 ½ oz (3 tbs) shallots—coarsely chopped (45 g)

¾ oz (1 tsp) turmeric (20 g)

¾ oz (1 tsp) belacan (20 g)

Note: Belacan, or fermented prawn paste, is available in some Asian foodstores.

Prepare grill.

Rub chicken with ginger and garlic. Set aside for 1 hour.

Mix the remaining ingredients in a saucepan and bring to a boil slowly, stirring constantly over low heat for 10 minutes until thickened.

Coat chicken with the sauce and sandwich between bamboo sticks. Place over glowing coals. Baste frequently and grill until both sides of chicken are evenly browned and cooked, about 45 minutes.

Ayam Bungus
"Money Bag" Chicken

Hyatt Kinabalu, Malaysia

Serves 4

½ oz (1 tbs) garlic—chopped (15 g)

2 oz fresh black mushrooms (shiitake)—diced (60 g)

5 ½ oz carrots—diced (150 g)

3 oz onions—diced and peeled (85 g)

7 oz boiled chicken—diced (200 g)

3 ½ oz shelled green peas (100 g)

½ tsp ground cinnamon (2 g)

salt and pepper to taste

3 oz (1 small) green bell pepper (85 g)

3 oz (1 small) red bell pepper (85 g)

8 scallions—discard white parts

4 spring roll wrappers

vegetable oil for deep-frying

8 fl oz (1 c) chicken stock (250 ml)

Sauté garlic until brown; add mushrooms, carrots, onions, chicken and peas.

Stir, then add cinnamon and season with salt and pepper.

Set ingredients aside and allow to cool.

Roast the green and red bell peppers on an open fire until their skins are completely charred.

Peel the skin off under running tap water, core peppers and discard pips.

Purée the red and green bell peppers separately and chill.

Divide the sautéed among the spring roll wrappers and gather in a bundle. Tie each with the green part of a scallion.

Deep-fry bundles in oil until golden brown.

Arrange on a plate and serve with chilled sauce.

Steamed Chicken Breast
with Lemon Dressing and Shredded Fresh Vegetables

Hyatt Regency Seoul, Korea

SERVES 4

3 ⅓ fl oz (6 ¾ tbs) lemon juice (100 g)

3 oz (¾ c) chopped green bell pepper (85 g)

3 oz (¾ c) chopped red bell pepper (85 g)

salt and pepper to taste

2 ¾ fl oz (5 ½ tbs) olive oil (80 ml)

4 ¼ oz red radishes (120 g)

4 ¼ oz (1 large) turnip—cooked (120 g)

4 ¼ oz (2 medium) carrots (120 g)

4 ¼ oz (1 large) beet (120 g)

4 ¼ oz (1 medium) cucumber (120 g)

4 ¼ oz (2 stalks) celery (120 g)

1 lb boneless chicken breasts—skinned (480 g)

¾ oz (1 tbs) garlic cloves (20 g)

Make lemon dressing by mixing lemon juice with the chopped green and red bell peppers.

Add olive oil and seasonings to taste.

Peel all vegetables and cut into fine strips.

Set aside.

Sprinkle chicken breasts with salt and rub with garlic cloves.

Steam chicken for 7 minutes.

Place breasts on a large platter.

Arrange vegetable strips around chicken.

Cover breasts with lemon dressing.

Serve hot.

ADOBONG MANOK
BARBECUED CHICKEN ADOBO WITH ATCHARA PICKLES

〰

HYATT REGENCY MANILA, PHILIPPINES

SERVES 4

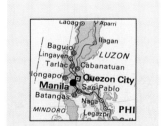

PICKLES AND VEGETABLES

1 ¼ oz (1 small) carrot (35 g)

1 ¼ oz (1 medium) cucumber (35 g)

1 ¼ oz (⅛ medium) white radish (35 g)

1 ¼ oz (¼ medium) red bell pepper (35 g)

5 fl oz (½ c) rice vinegar (120 ml)

6 oz (¾ c) brown sugar (180 g)

1 bay leaf

1 whole clove

½ tsp turmeric (2 g)

salt and pepper to taste

white pepper—freshly ground, to taste

Peel carrot, cucumber and radish and slice into juliennes. Julienne the pepper.

〰

Place vegetables in a bowl.

〰

Combine vinegar, brown sugar, bay leaf, clove and turmeric in a saucepan and bring to a boil.

〰

Season with salt and pepper, then pour hot mixture over vegetables. Cool and let stand 24 hours.

TO COOK AND SERVE

3 oz (1 small) tomato—cut into eighths for garnish (85 g)

Prepare grill.

〰

Drain and barbecue chickens until done, about 5 minutes.

〰

Serve with pickles, vegetables and tomato wedges.

CHICKEN MARINADE

8 fl oz (1 c) dark soy sauce (240 ml)

5 fl oz (⅔ c) vinegar (150 ml)

¾ oz (1 ½ cloves) garlic—pounded (20 g)

3 bay leaves

1 tsp peppercorns—lightly crushed (5 g)

4 lb (2 small) chickens—cut in half (2 kg)

In a large bowl, mix the soy sauce, vinegar, garlic, bay leaves and peppercorns.

〰

Add chickens and marinate, refrigerate for 24 hours.

Poussin Farci Aux Girolles
Spring Chicken Stuffed with Chanterelles

Rabat Hyatt Regency, Morocco
Serves 4

6 lb (4 small) spring chickens (2 ¾ kg)

1 ½ oz (3 tbs) butter (45 g)

14 oz chanterelles (395 g)

salt and pepper to taste

3 ½ oz (1 small) onion—chopped (100g)

2 oz (4 tbs) fresh coriander—chopped (55 g)

3 ½ fl oz (7 tbs) dry white wine (100 ml)

7 fl oz (¾ c) chicken stock (180 ml) (see glossary)

Preheat oven to 350° F (180° C).

Bone the chickens, starting from the neck, keeping thighs and drumsticks whole. Set aside.

Sauté mushrooms in butter, seasoning with salt and pepper.

Add onion and coriander, and cook over low heat until onions are soft.

Season cavity of each chicken and stuff with mushroom mixture.

Close up the chicken by sewing, then truss at neck.

Place chickens on roasting pan and bake until golden brown, about 30 minutes.

Remove and set aside. Keep warm.

Deglaze the roasting pan by placing over heat and adding wine, followed by chicken stock. Scrape up particles on bottom.

Reduce liquid by a third and season with salt and pepper.

Neatly arrange stuffed chickens on each plate and pour some sauce over. Serve.

DUCK BREAST WITH DATE SAUCE

HYATT REGENCY RIYADH, SAUDI ARABIA

SERVES 4

1 lb (4 medium) duck breasts—fillets with skin (455 g)

salt and pepper to taste

10 ½ oz dates (300 g)

⅔ oz (1 ½ tbs) butter (20 g)

2 oz (½ c) sugar (60 g)

1 tsp vinegar (5 ml)

4 fl oz (½ c) brown sauce (120 ml) (see glossary)

Preheat oven to 400° F (200° C). Lightly oil the bottom of a heatproof baking dish.

Clean duck breasts and trim off excess fat. Season with salt and pepper.

Place breasts skin side down in baking dish and place on top of stove.

Lighly sauté breasts until skin is browned, then turn and put dish in oven.

Bake breasts for approximately 6–8 minutes or until slightly pink in centre.

Peel dates, cut in half and remove stones.

○

Save 8 nice dates for presentation.

○

Pass the remaining dates through a sieve or purée in a liquidiser. Set aside.

○

Prepare the sauce by melting butter in a saucepan, then adding sugar. Boil until lightly caramelized.

○

Immediately add vinegar and stir with a wooden spoon.

○

Reduce liquid almost completely, then add the sauce.

○

Add puréed dates and pass mixture through a sieve to strain.

○

Reheat sauce and then ladle onto 4 warm plates.

○

Slice the duck breasts and arrange on top of sauce (see photo).

○

Garnish with fresh dates and serve.

GRILLED CHICKEN BREAST ON GARDEN GREENS

○

HYATT REGENCY SAIPAN, MARIANA ISLANDS

SERVES 4

CHICKEN

1 ½ lb chicken breasts—boneless (565 g)

salt and pepper to taste

2 oz (½ c) spinach—trimmed and cleaned (55 g)

2 oz (½ c) romaine (55 g)

2 oz (½ c) red-leaf lettuce (55 g)

1 oz (¼ c) witloof (Belgian endive) (30 g)

1 oz (¼ c) bean sprouts (30 g)

1 oz (¼ c) alfalfa sprouts (30 g)

1 oz (¼ c) radish sprouts (30 g)

2 oz (½ medium) yellow bell pepper—pips removed and neatly diced (55 g)

2 oz (½ medium) red bell pepper—pips removed and neatly diced (55 g)

8 cherry tomatoes

1 sprig basil

1 sprig thyme—chopped

HERB DRESSING

1 sprig thyme—finely chopped

1 sprig rosemary—finely chopped

1 sprig basil—finely chopped

4 fl oz (½ c) vinegar (120 ml)

8 fl oz (1 c) vegetable oil (240 ml)

1 green onion (scallion)—finely chopped

Season chicken breasts with salt and pepper. Grill until done.

○

Combine ingredients for dressing and mix well.

○

Place the greens and sprouts on platter.

○

Place chicken breasts on top. Sprinkle on diced peppers.

○

MEAT

RABBIT WITH PLUM BRIOCHE

HYATT AUCKLAND, NEW ZEALAND

SERVES 4

STUFFED RABBIT

2 boned rabbit loins with belly flap on

1 ½ fl oz (3 tbs) milk (45 ml)

1 oz (⅓ c) fresh white bread crumbs (30 g)

5 oz ground rabbit meat (140 g)

1 egg white

4 fl oz (½ c) double (heavy) cream (120 ml)

cayenne, salt and pepper to taste

1 ¾ oz morels—soaked briefly in water, drained, then coarsely diced (50 g)

½ oz (1 tbs) butter (15 g)

1 tsp each garlic, onion and chervil—chopped (5 g)

3 ½ oz caul fat (100 g)

8 fl oz (1 c) rabbit or chicken stock (240 ml) (see glossary)

1 ½ fl oz (3 ½ tbs) dry white wine (45 ml)

Preheat oven to 325° F (165° C).

○

Remove all sinew and fat from rabbit loins keeping flap intact.

○

Bring milk to a boil and add bread crumbs. Mix well and let cool.

○

Mix bread crumbs with ground rabbit meat, egg whites, cream, cayenne, salt and pepper. Chill.

○

Sauté morels in butter with chopped garlic, onion and chervil. Let cool.

○

Mix a small amount of stuffing with morels to bind together.

○

Spread alternate layers of morels and stuffing on rabbit loins, making sure it is not too full.

○

Enclose the flaps and wrap tightly in caul fat.

○

Roast slowly for 10–15 minutes, making sure you do not overcook.

○

Remove rabbit from pan and allow to rest.

○

Deglaze roasting pan with wine over medium heat, then add stock and reduce by ⅔. Strain.

○

Slice each rabbit loin into 3 even slices and arrange on individual plates with the plum brioche (recipe follows) alongside.

PLUM BRIOCHE

7 oz (4 small) firm red plum—peeled and pitted (200 g)

⅔ oz (1 tsp) sugar (20 g)

1 fl oz (2 tbs) water (30 ml)

1 tsp vinegar (5 ml)

4 small brioches

Boil the plum with sugar, water and vinegar until soft, about 2 minutes. Purée until smooth.

○

Cut tops off the brioche and scoop out centers to make small, hollow wells.

○

Fill each well with plum compote, allowing a small amount to run down sides of brioche. Replace tops.

KALBI JIM
BRAISED BEEF SHORT RIBS WITH CHESTNUTS AND JUJUBES

HYATT REGENCY CHEJU, KOREA

SERVES 4

MAIN DISH

3 ½ fl oz (7 tbs) soy sauce (100 ml)

1 ½ oz (3 tbs) sugar (45 g)

1 ½ oz (3 tbs) garlic—chopped (45 g)

1 ½ oz (3 tbs) ginger—cubed (45 g)

3 lb lean beef short ribs—cut into 2–
  2 ½ oz (55–70 g) pieces (1 ⅓ kg)

1 ¼ pt (3 c) water (710 ml)

5 ¼ oz (1 ¼ c) peeled chestnuts (150 g)

¾ oz gingko nuts (20 g)

1 ½ oz jujubes (Chinese red dates)
  (40 g)

1 ½ fl oz (2 ½ tbs) sake or medium dry
  sherry (40 ml)

ground black pepper to taste

*Note: Gingko nuts are abundant in
  Chinese and Japanese markets.
  They are oval, with a buff
  exterior. Jujubes are also readily
  available in Asian markets.*

Combine soy sauce, sugar, garlic,
ginger and black pepper.

Marinate short ribs for 1 hour.

Transfer ribs and marinade to a deep
pot, add water to cover and bring to a
boil; simmer 30 minutes.

Add chestnuts, gingko nuts, jujubes
and wine. Simmer until meat is
tender, about 2 hours.

Remove meat and keep warm.

Boil liquid until reduced by ⅓, then
put meat back in to heat through.

Place in serving bowls and garnish
(recipe follows).

GARNISH

1 egg—beaten

¼ oz (½ tbs) butter (7 g)

¾ oz (1 ½ tbs) pine-kernels (pignoli)—
  chopped (20 g)

Fry egg in butter like an omelet.

Cut into strips and combine with
pine-kernels.

POACHED FILLET OF BEEF
WITH OYSTER MUSHROOMS AND RED WINE SAUCE

HYATT KINGSGATE SYDNEY, AUSTRALIA

SERVES 4

SAUCE

8 fl oz (1 c) beef stock (240 ml) (see glossary)

¼ pt (½ c) dry red wine (120 ml)

3 oz (1 small) onion—diced (85 g)

salt and pepper to taste

3 oz (6 tbs) butter—chilled and cubed (85 g)

Mix stock, wine and onion in a saucepan and bring to a boil. Reduce by half.

○

Strain and boil again 3 minutes.

○

Season with salt and pepper.

○

Remove from heat and add cubed butter slowly, mixing until melted. Keep warm.

POACHED BEEF

1 ½ lb beef tenderloin—cut into 4 pieces (680 g)

salt and pepper to taste

2 oz (4 tbs) butter (55 g)

1 oz (½ medium) carrot—diced (30 g)

2 oz (½ medium) onion—diced (55 g)

1 oz (½ stalk) celery (30 g)

2 bay leaves

¼ oz (1 tbs) black peppercorns (7 g)

1 ½ pt (3 ¼ c) beef stock (800 ml) (see glossary)

Season beef with salt and pepper and brown on both sides with butter.

○

Add carrot, onion, celery, bay leaves and peppercorns to stock. Bring to a boil.

○

Lower heat to barely simmering, then add beef and poach 8–10 minutes or until medium rare. Keep warm.

TO ASSEMBLE AND SERVE

7 oz oyster mushrooms—sautéd in butter (200 g)

1 ⅛ lb seasonal vegetables—cooked (510 g)

Slice each piece of beef through the centre.

○

Pour 1 ½ tsp (¾ fl oz) (22 ml) of sauce onto each of 4 plates and arrange beef on top.

○

Accompany with oyster mushrooms and seasonal vegetables.

Parrillada Mixta
Mexican Mixed Grill

Hyatt Regency Cancun, Mexico

Serves 4

Sauce

2 oz (1 medium) serrano or other hot chilli—diced (60 g)

8 oz (2 medium) tomatoes—diced (225 g)

4 oz (1 medium) onion—diced (115 g)

¾ oz (1 large clove) garlic—diced (20 g)

1 fl oz (2 tsp) vegetable oil (30 ml)

1 oz (2 tbs) coriander—fresh chopped (30 g)

Sauté vegetables in oil until translucent and put in a liquidiser to purée.

Add the coriander and stir.

Mixed Grill

8 ½ oz chorizo (spicy Mexican sausage) (240 g)

10 oz pork cutlet (chop) (285 g) (see glossary)

8 ½ oz chicken legs (240 g)

8 ½ oz beef tenderloin—sliced into medallions (240 g)

salt and pepper to taste

1 fl oz (2 tbs) vegetable oil (30 ml)

5 oz (1 large) onion—sliced (150 g)

5 oz (½ medium each) red and green bell peppers—pips removed and julienned (150 g)

Season the sausage, pork cutlet, chicken legs and beef medallions and grill until done. Keep warm.

Heat oil in skillet and sauté vegetables until tender-crisp. Keep warm.

Note: Chorizo—pepperoni or any other spicy sausage may be substituted.

To Serve

10 oz (2 ½ c) guacamole (285 g) (see glossary)

10 oz (2 ½ c) refried beans (285 g) (see glossary)

3 ½ oz corn tortillas—softened and warmed in oven (85 g) (see glossary)

Arrange grilled meats on individual plates.

Place the sautéed peppers and onion alongside.

Serve sauce in a side dish with the guacamole, refried beans and tortillas.

Teriyaki Steak

Century Hyatt Tokyo, Japan

Serves 4

Marinade

1 ½ fl oz (3 ½ tbs) sake or medium-dry sherry (50 ml)

¼ oz (½ tbs) fresh ginger—grated (7 g)

1 ¾ oz (3 ½ tbs) soy sauce (50 ml)

½ oz (1 tbs) sugar (15 g)

Mix all ingredients.

Steaks

1 ½ lb (4 steaks) beef sirloin (600 g)

6 oz (1 medium) sweet potato—peeled (170 g)

4 cherry tomatoes

8 long thick strips green bell pepper

4 oz (½ c) cooked white rice (115 g) vegetable oil for deep-frying

Marinate the steaks for 15 minutes.

Cut sweet potato into quarters and boil till tender, about 10 minutes.

Grill the cherry tomatoes, about 2 minutes.

Deep-fry the bell pepper strips until crisp.

Shape the rice into individual small bowls.

Sauté steaks until medium rare (or to your liking), turning once.

Slice into wide strips and arrange on plates with the vegetables and rice and glaze with sauce (recipe follows).

Sauce

1 fl oz (2 tbs) soy sauce (30 ml)

1 fl oz (2 tbs) sake or white wine (30 ml)

½ oz (1 tbs) sugar (15 g)

1 tsp cornflour (cornstarch) (5 g) dissolved in 1 tbs water (15 ml)

Heat soy sauce, sake and sugar over low heat.

Thicken with cornflour mixture and heat another minute.

SPICY TENDERLOIN OF BEEF
ON A GRILLED FLOWER OF AUBERGINE AND TOMATO

HYATT REGENCY JERUSALEM, ISRAEL

SERVES 4

SAUCE

1 tsp vegetable oil (5 ml)

¼ oz (1 ½ tsp) onion—roughly chopped (7 g)

4 oz (1 medium) tomato—roughly chopped (115 g)

⅓ oz (2 tsp) tomato concentrate (paste) (10 ml)

1 tsp ground cumin (5 g)

1 tsp ground cardamom (5 g)

8 fl oz (1 c) dry red wine (240 ml)

1 tsp dried chilli—crushed (5 g)

¾ pt (2 c) brown veal or beef stock (480 ml) (see glossary)

salt and pepper to taste

Tabasco—for seasoning

Heat oil in a saucepan and lightly brown onion.

○

Add chopped tomato and tomato concentrate. Cook until mixture is stiff.

○

Add the cumin and cook 1 minute.

○

Add wine and chilli and simmer till reduced by half.

○

Add stock and reduce by ⅓.

○

Strain mixture through a fine sieve.

○

Season to taste with salt, pepper and Tabasco. Keep warm.

STEAKS

1 ½ lb (4 medium) beef steak fillets (680 g)

1 long aubergine (eggplant)—sliced crosswise ¼-inch (8 cm) thick

12 oz (3 medium) tomatoes—sliced crosswise ¼-inch (⅔ cm) thick (340 g)

8 fl oz (1 c) vegetable oil (240 ml)

salt and pepper to taste

2–3 springs fresh coriander

Dip the aubergine slices in oil and fry on a hot griddle for about 1 minute on each side.

○

Repeat the process for tomato slices, but cook only on one side for about ½ minute.

○

Season the steaks with salt and pepper. Cook to taste (i.e., well done, medium or rare). Keep warm.

TO SERVE

On 4 separate plates, neatly arrange 4 slices each of aubergine and 4 slices each of tomato (interwoven) in a ring around the centre of each plate. Set aside.

○

Place steaks in centre of each plate.

○

Surround the aubergine "flower" with sauce and garnish each plate with 3 coriander leaves.

○

Serve immediately, with steamed or saffron rice.

Noisettes d'Agneau Marco Polo
Fillets of Lamb Marco Polo

○

The Carlton Tower, A Park Hyatt Hotel, London, United Kingdom

Serves 4

1 ½ lb (12 slices) lamb fillet (680 g)

1 fl oz (2 tbs) olive oil (30 ml)

4 oz (1 small) green bell pepper—pips removed and diced (115 g)

4 oz (1 small) red bell pepper—pips removed and diced (115 g)

½ fl oz (1 tbs) brandy (15 ml)

¼ oz (1 tsp) green peppercorns (7 g)

½ fl oz (1 tbs) red port wine (15 ml)

4 fl oz (7 tbs) double (heavy) cream (100 ml)

3 oz (1 small) lemon—peeled and separated into segments (85 g)

1 oz (2 tbs) chives—chopped (30 g)

Cook lamb in a pan with olive oil until still pink, about 5 minutes.

○

Transfer to a serving dish and keep warm.

○

In the same pan, sauté the bell peppers; add the peppercorns, followed by the brandy and port wine.

○

Reduce by half, then add cream.

○

Reduce again until thickened.

○

When thickened add lemon segments and chives.

○

Pour over lamb and serve.

Filete de Porco Marinado con Entros e Pancake de Trigo
Marinated Pork on Chive, Coriander and Wholemeal Pancake

Hyatt Regency Macau, Macau

Serves 4

Pork

1 ¾ lb pork fillets—sliced into 4 medallions (800 g)

⅓ oz (1 tbs) chilli—diced (10 g)

2 fl oz (4 tbs) soy sauce (60 ml)

1 fl oz (2 tbs) honey (30 ml)

vegetable oil for frying

Mix the chilli, soy sauce and honey. Marinate pork medallions for 2 hours, turning 3–4 times.

Fry medallions until golden brown and well done, about 5 minutes.

Slice each medallion in half.

Pancake

10 oz (2 c) wholemeal (whole wheat) flour (285 g)

2 eggs

1 ½ pt (1 ½ c) milk (360 ml)

¾ oz (3 tbs) chives—chopped (20 g)

¾ oz (3 tbs) fresh coriander—chopped (20 g)

salt and pepper to taste

Whisk flour and eggs with small amount of milk to make paste.

Whisk until smooth, then add remaining milk, chives, coriander, salt and pepper.

Make 8 pancakes, one at a time, by spooning some batter onto hot griddle. Fry until lightly browned, then keep warm.

To Serve

Arrange 2 pancakes on plate and place pork medallions on top.

Serve with vegetables.

LAMB FILLET IN PHYLLO PASTRY

HYATT REGENCY SANCTUARY COVE, QUEENSLAND, AUSTRALIA

SERVES 4

LAMB

1 ¼ lb (4 pieces) boned lamb loin (560 g)

2 egg yolks

¾ oz (2 tbs) plain yoghurt (20 g)

½ tsp chives—chopped (2 g)

½ tsp basil—chopped (2 g)

3 oz (1 small) red bell pepper—pips removed and diced (85 g)

1 ½ oz button mushrooms—diced (45 g)

4 sheets phyllo dough—cut in half crosswise (6x18 cm) (see glossary)

2 oz (4 tbs) melted butter (55 g)

Preheat oven to 350° F (180° C).

Trim lamb into noisettes.

Place trimmings in a liquidiser with egg yolk, yoghurt, herbs and red pepper.

Purée; add the mushrooms and purée again until a smooth lamb mousse is formed.

Brush phyllo sheets with melted butter.

Using 2 sheets of phyllo dough, stack one on top of the other. Spread some lamb mousse in centre of sheets, then place a noisette over it.

Spread on a small amount of mousse, then roll up and tuck sides of phyllo dough underneath. Brush with more melted butter.

Repeat 3 times, making 4 bundles.

Bake for 15 minutes, or until dough is crispy and lamb is cooked to taste. Keep warm.

5 fl oz (⅔ c) dry white wine (150 ml)

3 oz (1 small) tomato—peeled, pips removed and chopped (85 g)

2 oz (½ medium) onion—chopped (55 g)

5 fl oz (⅔ c) lamb or chicken stock (150 ml) (see glossary)

1 tsp tomato concentrate (paste) (5 ml)

2 oz (½ c) pimiento (stuffed olives) (55 g)

salt and pepper to taste

Reduce wine by half in saucepan.

○

Add tomato and onion and cook for 10 minutes.

○

Add stock, tomato concentrate, olives, salt and pepper.

○

Simmer 5–10 minutes.

Place lamb bundles on individual plates.

○

Cut each in half, opening up and revealing lamb.

○

Place sauce around and serve with your choice of seasonal vegetables.

DAGING PANGGANG HITAM SAUS KACANG
GRILLED SIRLOIN STEAK WITH BLACK BEAN-OYSTER SAUCE

○

HYATT ARYADUTA JAKARTA, INDONESIA

SERVES 4

1 ½ oz (3 tbs) peanut or vegetable oil (45 ml)

1 tsp garlic—minced (5 g)

8 oz (2 medium) green bell peppers— pips removed and diced (225 g)

8 oz (2 medium) red bell peppers—pips removed and diced (225 g)

8 oz (1 c) black beans—cooked (225 g)

¼ pt (½ c) chicken stock (120 ml) (see glossary)

2 fl oz (4 tbs) oyster sauce (60 ml)

½ fl oz (1 tbs) Chinese or other semi-dry wine (15 ml)

1 lb 12 oz (4 medium) sirloin steaks (795 g)

salt and pepper to taste

oil or butter—for grilling

4 medium baked potatoes

8 oz (1 c) sour cream (240 ml)

In a wok, heat the oil and stir-fry the garlic, bell peppers and black beans for 2 minutes.

○

Add chicken stock, oyster sauce and Chinese wine.

○

Cook for another 2 minutes. Set aside.

○

Season the steaks with salt and pepper and rub some oil or melted butter on both sides of steaks. Grill to your liking.

○

To serve, pour sauce on half the plate.

○

Slice the sirloin on the diagonal and fan out slices on top of the sauce.

○

Add baked potatoes and sour cream.

SATAY DAGING LEMBU
BEEF SATAY

⌒

HYATT KUANTAN, MALAYSIA

SERVES 4

SATAY

12 oz tenderloin of beef—trimmed (340 g)

1 oz (2 tbs) fresh turmeric—finely ground (30 g)

1 tsp fennel seeds—finely ground (5 g)

1 tsp cumin seeds—finely ground (5 g)

1 ¾ oz (¼ c) sugar (50 g)

½ oz (1 tbs) salt (15 g)

1 fl oz (2 tbs) vegetable oil (30 ml)

20 bamboo skewers—soaked in water for 30 minutes

1 oz (1 stalk) lemongrass—crushed at thicker end for basting (30 g)

8 fl oz (1 c) coconut milk (240 ml) (see glossary)

4 oz (1 small) cucumber—chunked (115 g)

Slice beef into ¾-inch (2 cm) cubes.

⌒

Make marinade by combining the spices, sugar, salt and oil.

⌒

Marinate beef for at least 2 hours. Drain and reserve marinade.

⌒

Thread the beef cubes on the skewers.

⌒

Combine marinade with coconut milk and brush skewers with this mixture, using the lemongrass.

⌒

Grill over glowing charcoal, basting often until meat is done, about 3 minutes.

⌒

Serve with peanut sauce (recipe follows), rice cakes and cucumber wedges.

PEANUT SAUCE

2 ½ fl oz (5 tbs) vegetable oil (75 ml)

½ oz (1 clove) garlic—finely ground and peeled (15 g)

1 stalk lemongrass

1 tsp coriander—ground (5 g)

2 candlenuts (raw macadamia nuts)—finely ground

½ oz (1 tbs) shrimp paste (15 g)

10 mild fresh chillies (or to taste)—minced

5 oz (1 c) roasted peanuts—finely ground (150 g)

12 fl oz (1 ½ c) coconut milk (360 ml) (see glossary)

⅓ fl oz (2 tsp) tamarind juice—strained (10 ml) (see glossary)

¼ pt (½ c) water (120 ml)

3 ½ oz (½ c) sugar (100 g)

1 tsp salt (5 g)

Heat oil and fry garlic, lemongrass, coriander, candlenuts and shrimp paste until fragrant and oils separate, about 2 minutes.

⌒

Stir in chillies, then add peanuts and coconut milk.

⌒

Bring to a slow boil, add tamarind juice, water, sugar and salt. Simmer for 20 minutes. Discard lemongrass before serving.

Aussie Bucco

Hyatt On Collins, Melbourne, Australia

Serves 4

Oxtails

2 ¼ lb oxtails (1 kg)

3 ½ fl oz (7 tbs) olive oil (100 ml)

3 oz (1 small) onion—cubed (85 g)

2 oz (1 medium) carrot—cubed (55 g)

2 oz (1 stalk) celery—cubed (55 g)

½ oz (1 clove) garlic—chopped (15 g)

1 sprig rosemary—finely minced

5 fl oz (⅔ c) dry white wine (150 ml)

8 ½ oz (2 small) tomatoes—peeled and chopped (240 g)

3 fl oz (6 tbs) tomato concentrate (paste) (90 ml)

1 ¾ pt (4 ¼ c) brown veal stock (1 *l*) (see glossary)

1 bay leaf

juice of 1 navel orange

juice of 1 mandarin orange

juice of 1 lime

Brown oxtails in olive oil.

Add the onion, carrot, celery, garlic and rosemary. Sauté until softened.

Add wine, tomatoes, tomato concentrate, veal stock, bay leaf, orange and lime juices.

Simmer for 1 ¾ hours, or until meat is tender and sauce thick. Strain sauce. Keep warm.

Pizza

1 ¾ lb homemade or commercial pizza dough (795 g)

Preheat oven to 400° F (200° C).

Put pizza dough in large pan and bake halfway with a heavy weight on top, about 10 minutes.

Remove weight and finish baking until golden brown, about 10 minutes more. Keep warm.

Tomato Linguini

14 oz linguini—preferably flavoured and coloured with tomato (375 g)

1 oz (2 tbs) chives (30 g)

1 oz (2 tbs) butter (30 g)

Cook linguini in salted water until al dente.

Drain and toss with butter and chives. Keep warm.

To Assemble and Serve

zest of 1 orange—julienned

zest of 1 lime—julienned

3 ½ oz (½ c) sugar (100 g)

1 ¾ fl oz (3 ½ tbs) water (50 ml)

Place sugar and water in saucepan and boil until syrupy.

Toss in zests and simmer 12–15 minutes, until candied.

Place linguini on pizza crust.

Arrange oxtails on top of linguini and garnish with candied zests.

Surround linguini with sauce.

KERABU PERUT
TRIPE

HYATT SAUJANA, KUALA LUMPUR, MALAYSIA

SERVES 4

1 lb beef tripe (450 g)

8 oz (2 c) toasted coconut—grated (225 g)

15 green onions (scallions)—sliced (85 g)

1 fresh red chillies (or to taste)—diced

¾ oz belacan—toasted and pounded (20 g)

2 oz (2 stems) lemongrass—sliced. (55 g)

juice of 3 limes

4 lemon slices

salt and white pepper to taste

Rub tripe with salt.

Place in boiling water and cook until tender, about 2 hours.

Drain and cut into ½-inch (1 ¾ cm) strips.

Combine rest of ingredients in saucepan. Add tripe.

Mix well, reheat and adjust seasonings to taste.

SLICED BEEF WITH ASPARAGUS
IN POTATO BASKET

HYATT REGENCY SINGAPORE, SINGAPORE

SERVES 4

POTATO BASKET

5 oz (1 c) flour (150 g)

2 egg yolks

2 ½ fl oz (5 tbs) water (80 ml)

8 oz potatoes—peeled and thinly sliced crosswise (225 g)

vegetable oil—for deep-frying

Whisk flour, egg yolks and water in a bowl until smooth.

Wipe potato slices dry.

Dip ¼ of the potatoes, one at a time, into egg mixture, then arrange neatly in a 6–8 inch (15–20 cm) strainer.

Place another slightly smaller strainer over it and deep-fry until golden brown.

Blot with absorbent paper. Repeat 3 times, making remaining baskets.

BEEF AND VEGETABLES

2 ½ fl oz (5 tbs) vegetable oil (70 ml)

1 ¼ lb beef tenderloin—trimmed and sliced into thin strips 1-inch (2.5 cm) long (600 g)

7 oz asparagus—cleaned and trimmed (200 g)

3 ½ oz (1 large) carrot—peeled and julienned (100 g)

½ oz (2 tbs) shallots—minced (15 g)

½ oz (2 tbs) garlic—minced (15 g)

⅓ oz (2 tsp) fresh ginger—sliced very thinly into strips (10 g)

8 fl oz (1 c) chicken stock (240 ml) (see glossary)

1 tsp light soy sauce (5 ml)

1 tsp oyster sauce (5 ml)

1 tsp (5 g) cornflour (cornstarch)— dissolved in 1 tbs water (15 ml)

1 ½ fl oz (3 tbs) sherry (45 ml)

½ oz (2 tbs) green onion (scallions)— diced for garnish (15 g)

Heat wok with half the oil until hot.

Stir-fry tenderloin strips for 1 minute; set aside and keep warm.

Briefly blanch the asparagus and carrot in boiling water. Drain and refresh in ice water; drain again. Set aside.

Heat wok with remaining oil and sauté shallots, garlic and ginger until limp.

Lower heat and add stock, soy sauce and oyster sauce.

Simmer for 1 minute, then thicken with cornflour mixture.

Stir well, then add beef and vegetables.

Bring back to a boil and remove from heat.

Add sherry, mix and serve immediately on the potato basket. Garnish with green onion.

Kalbi Gui

Charcoal Broiled Beef Rib

◯

Hyatt Regency Seoul, Korea

Serves 4

4 lb beef rib (1.8 kg)—cut into 1-inch (2.5 cm) lengths

3 ½ fl oz (7 tbs) soy sauce (100 ml)

3 ½ fl oz (7 tbs) water (100 ml)

½ oz (1 clove) garlic—finely chopped (15 g)

⅓ oz (2 tsp) sesame seeds—ground (10 g)

1 tsp green onions (scallions)— chopped (5 g)

½ oz (1 tbs) sugar (15 g)

3 ½ fl oz (7 tbs) sake or dry white wine (100 ml)

3 oz (½ medium) pear—chopped (85 g)

3 ½ fl oz (7 tbs) oriental sesame oil (100 ml)

Carefully cut halfway into the bone from the middle of each rib. Cut lengthwise, leaving bone attached to meat, almost to the end of each rib. Flatten the meat away from the middle of each rib.

◯

Mix soy sauce, water, garlic, sesame powder and green onion.

◯

Pour mixture over beef and marinate overnight in the refrigerator.

Sprinkle sugar and rice wine over pear. Marinate 2 hours.

◯

Drain ribs and brush with sesame oil. Sauté in pan over medium heat or charcoal until tender, about 10 minutes.

◯

Serve with sweetened pears.

Note: If meat is slightly frozen, cutting will be easier. Or have butcher prepare ribs.

Lomo de Cerdo "La Place"
Lamb Loin "La Place"

Hyatt Cancun Caribe Resort & Villas, Mexico

Serves 4

Stuffed Lamb

3 ½ oz (7 tbs) butter (100 g)

3 ½ oz (¾ c) shallots—minced (100 g)

½ oz (1 clove) garlic—mashed (15 g)

3 ½ oz spinach—trimmed, cleaned, poached and drained (100 g)

1 ¼ lb boned lamb loin—trimmed (600 g)

salt and pepper to taste

Preheat oven to 350° F (180° C).

Heat butter in sauté pan and sauté the shallots and garlic for 3 seconds.

Add the spinach and cook for 1 minute.

Filling the cavity where the bone was, stuff the lamb with the spinach mixture.

Season lamb with salt and pepper and roast until medium-rare, about 30 minutes.

Slice lamb into ⅔-inch (1.5 cm) slices.

Serve with caper sauce (recipe follows) and seasonal vegetables.

Caper Sauce

3 ½ oz (¾ c) shallots—minced (100 g)

1 oz (2 tbs) butter (30 g)

¼ pt (½ c) dry white wine (120 ml)

½ fl oz (1 tbs) wine vinegar (15 ml)

6 fl oz (¾ c) lamb or beef stock (180 ml) (see glossary)

2 fl oz (4 tbs) double (heavy) cream (60 ml)

¾ oz (3 tbs) capers—chopped (20 g)

salt and pepper to taste

Sauté shallots in butter until golden brown.

Add wine, vinegar and stock. Simmer 15–20 minutes.

Purée mixture in a liquidiser and strain.

Add cream, capers and salt and pepper to taste. Keep warm.

Soegogi Sanjuk
Skewered Beef

⟨◯⟩

Hyatt Regency Pusan, Korea

Serves 4

Skewered Beef

1 ¼ lb beef tenderloin—trimmed and cut into strips (600 g)

7 oz young green onions—trimmed and cut slightly shorter than beef strips (200 g)

3 ½ oz ginseng—cut to same size as beef strips (100 g) (see glossary)

Marinate meat and vegetables in the seasoning sauce (recipe follows) for 1 hour in the refrigerator.

◯

Skewer the ingredients alternately, beginning and ending with the meat.

◯

Baste skewers and grill (or fry) until done, about 5 minutes.

Seasoning Sauce (Marinade)

½ oz (1 tbs) sugar (15 g)

1 fl oz (2 tbs) sake or white wine (30 ml)

1 fl oz (2 tbs) soy sauce (30 ml)

2 green onions—diced

1 ½ oz (3 cloves) garlic—crushed (45 g)

½ oz (1 tbs) sesame salt (15 g)

1 fl oz (2 tbs) oriental sesame oil (30 ml)

Mix all until well blended.

Note: If sesame salt is unavailable, substitute ground sesame seeds mixed with a pinch of salt.

DICED BEEF KUNG-PO

HYATT REGENCY XIAN, PEOPLE'S REPUBLIC OF CHINA

SERVES 4

12 oz beef fillets (340 g)

½ oz (1 tbs) light soy sauce (15 ml)

pinch salt

⅓ oz (2 tsp) cornflour (cornstarch) (10 g)

1 oz (¼ c) raw peanuts (30 g)

vegetable oil—for deep-frying

1 ½ fl oz (3 tbs) vegetable oil (45 ml)

½ oz (1 clove) garlic—minced (15 g)

1 oz (¼ c) green bell pepper—pips
removed and minced (30 g)

1 oz (¼ c) red bell pepper—pips
removed and minced (30 g)

1 oz (2 tbs) dried red chilli (30 g)

¼ oz (2 tbs) ginger—minced (5 g)

2 oz bamboo shoots (55 g)

1 oz (¼ c) green onion (scallions)—
chopped (30 g)

Cut beef into cubes. Marinate in
soy sauce, salt and cornflour for
30 minutes.

Deep-fry the peanuts till golden. Set
aside.

Sauté beef in oil until half done, about
3 minutes. Set aside.

Stir-fry the garlic, peppers, chilli and
ginger in same pan.

Add beef and peanuts and stir-fry until
well blended.

Transfer to a platter and sprinkle with
chopped green onions.

Lomo de Cerdo Gratinado con Ejote
Pork Loin with Vegetables

Hyatt Regency Acapulco, Mexico

Serves 4

Pork Loin

1 ⅓ lb boned pork loin (600 g)

14 oz green beans—strings removed (400 g)

3 ½ oz (7 tbs) butter (100 g)

¾ oz (⅓ c) fresh coriander—chopped (20 g)

3 egg yolks

3 ½ oz (1 c) bread crumbs (100 g)

salt and pepper to taste

Season pork with salt and pepper; grill for 10 minutes. Set aside. Preheat oven to 350° F (180° C).

Blanch the beans in boiling salted water, then run under cold water and drain.

Separate ¼ of the beans and cut into cubes for garnish.

Chop remaining beans coarsely, then put in a liquidiser to purée.

Heat the butter and sauté onion and coriander until onion is soft.

Remove from heat, season with salt and pepper and allow to cool.

Add the egg yolks, bread crumbs and puréed beans. Mix well until it forms a paste.

Spread paste on pork and bake until the paste turns golden brown, about 30 minutes.

Vegetables

2 oz (4 tbs) butter (55 g)

7 oz (2 small) onions—quartered (200 g)

5¼ oz (2 medium) leeks—sliced (145 g)

14 oz (3 medium) tomatoes—peeled and chopped (395 g)

⅓ oz (¼ c) mixture of chopped thyme, basil and oregano (10 g)

Melt butter in pan and sauté onion and leek until golden brown.

Add remaining ingredients and cook until mixture thickens. Keep warm.

Sauce

2 fl oz (4 tbs) vegetable oil (50 ml)

2 oz (4 cloves) garlic—chopped (50 g)

7 oz (2 small) onions—diced (200 g)

14 serrano or other hot chillies—diced

3 ½ oz (1 small) tomatoes—peeled and chopped (100 g)

6 fl oz (¾ c) dry white wine (200 ml)

salt and pepper to taste

Heat oil and sauté garlic, onion and chilli until golden brown.

Add tomato and cook until sauce thickens.

Add wine and season with salt and pepper.

Pour sauce into a liquidiser and blend at medium speed for 10 seconds.

Pour back into saucepan and keep warm.

To Garnish and Serve

3 ½ oz (2 small) carrots—cubed and boiled until tender (100 g)

3 ½ oz (1 c) cooked green beans—cut into large pieces (100 g)

Cut the pork loin crosswise into ½-inch (1.25 cm) slices.

Pour the sauce onto a plate. Arrange pork slices on sauce and place vegetables alongside. Garnish with carrots and green beans.

POACHED BABY BEEF TENDERLOIN

HYATT REGENCY COOLUM, QUEENSLAND, AUSTRALIA

SERVES 4

12 oz (4 steaks) trimmed baby beef or veal tenderloin (340 g)

¾ pt (2 c) vegetable stock (240 ml) (see glossary)

3 oz tofu (85 g)

pinch celery salt

4 oz (1 medium) red bell pepper—halved and pips removed (115 g)

4 oz (1 medium) green bell pepper—halved and pips removed (115 g)

4 oz (1 medium) yellow bell pepper—halved and pips removed (115 g)

1 fl oz (2 tbs) grape seed oil, cold pressed (30 ml)

4 oz (2 medium) fresh ripe apricots—stones removed (120 g)

¼ pt (½ c) dry white wine (120 ml)

fennel flowers—for decoration

pink peppercorns—for decoration

Wrap each steak in parchment paper and poach gently in vegetable stock.

Season tofu with celery salt and fry on griddle until browned.

Cut peppers into quarters.

Heat oil gently and toss in peppers. Sauté briefly.

Place apricots in liquidiser with wine and purée until creamy.

Arrange ingredients on plate. Garnish with fennel flowers and pink peppercorns.

BEEF BERLADA
BEEF TENDERLOIN IN CHILLI SAUCE

HYATT KINABALU, MALAYSIA

SERVES 4

7 oz (1 c) tapioca flour (200 g)

7 oz (1 c) cornflour (cornstarch) (200 g)

1 egg yolk

pinch saffron

8 fl oz (1 c) water (240 ml)

vegetable oil—for frying

1 ⅔ lb beef tenderloin (750 g)

salt and pepper to taste

1 ⅓ fl oz (8 tsp) sambal ulek (40 ml)

1 oz (2 tbs) butter (30 g)

½ oz (1 tbs) sugar (15 g)

4 oz (1 medium) green bell pepper —
pips removed and sliced into strips
(115 g)

4 oz (1 medium) red bell pepper—pips
removed and sliced into strips
(115 g)

4 oz bean sprouts (115 g)

4 oz (1 medium) onion—sliced into
rings (115 g)

Mix the tapioca and cornflour with the egg yolk.

In a separate bowl, mix saffron with water.

Slowly add this to the cornflour mixture until a smooth batter is formed.

Heat a serving ladle in very hot oil, then dip the bottom in the batter.

Wait a few seconds for the batter to stick, then deep-fry batter until golden brown. These are "golden cups."

Slice beef into individual portions.

Season with salt and pepper and grill to your liking.

Sauté sambal ulek in butter and add sugar. Stir constantly until dissolved.

Add grilled beef to sauté pan and stir to coat.

Sauté the peppers with the sprouts.

Place the sautéed vegetables in the "golden cups" and serve with beef.

Garnish with onion rings.

Note: Sambal ulek is an Indonesian hot tomato paste, available in specialty stores.

POACHED VEAL LOIN
FRESH TOMATO COULIS WITH GRATIN POTATOES

⌒

HYATT REGENCY MANILA, PHILIPPINES

SERVES 4

VEAL		COULIS

1 ¼ lb veal loin (600 g)

½ pt (1 ½ c) brown veal stock (360 ml) (see glossary)

Bring stock to a boil in large heavy pot.

⌒

Add the meat, lower heat and simmer 20 minutes.

⌒

Set aside and keep warm.

4 oz (1 medium) tomato—chopped (115 g)

2 oz (1 medium) onion—chopped (55 g)

½ oz (1 tbs) butter (15 g)

pinch of garlic—chopped

8 fl oz (1 c) brown veal stock (240 ml)

salt and pepper to taste

Sauté the tomato, onion and garlic in butter until soft.

⌒

Add stock and simmer till you have a thick sauce.

⌒

Strain and season with salt and pepper. Keep warm.

POTATOES

1 lb potatoes—peeled and thinly sliced crosswise (450 g)

8 fl oz (1 c) double (heavy) cream (240 ml)

salt and pepper, garlic and nutmeg to taste

Preheat oven to 350° F (180° C).

○

Place potato slices in buttered baking dish.

○

Mix cream with salt, pepper, garlic and nutmeg.

○

Pour over potatoes and bake for 40 minutes or until potatoes are soft.

TO GARNISH AND SERVE

1 lb assorted young vegetables— blanched (450 g)

Slice veal crosswise into thin pieces. Place on individual plates.

○

Pour on coulis and serve blanched vegetables on the side.

○

Serve with gratin potatoes.

PAN-FRIED LAMB MEDALLIONS
GREEN-OLIVE SABAYON WITH FIGS

⬯

HYATT REGENCY JEDDAH, SAUDI ARABIA

SERVES 4

1 ½ lb (8 pcs) lamb medallions (680 g)

salt and pepper to taste

2 oz (4 tbs) butter—preferably clarified (55 g)

3 egg yolks

¾ oz (1 ½ tbs) green olives—puréed (20 g)

½ fl oz (1 tbs) white grape juice (15 ml)

3 oz (¾ c) thin green beans (85 g)

10 oz (2 large) tomatoes—peeled, pips removed and sliced into strips (285 g)

4 figs preserved in syrup—cut in half

Season lamb medallions with salt and pepper to taste.

○

Pan-fry in butter until pink, about 8 minutes. Set aside and keep warm.

○

In a bowl, combine egg yolks, olive purée and grape juice.

○

Place bowl over hot water, whisking eggs continuously until frothy. Season to taste. This is the sabayon.

○

Blanch beans in boiling water and immediately immerse in cold water.

○

Drain, then briefly sauté with tomato strips.

○

Quickly grill fig halves until lightly singed.

○

To serve, arrange lamb on plates with sabayon and fig halves.

○

Garnish with sautéed beans and tomato strips.

LAMB CUTLETS WITH GOAT CHEESE

U.N. PLAZA HOTEL, A PARK HYATT HOTEL, NEW YORK, U.S.A.

SERVES 4

1 ½ lb (12 small) lamb cutlets (chops)
(680 g)

salt and pepper to taste

1 fl oz (2 tbs) olive oil (30 ml)

1 oz (2 tbs) butter (30 g)

2 oz (½ c) shallots—finely chopped
(55 g)

2 fl oz (4 tbs) Armagnac (60 ml)

½ oz (2 tbs) fresh rosemary—chopped
(15 g)

1 oz (2 tbs) chilled butter—cubed (30 g)

12 oz (12 slices) goat cheese 1.4-inch
(3 ½ cm) (340 g) thick

Season lamb cutlets with salt and
pepper.

⁃

Sauté cutlets in a large pan with olive
oil and butter for 2–3 minutes each
side. Set aside cutlets and keep warm.

⁃

Using same sauté pan, pour off excess
fat, then sauté shallots without
colouring.

⁃

Deglaze pan with the Armagnac,
flambé and let flames die down.

⁃

Add rosemary and reduce for 2 minutes.

⁃

Remove from heat and stir in chilled
butter.

⁃

Place three cutlets neatly on each
plate and top each cutlet with a slice
of goat cheese.

⁃

If plates are broilere-proof, place under
broiler until cheese starts to brown

⁃

Garnish with hot vegetables of your
choice. Spoon suace over cutlets and
serve.

MIXIOTE DE CORDERO
MIXIOTE OF LAMB

<hr />

HYATT HOTEL VILLAHERMOSA, MEXICO

SERVES 4

2 ¼ lb lamb stew meat—cut in large cubes or squares

4 dried Guajillo chillies—chopped

4 dried Cascabel chillies—chopped

1 lb (4 medium) tomatoes—chopped (450 g)

4 oz (1 medium) onion—minced (115 g)

4 oz (8 cloves) garlic—peeled and minced (115 g)

½ tsp dried oregano (2 g)

1 tsp ground cumin (5 g)

2 fl oz (4 tbs) pineapple or other fruit vinegar (60 ml)

salt and pepper to taste

4 maguey (agave) or banana leaves

Note: Guajillo and Cascabel chillies are fiery hot. If unavailable, substitute other hot chillies.

Place chillies, tomatoes, onion, garlic, oregano, cumin, vinegar, salt and pepper in a large pot. Bring to a boil, then simmer until thick, about 10 minutes.

Place a portion of lamb on each maguey or banana leaf; top with some sauce and wrap well, sewing with string.

Place lamb "packages" in a pan and place pan in steamer. Steam until lamb is cooked, approximately 2 hours.

Place "packages" on individual plates and serve hot.

LAL MAAS
SPICY LAMB CURRY

○

HYATT REGENCY DELHI, INDIA

SERVES 4

5¼ oz (1 ¼ c) ghee (clarified butter) (150 g) (see glossary)

7 oz (2 small) onions—sliced (200 g)

2 ¼ oz (5 cloves) garlic—crushed (60 g)

5 black cardamom seeds

5 green cardamom seeds

1 tsp cumin seeds (5 g)

2 ¼ lb boned leg of spring lamb (1 kg)

10 fresh red chillies

1 ¼ oz (2 ½ tbs) coriander—ground (35 g)

½ tsp turmeric (2 g)

8 oz (1 c) plain yoghurt (225 g)

½ oz (2 tbs) fresh ginger—sliced (15 g)

¼ pt (3 c) water (700 ml)

salt and pepper to taste

¾ oz (3 tsp) fresh coriander—chopped (20 g)

8 tomato wedges—for garnish

Heat ghee in large pan.

○

Sauté onions until golden brown, then add garlic and cardamom.

○

Sauté until golden, then add cumin seeds and lamb; fry for 10 minutes.

○

Add chillies, coriander, turmeric, salt and yoghurt. Simmer until most of the liquid has evaporated.

○

Add water and bring to a boil, cover and simmer, stirring occasionally until meat is tender and gravy is thick, about 2 hours.

○

Place curry in individual bowls.

○

Serve with ginger slices, chopped fresh coriander and tomato wedges.

Piccata de Veau au Citron Vert Tagliatelle a la Tomate et Basilic
Veal Piccata with Lime and Tagliatelle with Tomato and Basil

The Carlton Tower, A Park Hyatt Hotel, London, United Kingdom

Serves 4

1 lb green and white tagliatelle (450 g)

3 limes

1 lb (16 pieces) veal medallions—
pounded very thin (450 g)

2 eggs—beaten

2 fl oz (4 tbs) olive oil (60 ml)

4 oz (8 tbs) butter (115 g)

1 fl oz (2 tbs) Worcestershire sauce
(30 ml)

salt and pepper to taste

10 oz (2 large) tomatoes—peeled, pips
removed and julienned (285 g)

1 oz (¼ c) fresh basil—shredded (30 g)

Cook tagliatelle until al dente; drain
and keep warm.

Peel 2 limes with a potato peeler; save
skins. Remove any white part of skin;
slice peel into julienne. Blanch for 10
seconds in boiling water. Set aside.

Separate limes into segments. Set
aside.

Flour the veal very lightly; then dip in
beaten eggs.

Sauté quickly in half the olive oil and
butter. Remove from pan and keep
warm.

Deglaze the pan with the juice of
remaining lime and the
Worcestershire sauce. Add remaining
butter and stir well.

Stir in shredded lime peel and segments, then season with salt and
pepper.

In a large pan, pour in remaining olive
oil and butter.

Quickly toss in tomatoes and basil
leaves.

Add the tagliatelle, stir to coat and
transfer to a serving dish.

Place veal around tagliatelle, pour
sauce over and serve.

Veal Medallions with Macadamia Nut-Herb Crust
Served with Ginseng Sauce and Tofu Lasagna

Hyatt Regency Perth, Australia

Serves 4

Ginseng Sauce

½ tsp vegetable oil (3 ml)

2 ¼ oz (4 medium) shallots—minced (60 g)

¼ oz (½ medium clove) garlic—minced (7 g)

½ oz (1 tbs) fresh ginger—minced (15 g)

½ tsp vegetable oil (2 ml)

¼ pt (½ c) ginseng drink (120 ml)

6 fl oz (¾ c) brown stock (180 ml) (see glossary)

salt and pepper to taste

Sauté the shallots, garlic and ginger in oil.

Deglaze pan with ginseng and simmer until reduced by half.

Add stock and reduce again by half; adjust seasonings and keep warm.

Note: Ginseng drink is a stamina with Korean ginseng root as the main component. It is available in major Asian grocery stores.

Nut-Herb Crust and Veal

3 oz (¾ c) Macadamia nuts—crushed (85 g)

½ oz (1 tbs) butter (15 g)

⅓ oz (1 tbs) fresh herbs of your choice—chopped (10 g)

2 slices white bread—toasted and ground for crumbs (60 g)

¼ oz (1 tsp) Dijon mustard (7 g)

1 egg yolk

1 ½ lb (8 pcs) veal medallions (680 g)

salt and pepper to taste

½ fl oz (1 tbs) vegetable oil (15 g)

Sauté nuts in butter until golden brown.

Stir in herbs, bread crumbs, mustard and egg yolk.

Roll mixture into a cylinder and slice into 8 pieces.

Season veal with salt and pepper.

Sauté until medium rare, about 7–8 minutes. Keep warm.

Tofu Lasagna

7 oz (1 c) spinach—trimmed, cleaned and chopped (200 g)

½ oz (1 tbs) butter (15 g)

salt and pepper to taste

6 ½ oz (1 ½ medium) tomatoes—peeled, pips removed and chopped (185 g)

4 tofu squares—sliced ½-inch (1.25 cm) thick

8 fl oz (1 c) tomato coulis (240 ml) (see glossary)

Preheat oven to 200° F (100° C).

Sauté the spinach in butter until wilted.

Season with salt and pepper, then add tomatoes

In a pan, layer the tofu slices with some of the spinach-tomato mixture.

Pour coulis over and warm in oven.

Rice Cake

7 oz (1 c) sticky (glutinous) rice (200 g)

2 ¼ oz (¼ c) wild rice (60 g)

1 ¾ pt (4 c) chicken stock (1 *l*) (see glossary)

Bring 8 fl oz (1 c; 240 ml) stock to a boil and add wild rice. Simmer until cooked, about 45 minutes.

Bring remaining stock to a boil and add sticky rice. Simmer until almost tender, about 10 minutes.

Combine rices to blend well.

Grease a large sheet of aluminum foil with butter.

Place rice mixture on it and roll up tightly.

Steam for 10 minutes. Keep warm.

To Assemble and Serve

Place two rice cakes in centre of serving plate.

Put veal medallions on top of rice cakes.

Place macadamia crust on top.

Arrange the lasagna on the side of the plate and serve sauce separately.

CARVED SADDLE AND FILLET OF LAMB
WITH BRAISED LEEK AND NATURAL JUICES

HYATT AUCKLAND, NEW ZEALAND

SERVES 4

2 ½ oz (1 medium) leek (70 g)

5 fl oz (⅔ c) chicken stock (150 ml)
(see glossary)

4 oz lamb fillet (115 g)

1 ½ lb boned lamb loin (680 g)

½ oz (1 tbs) butter (15 g)

⅔ fl oz (4 tsp) brandy (20 ml)

2 fl oz (4 tbs) dry red wine (60 ml)

6 fl oz (¾ c) brown veal stock (180 ml)
(see glossary)

⅓ oz butter—chilled (10 g)

1 oz (2 medium) shallots—peeled (30 g)

4 oz pearl onions—peeled (115 g)

4 oz snow peas (115 g)

4 oz turnips—peeled and sliced (115 g)

2 oz (½ medium) tomato—blanched,
peeled and quartered (55 g)

Braise leek in chicken stock for
approximately 7 minutes.

○

Slice leek and reheat in reduced
chicken stock along with the shallots
and pearl onions.

○

Halve lengthwise and remove centre
for garnish; reduce stock by ⅔. Set
aside.

○

Put lamb fillet between sheets of
greaseproof paper and pound with
mallet.

○

Enclose leek halves and roll up. Secure
with string.

○

Pan-roast the loin until still pink,
about 20 minutes. Remove from heat
and keep warm.

○

Sauté the fillet in butter until light
pink, about 5 minutes. Transfer to pan
with loin.

○

Deglaze skillet with brandy, wine and
veal stock. Reduce by ⅔. Remove from
heat and swirl in chilled butter. Keep
warm.

○

Slice lamb loin fillet and arrange on
individual plates with leek-onion
mixture alongside. Spoon sauce over
this. If desired, serve with seasonal
vegetables of your choice.

GRILLED TENDERLOIN OF BEEF AND LAMB CHOP

HYATT REGENCY SAIPAN, MARIANA ISLANDS

SERVES 4

4 ¼ lb beef tenderloin steaks (460 g)

4 ¼ lb lamb cutlets (chops) (460 g)

salt to taste

¼ oz (1 ½ tsp) mixed fresh herbs (7 g)

6 oz green beans—blanched briefly and sliced on an angle 1-inch (2.5 cm) thick (170 g)

½ oz (1 tbs) butter (15 g)

5 oz (1 large) onion—sliced (140 g)

3 ¾ oz (1 small) red bell pepper—pips removed and diced (105 g)

3 ¾ oz (1 small) yellow bell pepper—pips removed and diced (105 g)

8 oz (4 small) aubergine (eggplant) (225 g)

4 fresh red chillies—for garnish

4 sprigs thyme—for garnish

4 sprigs basil—for garnish

Season steaks and cutlets with salt and herbs.

Sauté or grill until done, about 20 minutes. Set aside and keep warm.

Make crosswise slices of aubergine, about ½-inch (¾ cm) wide.

Blanch lightly.

Heat pan with butter. Sauté onion and beans lightly, about 5 minutes. Add diced peppers and sauté for 30 seconds more.

Place aubergines on top of the sautéed vegetables and cover pan. Steam for 20 minutes, or until aubergines are tender.

Arrange beef steaks and lamb chops neatly on individual plates. Place vegetables around side.

Garnish with chillies and fresh herbs.

Veal Roulades in Citrus Glaze
with Saffron Linguini

○

Hyatt Regency Manila, Philippines

Serves 4

Roulades and Lemon Sauce

1 lb boneless veal roast (450 g)

1 ½ oz (3 tbs) olive oil (45 ml)

⅓ oz (1 clove) garlic—minced (10 g)

⅓ oz (1 medium) shallot—minced (10 g)

8 oz (2 medium) tomatoes—peeled, pips removed and chopped (225 g)

½ oz (1 tbs) fresh basil—chopped (15 g)

4 oz (1 small) avocado—halved, peeled, stone removed and sliced into 8 pieces (115 g)

4 oz spinach—blanched and drained (115 g)

8 fl oz (1 c) chicken stock (240 ml) (see glossary)

1 ½ fl oz (3 tbs) lemon juice (45 ml)

6 fl oz (¾ c) double (heavy) cream (180 ml)

grated zest of 1 lemon

½ oz (1 tbs) butter—chilled and cubed (15 g)

salt and pepper to taste

Cut the veal into 8 thin slices.

○

Place each slice between 2 pieces of greaseproof paper and pound until thin. Lay slices flat and season with salt and pepper.

○

Heat olive oil in a pan and sauté garlic and shallots briefly without colouring.

○

Add tomatoes and basil and cook for 3 minutes. Let cool.

○

Place a thin layer of spinach on each slice of veal, covering it entirely.

○

Spread tomato mixture evenly on the spinach.

○

Place a slice of avocado at the base and roll veal as tightly as possible. Secure with a toothpick.

○

Arrange roulades in sauté pan and pour in stock. Cover pan and place over low heat. Simmer roulades for 6–8 minutes. Transfer to warmed platter.

○

Add lemon juice to stock and reduce mixture to ⅓ c (80 ml). Add heavy cream and lemon zest and reduce to desired consistency.

○

Remove from heat and swirl in chilled butter. Season with salt and pepper. Keep warm.

Linguini and Vegetables

5 saffron threads

8 oz linguini (225 g)

½ oz (1 tbs) butter (15 g)

6 oz thin green beans—blanched (175 g)

4 oz cauliflower—blanched (115 g)

salt and pepper to taste

Bring a large pot of salted water to boil. Add saffron and stir.

○

When water turns orange, drop in linguini and cook until al dente. Drain well and keep warm.

○

Melt butter in a pan and briefy sauté beans and cauliflower. Season with salt and pepper. Keep warm.

To Serve

Arrange roulades, linguini and vegetables on plates as shown in photo.

○

Serve sauce separately.

VEAL AND VEGETABLE ROLL
LIGHT PLUM SAUCE WITH RICE POCKETS

⌒

HYATT REGENCY SINGAPORE, SINGAPORE

SERVES 4

VEAL AND VEGETABLE ROLL

6 oz (16 small) veal medallions (175 g)

3 ½ oz (1 small) red bell pepper—pips removed and julienned (100 g)

3 ½ oz (1 small) green bell pepper—pips removed and julienned (100 g)

3 ½ oz (2 small) carrots—julienned (100 g)

2 oz enoki mushrooms (55 g)

salt and pepper to taste

MARINADE

1 ½ fl oz (3 tbs) soy sauce (45 ml)

1 ½ fl oz (3 tbs) sake or white wine (45 ml)

1 ½ fl oz (3 tbs) brown veal stock (45 ml) (see glossary)

⅓ oz (1 ½ tsp) fresh ginger—grated (10 g)

⅓ oz (2 tsp) green onion (scallions)—sliced (10 g)

½ oz (1 clove) garlic—chopped (15 g)

⅓ oz (2 tsp) sugar (10 g)

¼ oz (1 tsp) white sesame seeds (3 g)

Pound veal medallions into thin squares.

⌒

Combine marinade ingredients and use to marinate veal, refrigerating for 24 hours.

⌒

Bring salted water to a rolling boil and blanch the bell peppers and carrots for 1 or 2 minutes. Refresh in ice water and drain.

⌒

Mix in mushrooms and season.

⌒

Place a small amount of the vegetable mixture at the end of each veal medallion.

⌒

Roll up and secure with a toothpick. Set aside. Reserve marinade.

RICE POCKETS

1 ½ fl oz (3 tbs) vegetable oil (45 ml)

1 ½ oz (1 ½ medium) shallots—minced (45 g)

¾ oz (1 large clove) garlic—minced (20 g)

3 ½ oz shrimp—peeled and cubed (100 g)

3 eggs—beaten

2 oz crabmeat (60 g)

2 oz (½ c) asparagus—diced and blanched (60 g)

2 oz (½ c) carrots—diced and blanched (60 g)

2 oz (½ c) bean sprouts (60 g)

8 oz (3 c) cooked white rice (240 g)

¾ fl oz (1 ½ tbs) dark soy sauce (20 ml)

¾ fl oz (1 ½ tbs) light soy sauce (20 ml)

⅓ oz (1 ½ tbs) scallions—diced (20 g)

salt and pepper to taste

4 spring roll wrappers

vegetable oil—for deep-frying

Heat wok with oil and sauté shallots and garlic without coloring.

⌒

Add shrimp and sauté briefly; add beaten egg and stir-fry to break apart.

⌒

Add the crabmeat and vegetables, then add cooked rice.

⌒

Stir-fry well, then pour in soy sauces and scallions.

⌒

Season with salt and pepper.

⌒

Divide fried rice into 4 portions; place one portion on each spring roll wrapper.

⌒

Wet edges with water and pinch together at top.

⌒

Deep-fry in oil until crispy, about 5 minutes.

PLUM SAUCE

2 ¾ fl oz (5 ½ tbs) brown veal stock (80 ml) (see glossary)

2 ½ fl oz (5 tbs) plum sauce (75 ml)

½ oz (1 tbs) butter—chilled (15 g)

Bring stock, 5 ½ tbs (2 ¾ fl oz) (80 ml) of reserved marinade and plum sauce to a boil. Reduce by ¼.

○

Remove from heat and swirl in butter. Keep warm.

TO ASSEMBLE AND SERVE

Grill or sauté veal rolls until evenly cooked, about 10 minutes.

○

Arrange veal rolls and spring rolls neatly on individual plates.

○

Serve plum sauce separately.

Wanton vom Rinderfilet Gefüllt mit Gänseleber in Portweinsauce

Wonton of Beef Fillet stuffed with Goose Liver in a Port Wine Sauce

◯

Hyatt Regency Cologne, Germany

SERVES 4

1 ¼ lb (12 thin slices) fillets of beef (600 g)

12 oz (12 slices) goose liver (340 g)

12 wonton skins

vegetable oil—for deep-frying

Put a slice of liver and a slice of beef on a wonton skin and wrap well, moistening edges to seal. Repeat to have 12 wontons.

◯

Deep-fry wontons. Keep warm.

◯

Place an equal amount of sauce on individual plates and put the wontons on top of sauce. Serve.
(See glossary for Port Wine Sauce.)

LAMB'S FRIES WITH BRAISED SHALLOTS

HYATT ON COLLINS, MELBOURNE, AUSTRALIA

SERVES 4

(2 tbs) lamb's fries (testicles) (450 g)

1 fl oz olive oil (30 ml)

8 fl oz (1 c) lamb stock (237 ml)   (see glossary)

6 oz (1 ½ c) shallots—peeled (170 g)

8 oz (1 large) sabago or other baking potato—cut into thin slices (225 g)

3 ½ oz (¾ c) red onion slices (100 g)

2-4 chives—for garnish

salt and pepper to taste

Slice lamb's fries thinly and sear in half the olive oil in a hot pan. Do not overcook.

In a saucepan braise shallots in 2 fl oz (4 tbs) stock until soft (60 ml).

Sauté onion slices and potatoes in remaining olive oil until translucent.

Add remaining stock and season with salt and pepper.

Place potatoes and onions in centre of serving plate and arrange lamb's fries on top, surrounded by shallots.

Lightly glaze lamb's fries with sauce and garnish plate with chives.

FISH AND SEAFOOD

CREVETTES GEANTES GRILLEES AVEC SAUCE VANILLE
GRILLED SHRIMP WITH VANILLA SAUCE

○

HYATT REGENCY TAHITI, FRENCH POLYNESIA

SERVES 4

SHRIMP

1 ¼ lb (12 large) shrimp or prawns—peeled and deveined (560 g)

salt and pepper to taste

1–2 fl oz (2–4 tbs) vegetable oil (30–60 ml)

12 oz (1 ½ c) wild rice—soaked overnight (340 g)

8 chives—cut into 3-inch (7.5 cm) pieces

Season shrimp with salt, pepper and oil

○

Grill until done, approximately 5 minutes. Keep warm.

○

Drain rice and cook until tender, about 45 minutes.

○

Serve grilled shrimp with wild rice and vanilla sauce (recipe follows).

○

Garnish with chives.

VANILLA SAUCE

1 ½ oz (3 medium) shallots—peeled and chopped (45 g)

2 fl oz (4 tbs) dry white wine (60 ml)

8 fl oz (1 c) fish stock (240 ml) (see glossary)

1 vanilla bean—halved lengthwise

8 fl oz (1 c) double (heavy) cream (240 ml)

salt and pepper to taste

Place shallots and wine in saucepan. Cook vigorously, reducing until almost dry.

○

Add stock and vanilla bean and reduce by half or until thick enough to coat back of a spoon.

○

Add cream and simmer gently until thickened.

○

Season with salt and pepper.

○

Strain in a sieve. Keep warm.

GRILLED BABY OCTOPUS
WITH OLIVE DRESSING

○

HYATT ON COLLINS, MELBOURNE, AUSTRALIA
SERVES 4

OCTOPUS

1 ¼ lb baby octopus (560 g)

8 fl oz (1 c) olive oil (240 ml)

juice of 4 lemons

3 ½ oz (¾ c) red and green bell pepper strips (100 g)

1 tbs clarified butter (15 ml) (see glossary)

Marinate octopus overnight in olive oil and lemon juice.

○

Drain and grill until tender, about 20 minutes.

○

Sauté red and green peppers briefly in butter.

OLIVE DRESSING

¾ fl oz (1 ½ tbs) Dijon mustard (20 ml)

3 fl oz (6 tbs) rice wine vinegar (100 ml)

2 ½ oz (⅓ c) black olive purée (70 g)

2 oz (½ c) shallots—minced (55 g)

juice of 1 lemon

¼ tsp black peppercorns—cracked

3 fl oz (6 tbs) salad oil (100 ml)

8 fl oz (1 c) olive oil (240 ml)

Whisk all ingredients together, then pass through fine sieve.

TO GARNISH AND SERVE

1 tsp capers (2.5 g)

Place sautéed peppers on individual plates.

○

Arrange grilled octopus in centre of each plate.

○

Drizzle dressing and sprinkle with capers.

STEAMED SEAFOOD IN PAPER BARK
WITH LEMON-BUTTER BELL PEPPER SAUCE

HYATT REGENCY COOLUM, QUEENSLAND, AUSTRALIA

SERVES 4

SEAFOOD

- 4 12-inch (30 cm) squares paper bark or parchment paper
- 1 ½ lb (4 pieces) snapper fillets (680 g)
- 12 Tasmanian or sea scallops
- 4 oz (1 large) leek—cut at a 45 degree angle ⅓-inch (1 cm) thick (115 g)
- 12 mussels—cleaned and debearded
- 2 ears of corn—cut into 1-inch (2.5 cm) lengths
- 8 brussels sprouts—halved
- 1 tsp cracked black peppercorns (3–4 g)
- 1 tsp sea salt

Preheat oven to 400° F (200° C).

Combine all (except paper bark and fish fillets) and divide equally into 4 parts.

Place fillets onto centre of each piece of bark and spoon mixture on top.

Fold all corners of each paper bark toward the centre and tie with a string to form a parcel.

In a deep ovenproof dish filled ½-inch (1.25 cm) deep with water, arrange the 4 parcels and steam in oven for 20 minutes.

Place each parcel on a plate. Remove and discard string.

Open parcel and pour in a small amount of sauce (recipe follows).

LEMON-BUTTER BELL PEPPER SAUCE

- 2 fl oz (4 tbs) lemon juice (60 ml)
- 3 ½ oz (7 tbs) softened butter (100 g)
- 3 oz (1 small) red bell pepper—finely sliced (85 g)
- 2 sprigs lemon balm (leaves)—finely chopped

In a small saucepan heat lemon juice and reduce by half.

Remove from heat and add butter.

Return to heat and add pepper and lemon balm. Stir.

MIN SHA NIAN TOFU
STEAMED TOFU STUFFED WITH PRAWNS

HYATT TIANJIN, PEOPLE'S REPUBLIC OF CHINA
SERVES 4

9 ¾ oz small prawns—peeled and minced (275 g)

1 egg white—whisk and discard half

salt and pepper to taste

1 lb tofu (450 g)

1 fl oz (2 tbs) dark soy sauce (30 ml)

1 green onion—cut into 2-inch (5 cm) strips

1 tbs fresh ginger—grated (7 g)

1 tbs fresh red chilli—finely chopped with pips discarded (15 g)

3 ½ tbs peanut oil (50 ml)

Blend minced prawns with egg white, salt and pepper. Set aside.

Cut tofu cake into 8 rectangles by halving the block lengthwise, then making 4 cuts crosswise.

With a melon baller, scoop a well in the centre of each rectangle, going only halfway through.

Place a small amount of prawn filling in each well.

Set on a plate which fits into a steamer rack.

Cover and steam for 5 minutes.

Spoon the soy sauce into a heated serving dish.

Carefully transfer tofu squares to dish.

Sprinkle with green onion, ginger and chilli.

Heat peanut oil in a small pan and pour evenly over the tofu.

Serve hot.

WOK-SEARED SCALLOPS AND PEARS

GRAND HYATT HONG KONG, HONG KONG
SERVES 4

12 oz (2 medium) pears—cored and
sliced crosswise into 8 round pieces
(340 g)

4 oz shrimp or prawns—shelled and
minced (115 g)

8 oz scallops (225 g)

2 oz boiled ham—sliced into 8 small
diamond shapes (60 g)

8 leaves coriander

1 oz (3 ½ tbs) cornflour (cornstarch)
(30 g)

vegetable oil—for deep-frying

Spread the minced shrimp evenly on
one side of each of the pear rounds.
Top each with a scallop.

Press the ham and coriander sprigs on
each of the scallops.

Dust each with cornflour and gently
fry in ½-inch (1.25 cm) hot oil until
golden brown, about 3 minutes.

Place pear slices on individual dishes
and serve warm.

Sautéed Shrimp Szechuan Style

Hyatt Regency Xian, People's Republic of China

Serves 2

⅓ oz (2 tsp) cornflour (cornstarch) (10 g)—dissolved in 2 tsp (10 ml) water

10 oz shrimp or prawns—shelled (280 g)

1 ½ fl oz (3 tsp) vegetable oil (15 ml)

½ tsp garlic—minced (2 g)

½ tsp ginger—minced (2 g)

½ oz (2 tbs) red bell pepper—cored and diced (15 g)

¾ tsp chilli oil (4 ml)

salt and pepper to taste

Mix salt and pepper with cornflour and use to marinate shrimp for 30 minutes.

Sauté shrimp slightly until opaque, then set aside.

Heat wok with oil and stir-fry the garlic and ginger.

Add red pepper, chilli oil and shrimp.

Stir-fry until shrimp are done, about 5 minutes.

Shrimp Kelaguin

Marinated Shrimp in Lemon Juice

Hyatt Regency Saipan, Mariana Islands

Serves 4

1 lb (16 jumbo) shrimp—peeled and deveined (450 g)

2 ½ oz (½ c) coconut—shredded (70 g)

1 fresh red chilli—chopped

½ oz (2 tbs) onion—minced (14 g)

juice of 2 lemons

salt and pepper to taste

2 lb (2 small) cantaloupe (900 g)

Blanch shrimp for approximately 2 minutes. Chop and set aside.

Combine remaining ingredients except cantaloupe. Season with salt and pepper.

Cut cantaloupes in half, scoop out pips and fill with shrimp mixture. Serve.

KOKODA
WHITE FISH MARINATED IN COCONUT

HYATT REGENCY DUBAI, UNITED ARAB EMIRATES

SERVES 4

2 coconuts

3 ¼ lb white fish fillet (1 ½ kg)

4 oz (1 medium) onion—chopped (115 g)

1 fresh green chilli—pips removed and flesh finely chopped

4 lemons—squeezed for juice

5 oz (1 large) tomato—skinned, pips removed and finely chopped (150 g)

4 sprigs chives or green onions (green part only)

Pierce coconuts in "eyes" to drain off water and then crack coconuts in half. Pry out flesh, save shells with some flesh and use remaining coconut flesh to extract 8 fl oz (1 c; 240 ml) milk (see glossary).

Slice fish fillets into cubes, then mix with onion and marinate in lemon juice for at least 2 hours.

Drain fish and add coconut milk just before serving.

To serve, arrange each coconut shell on a dish. Fill with marinated fish mixture.

Sprinkle with chopped chilli and tomato.

Garnish with chives or green onion.

BLACK PEPPER PRAWN WITH KAILAN

⌒

HYATT REGENCY SINGAPORE, SINGAPORE
SERVES 4

PRAWNS

24 king or jumbo prawns

1 tsp black peppercorns—crushed (5 g)

2 fl oz (4 tbs) vegetable oil (60 ml)

4 oz (1 medium) onion—sliced (115 g)

1 ½ oz (3 cloves) garlic—chopped (45 g)

1 fresh red chilli—pips removed and diced

4 oz (1 medium) green bell pepper—pips removed and cubed (115 g)

5 fl oz (⅔ c) chicken stock (150 ml) (see glossary)

1 tsp light soy sauce (5 ml)

¼ oz (1 tbs) cornflour (cornstarch) (7g)—dissolved in 1 tbs (15 ml) water

Season prawns with peppercorns.

⌒

Heat wok with oil. Stir-fry prawns for 3 minutes, then set aside.

⌒

In the same wok, sauté onion, garlic, chilli and green pepper for 1 minute.

⌒

Lower heat and add stock and soy sauce.

⌒

Bring to a boil, then stir in cornflour mixture. Stir until thickened.

⌒

Add prawns and stir for 10 seconds.

⌒

Transfer to a large platter and serve with Chinese broccoli (recipe follows) or Western broccoli.

KAILAN

10 oz young kailan (gaailaan), or Chinese broccoli—peeled and trimmed (285 g)

salt and pepper to taste

½ fl oz (1 tbs) oyster sauce (15 ml)

Add kailan to a pot with salted, boiling water.

⌒

Cook 30 seconds, then drain.

⌒

Season kailan with salt, pepper and oyster sauce.

Pescado Tixin-Xic
Fish in Annato Sauce

⌣

Hyatt Regency Cancun, Mexico
Serves 4

1 ¾ lb trout, baby grouper or baby red snapper (800 g)

5 ¼ oz (1 c) annatto paste (150 g)

6 fl oz (¾ c) orange juice (180 ml)

½ fl oz (1 tbs) lime juice (15 ml)

1 oz (1 clove) garlic—chopped (30 g)

¼ oz (½ small) red chilli—dried (5–7 g)

¾ oz (1 ½ tbs) cumin—ground (20 g)

1 tsp salt

5 bay leaves—crushed

⅓ oz (2 tsp) whole cloves (10g)

3 ½ oz (1 small) white onion—chopped (100 g)

1 tsp black pepper (5 g)

1 ½ fl oz (3 tbs) cider vinegar (45 ml)

1 fl oz (2 tbs) vegetable oil (30 ml)

6 banana leaves or squares of aluminum foil

4 ½ oz (1 large) red onion—sliced into rings and sprinkled with salt (130 g)

Dissolve the annatto paste by mixing it with the orange and lime juices.

⌣

Place the garlic, chilli, cumin, salt, bay leaves and cloves into a liquidiser; blend until smooth, then transfer to a bowl.

⌣

Add the onion, black pepper and annatto paste along with the vinegar. If desired, thin mixture with a little vegetable oil.

⌣

Coat fish with annatto mixture and marinate for at least 3 hours, basting frequently.

⌣

Place fish with some marinade on each banana leaf or foil square and wrap well.

⌣

Preheat oven to 400° F (200° C).

⌣

Place on an ovenproof clay plate or tray and bake for 15–20 minutes.

⌣

Serve immediately with rice and salted red onion rings.

Note: Annatto paste is made from achiote, the seed of the annatto tree. It is sometimes sold already prepared, or you can make your own at home.

Pan-Fried Red Snapper
In Chilli Bean Sauce

Hyatt Regency Xian, People's Republic of China
Serves 4

1 ½ lb red snapper (590 g)

salt

vegetable oil—for deep-frying

1 tsp fresh ginger—minced (5 g)

1 tsp garlic—minced (5 g)

1 tsp celery—minced (5 g)

pinch diced red bell pepper

½ fl oz (3 tsp) chilli bean sauce or chilli sauce (15 ml)

⅓ fl oz (2 tsp) vegetable oil (10 ml)

⅓ fl oz (2 tsp) tomato ketchup (10 ml)

1 tsp sugar (5 g)

⅓ fl oz (2 tsp) vinegar (10 ml)

2 ½ fl oz (5 tbs) chicken stock (80 ml) (see glossary)

⅓ oz (2 tsp) salt (10 g)

¾ oz (4 tsp) cornflour (cornstarch) (20 g)

⅓ fl oz (2 tsp) water (10 ml)

½ oz (1 tbs) green onion—minced (15 g)

½ tsp scallions—minced (see glossary)

Remove scales from fish. Clean and dry well.

With knife make 3 light diagonal slits on each side of fish.

Sprinkle salt over fish and set aside for a few minutes.

Deep-fry fish in vegetable oil until golden brown, about 10 minutes.

Set aside on a plate and keep warm.

In a wok, stir-fry ginger, garlic, celery and red pepper in oil.

Add chilli bean sauce, ketchup, sugar, vinegar, stock and salt.

Mix cornflour with water, then stir into wok. Stir to thicken sauce.

Top the fish with sauce and sprinkle green onion on top before serving.

IKAN SATAY

SATAY FISH

HYATT REGENCY SINGAPORE, SINGAPORE

SERVES 4

FISH

4 lb (2 medium) red snapper (900 g)

1 tsp ground cumin (5 g)

1 ½ oz (1 ½ tbs) shallots (45 g)

1 tsp coriander—ground (5 g)

1 tsp turmeric (5 g)

1 tsp sugar (5 g)

1 fl oz (2 tbs) vegetable oil (30 ml)

2 oz (1 stalk) lemongrass—finely diced (55 g)

1 oz (1 tbs) roasted peanuts (30 g)

pinch ground cinnamon (2 g)

juice of 2–3 limes

salt and pepper to taste

With a sharp knife, score each side of the fish.

Clean, wash and dry fish, then rub generously with lime juice.

Meanwhile, place remaining in large mortar and grind well with pestle or place in liquidiser and blend until fine and well mixed.

Rub mixture on both sides of each fish and marinate for 1 hour.

Place fish on hot grill and grill over medium-high heat until done, turning once.

Serve with peanut sauce (recipe follows).

PEANUT SAUCE

10 oz (1 ¼ c) roasted peanuts (300 g)

4 oz (2 stalks) lemongrass (115 g)

1 ½ oz (1 ½ tbs) fresh ginger—grated (40 g)

3 ¼ oz (1 small) onion—sliced (90 g)

½ fl oz (1 tbs) vegetable oil (15 ml)

½ oz (1 tbs) fresh red chillies—crushed (15 g)

6 fl oz (¾ c) tamarind juice (180 ml) (see glossary)

3 oz (½ c) sugar (100 g)

salt and pepper to taste

Grind peanuts until a paste. Set aside.

Pound lemongrass and ginger in a mortar until a paste forms.

Stir-fry onion in oil until limp.

Add chillies, ginger paste and peanuts. Stir in tamarind juice, sugar and salt.

Simmer until smooth and slightly thickened.

KARI IKAN

FISH CURRY

HYATT KINABALU, MALAYSIA

SERVES 4

1 ½ fl oz (3 tbs) vegetable oil (45 ml)

3 ½ oz (¾ c) onion—diced (100 g)

1 oz (2 large cloves) garlic—minced (50 g)

1 oz (2 tbs) fresh ginger—grated (25 g)

1 oz (2 tbs) medium-hot curry powder (30 g)

1 ¾ oz (1 large) fresh red chilli (50 g)

1 ¼ lb (4 medium) snapper fillets (560 g)

¾ pt (2 c) coconut milk (500 ml) (see glossary)

8 ½ oz (12 thin spears) fresh asparagus tips (250 g)

4 star anise (optional)

2 cherry tomatoes—each cut into 4 wedges

Prepare the sauce by heating oil in a large frying pan.

Fry the onion, garlic and ginger until golden brown.

Add curry powder and chilli and fry for 2–3 minutes, stirring continuously.

Add coconut milk and simmer over low heat for 10 minutes.

Meanwhile, roll up fish fillets with a few asparagus in each.

Poach fish "bundles" in curry sauce for about 10 to 15 minutes.

To serve, place fish bundles on plates glazed with curry sauce. Garnish with cherry tomatoes and star anise (if desired).

SALMON STEAK A LA RICHELIEU

ATRIUM HYATT BUDAPEST, HUNGARY

SERVES 4

SALMON STEAK

1 ½ lb salmon steaks—cut into 1-inch (2.5 cm) thick (680 g)

3 ¾ oz (7 tbs) butter (100 g)

½ lb cocktail shrimp—peeled (200 g)

½ lb mussels—beards removed (200 g)

½ lb mushrooms—chanterelles, if possible (200 g)

1 ½ fl oz (3 tbs) brandy (45 ml)

salt to taste

Sauté salmon in butter until done, about 10 minutes. Keep warm.

In another pot, steam shrimp. Set aside.

Steam mussels until open; discard any that did not open. Remove from shells and mix with shrimp.

Lightly sauté mushrooms, then add to shrimp.

Place shrimp, mussels and mushrooms in skillet. Add brandy and flame.

Season to taste.

HOLLANDAISE SAUCE

6 egg yolks

8 fl oz (1 c) double (heavy) cream (240 ml)

4 oz (½ c) butter—melted (115 ml)

1 ½ fl oz (3 tbs) brandy (45 ml)

lemon juice to taste

Place yolks and cream in a double boiler.

Whisk vigorously until thickened.

Remove from heat and whisk in melted butter very slowly.

Stir in brandy and lemon juice. Keep warm.

Tamal de Marisco con Salsa Newburg
Seafood Tamales with Newburg Sauce

Hyatt Regency Acapulco, Mexico

Serves 4

Newburg Sauce

1 ½ oz (3 tbs) butter (45 g)

½ lb lobster or prawn shells—cleaned and crushed (225 g)

2 fl oz (4 tbs) brandy (60 ml)

¾ oz (3 tbs) flour (45 g)

1 oz (2 tbs) paprika (30 g)

1 pt (¼ c) milk (500 ml)

2 sprigs fresh thyme

3 bay leaves

10 black peppercorns—crushed

Melt butter in a saucepan and sauté the crushed shells until they turn bright orange. Discard shells.

Pour in brandy and flame immediately.

Add flour, stir, then add paprika, stirring continuously for 2 minutes.

Pour in milk and whisk until smooth.

Add thyme, bay leaves and crushed peppercorns.

Simmer over very low heat for 20–30 minutes.

Strain the sauce and divide into 2 portions.

Tamales

3 oz baby octopus—cleaned (85 g)

2 oz (½ medium) onion—sliced (45 g)

½ oz (1 cloves) garlic—crushed (15 g)

3 oz shrimp or prawns—shelled (85 g)

3 oz scallops (85 g)

3 oz squid (85 g)

8 clams

juice of 4 lemons

salt and pepper to taste

1 tsp Worcestershire sauce (5 ml)

4 ½ oz (¾ c) masa harina or cornmeal (125 g)

3 oz (6 tbs) shortening or lard (85 g)

4 corn husks or banana leaves—cut into 12-inch (30 cm) squares— softened in hot water and dried

Put the octopus in a saucepan filled with water. Add onion slices and garlic.

Bring to a boil, then simmer for 30 minutes or until tender. Drain.

Put octopus and remaining seafood in a bowl and marinate with lemon juice, salt and pepper and Worcestershire sauce for 20 minutes.

Mix the cornmeal, shortening and one portion of newburg sauce until smooth.

Divide dough equally into 4 portions.

Spread the cornmeal dough on the husks or banana leaves, and wrap to shape into 4x5-inch (12.5 cm) squares, ½-inch (1.25 cm) thick.

Spread the seafood mixture on dough. Fold the husk or leaf over dough to cover entirely.

Place tamales on a steamer rack and steam, covered, for 50 minutes. Spread a portion of the sauce on 4 plates.

Unwrap the tamales and discard wrappers.

Place tamales on sauce and serve.

Note: Masa harina is ground, dried husked corn, used in Mexico for making tamales and tortillas. Substitute white cornmeal if unavailable.

Lobster Stir-Fry with Steamed Vegetables

Hyatt Regency Hong Kong, Hong Kong

SERVES 4

2 lb lobster—boiled and shelled and deveined (1 kg)

1 lb broccoli—cut into flowerettes (455 g)

½ tsp salt (2 g)

½ fl oz (1 tbs) vegetable oil (15 ml)

8 slices fresh ginger (85 g)

½ tsp garlic—crushed (2 g)

½ tsp cornflour (cornstarch) (2 g)

2 ½ fl oz (5 tbs) fish or chicken stock (80 ml) (see glossary)

8 baby carrots—with 2 inches (5 cm) of stem—peeled and blanched

Chop lobster meat into cubes.

○

Blanch broccoli in salted water. Drain, set aside and keep warm.

○

Heat wok with oil until very hot.

○

Add lobster meat and stir-fry until meat turns red. Remove and set aside.

○

Lower heat and add ginger and garlic. Stir-fry for 2 minutes.

○

Mix cornflour with stock and add to the wok to thicken mixture.

○

Add lobster meat to wok, stir, and simmer 2 minutes over low heat. Add a small amount of water if sauce reduces too much.

○

Season with salt and pepper, then transfer to individual plates.

○

Garnish with blanched broccoli and baby carrots.

Ikan Bakar Tuna Dengan Tiga Maoam Kacang
Grilled Tuna and Beans

Hyatt Aryaduta Jakarta, Indonesia
Serves 4

1 ¾ lb tuna fillet (800 g)

salt and pepper to taste

juice of 4 lemons

olive oil—for coating fish

4 oz (½ c) dried white beans (115 g)

4 oz (½ c) dried red beans (115 g)

4 oz (½ c) split peas (115 g)

4 oz (½ c) lentils (115 g)

2 fl oz (4 tbs) olive oil (60 ml)

2 oz (½ c) shallots—chopped (30 g)

1 oz (2 cloves) garlic—chopped (30 g)

5 ½ oz (1 large) tomato—peeled, pips removed and diced (160 g)

1 oz (¼ c) chives—chopped (30 g)

7 oz (¾ c) leek—julienned (200 g)

½ oz (1 tbs) lemon thyme—crushed (15 g)

2–3 leaves curly endive (chicory)

Soak beans, peas and lentils overnight in water; then boil them separately until tender. Drain.

Cut tuna fillet into 4 even slices.

Season with salt and pepper and juice of 2 lemons.

Rub with small amount of olive oil and grill over hot charcoal until done, about 15 minutes.

Heat olive oil in pan and sauté shallots and garlic until golden brown.

Add beans, peas and lentils and cook 3 minutes.

Add tomatoes, chives, leek, juice of 2 lemons and thyme.

Mix thoroughly and heat for 10–15 minutes.

To serve, spoon bean mixture onto 4 plates and arrange the tuna slices on top.

TANDOORI POMFRET

HYATT REGENCY DELHI, INDIA

SERVES 4

FISH AND MARINADE

1 lb (4 medium) pomfret or butterfish (450 g)

2 fl oz (4 tbs) lemon juice (60 ml)

1 oz (¼ c) ginger garlic paste (30 g)

⅓ oz (2 tsp) garam masala (10 g)

⅓ oz (2 tsp) chilli paste (10 g)

⅓ oz (2 tsp) fresh ginger—chopped (10 g)

¾ oz (2 tbs) fresh chilli—chopped (20 g)

1 oz (½ c) fresh coriander—chopped (30 g)

¼ oz (1 tsp) ajwain or anise seed (7 g)

7 oz (¾ c) plain yoghurt (200 g)

Note: Ginger garlic paste is made easily by pounding in a mortar a combination of 1 part fresh ginger, 1 part garlic and a dash of water to make a smooth paste. Garam masala and ajwain are available in Indian groceries.

Make 3 diagonal slices (slits) on each side of pomfret.

Mix remaining to make a marinade.

Rub this on fish and marinate for 2–3 hours in the refrigerator.

Cook fish in a clay oven (tandoori) for 5 minutes or until pomfret are done. If desired bake in covered ovenproof dish in 400° F (200° C) oven for 10 minutes.

Serve with a green salad and lemon wedges.

Cola de Langosta Escalfada en Manzanilla, Salsa de Chile Y Frijoles Negros

Lobster Tails Poached in Camomile Tea

Hyatt Regency Acapulco, Mexico

Serves 4

Lobster

3 ½ oz (1 small) onion—cubed (100 g)

7 oz (3 large) carrots—cubed (200 g)

1 oz (¼ c) fresh coriander (30 g)

2 oz (½ c) camomile tea (55 g)

4 lobster tails

Put onion, carrots, coriander and tea in deep pot with enough water to cover vegetables.

○

Bring water to a boil and place lobster in pot.

○

Boil for 10 minutes, then set lobster tails aside.

○

Save ¾ pt (1 ½ c ; 355 ml) of the broth for sauce. Save remainder to reheat the lobster.

Black Beans

3 ½ oz (⅓ c) black beans—soaked overnight (100 g)

salt to taste

2 sprigs fresh coriander

Boil beans in salted water with coriander until tender.

○

Drain and set aside.

Vegetables

¾ pt (2 c) vegetable oil (500 ml)

3 ½ oz (1 small) green bell pepper (100 g)

3 ½ oz (1 small) red bell pepper (100 g)

3 ½ oz (1 small) yellow bell pepper (100 g)

2 oz (4 tbs) butter (55 g)

7 oz (2 small) onion—sliced (200 g)

2 oz (½ stalk) leek—julienned (55 g)

10 ½ oz (2 large) tomatoes—peeled and sliced (300 g)

¾ oz (3 tbs) fresh coriander—chopped (20 g)

salt and pepper to taste

Heat oil in a deep pan and fry peppers until skins blister.

○

Remove from heat and peel peppers. Halve them and remove veins and pips.

○

Cut pepper into strips.

○

Heat butter in sauté pan and sauté onions, leek, tomatoes and coriander.

○

Season with salt and pepper, then add the pepper strips.

○

Stir well and remove from fire.

Chilli Sauce

2 oz (4 tbs) butter (55 g)

1 oz (¼ c) flour (30 g)

9 fl oz (1 c) double (heavy) cream (237 ml)

2 Serrano or other hot chillies—chopped

2 oz (½ medium) green bell pepper—pips removed and chopped (55 g)

½ tsp thyme (2 g)

½ oz (1 tbs) fresh coriander—chopped (15 g)

Melt butter in saucepan and whisk in flour. Cook 1 minute.

○

Simmer on low heat until thickened.

○

Add pepper, chilli, thyme and coriander. Remove from heat after 2 minutes.

○

Reheat lobster tails briefly in leftover broth or hot water.

○

Remove shells and slice each tail into 5 medallions.

○

Place vegetables in centre of plate. Arrange lobster medallions on side and pour sauce on lobster.

○

Garnish with black beans.

FILETE DE HUACHINANGO EN MIXIOTE
FILLET OF RED SNAPPER BOILED IN A MIXIOTE LEAF

HYATT REGENCY GUADALAJARA, MEXICO
SERVES 4

FISH

1 ½ lb red snapper fillets (680 g)

salt and pepper to taste

juice of 1 lemon

¾ pt (½ c) mixiote sauce (354 ml) (recipe follows)

6 fl oz (¾ c) fish stock (180 ml) (see glossary)

1 fl oz (2 tbs) dry white wine (30 ml)

4 mixiote (agave) leaves or parchment paper squares

5 ¾ oz (1 c) mushrooms—sliced and sautéed for garnish (165 g)

6 oz (1 ½ c) broccoli flowerettes, sautéed for garnish (165 g)

6 oz (2 ½ c) cooked white rice (165 g)

1 tsp parsley—chopped for garnish (5 g)

Season fish fillets with salt and pepper, then rub with lemon juice.

In a large pan gently heat mixiote sauce, stock and wine.

Lower heat and poach fish for 3 minutes.

Remove fillets from liquid and place on mixiote leaves.

Reduce liquid by ½ over high heat.

Pour a small amount of sauce over fish fillets and wrap each in mixiote leaf. Tie with string.

Put the 4 packages under broiler for approximately 5 minutes. Then arrange each package on a hot plate.

Garnish with mushrooms, broccoli and rice.

Sprinkle parsley on rice for color.

MIXIOTE SAUCE

5 ¼ oz (1 c) achiote (150 g)

8 fl oz (1 c) orange juice (240 ml)

2 fl oz (4 tbs) distilled white vinegar (60 ml)

¾ pt (2 c) fish stock (500 ml) (see glossary)

1 ¾ fl oz (3 ½ tbs) vegetable oil (50 ml)

⅓ oz (1 small clove) garlic—chopped (10 g)

1 ¾ oz (½ small) onion—chopped (50 g)

⅛ oz (1 tsp) fresh marjoram—chopped (3 g)

3 fresh coriander leaves—chopped

salt and pepper to taste

In a bowl, blend achiote orange juice, vinegar and fish stock.

Heat oil in pan and sauté garlic and onion until golden brown.

Add achiote mixture and stir.

Cook gently for 5 minutes.

Pass through a sieve.

Add herbs, salt and papper to taste.

Note: Achiote is the seed of the annatto tree. It is sometimes sold in a paste form, but most often only the hard seeds are available, usually in Mexican groceries.

Marinated Scallops with Smoked Salmon

Hyatt Regency Seoul, Korea

Serves 4

8 fl oz (1 c) dry white wine (240 ml)

1 oz (¼ c) onion—chopped (30 g)

pinch each thyme, crushed bay leaf, ground coriander, mustard seeds and peppercorns

1 fl oz (2 tbs) vinegar (30 ml)

½ lb scallops (250 g)

5 ¼ oz smoked salmon (150 g)

⅓ fl oz (2 tsp) lemon juice (10 ml)

⅓ fl oz (2 tsp) olive oil (10 ml)

Pour white wine into a saucepan and bring to a boil.

Add onion, herbs, spices and vinegar. Mix well.

Add scallops and remove from heat.

Let scallops cool in stock at room temperature.

Drain and slice scallops. Slice salmon.

Make vinaigrette by mixing lemon juice and olive oil.

To serve, arrange scallops and salmon in a circular pattern on a large platter.

Arrange salad leaves around seafood. Top with lemon vinaigrette.

Victorian Lobster and John Dory

Hyatt On Collins, Melbourne, Australia
Serves 4

1 lb mixed raw vegetables—sliced
(455 g)

4 oz wood ears or other wild mushrooms—soaked overnight and
drained (115 g)

8 fl oz (1 c) fish stock (240 ml)
(see glossary)

5 oz (10 tbs) butter—cut into cubes
and chilled (150 g)

12 oz (2 large) lobster tails (340 g)

8 oz (2 large) John Dory or St. Peter's
fish fillets—sliced in half lengthwise
(225 g)

salt and pepper to taste

4 very large spinach leaves or
parchment paper

1 fl oz (2 tbs) Oriental sesame oil
(30 ml)

fresh herbs—for garnish

In a large pan, sauté mixed vegetables
until tender, then add wood ears.

Deglaze pan with fish stock and
simmer until thickened.

Remove from heat and swirl in
chilled butter cubes. Keep warm.

Semi-cook the lobster tails by boiling
or steaming 4–5 minutes.

Remove shells and cut tails into
medallions (4 crosswise slices per
tail).

Season the fillets with salt and
pepper, then gently wrap in spinach
leaves.

Very lightly brush the lobster medallions and wrapped fish with sesame
oil.

Set on a steamer and steam 5–7
minutes.

Arrange vegetables on a plate with
lobster medallions and fish on top.
Pour on sauce.

Garnish with herbs.

POACHED FILLET OF SOLE
WITH BLACK BEANS IN WHITE WINE SAUCE

HYATT REGENCY MANILA, PHILIPPINES

SERVES 4

POACHED SOLE

20 oz sole fillet (600 g)

2 fl oz (4 tbs) dry white wine (60 ml)

salt and pepper to taste

1 tsp butter (5 g)

3 oz (6 tbs) water (90 ml)

Preheat oven to 300° F (150° C).

Arrange fillets in buttered baking dish. Sprinkle with white wine, salt and pepper.

Poach in oven for 10 minutes. Keep warm.

WHITE WINE SAUCE

2 fl oz (4 tbs) fish stock (60 ml) (see glossary)

2 fl oz (4 tbs) dry white wine (60 ml)

1 fl oz (2 tbs) double (heavy) cream (30 ml)

1 tsp butter (5 g)

Bring stock and wine to a boil in saucepan.

Add cream and cook until sauce thickens.

Take off the heat. Stir in butter and blend well.

SERVING INSTRUCTIONS

4 large spinach leaves—cleaned

1 lb (4 small) potatoes—peeled (450 g)

3 oz (3 tbs) cooked black beans (100 g)

4 oz cooked pearl onions (115 g)

½ oz (1 tbs) butter (15 g)

With a melon baller, scoop balls from potatoes and cook in boiling water for 5 minutes, or until tender.

Sauté onions in butter until glazed.

Place spinach on individual plates. Put fish fillets on spinach leaves, then drizzle on sauce.

Garnish with beans, onions and potatoes.

Tuna with Corn Salsa

Hyatt Regency Manila, Philippines
Serves 4

Fish

1 ¼ lb (4 slices) tuna fillets (560 g)

salt and pepper to taste

1 tsp dill—chopped (2 g)

⅓ oz (1 tbs) mustard seeds—lightly crushed (8 g)

⅓ oz (1 tbs) sesame seeds (10 g)

2 fl oz (4 tbs) vegetable oil (60 ml)

Season tuna with salt, pepper and dill.

○

Coat with mustard and sesame seeds.

○

Heat oil in pan and sauté tuna on both sides until medium-rare. Remove from pan and keep warm.

Corn Salsa

1 ½ oz (⅓ c) corn kernels (45 g)

2 oz (½ c) onion—diced (55 g)

2 oz (½ c) green bell pepper—cored and diced (55 g)

1 ½ oz (⅓ c) red bell pepper—cored and diced (45 g)

½ fl oz (1 tbs) vegetable oil (15 ml)

2 fl oz (4 tbs) dry white wine (60 ml)

6 fl oz (¾ c) fish stock (180 ml) (see glossary)

¼ oz (1 tbs) cornflour (cornstarch) (7 g)

Sauté corn, onion and bell peppers in oil until tender.

○

Add wine and simmer until reduced by half.

○

Dissolve cornflour in 3 tbs (45 ml) of fish stock.

○

Add remainder of stock to pan and simmer 2 minutes.

○

Thicken salsa with cornflour mixture and simmer until slightly thickened. Keep warm.

Garnish and How to Serve

16 asparagus spears—peeled and blanched

1 lb potatoes—cut into balls with melon scoop and cooked in salted water until tender

Spoon the salsa onto a serving plate.

○

Place tuna slices over the sauce and surround with the asparagus and potatoes as shown in photo.

POMFRET "SANDWICH"
COATED WITH BLACK AND WHITE SESAME SEEDS

HYATT REGENCY SINGAPORE, SINGAPORE
SERVES 4

FISH

3 lb (4 baby) pomfret or butterfish—filleted (1 ⅓ kg)

salt and pepper to taste

juice of 2 lemons

⅓ oz (1 tsp) fresh coriander—chopped (10 g)

flour—for dusting

2 eggs—beaten

1 oz (1 tbs) white sesame seeds (30 g)

1 oz (1 tbs) black sesame seeds (30 g)

1 ½ fl oz (3 tbs) peanut or vegetable oil (45 ml)

Season fish fillets with salt, pepper, lemon juice and coriander.

○

Dust fillets lightly with flour, dip in egg, and coat evenly with the black and white sesame seeds.

○

Heat oil in non-stick pan and fry fillets 3 minutes each side until done and crisp. Keep warm.

SAUCE

¾ fl oz (1 ½ tbs) peanut or vegetable oil (20 ml)

1 oz (¼ c) shallots—minced (30 g)

⅓ oz (2 tsp) garlic—minced (10 g)

¼ oz (1 ½ tsp) fresh ginger—grated (5-7 g)

1 ½ fl oz (3 tbs) dry white wine (45 ml)

⅓ oz (2 tsp) turmeric (10 g)

8 fl oz (1 c) chicken stock (240 ml) (see glossary)

1 stalk lemongrass—minced

4 fl oz (½ c) double (heavy) cream (150 ml)

salt, pepper and lemon juice to taste

1 oz (2 tbs) butter—room temperature (30 g)

Heat oil in pan and sauté shallots, garlic and ginger for 2 minutes.

○

Add turmeric and cook another minute.

○

Deglaze with wine, then add stock and lemongrass.

○

Simmer 5 minutes, then add cream and reduce sauce by half.

○

Season with salt and pepper and lemon juice.

○

Pour sauce into liquidiser and blend 2 minutes.

○

Add butter and blend another 30 seconds.

○

Strain sauce through fine sieve. Keep warm.

TO GARNISH AND SERVE

8 oz asparagus spears (240 g)

½ oz (1 tbs) butter (15 g)

2 oz (4 tsp) salmon caviar (60 g)

salt

Blanch the asparagus in salted boiling water until tender but firm, about 5 minutes.

○

Drain in ice water to retain color.

○

Transfer to skillet and lightly sauté in butter to glaze.

○

Arrange dish with fish, asparagus, sauce and caviar as shown in photo.

Alimango Tausi

Stuffed Crab with a Sauce of Black Beans, Ginger and Egg

◯

Hyatt Regency Manila, Philippines

Serves 4

Stuffed Crab

1 ¾ lb (8 medium) crabs (800 g)

1 ½ fl oz (3 tbs) vegetable oil (45 ml)

2 oz (½ medium) onion—chopped (55 g)

2 ½ oz (5 cloves) garlic—chopped (70 g)

½ oz (1 tbs) fresh ginger—chopped (10 g)

2 oz (1 medium) carrot—diced (55 g)

1 ½ oz (½ small) red bell pepper—cored and diced (45 g)

1 ½ oz (½ small) green bell pepper—cored and diced (45 g)

3 oz (¾ c) fermented black beans—rinsed, drained and chopped (85 g)

7 oz (¾ c) shrimp—diced (200 g)

2 egg yolks

1 ½ tbs rice wine or medium-dry sherry (20 ml)

salt and white pepper to taste

vegetable oil—for deep-frying

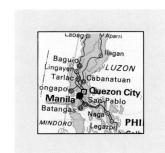

Steam crabs until they turn red, about 5 minutes.

◯

Carefully pick meat and break claws. Discard cartilage but save carapace (shell for body).

◯

Heat oil in pan and sauté onion, garlic and ginger.

◯

Add remaining vegetables and beans and sauté until tender.

◯

Set aside to cool, then mix in crabmeat, shrimp, egg yolks and the wine. Season with salt and pepper.

◯

Rinse crab carapace and dry well. Stuff mixture into hollowed out shells.

◯

Heat oil (375° F; 190° C) and deep-fry the stuffed crabs for approximately 8 minutes.

◯

Place 2 stuffed crabs on each plate. Serve with sauce (recipe follows)

Sauce

1 ½ fl oz (3 tbs) vegetable oil (45 ml)

2 oz (4 cloves) garlic—chopped (55 g)

½ oz (1 tbs) fresh ginger—chopped (15 g)

3 ½ oz (1 c) fermented black beans—washed, drained and chopped (100 g)

3 oz (1 small) tomato—peeled, diced and pips removed (100 g)

14 fl oz (1¾ c) chicken stock (400 ml) (see glossary)

2 fl oz (4 tbs) oyster sauce (60 ml)

¼ oz (1 tbs) cornflour (cornstarch) (7 g)

¾ fl oz (1 ½ tbs) rice wine (20 ml)

2 eggs—beaten

½ oz (1 tbs) chives—chopped (20 g)

Heat oil in wok and sauté the garlic, ginger, beans and tomato for 2 minutes without browning.

◯

Add stock and oyster sauce, then bring to a boil.

◯

Dissolve cornflour in rice wine and add to sauce to thicken.

◯

Whisk in the beaten eggs and chives. Do not overcook eggs.

Hivana
Marinated Raw Fish

○

Hyatt Kinabalu, Malaysia
Serves 4

14 oz Tengiri fillet or other mackerel fillet (400 g)

2 ½ oz (½ c) young ginger—grated (70 g)

5 ⅓ oz (1 large) onion—peeled and sliced (150 g)

salt to taste

juice of 4 large limes

1 oz (1 small) fresh red chilli—crushed and chopped (30 g)

½ bambagan stone—grated

Cut fish into thin slices. Place in a bowl with above.

○

Mix well and marinate for 30 minutes.

○

Chill before serving.

Note: Bambagan stone is sometimes available in Asian stores. Omit if unavailable.

IKAN REBUS DENGAN SAYUR GORENG

FISH WITH GRILLED VEGETABLES

⟨◦⟩

HYATT KINABALU, MALAYSIA

SERVES 4

1 ¼ lb (4 medium) skinless red snapper fillets (560 g)

6 oz (3 medium) carrots—peeled and cubed (170 g)

8 fl oz (1 c) chicken stock (240 ml) (see glossary)

salt and pepper to taste

8 oz (2 medium) courgettes (zucchini)—sliced ¾-inch (2 cm) thick (225 g)

10 oz (4 large) red bell peppers—sliced ¾-inch (2 cm) thick (285 g)

8 oz (2 medium) aubergine (eggplant)—sliced ¾-inch (2 cm) thick (225 g)

1 lb (8 medium) leeks—sliced ¾-inch (2 cm) thick (450 g)

With a sharp knife, cut fillets into thick slices and steam until done, about 5 minutes.

Boil the carrots in stock until soft. Drain and purée in a liquidiser until smooth. Season with salt and pepper. Set aside.

Grill courgettes, peppers, aubergine and leeks on both sides until lightly browned.

To serve, neatly arrange the steamed fish and grilled vegetables on top of carrot sauce.

Scallops, Edible Flower Pasta and Fresh Figs

Hyatt Regency Coolum, Queensland, Australia

Serves 4

¼ oz (1 tsp) jasmine tea (5 g)

1 lb sea scallops (450 g)

½ lb pasta dough, preferably made with rice flour (225 g) (see glossary)

2 oz (4 tbs) assorted edible flowers (60 g)

4 oz (1 c) fresh pineapple—peeled, cored and diced (115 g)

1 ½ fl oz (3 tbs) vegetable stock (45 ml) (see glossary)

4 fl oz (½ c) dry white wine (120 ml)

½ oz (1 tbs) lime rind—grated (15 g)

½ oz (1 tbs) rice starch (5 g)—dissolved in 1 tbs (15 ml) cold water

6 ¾ tbs grape seed oil—cold pressed (100 ml)

6 oz fresh figs (170 g)

½ oz (1 tbs) fresh red chilli—minced (15 g) chive flowers—for decoration

Brew approximately ¾ pt (1 ⅔ c ; 480 ml) jasmine tea and use to steam scallops for 3–5 minutes.

Roll out half the pasta dough until very thin and cover with the flowers.

Roll out the other half and use to top the flowers, then run both layers as one through the thinnest possible setting of a pasta machine.

Cut into fettucine noodles and cook until al dente, about 2 minutes.

Poach the pineapple in stock and wine until tender, about 1 minute.

In a liquidiser, blend pineapple to a fine purée, then place purée back in saucepan and reheat, adding grated lime rind. Thicken with rice starch mixture.

Arrange the scallops and pasta on a plate as shown in photo. Add pineapple sauce.

Pour grape seed oil over all. Garnish with figs, chilli and chive flowers.

MANTIS SHRIMP
IN PASTRY PARCELS

<hr>

HYATT REGENCY HONG KONG, HONG KONG
SERVES 4

SHRIMP

20 mantis shrimp, jumbo shrimp or prawns (680 g)

6 oz (24 sheets) phyllo dough (175 g)

3–4 oz (¾–1 c) butter—melted (85–115 g)

8 oz (1 medium) tomatoes—sliced crosswise (225 g)

2 oz thin green beans (haricot verts) (60 g)

1 ½ oz (1 small) carrot (40 g)

1 ½ oz (¼ head) cauliflower (40 g)

2 oz fresh basil (60 g)

4 green onions (green part only)

Preheat oven to 300° F (150° C).

In salted water boil shrimp until tender, about 10 minutes.

Peel and use shrimp shells for sauce. (Note: keep 4 shrimp with tails intact for decoration.) Dice remaining shrimp.

Cut phyllo sheets into 8-inch (20 cm) squares.

With a pastry brush coat each sheet with melted butter on one side.

Layer 6 sheets in a stack and repeat 4 times. In centre of each square place 1 tomato slice with a basil leaf, then add 4 pieces of shrimp.

Enclose filling within the square to form a parcel (or square "envelope"). Create a small hole at the top using the handle of a wooden spoon.

Tie each parcel with a strip of green onion. Do not close completely.

Fill the parcels with a small amount of sauce (recipe above).

Bake for 10 minutes in preheated oven.

Meanwhile, boil vegetables until tender and cut into small cubes. Coat vegetables with half of the remaining melted butter and arrange on plates as shown in picture.

Offer remaining sauce separately.

SAUCE

3 tbs olive oil (45 ml)

1 ½ oz shrimp shells—crushed (40 g) (see shrimp recipe)

1 oz (2 tbs) butter (30 g)

¼ oz (1 tbs) shallots—chopped (7 g)

1 ¾ oz (⅓ c) celeriac (celery root)— diced (50 g)

1 oz (½ small) carrot—diced (30 g)

¼ oz (½ clove) garlic—chopped (7 g)

2 ½ fl oz (5 tbs) cognac (75 ml)

5 fl oz (⅔ c) dry white wine (150 ml)

8 fl oz (1 c) fish stock (240 ml) (see glossary)

1 tsp beef bouillon concentrate (5 g)

1 tsp dried tarragon

5 ¼ oz (1 large) tomato—peeled, diced (150 g)

5 tbs double (heavy) cream (75 ml)

1 tsp parsley—chopped

salt and pepper to taste

2 tsp cayenne (10 g)

Heat oil in large pan and stir-fry shrimp shells until they turn bright red.

Discard oil and add half the butter.

Fry shallots, celeriac, carrot and garlic until shallots are transparent.

Add cognac, ignite, and allow flame to die down.

Add wine, fish stock, powdered bouillon, tarragon and tomatoes.

Bring to a boil, then cover and simmer gently for 8–10 minutes.

Strain sauce into another saucepan. Reduce sauce over medium heat until it begins to thicken.

Whisk in remaining butter, cream and parsley.

Season with salt, pepper and cayenne. Keep warm.

Ikan Kukus Dengan Daun Pisang
Steamed Red Snapper in Banana Leaves

Hyatt Kuantan, Malaysia

Serves 4

1 ¼ lb red snapper fillets—cut into 4 pcs (500 g)

juice of 2 lemons

salt and pepper to taste

1 ½ oz (3 cloves) garlic—minced (45 g)

7 oz (1 ¾ c) coconut—grated (200 g)

1 tsp turmeric (10 g)

¾ oz (2 tsp) black pepper— ground (20 g)

8 oz (2 medium) tomatoes—cut into wedges, for garnish (225 g)

1 lemon or lime—cut into wedges

1 banana leaf—washed, dried and cut into 4 squares (12-inch) (30 cm)

Season the fillets with lemon juice, salt and pepper.

Mix garlic, coconut, turmeric and ground pepper.

Spread this mixture evenly on the 4 banana leaf squares.

Arrange each fillet on top of mixture and wrap with banana leaf; tie closed.

Steam for 15 minutes.

Put a fish package on each plate and garnish with tomato and lemon or lime wedges.

Note: If banana leaves are unavailable, substitute squares of parchment paper or foil.

OYSTERS IN HOISIN SAUCE

GRAND HYATT TAIPEI, TAIWAN
SERVES 4

32 oysters—shucked

2 fl oz (4 tbs) Oriental sesame oil
(60 ml)

1 oz (2 tbs) green onions—minced
(30 g)

1 ½ oz (3 tbs) black beans—soaked
overnight and drained (fermented)
(45 g)

1 ½ fl oz (3 tbs) hoisin sauce (45 ml)
(see glossary)

⅓ oz (1 tsp) cornflour (cornstarch)
(10 g)—dissolved in a little cold
water

1 fresh red chilli—cut into strips

1 ¼ lb (4 medium) tomatoes—for
tomato roses (optional) (570 g)

*Note: To make tomato rose, carefully
cut a long strip of pulp from a
peeled tomato, much as you
would peel a lemon or orange.
Roll strip into a tight curl and
slightly open up edges of one
side of curl to form a "rose".*

Wash oysters with salt water and
rinse. Drain.

Steam for 15 seconds in boiling water.
Set aside.

Heat sesame oil, stir-fry the green
onions and black beans until onions
are limp.

Add soy sauce, hoissin sauce and
cornflour mixture. Stir and cook until
sauce is thickened.

Neatly arrange bean mixture on
4 plates. Place oysters on top (8 oysters
per plate).

Garnish with chilli strips and tomato
rose, if desired.

RED EMPEROR FILLET WITH PLUM SAUCE

HYATT REGENCY COOLUM, QUEENSLAND, AUSTRALIA

SERVES 4

1 ¼ lb (4 pc) red emperor or salmon trout fillets—skin on (560g)

6 oz (1 medium) orange (170 g)

8 oz (½ medium) grapefruit (225 g)

1 lime

2 fl oz (4 tbs) honey (40 g)

1 fl oz (2 tbs) lemon or white wine vinegar (30 ml)

½ oz (1 tbs) fresh red chilli—chopped and pips removed (20 g)

4 oz (1 medium) Santa Rosa or other fleshy red plum—chopped (115 g)

⅓ oz (2 tsp) rice starch or rice flour (7 g)

2 ½ oz (5 tbs) dry white wine (75 ml)

6 oz (1 medium) chayote—skin on, thinly sliced (170 g)

2 ½ oz (5 tbs) vegetable stock (7ml) (see glossary)

purple fennel—for garnish

Cook fish fillets by either poaching, broiling, grilling, or pan-frying. Keep warm.

Separate orange, grapefruit and lime into sections, reserving juice that drips off.

Heat honey, vinegar, reserved fruit juices, chilli and plum, over low heat.

Dissolve rice starch in wine, then add to pan and cook until sauce thickens. Remove from heat.

Poach the chayote slices in stock for 1 minute.

Place all the items onto 4 individual plates and garnish with fennel as illustrated.

LOBSTER STEW IN FENNEL LEAVES

HYATT CONTINENTAL MONTREUX, SWITZERLAND
SERVES 4

1 ¾ pt (4 ¼ c) water (1 *l*)

2 ½ fl oz (5 tbs) vinegar (100 ml)

salt and pepper to taste

3 lb (2 medium) lobsters (1 ⅓ kg)

2 fennel bulbs with leaves

1 ¾ oz (3 ½ tbs) butter (50 g)

1 ¾ oz (⅓ c) shallots—chopped (50 g)

2 ½ fl oz (5 tbs) dry white wine (100 ml)

2 ½ fl oz (5 tbs) fish stock (100 ml) (see glossary)

1 ½ fl oz (3 tbs) double (heavy) cream (45 ml)

⅓ oz (2 tsp) dill—chopped for garnish (10 g)

In a deep pot bring water, vinegar, salt and pepper to a rolling boil.

Drop lobster in, cover and boil for 15 minutes. Drain.

Cut lobster in half lengthwise; carefully remove meat from shell and dice meat. Set aside.

Cut fennel leaves from bulbs and set aside.

Separate bulbs into "leaves" and blanch quickly in salted boiling water. Set aside.

Melt butter in sauté pan and add shallots. Add lobster meat; sauté briefly. Add white wine; simmer for 1 minute.

Remove lobster meat and set aside.

Add the fish stock and cream to sauté pan and reduce by half.

Turn off heat, return lobster meat and check the seasonings.

Arrange blanched fennel bulbs on a dinner plate. Stuff them with the lobster stew and sprinkle with chopped dill.

Garnish with fresh fennel leaves on the side. Serve with wild rice.

Platillo Tipico de Tabasco
Traditional Tabasco's Dish

◯

Hyatt Hotel Villahermosa, Mexico
Serves 4

1 lb (1 medium) pejelegarto (450 g)

1 oz (¼ c) red onion—chopped (30 g)

4 oz (1 medium) green bell pepper—pips removed and chopped (115 g)

⅓ fl oz (2 tsp) lemon juice (10 ml)

⅓ oz (1 tbs) fresh coriander—chopped (10 g)

salt and pepper to taste

1 carrot, 4 lettuce leaves, 4 avocado slices and lemon quarters—for garnish

2 tsp olive oil (10 ml)

Note: Pejelegarto is a local freshwater fish that is smoked. Smoked mackerel may be substituted.

Grill the pejelegarto, then remove skin and all the bones.

◯

Mix onion, pepper, coriander, lemon juice, salt and pepper. Add olive oil.

◯

Present fish in an oval dish dressed with onion mixture.

◯

Decorate with carrots, lettuce, avocado and lemon.

Steamed Garfish
with White Champagne Butter and Shiitake Mushrooms

Hyatt Regency Adelaide, Australia

Serves 4

Garfish

1 lb boned gar (450 g)

½ tsp shallots—finely chopped (2 g)

⅓ fl oz (2 tsp) butter (10 ml)

1 tsp champagne (or other sparkling wine) (5 ml)

1 ¼ pt (3 c) fish stock (700 ml) (see glossary)

Preserve gar head.

Sauté shallots in butter.

Add champagne and stock and bring to a boil. Lower heat until barely simmering.

Add gar, cover with buttered parchment paper and simmer gently for 3–5 minutes.

Transfer gar to a serving platter. Keep warm.

Strain stock and reduce over high heat until 4 tbs (60 ml) are left.

Note: Gar is an elongated fish with a multi-toothed beak. Any needlefish can be substituted, or use eel.

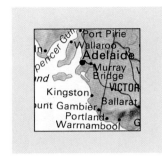

Duxelles

2 oz oyster mushrooms (55 g)

¾ oz pine mushrooms (20 g)

¾ oz field mushrooms (20 g)

¾ oz cepes (20 g)

1 tsp shallots—minced (5 g)

½ oz (1 tbs) butter (15 g)

⅓ fl oz (2 tsp) dry white wine (10 ml)

⅓ fl oz (2 tsp) double (heavy) cream (10 ml)

¼ oz (1 tbs) parsley—coarsely chopped (5 g)

salt and pepper to taste

Set aside 8 oyster mushrooms.

Slice rest of the mushrooms.

Sauté shallots in butter, then add whole oyster mushrooms until cooked, about 2 minutes.

Transfer to a plate and keep warm.

Into the same pan, sauté the remaining sliced mushrooms until light brown.

Season with salt and pepper, then deglaze pan with wine.

Add cream and reduce until thickened.

Add parsley.

Note: Depending on availability, you may have to substitute other wild mushrooms in season.

Champagne Buerre Blanche

4 fl oz (½ c) champagne (120 ml)

1 oz (2 medium) shallots—finely chopped (30 g)

⅓ fl oz (2 tsp) creme fraiche (10 ml) (see glossary)

2 oz (4 tbs) butter—chilled and cubed (55 g)

4 oz (1 large) tomato—peeled, pips removed and diced (115 g)

4 button mushrooms—diced

Put all the champagne except 3 tbs (45 ml) and shallots in a small saucepan and reduce over medium heat until almost dry. Set aside.

Add creme fraiche and remove from heat.

Slowly whisk in the butter.

Add the highly reduced champagne, stock, tomato and mushrooms.

Reheat gently and pour in remaining champagne. Keep warm.

To Assemble and Serve

Place a spoonful of duxelles on the side of the fish.

With a spoon, cover part of the gar with the champagne beurre blanche.

Garnish with whole oyster mushrooms.

MARRON WITH ORANGE NOODLES AND AVOCADO SAUCE

HYATT REGENCY ADELAIDE, AUSTRALIA

SERVES 4

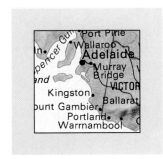

SAUCE

½ fl oz (1 tbs) vegetable oil (15 ml)

½ oz (1 tbs) onion—chopped (15 g)

½ oz (1 tbs) celery—chopped (15 g)

½ oz (1 tbs) carrot—chopped (15 g)

3 oz (1 small) tomato—peeled, pips removed, chopped (85 g)

4 marron (see recipe below)—cleaned, quartered, then crushed

4 fl oz (½ c) dry white wine (120 ml)

1 ¼ pt (3 c) fish stock (700 ml) (see glossary)

5 tbs double (heavy) cream—whipped (80 ml)

1 oz (2 tbs) butter—cubed and chilled (30 g)

¼ avocado—peeled and cubed

juice of ½ lime

Heat oil in a deep pot and sauté onion, celery and carrot until tender.

Add tomato and sauté until most of the juices have evaporated.

Add the marron bodies, pour in wine and ignite.

When flames are extinguished, add the stock.

Bring to a boil, then simmer 40 minutes, skimming frequently.

Strain liquid through a muslin cloth, then return to pot and reduce liquid by ½.

Measure 6 fl oz (¾ c; 180 ml) of the reduced liquid and set remainder aside for another use.

Place liquid in a saucepan over low heat and stir in whipped heavy cream.

Reduce again until thickened.

Remove from heat; whisk in chilled butter.

Add avocado cubes and lime juice.

Keep warm.

ORANGE NOODLES

6 fl oz (¾ c) orange juice (180 ml) zest of 1 orange—chopped and blanched

1 fl oz (2 tbs) peanut oil (30 ml)

2 eggs

¾ oz (1 ½ tbs) butter (20 g)

13 oz (2⅓ c) flour (370 g)

1 ½ tsp salt (8 g)

In a saucepan, reduce orange juice by ½.

Cool, then whisk in zest, oil, eggs and butter. Set aside.

Mix flour and salt in a bowl.

Make a well in the centre and gradually incorporate flour into the orange mixture.

Knead until smooth, about 5 minutes.

Wrap and chill for 2 hours.

Pass dough through a pasta maker to form spaghetti-type noodles.

Cook pasta in boiling salted water until al dente, about 3 minutes.

Drain and keep warm.

MARRON

4 marron or baby lobsters—cooked (12 oz or 340 g each)

3 oz (½ medium) avocado—sliced thinly in 12 segments (85 g)

Preheat oven to 350° F (180° C).

○

Separate heads from tails of marron and use bodies for sauce.

○

Shell the tails and slice into medallions.

○

Place medallions in baking dish, cover with buttered parchment and heat gently in oven for 5 minutes.

○

Warm avocado segments in the oven for a few seconds.

TO ASSEMBLE AND SERVE

Arrange noodles on individual plates.

○

Set avocadoes on the noodles, surrounded by the marron medallions.

○

Gently pour sauce over medallions and serve.

Ammeijoas Na Cataplana
Clam Hot Pot

◯

Hyatt Regency Macau, Macau
Serves 4

1 ½ oz (3 large cloves) garlic—peeled (40 g)

4 fl oz (½ c) olive oil (120 ml)

8 fl oz (1 c) dry white wine (240 ml)

1 ¼ lb (4 medium) tomatoes—cut into chunks

2 fl oz (4 tbs) tomato concentrate (paste) (60 ml)

2 mild fresh red chillies

3 ½ oz Parma ham (prosciutto)—julienned (100 g)

3 oz Portuguese or other spicy sausage—julienned (85 g)

1 ¾ lb small clams—washed well (800 g)

1 oz (2 tbs) fresh coriander—chopped (30 g)

Preheat oven to 320° F (160° C).

◯

Sauté garlic in olive oil for 3 minutes.

◯

Deglaze pan with wine and simmer 2 more minutes. Set aside.

◯

Put tomatoes, tomato concentrate and chillies in liquidiser and purée.

◯

In a deep saucepan or casserole, place all ingredients together with the clams. Cover pot and bake for 15–20 minutes, or until clams open.

◯

Serve with rice or bread.

DALGOGI GOOI
GRILLED JOHN DORY ON TOFU IN YOGHURT SAUCE

HYATT REGENCY CHEJU, KOREA

SERVES 4

¾ oz (1 ½ tbs) butter (20 g)

2 ¼ oz (½ c) onion—chopped (60 g)

⅓ oz (2 tsp) celery—sliced (10 g)

1 ½ fl oz (3 tbs) dry white wine (45 ml)

3 oz (⅓ c) plain yoghurt (85 g)

½ lb tofu—blanched in hot water and cut into thick strips (225 g)

1 ¼ lb John Dory or St. Peter's fish fillets—boned and skinned (600 g)

1 fl oz (2 tbs) lemon juice (20 ml)

8 oz (2–3 medium) courgettes (zucchini)—julienned, blanched, iced and strained (225 g)

salt and pepper to taste

Heat butter and sauté onion and celery until limp.

Add wine and yoghurt and simmer 10 minutes.

Place in a liquidiser and purée, then strain into a saucepan and keep warm.

Place tofu slices on individual plates.

Wash and dry fillets, then season with lemon juice. Grill until tender, about 10 minutes.

Sauté courgettes, seasoning with salt and pepper.

Place grilled fish fillets on top of tofu with courgettes on the side.

Dress plates with yoghurt celery

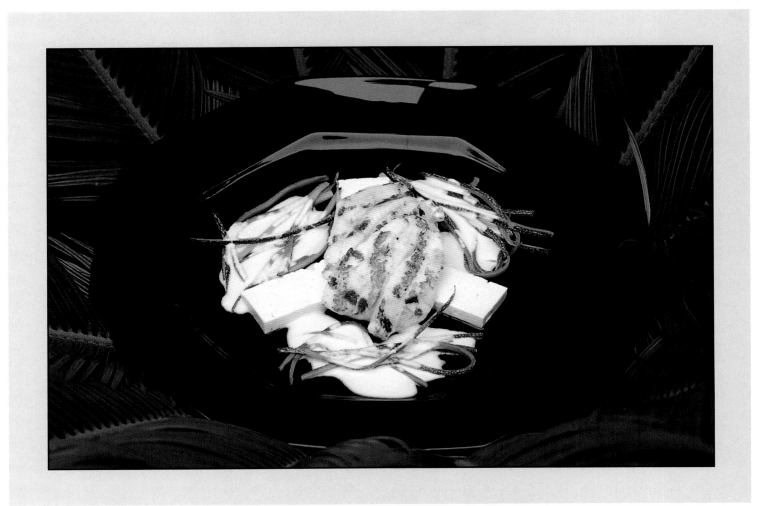

PASTA AND NOODLES

Mee Goreng Bakul
Fried Noodle Basket

Hyatt Kinabalu, Malaysia

Serves 4

14 oz fresh thin egg noodles or
vermicelli (395 g)

vegetable oil—for deep-frying

½ oz (2 tbs) onion—chopped (15 g)

¼ oz (½ clove) garlic—chopped (5–7 g)

1 tsp vegetable oil (5 ml)

3 ½ oz squid—cleaned and sliced into
rings (100 g)

3 ½ oz chicken—cut into chunks
(100 g)

3 ½ oz grouper or other firm white
fish—cut into large cubes (100 g)

3 ½ oz prawns—peeled and deveined
(100 g)

2 oz snow peas—strings removed (50 g)

2 fl oz (4 tbs) oriental sesame oil
(60 ml) (see glossary)

salt and pepper to taste

½ pt (1¼ c) chicken stock (250 ml)
(see glossary)

2 ½ fl oz (5 tbs) cornflour (cornstarch)
dissolved in 6 fl oz (3 tbs) cold water
(150 ml)

1 lb (4 medium) tomatoes (450 g)

3 oz (½ head) lettuce—shredded (85 g)

2 oz (1 medium) carrot—peeled and
sliced into rounds (55 g)

1 fresh red chilli—thinly sliced

Place ¼ of the noodles in a stainless
steel sieve and deep-fry in hot oil until
golden brown. Set aside and repeat
3 times for remaining baskets.

Sauté the onion and garlic in oil until
glazed.

Add squid, chicken, fish and prawns
and sauté for 5 minutes.

Add snow peas. Stir and season with
sesame oil, salt and pepper. Remove
from pan and set aside.

Add stock to pan, heat to boiling and
thicken with cornflour mixture.

Add seafood mixture and bring to a
boil.

Line serving plates with tomato slices
and lettuce.

Neatly arrange noodle baskets on
individual plates and place sautéed
mixture in the centre.

Garnish with sliced carrot and chilli.

SPAGHETTI WITH SMOKED SALMON, ORANGES AND GREEN PEPPERCORNS

HYATT CONTINENTAL MONTREUX, SWITZERLAND

SERVES 4

7 oz spaghetti (200 g)

1 ¾ oz (3 ½ tbs) shallots—minced (50 g)

1 ¾ oz (3 ½ tbs) butter (50 g)

3 fl oz (6 tbs) dry white wine (100 ml)

¾ pt (1 ½ c) double (heavy) cream (480 ml)

5 ¾ oz smoked salmon—julienned (160 g)

3 fl oz (6 tbs) orange juice (100 ml)

1 ¾ oz (3 ½ tbs) green peppercorns (50 g)

salt and pepper to taste

12 oz (2 large) oranges—peeled and separated into segments (340 g)

Cook spaghetti until al dente. Drain and keep warm.

Sauté shallots in butter.

Deglaze pan with wine, then add cream and reduce by ½.

Add spaghetti, most of the salmon (save a few slices for garnish), orange juice and peppercorns.

Mix gently and season with salt and pepper if needed.

Put pasta on individual plates.

Garnish with orange segments and reserved salmon slices.

Fusilli with Avocado, Mango, Prawns and Scallops

Hyatt Regency Saipan, Mariana Islands

Serves 4

Main Dish

9 oz fusilli (spirals) pasta (250 g)

2 oz (½ medium) onion—chopped (55 g)

3 oz (6 tbs) butter (85 g)

8 jumbo prawns—peeled, deveined and cut in half

8 sea scallops—cut in half (340 g)

6 oz (1 medium) avocado—peeled and diced (175 g)

6 oz (1 small) mango—peeled and diced (175 g)

salt and pepper to taste

8 cherry tomatoes—for garnish

1 sprig basil—for garnish

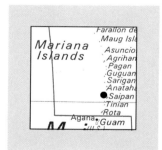

Cook pasta in a large pot of boiling salted water until al dente, about 8–10 minutes. Drain well.

In a skillet, sauté onion in half the butter. Add prawns and scallops and cook lightly, about 5 minutes. Set aside.

Melt remaining butter in skillet and add pasta. Heat and stir for 2 minutes.

Add avocado, mango.

Season with salt and pepper, then add scallops and prawns. Heat for a few seconds.

Transfer to a platter and garnish with cherry tomatoes and basil.

Sprinkle on chopped fresh herbs and serve.

SUNFLOWER SEED BREAD

HYATT REGENCY DUBAI, UNITED ARAB EMIRATES

SERVES 4

½ tsp milk (2.5 ml)

1 tsp water (5 ml)

¼ tsp vegetable oil (1.25 ml)

1 tsp fresh yeast (5 g)

pinch sugar

¼ tsp wholemeal (whole wheat) flour
(1.25 ml)

⅓ oz (2 tsp) salt (10 g)

⅓ oz (2 tsp) sugar (10 g)

5 ½ fl oz (⅔ c) water (160 ml)

8 ¾ oz (2 ¼ c) rye flour (245 g)

3 oz (2 tbs) sunflower seeds (85 g)

⅓ oz (2 tsp) cornstarch (cornflour) (10 g)

1 oz (2 tbs) sugar (30 g)

(2 tsp) sunflower seeds—for garnish
(30 g)

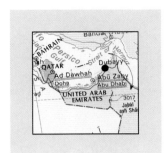

In a saucepan, heat milk, 1 tsp water
and oil until lukewarm. Add yeast and
pinch of sugar. Set aside for 15 minutes to prove. When mixture is light
and bubbly (about 3–5 minutes), stir in
wholemeal flour and salt. Cover and
set mixture aside at room temperature
for 3–5 days, stirring twice a day.

Preheat oven to 425° F (200° C).

Mix the 2 tsp of sugar and ⅔ c water.
Add to above yeast mixture.
Gradually knead in rye flour. Knead
well with hands or with a mixer, using
a dough hook. Cover and keep dough
in a warm place for 10 minutes. Add
sunflower seeds (3 oz) and knead
again. Shape into a loaf and place in
oiled loaf tin.

Mix cornstarch and 1 oz sugar together
and sprinkle over loaf. Make a shallow
slit (lengthwise) along centre of loaf
and fill with 1 oz sunflower seeds.
Bake in oven for 30 minutes, then
lower temperature to 350° F (180° C).
Bake for another 20 minutes.

Remove loaf from the tin and cool on
a wire rack.

Fettuccine aux Crevettes et Coquilles Saint Jacques Parfumées au Gingembre et Basilic
Seafood Fettuccine with Basil and Ginger

———○———

Hyatt Regency Tahiti, French Polynesia

Serves 4

2 oz (4 tbs) butter (55 g)

8 oz large prawns—peeled (225 g)

8 oz sea scallops (225 g)

3 oz (¾ c) shallots (85 g)

½ oz (1 tbs) fresh basil—chopped (15 g)

8 fl oz (1 c) dry white wine (240 ml)

1 oz (¼ c) fresh ginger—chopped (30 g)

¾ pt (1 ½ c) double (heavy) cream (355 ml)

7 oz fettuccine (200 g)

salt and pepper to taste

4 basil leaves—for garnish

Melt butter in large skillet.

○

Add prawns and sauté until pink.

○

Add scallops and cook a few minutes until firm. Set prawns and scallops aside.

○

In same skillet, sauté shallots until limp. Stir in the basil and ginger and cook for 1 minute.

○

Add wine and over high heat reduce to about 4 tbs (60 ml).

○

Add cream and simmer 3 minutes. Keep warm.

○

Cook fettuccine in salted boiling water until al dente.

○

Drain and add to skillet. Stir well.

○

Add scallops and prawns to pasta, season with salt and pepper and serve, garnished with basil leaves.

MACARRONES TAPATIOS
MACARONI WITH MEXICAN SAUSAGE

○

HYATT REGENCY GUADALAJARA, MEXICO

SERVES 4

5 pt (4 ¾ qt) water (3 𝑙)

2 ½ fl oz (5 tbs) vegetable oil (90 ml)

salt

1 ¼ lb macarrones or any other tubular pasta (600 g)

1 lb chorizo (Mexican sausage)—sliced (450 g)

1 ½ oz (3 tbs) butter (45 g)

8 oz green chilli (225 g)

4 fl oz (½ c) double (heavy) cream (120 ml)

½ tsp fresh marjoram (5 g)

4 ¼ oz mild melting cheese, like Monterey Jack or mozzarella—grated (120 g)

4 ¼ oz (1 medium) green bell pepper—peeled, pips removed and cut into 4 long slices (120 g)

Note: Chorizo is a long, dry sausage flavoured with chillies and garlic. It may contain only pork or beef or a combination of both. Pepperoni sausage may be substituted.

Bring water with oil and some salt to a boil, then add pasta. Cook until al dente.

○

Drain pasta and set aside.

○

Sauté sausages in butter for 3 minutes.

○

Add pasta and mix completely. Keep warm.

○

In a separate pan, heat the chilli sauce, cream and marjoram.

○

Arrange pasta on individual plates.

○

Sprinkle each with grated cheese and top with green pepper slices.

○

Pour sauce around the pasta on each plate and serve.

SEAFOOD CANNELLONI
WITH THREE SAUCES

◯

HYATT REGENCY SANCTUARY COVE, QUEENSLAND, AUSTRALIA

SERVES 4

CANNELLONI

2 oz meat from sand crabs or other crabs (50 g)

2 oz pippies or other clam meat (50 g)

2 oz prawns—peeled and cooked (50 g)

2 oz small shrimp—peeled and cooked (50 g)

2 oz small scallops (50 g)

2 oz squid rings (50 g)

2 oz lobster meat (50 g)

¾ oz (1 ½ tbs) butter (20 g)

3 ½ oz (1 small) onion—chopped (100 g)

1 oz (2 cloves) garlic—chopped (30 g)

1 ¾ fl oz (3 ½ tbs) double (heavy) cream (52 ml)

3 ½ oz (1 small) tomato—pips removed and chopped (100 g)

¾ oz (4 tsp) Parmesan cheese—grated (20 g)

salt and pepper to taste

8 cannelloni sheets

8 (long leaves) green onion (scallions)—blanched

Dice seafood coarsely.

◯

Melt butter in a large pan and sauté onion and garlic.

◯

Add the seafood and sauté gently for 3 minutes.

◯

Add the cream and tomato; bring to a boil, then simmer for 5 minutes.

◯

Remove pan from heat; add Parmesan, salt and pepper.

◯

Cook the cannelloni sheets in salted boiling water until al dente, about 3 minutes.

◯

Refresh in cold water and drain.

◯

Put equal amounts of filling in the 8 cannelloni sheets and roll up, with the ends folded in.

◯

Tie with green onion leaves and reheat gently in a warm oven.

◯

Serve with the three following sauces.

WHITE WINE SAUCE

1 ¾ oz (3 ½ tbs) dry white wine (50 ml)

3 ½ fl oz (7 tbs) double (heavy) cream (100 ml)

⅓ oz (2 tbs) chilled butter (10 g)

⅓ oz (1 tbs) cornflour (cornstarch)— dissolved in 2 tbs (30 ml) wine or water (10 g)

nutmeg, thyme, salt and pepper to taste.

Bring wine, nutmeg, and thyme to a boil.

◯

Add cream and simmer for 5 minutes.

◯

Add cornflour mixture and stir until thickened.

◯

Season with salt and pepper; remove from heat and swirl in the butter.

◯

Serve hot.

BLACK BEAN SAUCE

1 tsp black bean paste (10 g) (see glossary)

¼ oz fresh ginger—grated (5–7 g)

½ oz (1 clove) garlic—chopped (15 g)

3 fl oz (6 tbs) chicken stock (100 ml) (see glossary)

⅓ fl oz (2 tsp) soy sauce (10 ml)

Mix ingredients in a small saucepan.

◯

Bring to a boil and adjust seasonings to taste.

Tomato Sauce

¾ oz (1 ½ tbs) butter (20 g)

3 oz (1 small) onion—chopped (85 g)

7 oz (1 ½ medium) tomatoes—peeled and chopped (200 g)

1 strip of bacon

rosemary, basil, oregano,

salt and pepper to taste

¾ oz (½ tbs) double (heavy) cream (20 ml)

Melt butter in pan. Sauté onion and bacon for 5 minutes.

○

Stir in tomatoes and herbs. Simmer for another 15 minutes.

○

Purée in a liquidiser, adjust seasonings and stir in cream.

CANNELLONI DAN KARE RAVIOLI DENGAN KEJU RICOTTA
CANNELLONI AND CURRIED RAVIOLI WITH RICOTTA

BALI HYATT, INDONESIA

SERVES 4

RICOTTA FILLING

14 oz spinach—trimmed and cleaned (400 g)

10 oz ricotta cheese (300 g)

1 egg—beaten

2 oz (½ c) Parmesan cheese—grated (50 g)

salt and pepper to taste

Blanch spinach for 1 minute in boiling water.

Drain and refresh in ice water.

Drain again, put in a cheesecloth. Squeeze out excess moisture.

Chop spinach coarsely.

Crumble ricotta into a bowl and add spinach, parmesan and egg.

Season with salt and pepper. Set aside.

CANNELLONI

6 eggs

pinch salt (10 g)

1 fl oz (2 tbs) olive oil (30 ml)

1 lb (3 ¼ c) flour (500 g)

In a large bowl, lightly whisk eggs, salt and olive oil.

Add about ¼ of the flour, then whisk until smooth.

Add the remaining flour, then mix with your hands or a wooden spoon.

Knead until smooth, about 5 minutes. Let rest for 30 minutes.

Divide dough into several pieces, the size of a golf ball.

CURRIED RAVIOLI

½ recipe for cannelloni (see below)

1 ½ oz (3 tbs) curry powder (40 g)

Knead the curry powder into the dough. Let rest for 30 minutes.

Divide into balls the size of a golf ball and roll the balls in to 2 ½ -inch (6.25-cm) squares. Keep covered with a moist towel to prevent drying.

Fill each square with 1 tsp (5 g) of ricotta mixture and fold diagonally; moisten the edges with water to seal.

Place balls in a bowl and cover with a damp cloth.

Roll each piece into a 4x5-inch (10x12.5 cm) rectangle, rolling from centre outward. Trim into neat rectangles.

Cook cannelloni in boiling salted water until al dente, about 3 minutes.

Drain well and spread on a towel to drain.

Fill each cannelloni square with 2 tbs (55 g) of ricotta mixture and roll into a cylinder. Keep warm.

TOMATO CONCASSE

1 oz (2 cloves) garlic—chopped (25 g)

18 oz (5 large) tomatoes—peeled, pips removed and chopped (500 g)

1 fl oz (2 tbs) olive oil (25 ml)

½ oz (1 tbs) shallots—minced (15 g)

salt and pepper to taste

¾ oz (1 ½ tbs) fresh basil—chopped (10 g)

Sauté garlic and shallots in olive oil for 2 minutes.

Add tomatoes, season with salt and pepper and simmer 10-15 minutes.

Remove from heat and add basil. Keep warm.

TO ASSEMBLE AND SERVE

fresh basil leaves—for garnish

Cook ravioli in boiling salted water until al dente, about 2 minutes. Drain.

Place 2 cannelloni on each plate.

Arrange 2 ravioli on each plate, splitting one open to reveal filling.

Spoon tomato concasse in front of cannelloni.

Garnish with basil leaves and serve.

Kodok Kecap Dengan
Cabe Taoge dan Mie Hun Goreng
Glazed Frogs' Legs with Sweet Soy Chillies and Glass Noodles

Bali Hyatt, Indonesia

Serves 4

Frogs' Legs

12 oz frogs' legs (320 g) juice of 3 limes

1 ½ oz (3 tbs) fresh ginger—grated (40 g)

salt and pepper to taste

flour—for dusting

vegetable oil—for deep-frying

5 fl oz (⅔ c) sweet soy sauce (160 ml)

Marinate the frogs' legs in a mixture of lime juice, ginger, salt and pepper for 15 minutes.

Lightly dust the frogs' legs with flour, then deep-fry in hot oil until golden brown.

Drain on paper towels.

Heat soy sauce until boiling.

Dip frogs' legs in hot soy sauce, then place legs on a baking tray and put under broiler for 1–2 minutes to crisp.

Note: Sweet soy sauce is an Indonesian ingredient, commonly called kecap manis. It is available in some Asian groceries.

Glass Noodles

3 ½ oz glass (cellophane) noodles (100 g)

vegetable oil—for deep frying

⅓ oz (2 tsp) carrot—julienned (15 g)

⅓ oz (2 tsp) bean sprouts (15 g)

⅓ oz (2 tsp) red bell peppers—pips removed and julienned (15 g)

⅓ oz (2 tsp) leeks—julienned (15 g)

Deep-fry the noodles until golden brown and crispy.

Quickly blanch vegetables until tender-crisp. Drain well.

Arrange noodles on a plate. Arrange frogs' legs over and sprinkle vegetables on top.

Arroz de Marisco
Seafood Rice

Hyatt Regency Macau, Macau

Serves 4

8 oz (3 c) cooked rice (225 g)

1 oz (2 tbs) garlic—chopped (30 g)

2 fl oz (4 tbs) olive oil (60 ml)

8 fl oz (1 c) water (240 ml)

8 fl oz (1 c) dry white wine (240 ml)

1 ¼ lb (5 large) tomatoes—cut into chunks and puréed (565 g)

salt and pepper to taste

10 oz prawns—cleaned and washed (300 g)

14 oz mussels—washed and debearded (400 g)

7 oz clams—cleaned and washed (200 g)

8 oz (2 c) crabmeat (225 g)

4 eggs

1 oz (2 tbs) fresh coriander—chopped (30 g)

Sauté rice and garlic in olive oil in a large pot.

Add water, wine and tomato purée.

Season with salt and pepper, cover pot and bring to a boil.

After 5 minutes, add seafood and simmer another 15 minutes. If rice gets too dry, add some fish stock or water.

Stir in crabmeat, then break the eggs onto the rice and slowly stir in.

Arrange on 4 plates and garnish with coriander.

Couscous Bil Jobna
Gratin of Couscous with Parmesan

◯

Casablanca Hyatt Regency, Morocco

Serves 4

Couscous

**8 oz (1 c) couscous (semolina grain)
(250 g)**

½ oz (1tbs) vegetable oil (15 ml)

1 oz (2 tbs) butter—melted (30 g)

2 ½ fl oz (5 tbs) water—salted (75 ml)

Mix couscous with oil and place in a
steamer over boiling water.

◯

Steam for 30 minutes.

◯

Transfer couscous to a large dish and
with the round bottom side of a ladle
carefully smash the grains. Sift grains
through your fingers to separate.

◯

Let couscous cool, then pour salted
water through it.

◯

Let couscous rest for 15 minutes, then
repeat procedure 2 more times.

◯

Transfer couscous to a large dish, stir
and add the melted butter, mixing
well.

Gratin

**8 fl oz (1 c) double (heavy) cream
(240 ml)**

½ tsp nutmeg—grated (2.5 g)

salt and pepper to taste

3 egg yolks

**2 oz (½ c) Parmesan cheese—grated
(60 g)**

In a saucepan, simmer cream with
nutmeg, salt and pepper, until
thickened.

◯

Lower heat and whisk in egg yolks.

◯

Place couscous in a large boiler-proof
gratin dish, cover with cream and
sprinkle with Parmesan cheese.

◯

Put under a broiler until top is golden
brown, about 5 minutes.

Chapoh'as

Korean Rice Noodles with Vegetables

⟡

Hyatt Regency Pusan, Korea

Serves 4

7 oz rice noodles or vermicelli—dried (200 g)

1 ¾ oz (1 small) carrot (50 g)

1 ¾ oz shiitake mushrooms—fresh (50 g)

1 ¾ oz (1 medium) leek—trimmed (50 g)

1 ¾ oz spinach trimmed, cleaned (50 g)

3 oz (1 small) onion (80 g)

1 oz (2 cloves) garlic (30 g)

½ fl oz (1 tbs) vegetable oil (15 ml)

salt to taste

2 eggs—beaten

1 fl oz (2 tbs) soy sauce (30 ml)

1 tsp oriental sesame oil (5 ml) (see glossary)

½ tsp sesame seeds—for garnish (2.5 g)

Soak noodles in water for 30 minutes. Drain.

⟡

Cut vegetables into thin strips and stir-fry lightly in vegetable oil.

⟡

Fry the beaten eggs as for an omelet, then cut into thin strips.

⟡

In a wok, stir-fry the noodles with the soy sauce and sesame oil.

⟡

Place mixture on a plate; garnish with egg strips and sesame seeds.

GREEN CHILLI CANNELLONI
WITH ROASTED RED PEPPER SAUCE

HYATT REGENCY MANILA, PHILIPPINES

SERVES 4

GREEN CHILLI CANNELLONI

⅓ oz (1 small) fresh green chilli—pips removed and diced (10 g)

spinach—trimmed, cleaned, cooked, drained and diced (50 g)

1 ½ fl oz (3 tbs) water (50 ml)

½ tbs vegetable oil (7 ml)

10 oz (2 c) flour (300 g)

1 egg

Put the chilli, spinach, water and oil in a liquidiser and purée.

On a board, mound the flour and make a well in the centre.

Put the egg and green purée in the centre and work it into the flour with your hands until completely incorporated, and a dough is formed.

Roll dough into a ball; wrap and set aside in refrigerator for 20 minutes.

Roll out dough to ⅛-inch (½ -cm) thick and cut into 3x4-inch (7.5x10-cm) rectangles.

Cook dough rectangles in boiling salted water until al dente, about 3 minutes.

Cool cannelloni sheets in ice water, then drain well.

Place 2 tbs (30 g) filling (receipe follows) on each sheet and roll up tightly like a cigar. Set aside.

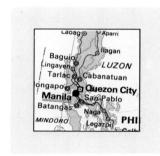

FILLING

2 oz (½ medium) onion—chopped (50 g)

½ oz (1 clove) garlic—minced (2 g)

2 oz (1 medium) carrot—julienned (50 g)

5 oz ham—diced (140 g)

1 oz (2 tbs) butter (30 g)

2 oz (½ medium) tomato—peeled, pips removed and diced (40 g)

1 tsp oregano—fresh, chopped (5 g)

3 oz mozzarella cheese—shredded (90 g)

Sauté the onion, garlic, carrot and ham in butter.

Add tomato and oregano.

Let cool, then stir in cheese.

ROASTED RED BELL PEPPER SAUCE

5 ¼ oz (1 large) red bell pepper (150 g)

½ tsp shallots—chopped (2.5 g)

½ tsp garlic—chopped (2.5 g)

½ fl oz (1 tbs) vegetable oil (15 ml)

12 fl oz (1 ½ c) double (heavy) cream (350 ml)

1 ½ oz (⅓ c) red bell pepper—pips removed and julienned for garnish (40 g)

1 oz (¼ c) leeks—julienned for garnish (25 g)

2 black olives—for garnish

salt and pepper to taste

Preheat oven to 300° F (150°C).

Roast bell pepper directly over open flame until skin has charred.

Rinse under tap water and then peel.

Slice pepper in half, discard pips, then coarsely dice.

Sauté garlic and shallots in oil.

Add cream and simmer until reduced by ½ .

Add roasted pepper and cook for 2 minutes.

Put mixture in a liquidiser and purée until smooth. Season with salt and pepper.

Oil a medium baking pan and arrange cannelloni in bottom. Pour on some sauce to keep moist, warm in oven for 25 minutes.

Spread sauce on individual plates. Place cannelloni on top and surround with red pepper garnish. Top with leeks and olives (see photo).

Lasagnette con Guisado de Mariscos
Seafood Ragout and Lasagnette

○

Hyatt Regency Cancun, Mexico
Serves 4

1 ½ fl oz (3 tbs) olive oil (45 ml)

½ oz (1 tbs) garlic—chopped (15 g)

1 oz (2 tbs) onion—chopped (30 g)

4 oz lobster meat (120 g)

4 oz (30-40 small) prawns—peeled and deveined (120 g)

4 oz squid—cleaned and sliced into rings; save head (120 g)

8 oz (4 large) fresh water crayfish—steamed, then tails peeled and bodies discarded (225 g)

3 oz salmon fillet—1-inch (2x2-cm) cubes (85 g)

12 mussels—cleaned and debearded

12 oz fresh lasagnette or other pasta (320 g)

3 oz (¾ c) broccoli flowerettes—cooked (85 g)

3 oz (¾ c) carrots—cooked (85 g)

3 oz (¾ c) red bell pepper—pips removed and julienned (85 g)

2 ¼ oz (½ c) green beans—cooked (60 g)

2 ¼ oz (½ c) green bell pepper—pips removed and julienned (60 g)

basil leaves—for garnish, julienned

Note: Freshwater crayfish, or ecrevisse, are found in streams. Only the tail is eaten. If unavailable, substitute small prawns.

In a large sauté pan, heat olive oil and sauté garlic and onion.

○

Add prawns, squid (including head), crayfish and lobster.

○

Cook for 3 minutes.

○

Add salmon and mussels and cook another 3 minutes. Remove from heat.

○

Cook pasta until al dente, about 2–3 minutes.

○

Add pasta to the seafood along with vegetables; stir.

○

Transfer pasta mixture to plates. Garnish with basil.

RED BELL PEPPER FETTUCCINE
WITH BACON, MUSHROOMS, WALNUTS AND A WINE-CREAM SAUCE

⚬

HYATT KINGSGATE SYDNEY, AUSTRALIA

SERVES 4

1 lb red bell pepper fettuccine (450 g)

5 oz (1 ¼ c) bacon strips—diced (150 g)

3 ½ oz (1 c) button mushrooms— sliced (100 g)

4 oz (1 large) onion—chopped (115 g)

salt and pepper to taste

4 fl oz (½ c) dry white wine (120 ml)

8 fl oz (1 c) double (heavy) cream (240 ml)

3 oz (¾ c) shallots—minced for garnish (100 g)

3 oz (¾ c) walnuts—shelled and chopped for garnish (100 g)

Cook fettuccine in boiling water until al dente. Drain.

⚬

Heat a pan and sauté bacon until half-cooked.

⚬

Discard the fat. Add the mushrooms and onion to the pan and sauté until bacon is cooked.

⚬

Discard any fat, then add wine and simmer a few more minutes until lightly thickened.

⚬

Add cream, salt and pepper to taste.

⚬

Remove pan from heat and immediately add fettuccine.

⚬

Serve hot with shallots and walnuts sprinkled on top.

CRAB WONTONS
WITH RATATOUILLE

HYATT ON COLLINS, MELBOURNE, AUSTRALIA

SERVES 4

CRAB WONTONS

12–20 wonton wrappers

3 ½ oz (¾ c+1 lbs) crabmeat (100 g)

1 oz (1 small bunch) chives—chopped (30 g)

1 egg white—beaten

Mix crabmeat with chives until well blended.

Place 1 tsp of crab filling in the centre of each wonton wrapper.

Brush margins of wonton with egg white.

Top with another wonton, sealing edges well. Make certain that there is no air caught between layers.

Trim the wontons with a small knife to eliminate excess dough around filling.

Cook in simmering water for 2 minutes, then drain.

RATATOUILLE

4 oz (1 small) aubergine (eggplant) (115 g)

3 oz (1 small) green bell pepper (85 g) pips removed

3 oz (1 small) red bell pepper (85 g) pips removed

3 oz (1 small) onion (85 g)

1 fl oz (2 tbs) olive oil (30 ml)

½ tbs fresh herbs—chopped (15 g)

1 fl oz (2 tbs) tomato concentrate (paste) (30 ml)

Dice vegetables and Sauté in olive oil.

Add fresh herbs, and then tomato concentrate.

Stir well and keep warm.

TO ASSEMBLE AND SERVE

basil leaves—julienned

8 fl oz (1 c) lemon butter sauce (240 ml) (see glossary)

empty crab shell for garnish—cleaned

Form a mound of ratatouille on a serving plate.

Place wontons alongside.

Garnish plate with basil leaves and neatly spoon on lemon butter sauce. Decorate with crab if desired.

PENNE WITH SHIITAKE MUSHROOMS AND SMOKED CHICKEN

U.N. PLAZA HOTEL, A PARK HYATT HOTEL, NEW YORK, U.S.A.

SERVES 4

2 ½ oz (2 large cloves) garlic (70 g)

2 oz (4 tbs) duck fat (55 g)

4 ½ fl oz (9 tbs) olive oil—for sautéing (135 ml)

1 lb penne or other tubular pasta (450 g)

2 oz (½ c) shallots—chopped (60 g)

12 oz shiitake mushrooms—cleaned and stems removed; sliced ¼-inch (6-mm) thick (340 g)

12 oz smoked chicken or turkey breast—sliced ¼-inch (6-mm) thick (340 g)

2 oz (½ c) sun-dried tomatoes— julienned (60 g)

8 fl oz (1 c) double (heavy) cream (240 ml)

2 oz (4 tbs) butter—chilled, cubed (60 g)

1 oz (¼ c) herbs—fresh and chopped for garnish (30 g)

Simmer garlic in duck fat for at least 45–60 minutes without colouring. Remove and crush garlic to a purée.

Cook pasta in salted boiling water with 1 ½ oz (3 tbs) (45 ml) olive oil until al dente. Drain.

In a large nonstick pan, heat 3 fl oz (6 tbs) (45 ml) oil and sauté the shallots, mushrooms and garlic.

Add the chicken or turkey strips and sun-dried tomatoes and sauté 5 seconds.

Add the cream and simmer until thickened.

Remove pan from heat and add the butter piece by piece, rotating and shaking the pan.

Return mushrooms to the pan, mix, then add pasta and toss gently.

Just before serving, check seasonings and granish with the herbs. Serve.

YUM WOON SEN

HOT AND SPICY GLASS NOODLES, SHRIMP AND PORK SALAD

GRAND HYATT ERAWAN BANGKOK, THAILAND

SERVES 4

¼ oz (6 large) dried tree ears (7 g)

7–8 oz (½ lb) glass (cellophane) noodles (200-225 g)

1 ½ fl oz (3 tbs) vegetable oil (45 ml)

1 oz (¼ c) dried shrimp (30 g)

12 oz (¾ lb) lean pork—coarsely ground or hand-chopped (340 g)

1 ½ oz (⅓ c) shallots—sliced (45 g)

2 oz (1 small) onion—cut into quarters and thinly sliced (55 g)

1 ½ oz (⅓ c) green onions (scallions)— thinly sliced (45 g)

1 ½ oz (⅓ c) celery leaves—inner, tender leaves (45 g)

2 fl oz (⅓ c) fish sauce (60 ml) (see glossary)

2 fl oz (⅓ c) lemon juice (60 ml)

⅓ oz (1 ½ tsp) sugar (10 g)

¾ oz (4 tsp) hot red chilli—minced, pips removed (20 g)

16 shrimp—peeled, deveined and boiled until cooked

4 oz (½ c) coriander leaves (115 g)

16 lettuce leaves—of your choice, washed and dried

Note: Tree ears, also called wood ears or cloud ears, are available in Asian or Chinese food markets.

Soak the tree ears in ¾ pt (2 c; 475 ml) warm water for about 15 minutes. Rinse off and discard knotty parts. Slice into thin strips and set aside.

○

Pour boiling water over noodles and let stand about 5 minutes. Drain. Using scissors, cut noodles into 3 to 4-inch (7.5-10 cm) lengths. Set aside.

○

In a pan, heat the 2 tbs (30 ml) oil and fry the dried shrimp until just crisp. Drain.

○

Heat remaining 1 tbs (15 ml) oil in another pan and stir-fry the pork over high heat until thoroughly cooked. Drain.

○

Combine the noodles, fried shrimp and pork in a bowl.

○

Mix the shallots, onion, green onions, celery leaves and tree ears. Add the fish sauce, lemon juice, sugar and minced chilli. Pour over bowl of noodles and toss until well-combined.

○

Cut the boiled shrimp in thirds diagonally, reserving 4 whole ones for garnish. Toss shrimp and coriander leaves over the noodles.

○

Cover 4 plates neatly with lettuce leaves. Arrange noodles in centre, garnished with the whole shrimp. Serve at room temperature.

Mee Mamak

Fried Noodles

Hyatt Kuantan, Malaysia

Serves 4

3 ½ oz (1 small) onion—sliced (100 g)

2 oz (4 cloves) garlic—chopped (55 g)

½ fl oz (1 tbs) vegetable oil (15 ml)

7 oz pork tenderloin—sliced into 1-inch (2.5-cm) strips (200 g)

2 oz (4 tbs) chilli paste (55 g)

2 oz (4 tbs) chilli sauce (55 g)

2 oz (4 tbs) tomato concentrate (paste) (55 g)

1 pt (2 ½ c) chicken stock (500 ml) (see glossary)

1 ¼ lb fresh egg noodles or fresh fettuccine (600 g)

3 eggs—beaten

5 ¼ oz mustard greens—coarsely chopped (145 g)

3 ½ oz bean sprouts (100 g)

salt to taste

Sauté onion and garlic in oil until soft but not brown.

Add the pork and stir fry for 5 minutes.

Add the chilli paste, chilli sauce and tomato purée.

Stir for 2 minutes, then pour in stock.

Simmer for 3 minutes, then add the noodles.

Stir noodles in mixture until most liquid has been absorbed.

Add the eggs and break up as they harden.

Add mustard greens and bean sprouts; then, season with salt.

FRIED KWAY TEOW
FRIED RICE NOODLES WITH VEGETABLES AND SEAFOOD IN SOY SAUCE

HYATT REGENCY SINGAPORE, SINGAPORE

SERVES 4

¾ fl oz (1 ½ tbs) corn oil (20 ml)

1 oz (2 cloves) garlic—crushed (30 g)

1 fresh chilli—crushed

2 lb (1 medium) chicken breast—whole, boned, skinned and cubed (900 g)

5 oz squid—cleaned and sliced into rings (150 g)

7 oz medium prawns—peeled (200 g)

1 tsp light soy sauce (5 ml)

1 tsp dark soy sauce (5 ml)

salt and pepper to taste

5 ¾ oz bean sprouts (160 g)

12 oz fresh rice noodles—(kway teow) (320 g)

4 fresh red chillies—pips removed and sliced for garnish

Note: Kway teow are fresh noodles that come in a variety of sizes. Use flat noodles here, or substitute dried noodles that have been soaked in warm water.

Heat the oil in a deep pan and sauté garlic and chilli until fragrant.

Raise heat and stir-fry chicken cubes for 2 minutes.

Add squid and prawns and stir-fry for another 2 minutes.

Stir in the soy sauces, salt and pepper and bean sprouts.

Add noodles, mix thoroughly and stir-fry for 2 more minutes.

Garnish with chillies and serve immediately.

Lachs und Spinat im Reisblatt
Salmon and Spinach Baked in Rice Paper

◯

Hyatt Regency Cologne, West Germany

Served 4

Salmon and Rice Paper

4 oz rice paper (115 g)

12 oz salmon fillets—cooked and sliced into thin strips (340 g)

12 oz spinach—trimmed, cleaned, blanched and drained (340 g)

salt and pepper to taste

1 oz (2 tbs) butter (30 g)

Note: Vietnamese rice paper is brittle when dry but pliable when moistened. It is available in most Asian groceries. You may also substitute phyllo dough.

Preheat oven to 350 ° F (180 °C).

◯

Cover rice paper with a damp cloth to soften.

◯

Heat spinach in butter and season with salt and pepper.

◯

Lay out a softened rice paper sheet and spread half the spinach over the sheet. Arrange half the salmon strips on top.

◯

Repeat layer and finish with a rice paper sheet on top.

◯

With a large cookie cutter (or rim of a drinking glass), make 4 circles from the layers, then cut out with a sharp knife.

◯

Bake for 7 minutes, or until rice paper is crisp.

◯

Serve with beetroot sauce (recipe follows) and your choice of seasonal vegetables

Beetroot Sauce

2 fl oz (4 tbs) white sauce (60 ml) (see glossary)

2 oz (½ c) beetroot—chopped (55 g)

4 fl oz (½ c) double (heavy) cream— whipped (120 ml)

Heat white sauce and beetroot in a saucepan.

◯

Strain, cool, then fold in whipped cream. Keep hot.

KHAO PHAT
THAI FRIED RICE

GRAND HYATT ERAWAN BANGKOK, THAILAND

SERVES 4

1 ½ fl oz (3 tbs) peanut oil (45 ml)

8 oz (2 medium) onions—finely chopped (225 g)

6 oz (1 large) pork chop—boned and meat finely diced (175 g)

8 oz prawns—shelled, deveined and coarsely diced (250 g)

6 ½ oz crabmeat (185 g)

3 eggs—beaten

10 oz (4 c) cold steamed rice (280 g)

1 fl oz (2 tbs) fish sauce (30 ml)

½ fl oz (1 tbs) chilli sauce (15 ml)—optional

1 fl oz (2 tbs) tomato concentrate (paste) (30 ml)

4 oz (1 c) green onions (scallions)—chopped

1 oz (4 tbs) fresh coriander leaves—chopped (30 g)

salt and pepper to taste

Heat oil in a large wok or frying pan. Sauté the onions over medium low heat until soft. Increase heat to high and stir-fry diced pork for about five minutes. Then add prawns and crabmeat and stir-fry 3 minutes longer.

Meanwhile, season beaten eggs with salt and pepper and pour into centre of wok. Stir until it just begins to set, then add cooled rice and stir well. Continue tossing and stirring until rice is heated through. Sprinkle fish sauce, optional chilli sauce over and stir in the tomato concentrate. Stir thoroughly until rice has an even, reddish color. Remove from heat and toss in the green onions. Transfer to a plate and sprinkle the chopped coriander leaves over the fried rice.

TORTELLINI
WITH CURRY CREAM SAUCE AND SMOKED SALMON

○

HYATT KINGSGATE SYDNEY, AUSTRALIA

SERVES 4

PASTA

1 ¼ lb tortellini (600 g)

salt to taste

4 ¼ oz smoked salmon—coarsely diced (120 g)

4 sprigs watercress

Cook tortellini in salted boiling water until al dente.

○

Drain well and place in individual bowls.

○

Pour sauce (recipe follows) over and sprinkle with salmon.

○

Garnish with watercress and serve.

CURRY CREAM SAUCE

1 ½ fl oz (3 tbs) olive oil (45 ml)

4 oz (1 large) onion—finely chopped (115 g)

2 ½ oz (5 cloves) garlic—finely chopped (70 g)

4 fl oz (½ c) dry white wine (120 ml)

8 fl oz (1 c) double (heavy) cream (240 ml)

½ oz (1 tbs) curry powder (15 g)

salt and pepper to taste

Heat olive oil and sauté onion and garlic until golden.

○

Add wine and reduce by ½ .

○

Add cream, curry powder, salt and pepper to taste.

Homemade Tagliatelle
with Sea Scallops and Asparagus Tips in Garlic Cream

Hyatt Regency Hong Kong, Hong Kong

Serves 4

1 ¼ lb sea scallops (565 g)

½ lb (2 c) thin asparagus tips (225 g)

14 fl oz (1 ¾ c) half-and-half (400 ml)

2 oz (4 cloves) garlic—peeled and lightly crushed (55 g)

1 oz (¼ c) chives—chopped (30 g)

1 oz (¼ c) red bell pepper—pips removed and chopped (30 g)

1 lb saffron tagliatelle (400 g) (see glossary)

4 leaves basil—for garnish

4 leaves chervil—for garnish

Briefly grill or sauté sea scallops, until cooked, about 5 minutes. Set aside.

Steam asparagus until tender, about 3 minutes.

Simmer half-and-half and garlic over medium heat until reduced by ¼ .

Strain cream and add chives and red pepper.

Cook tagliatelle in salted water until al dente.

Drain pasta and mix with sauce. Add garnish of basil and chervil. Serve.

Note: Half-and-half is a 50-50 mixture of whole milk and double (heavy) cream.

Lasagna with Sweetbreads and Oysters

Hyatt Regency Riyadh, Saudi Arabia

Serves 4

24 oysters

1 lb sweetbreads (450 g)

2 oz (½ c) carrot—diced (55 g)

2 oz (½ c) celery—diced (55 g)

2 oz (½ c) leeks (white part only)— diced (55 g)

1 bay leaf

2 whole cloves

5 pt (3 qt) water (3 *l*)

salt and pepper to taste

1 lb lasagna noodles (450 g)

½ oz (1 tbs) butter (15 g)

½ oz (⅓ c) onion—chopped (40 g)

6 fl oz (¾ c) dry white wine (180 ml)

¾ pt (2 c) double (heavy) cream (500 ml)

1 tsp chives—chopped (3 g)

juice of ½ lemon

1 tsp Parmesan cheese—for garnish (5 g)

Shuck the oysters, saving the liquid.

Clean the sweetbreads (removing membranes and sinew) and rinse under cold water.

To a stockpot, add the carrot, celery, leek, bay leaf, cloves, water, salt and pepper. Bring to a boil, reduce heat, then add sweetbreads. Simmer 3–5 minutes.

Break the sweetbreads into small pieces using your hands.

Strain the stock, then boil until reduced to 1 pt (2 c; 475 ml).

Cook the lasagna in salted water until al dente.

Melt the butter in a sauté pan and quickly sauté the oysters on both sides. Set aside.

In the same pan, quickly sauté onion. Add wine, stock and cream. Reduce until thickened, then add the sweetbreads, oysters and chives. Simmmer for about 2 minutes.

Layer the lasagna noodles in a heatproof pan. Spread some sweetbread-oyster ragout over noodles and cover with another noodle layer. Repeat several times.

Spread lasagna layer with remaining sauce and sprinkle grated cheese over it. Brown lightly in a broiler or grill, and serve.

PERFECT BALANCE

TERRINE DARI TERONG DENGAN TAOG DAN JAMUR
AUBERGINE TERRINE WITH BEAN SPROUT AND MUSHROOM SALAD

BALI HYATT, INDONESIA

SERVES 4

TERRINE

3 ⅓ lb small, slender aubergine (eggplant) (1 ½ kg)

½ fl oz (3 tbs) olive oil (45 ml)

1 oz (2 cloves) garlic—minced (30 g)

½ oz (1 tbs) shallots—minced (15 g)

1 oz (2 tbs) onion—minced (30 g)

½ tsp fresh thyme (5 g)

¼ oz (1 tbs) basil—fresh, minced (15 g)

8 oz (2 medium) tomatoes—peeled, pips removed and chopped (225 g)

salt and pepper to taste

oil for coating aubergine

Preheat oven to 330° F (180° C).

Halve the aubergine lengthwise; set 3 halves aside for later use. Coat a baking pan with olive oil and place aubergine, cut side down, on pan. Bake for 15 minutes, or until tender.

Scoop out pulp and chop finely.

Sauté the garlic, onion, thyme, basil and tomatoes in remaining olive oil for 10 minutes. Remove from heat and add the aubergine.

Slice the remaining aubergine halves into ⅛-inch (½ cm) slices.

Spread slices on a baking pan, drizzle with oil and bake for 5 minutes, or until tender.

Use aubergine slices to line the bottom of individual soup bowls and top with aubergine mixture.

Weight the tops of the soup bowls to compress aubergine and chill to firm up.

Unmold aubergine terrines onto individual plates and serve with salad (recipe follows).

SALAD

4 oz (1 c) bean sprouts (100 g)

3 oz (¾ c) button mushrooms (85 g)

1 ½ oz (½ medium) tomato—peeled and pips removed (45 g)

juice of 1 lime

In a bowl, toss bean sprouts, mushrooms and tomato with the lime juice, salt and pepper.

Add dressing (recipe follows) and toss again.

DRESSING

3 fl oz (6 tbs) water (90 ml)

1 fl oz (2 tbs) oriental sesame oil (30 ml)

1 fl oz (2 tbs) rice vinegar (30 ml)

⅓ oz (2 tsp) fresh coriander—chopped (10 g)

1 oz (2 tbs) leeks—sliced (30 g)

⅓ oz (2 tsp) ginger—sliced (10 g)

¾ oz (1 ½ tbs) shallots—sliced (20 g)

salt and pepper to taste

Mix dressing ingredients.

PALETA DEL PINTOR CON ADERZO DE YOGHURT Y AVELLUNUS
PAINTER'S PALETTE WITH HAZELNUT-YOGHURT DRESSING

HYATT CANCUN CARIBE RESORT & VILLAS, MEXICO

SERVES 4

PAINTER'S PALETTE

2 ⅓ lb watermelon (1 kg)

3 large mangoes

6 oz (2 medium) pitaya or cactus pear (170 g)

12 oz (2 medium) oranges (340 g)

1 lb (½ medium) cantaloupe (455 g)

3–4 fresh mint leaves—for garnish

Peel the fruit, remove stones or pips and cut in different shapes.

Creatively arrange assorted fruits on individual plates and garnish with mint leaves.

Serve with the hazelnut-yoghurt dressing (recipe follows).

Note: Pitaya or cactus pear are fruits of Mexican cactus. Any other tropical fruit of choice may be substituted.

HAZELNUT-YOGHURT DRESSING

8 fl oz (1 c) plain yoghurt (237 ml)

3 ½ oz (¾ c) hazelnuts (filberts)— chopped (100 g)

juice of ½ lime

1 fl oz (2 tbs) honey (30 ml)

Combine ingredients and mix well.

Perroquet Poché Dans Son Court-Bouillion au Gingembre
Parrotfish Poached in a Ginger Court-Bouillon

Hyatt Regency Tahiti, French Polynesia

Serves 4

Poached Fish, Vegetables and Garnish

½ oz (1 tbs) ginger—julienned (15 g)

4 oz (2 medium) carrots—peeled and sliced into thin rounds (115 g)

4 oz (1 small) courgette (zucchini)—sliced into thin rounds (115 g)

4 oz (1 small) turnip—tournéed (115 g)

4 oz green beans (115 g)

1 ¾ lb parrotfish (795 g)

1 lemon—in wedges for garnish

4 leaves basil—for garnish

Blanch vegetables separately in salted boiling water. Cool in ice water and let dry.

Bring the court-bouillon (recipe follows) to barely a simmer (do not boil) and gently poach the fish until cooked.

Carefully transfer fish (without breaking it) into a big, oval serving dish.

Quickly dip the vegetables in hot court-bouillon to heat them through.

Arrange vegetables over or around the fish, with a little court-bouillon poured on top. Garnish with lemon wedges and basil leaves.

1 ¾ pt (4 ¼ c) water (1 *l*)

4 oz (1 medium) onion—cubed (115 g)

2 oz (1 medium) carrot—cubed (55 g)

2 oz (1 stalk) celery—cubed (55 g)

3–4 sprigs parsley

8 black peppercorns

1 fl oz (2 tbs) white wine vinegar (30 ml)

12 fl oz (1 ½ c) dry white wine (355 ml)

½ oz (1 tbs) salt (15 g)

1 oz (2 tbs) fresh ginger—peeled and sliced (30 g)

Place all ingredients in a stockpot and bring to a boil. Simmer for 30 minutes.

○

Strain and reserve liquid; discard solids.

Note: Parrotfish live in warm waters and their harvest is restricted in some parts of the world. If unavailable, substitute pompano.

To tournée, from the French meaning "to turn," refers to cutting vegetables into a regular form for uniform cooking. The vegetable is turned as it is cut.

FILETES DE HAUCHINANGO POCHADOS CON LEGUMBRES AL NATURAL
POACHED RED SNAPPER FILLETS WITH RAW VEGETABLES

○

HYATT REGENCY ACAPULCO, MEXICO
SERVES 4

1 lb red snapper fillet (455 g)

2 fl oz (4 tbs) orange juice (60 ml)

2 fl oz (4 tbs) lemon juice (60 ml)

1 ¾ pt (3 ½ c) water (1 *l*)

6 drops vinegar

2 oz sprigs parsley

2 oz (1 stalk) celery (55 g)

3 oz seasonal fruits—sliced into bite-size pieces (85 g)

3 oz (¾ c) button mushrooms—sliced (85 g)

1 ½ oz bean sprouts (45 g)

1 ½ lb (4 medium) tomatoes—sliced into thin wedges (680 g)

8 oz (2 c) cottage cheese (225 g)

Marinate the fish fillets in a mixture of the orange and lemon juice.

○

In a large pot, bring water to a boil. Add parsley sprigs and celery stalk.

○

Lower heat to a bare simmer and poach fish for 5 minutes.

○

Transfer to serving plates.

○

Arrange the fruits, vegetables and cottage cheese attractively around fish fillets.

Yoghurt-Marinated Chicken and Vegetable Skewers
with Yellow Lentils

Hyatt Regency Manila, Philippines

Serves 4

Chicken and Marinade

1 lb boneless chicken breast—cut into 1-inch (2.5 cm) cubes (450 g)

3 ½ oz (⅓ c) yoghurt (100 g)

3 fl oz (6 tbs) olive oil (90 ml)

pinch (1 tbs) fresh rosemary (2 g)

pinch (1 tbs) fresh basil chopped (2 g)

pinch (1 ½ tsp) fresh thyme (2 g)

½ oz (1 clove) garlic—peeled and chopped (15 g)

1 fl oz honey (30 ml)

zest of 1 lime—diced

salt and pepper to taste

Combine all ingredients, except chicken to create marinade.

○

Using half the marinade, combine with chicken, and marinate for at least 2 hours.

○

Drain chicken.

○

Arrange chicken on skewers and grill over charcoal fire on both sides till done; about 5 minutes.

Vegetable Skewers

1 ½ oz (½ small) red bell pepper—cut into 1 ½-inch (about 4 cm) cubes (45 g)

1 ½ oz (1 small) green bell pepper—cut into 1 ½-inch (about 4 cm) cubes (45g)

8 button mushrooms—stems removed

3 oz (1 small) tomato—quartered (85 g)

4 ½ oz (3 large) white part of leeks—cut into 1 ½-inch (about 4 cm) strips (130 g)

Place the vegetables in remaining marinade (see Chicken recipe).

○

Marinate for at least 2 hours.

○

Arrange the vegetables alternately on wooden skewers. Grill on both sides along with chicken.

Lentils

⅓ oz (2 tsp) butter (10 g)

½ oz (1 tbs) onions—diced (15 g)

1 ¾ fl oz (3 ½ tbs) dry white wine (50 ml)

14 fl oz (1 ¾ c) chicken stock (415 ml) (see glossary)

3 ½ oz (1 c) yellow lentils—soaked in cold water for at least 2 hours and drained (100 g)

In a saucepan, sauté onion in butter till transparent.

○

Add wine and reduce by ½.

○

Add chicken stock and lentils, and simmer covered until tender, stirring occasionally and cooking until stock is absorbed, about 45 minutes.

To Serve

4 sprigs fresh coriander

Arrange the chicken and vegetable skewers side by side on 4 individual plates.

○

Garnish with coriander sprigs and serve with lentils.

Sate Sayuran Dengan Saos Kacang

Vegetable Satay with Peanut Sauce

⌒

Bali Hyatt, Indonesia
Serves 4

Satay

4 oz (1 medium) tomato—cut in wedges (115 g)

4 oz (½ medium) cucumber (115 g)

4 oz (1 c) button mushrooms (115 g)

4 oz (1 medium) red bell pepper (115 g)

4 oz (1 medium) turnip (115 g)

4 oz (1 medium) carrots (115 g)

4 oz (1 small) courgette (zucchini) (115 g)

juice of 3 limes

salt and pepper to taste

Cut the cucumber, pepper, turnip, carrots and courgette into large cubes.

⌒

Mix in a bowl with tomato wedges and mushrooms.

⌒

Pour in lime juice, sprinkle with salt and pepper and marinate for several hours.

⌒

Drain the vegetables and place alternately on wooden skewers. Barbecue over charcoal grill for 2–3 minutes. Serve with peanut sauce (recipe follows) and steamed rice.

Peanut Sauce

1 lb raw peanuts or ground nuts— shelled and skinned (450 g) vegetable oil—for deep-frying

1 ¾ fl oz (3 ½ tbs) peanut oil (52 ml)

2 oz (4 cloves) garlic—chopped (55 g)

¾ oz (1 small) fresh red chilli— chopped and pips removed (20 g)

1 ½ oz (¼ c) brown sugar (45 g)

1 oz (2 tbs) black bean paste (30 g)

1 stalk lemongrass—crushed

¾ fl oz (1 ½tbs) sweet soy sauce (22ml)

1 ¼ pt (2 ½ c) coconut milk (590 ml) (see glossary)

salt to taste

⅓ oz (1 tsp) cardamom—crushed (10 g)

Deep-fry peanuts in vegetable oil until golden brown.

⌒

Grind nuts in a mortar and pestle or liquidiser. Set aside.

⌒

Heat peanut oil and sauté garlic, chillies, and cardamom for 2 minutes.

⌒

Add brown sugar, bean paste, lemongrass and soy sauce.

⌒

Stir until sugar dissolves, then add ground nuts and sauté for another 2 minutes.

⌒

Pour in coconut milk, bring to a boil, then simmer, stirring constantly, for approximately 12 minutes.

⌒

Discard lemongrass and season sauce with salt.

Note: Sweet soy sauce is an Indonesian ingredient, commonly called Kecap Manis. It is available in Asian groceries.

PECHUNGA DE POLLO CON PAPAYA
CHICKEN BREAST WITH PAPAYA

HYATT REGENCY ACAPULCO, MEXICO

SERVES 4

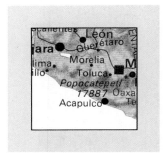

CHICKEN

8 fl oz (1 c) orange juice (237 ml)

1 ½ lb (4 large) chicken breasts halved—skinless and boneless (600 g)

1 ½ fl oz (3 tbs) vinegar (45 ml)

Mix the orange juice and vinegar in a saucepan and simmer for 5 minutes.

Poach chicken breasts in mixture until cooked, about 15 minutes.

Remove chicken breasts and reserve cooking liquid.

PAPAYA

14 oz (1 large) papaya (395 g)

8 fl oz (1 c) orange juice (237 ml)

Peel papaya, halve, remove pips and cut flesh into large cubes.

Briefly poach papaya cubes in orange juice.

Drain and reserve poaching liquid.

GARNISH AND SAUCE

8 oz (2 c) white rice (225 g)

1 leek—thinly sliced

Cook rice and keep warm.

Combine and simmer the poaching liquids of the chicken and papaya; reduce by ½.

Place chicken breasts and papaya cubes on individual plates.

Garnish with sliced leek.

Serve with rice and drizzle sauce over chicken.

Blanc de Volaille aux Poivrons Rouges
Breast of Chicken with Red Pepper

⟁

The Carlton Tower, A Park Hyatt Hotel, London, United Kingdom
Serves 4

4 oz (1 medium) red bell pepper (115 g)

1 lb (4 medium) chicken breasts— boneless and skinless (455 g)

salt and pepper to taste

8 green onions (scallions)

Roast red pepper in a hot 400° F (200° C) oven until skin blisters.

Discard skin and seeds.

Place pepper in a liquidiser to purée.

Season chicken breasts with salt and pepper and grill until done, about 10 minutes.

Spread red pepper purée on a plate.

Arrange chicken breasts on top and garnish with green onions.

LATTICE OF OCEAN AND CORAL TROUT

◯

HYATT REGENCY SANCTUARY COVE, QUEENSLAND, AUSTRALIA
SERVES 4

TROUT

10 oz ocean trout fillets (280 g)

10 oz coral or salmon trout fillet (280 g)

½ pt (1 c) fish stock (240 ml) (see glossary)

4 ½ oz spinach—trimmed and washed (120 g)

¾ oz (1 ½ tbs) butter (20 g)

Preheat oven to 400°F (200°C)

◯

Cut fillets in half lengthwise, then flatten with flat side of a knife until a little less than ½ inch (1 cm) thick. Cut each piece into 8 uniform strips ½ inch (1 cm) by 5 inches (12 cm).

◯

Weave alternating strips in 4 lattice patterns and place on buttered baking dish with stock. Poach in oven for 10 minutes or until firm.

◯

Blanch spinach in boiling water for 10 seconds. Drain, and immediately refresh in cold water.

◯

Sauté spinach in butter and arrange on individual plates.

◯

Place fish lattice over spinach, surround with noisette potatoes and spoon on coulis (recipes follow).

COULIS

7 oz (2 small) red bell peppers (200 g)

8 fl oz (1 c) fish stock (200 ml)

1 ½ oz (3 tbs) lemon juice (45 ml)

salt and pepper to taste

Cook pepper in stock until soft, about 3 minutes.

◯

Season with salt, pepper and lemon juice.

◯

Purée in a liquidiser and strain through a fine sieve. Keep warm.

NOISETTE POTATOES

1 lb (12 small) potatoes (560 g)

Peel and wash potatoes.

◯

With a melon baller, scoop potatoes into small balls and cook in boiling water until done, about 3–4 minutes. Keep warm.

ROYAL MIKADO
WITH RICE CAKE

CENTURY HYATT TOKYO, JAPAN
SERVES 4

ROYAL

½ fl oz (1tbs) sake or dry white wine (15 ml)

3 oz chicken breast—boneless and skinless; diced (85 g)

3 eggs—beaten

¾ pt (2 c) milk—scalded (480 ml)

1 ½ oz cheese—your choice (45 g)

3 oz (½ medium) potato—peeled and boiled (85 g)

2 ¼ oz (½ c) green beans—blanched (60 g)

1 ½ oz (⅓ c) nuts—your choice (45 g)

salt and pepper to taste

Sprinkle sake over chicken.

Dice cheese, potato, beans and nuts.

Stream hot milk into beaten eggs. Whisk well, then add salt and pepper. Strain mixture through a cheesecloth.

Place chicken, vegetables, cheese and nuts into bottom of individual cups or ramekins.

Pour milk mixture into cups.

Cover each cup or ramekin with plastic wrap and place on steamer racks.

Put rack in steamer over hot water and steam until set, about 20 minutes.

Serve with rice cake (recipe follows).

RICE CAKE

8 oz (2 c) white rice—boiled (225 g)

1 fl oz (2 tbs) vinegar dressing (30 ml)

1 egg—beaten and fried; sliced into strips

1 ½ oz (3 tbs) green peas (45 g)

2 ¼ oz carrots—cooked and glazed with 1 tsp (2.5 g) sugar, then diced (60 g)

4 chestnuts—glazed and diced

1 ½ oz tofu—deep fried and diced (45 g) (see note)

Sprinkle dressing over rice, then stir in remaining ingredients.

Shape rice as shown in photo, then unmould onto plate.

Note: Sake is the traditional Japanese wine made from rice.
A simple vinegar dressing can be made by mixing 2 tbs (30 ml) vinegar with ½ tsp sugar and a pinch of salt.
Boneless ham can be used as an alternative to the tofu.

CABBAGE AND RICE POPIAH
WITH CRAB CREAM SAUCE

HYATT REGENCY SINGAPORE, SINGAPORE

SERVES 4

SUSHI

7 oz (2 ¾ c) cooked rice (200 g)

¾ oz (1 ½ tbs) Japanese pickles (20 g)

¼ oz (1 tsp) turmeric (5 g)

¾ oz (1 ½ tbs) sweet pickled ginger—sliced (20 g)

¾ oz (1 ½ tbs) corn kernels—cooked, fresh or canned (20 g)

¼ oz (½ stalk) spring onion (scallion)—sliced (5 g)

¾ oz (1 ½ tbs) pecan nuts—coarsely chopped (20 g)

¾ oz (1 ½ tbs) asparagus tips—cooked (20 g)

¼ small fresh red chilli—finely chopped

4 leaves Chinese cabbage (bok choy)

4 leaves nori

salt and pepper to taste

In a deep bowl, combine rice, pickles, turmeric, pickled ginger, corn, green onion, pecan nuts, asparagus and chilli.

○

Stir in 5 tbs (50 ml) crab cream sauce (see below) and salt and pepper to taste. Mix until blended.

○

In a wide pan, bring salted water to a boil.

○

Blanch cabbage leaves briefly till wilted.

○

Drain and immediately cool in ice water, then dry well.

○

Place a cabbage leaf on a sushi mat.

○

Cover with 1 sheet of nori.

○

Spread evenly about 2 oz (5 tbs; 60 g) of the rice mixture to edges of nori and roll up tightly; remove sushi mat.

○

Slice crosswise into 5 even pieces.

○

Repeat for remaining cabbage leaves, seaweed and rice mixture, to have 4 rolls, or 20 slices.

○

Serve with remaining sauce (below).

Note: Nori, or laver, is a Japanese seaweed most commonly used as the wrapping for sushi. It is available in Asian food stores.

Japanese pickles and pickled vegetables are sold in Asian markets.

CRAB CREAM SAUCE

4 fl oz (½ c) plain yoghurt (120 ml)

4 fl oz (½ c) sour cream (120 ml)

3 oz crabmeat (85 g)

4 oz (1 large) tomato—peeled, pips removed and sliced (115 g)

⅔ oz fresh coriander—chopped (7 g)

⅔ fl oz (4 tsp) tomato juice (20 ml)

salt and pepper to taste

Combine yoghurt and sour cream Add remaining and blend well.

○

Season to taste with salt and pepper.

Note: If desired, add some chopped chilli or Tabasco for a spicier sauce.

VEGETARIAN TERRINE

HYATT ON COLLINS, MELBOURNE, AUSTRALIA
SERVES 4

2 sheets gelatine or 1 envelope
   unflavoured, powdered gelatine

⅔ pt (1 ¼ c) sour cream (300 ml)

4 oz (1 medium) red bell pepper seeded
   and sliced crosswise (115 g)

4 broccoli flowerettes—blanched

8 oz (2 medium) tomatoes—pips
   removed and sliced crosswise (225 g)

16 thin green beans—blanched

8 ears baby (miniature) corn

9 baby carrots—blanched

In a saucepan, dissolve gelatine in sour
cream over low heat and keep warm.

Line a 1-pint triangular mould with
plastic wrap

Place broccoli flowerettes on bottom
and pour in a little of the sour cream
mixture.

Chill until lightly set.

Repeat this step, laying in the red
pepper rings, beans, tomato, corn and
carrots, placing a layer of sour cream
between each and chilling lightly after
each layer.

Cover and chill until set.

Serve with a light salad or vegetable
dressing or your choice.

*Note: Miniature corn is sold in jars in
   Asian markets.*

SPINACH AND MUSHROOM SALAD
WITH STEAMED PRAWNS IN A TOMATO AND COTTAGE CHEESE VINAIGRETTE

HYATT REGENCY PERTH, AUSTRALIA

SERVES 4

SALAD

24 spinach leaves—trimmed washed and dried

28 king or jumbo prawns—steamed, peeled and deveined

2 fl oz (2 tsp) lemon juice (60 ml)

16 (medium) button mushrooms—sliced

15 (small) oyster mushrooms—halved

Arrange spinach on individual plates.

Neatly adorn with the prawns.

Mix lemon juice with the mushrooms and distribute among plates.

Drizzle vinaigrette (recipe following) over salad and serve.

VINAIGRETTE

4 oz (1 medium) tomato—peeled, pips removed and chopped (115 g)

1 ½ oz (⅓ c) cottage cheese (40 g)

4 fl oz (½ c) vegetable oil (120 ml)

2 fl oz (4 tbs) white wine vinegar (60 ml)

1 tsp lemon juice (5 ml)

salt and pepper to taste

Mix ingredients until well blended.

CHICKEN BREASTS WITH TURMERIC YOGHURT

HYATT AUCKLAND, NEW ZEALAND

SERVES 4

1 pt (2 c) low-fat, plain yoghurt (475 ml)

½ oz (1 tbs) turmeric (15 g)

⅓ oz (2 tsp) garlic—chopped (10 g)

⅓ oz (2 tsp) fresh ginger—chopped (10 g)

1 lb (4 medium) chicken breasts—halves skinless and boneless (450 g)

⅔ oz (4 tbs) onion—chopped (20 g)

⅔ oz (4 tsp) polyunsaturated margarine (20 g)

¾ fl (1 ½ tbs) chicken stock (20 ml) (see glossary)

Make marinade by combining yoghurt, turmeric, garlic and ginger.

Coat chicken breasts with marinade and refrigerate for 24 hours.

Sauté onion in margarine without browning.

Add stock and reduce by ½.

Drain chicken breasts (reverse marinade), then add to pan and simmer about 15 minutes.

Lower heat and add the yoghurt marinade. Stir constantly ensuring that the sauce simmers for a few seconds (do not boil or sauce will curdle).

Arrange chicken breasts neatly on 4 warm plates.

Coat chicken with half the sauce and serve remainder on side.

CHICKEN AND BANANA

WITH CURRY SAUCE

HYATT REGENCY SANCTUARY COVE, AUSTRALIA

SERVES 4

CHICKEN

1 lb (4 medium) chicken breast halves—skinless and boneless (455 g)

5 ½ oz (2 small) bananas—peeled and mashed (155 g)

1 pt (2 c) chicken stock (475 ml) (see glossary)

10 oz (1 small) spaghetti squash—cooked until tender (285 g)

2 oz (½ medium) green bell pepper—julienned and blanched (55 g)

2 oz (½ medium) red bell pepper—julienned and blanched (55 g)

1 oz (2 tbs) butter (30 g)

salt and pepper to taste

3 ½ oz (⅔ c) wild rice—cooked until tender but firm (100 g)

3 ½ oz (⅔ c) long-grain rice—cooked until tender (100 g)

5 ¼ oz (1 ¼ c) snow peas—blanched (145 g)

Flatten chicken breasts and spread mashed banana over each piece; roll and tie with string. Poach rolled breasts in chicken stock until cooked, about 8 minutes.

○

Mix spaghetti squash and peppers, then sauté in butter. Season and arrange on a platter.

○

Slice chicken rolls on the bias and arrange over the vegetables.

○

Mix the rice and heat in remaining butter. Season and press into 8 oz (1 c ; 240 ml) moulds or ramekins. Unmould and decorate with snow peas and serve with sauce (recipe follows).

Note: Spaghetti squash is a yellow winter squash that, when cooked, has an interior that shreds to resemble spaghetti.

CURRY SAUCE

¼ oz (1 ½ tsp) curry powder (8 g)

1 ½ oz (½ small) onion—chopped (40 g)

1 ½ fl oz (3 tbs) dry white wine (40 ml)

2 ½ fl oz (5 tbs) chicken stock (80 ml) (see glossary)

2 ½ oz (½ c) plain yoghurt (60 g)

In a small saucepan, combine curry powder, onion, wine and chicken stock.

○

Place over moderate heat and reduce until slightly thickened.

○

Remove from heat and stir in yoghurt slowly.

○

Pour into a liquidiser and purée until smooth.

PINEAPPLE JUICE-POACHED QUAILS
WITH FRUIT AND GINGER SAUCE

HYATT REGENCY HONG KONG, HONG KONG
SERVES 4

24 quail breasts

3 ½ pt (8 ½ c) pineapple juice (2 *l*)

8 oz (2 c) fresh ginger—peeled and grated (200 g)

8 oz (2 medium) green apples—peeled and diced (225 g)

4 oz (2 medium) apricots—peeled and sliced (115 g)

8 fl oz (1 c) plain yoghurt (240 ml)

½ oz (1 clove) garlic—chopped (15 g)

8 fl oz (1 c) milk (200 ml)

4 oz (1 c) chives—chopped (115 g)

24 raisins

4 oz (1 medium) red bell pepper—cored and chopped for garnish (115g)

4 chervil leaves—for garnish

1 slice ginger—julienned, for garnish

Poach quail breasts in pineapple juice for 7 minutes. Remove and keep warm.

Blend ginger with a little pineapple juice to form a paste of a mousse consistency, then add apples and apricots. Set aside.

Blend yoghurt, garlic and milk in a liquidiser, then strain.

Add chives and raisins to yoghurt mixture, and heat until warm. Do not allow to boil.

Arrange 6 quail breasts on each plate. Pour on sauce and garnish with red pepper, chervil and ginger.

ESSENZ VON GEFLÜGEL MIT KLEINEN GEMÜSEN
CHICKEN POT AU FEU

HYATT REGENCY COLOGNE, GERMANY
SERVES 4

14 oz (2 medium) chicken breast
halves—skinless and boneless
(400 g)

1 ½ pt (3 ½ c) chicken stock (800 ml)
(see glossary)

5 ½ oz (⅔ c) carrots (160 g)

5 ½ oz (⅔ c) white turnip (160 g)

8 oz (2 medium) potatoes (320 g)

5 ½ oz (⅔ c) snow peas—blanched,
drained (160 g)

6 oz (⅔ c) spinach—trimmed, washed,
blanced, drained (160 g)

Poach chicken in stock until cooked,
about 10 minutes.

Slice or cut chicken into strips or
cubes. Reserve stock.

Dice carrots, turnips and potatoes.
Blanch in stock until tender but firm,
about 5 minutes.

Arrange vegetables in layers on both
upper ends of an oval baking dish.

Add chicken to center and fill with
stock.

Garnish with herbs and serve.

Tahu Buah dan Kaoang Dalam Kulit
Tofu, Fruit and Nuts in a Tortilla Shell

Hyatt Aryaduta Jakarta, Indonesia

Serves 4

8 oz (2 medium) apples (225 g)

3 ½ oz (¾ c) pineapple—fresh, cubed (100 g)

3 ½ oz (¾ c) papaya—cubed (100 g)

3 ½ oz (¾ c) honeydew melon—cubed (100 g)

3 ½ oz (¾ c) strawberries—washed, hulled and quartered (100 g)

3 ½ oz (¾ c) dark grapes—halved (100 g)

5 ½ oz (1 ¼ c) walnuts (145 g)

5 ¼ oz (1 ¼ c) hazelnuts (filberts) (145 g)

1 ¾ lb tofu—cubed (795 g)
4 corn tortillas

⅜ pt (¾ c) honey (175 ml)

juice of 4 limes

4 fresh mint leaves—for garnish

Peel and core the apples, then cut into small cubes.

Mix apples with other fruit in a large bowl.

Crush the nuts and add to fruit along with the tofu.

Deep-fry the tortillas until golden brown. While still warm, shape into cups and let cool.

Place the fruit mixture in the tortilla shells and put 1 shell on each plate.

Mix the honey and lime juice, then drizzle on top of fruit.

Garnish with mint leaves.

Chicken Breast in a Light Ginger Sauce

Hyatt Regency Pusan, Korea

Serves 4

1 pt (2 c) chicken stock (475 ml) (see glossary)

⅓ oz (2 tsp) ginger—minced (10 g)

1 ½ lb (4 medium) chicken breast halves—boned and skinned (680 g)

1 tsp vegetable oil (5 ml)

3 oz (1 small) red bell pepper—julienned (85 g)

3 oz (1 small) green bell pepper—julienned (85 g)

3 oz (¾ c) bean sprouts (80 g)

2 fl oz (4 tbs) oyster sauce (60 ml)

1 tsp cornflour (cornstarch)—dissolved in 1 tsp (5 ml) water

1 stalk green onion (scallion)—minced—for garnish

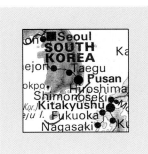

Boil chicken stock with ginger for 5 minutes to flavour.

Lower heat to a simmer and poach chicken breasts until cooked, about 7 minutes.

In a sauté pan, heat oil and sauté the peppers and sprouts until fragrant, about 3 minutes.

Remove from pan and set aside.

Add 6 tsp (90 ml) of stock and the oyster sauce to the sauté pan.

Bring to a boil, lower heat and simmer for 2 minutes, then thicken with the cornflour mixture.

Remove pan from heat and add the sautéed vegetables.

Divide vegetable mixture among 4 plates.

Arrange chicken breasts on vegetables and garnish with green onion.

VEGETARIAN

Oriental Salad

Hyatt Regency Dubai, United Arab Emirates
Serves 4

3 ½ oz (1 small) green bell pepper—halved, pips removed and cut into strips (100 g)

½ oz (1 tbs) mint leaves (15 g)

½ oz (1 tbs) fresh parsley (15 g)

3 oz (3 medium) radishes—sliced thinly, crosswise (85 g)

10 ½ oz (2 large) tomatoes—cubed (300 g)

3 ½ oz (1 c) romaine lettuce—shredded (100 g)

½ oz (1 small clove) garlic—pounded (15 g)

3 ½ fl oz (7 tbs) olive oil (105 ml)

1 fl oz (2 tbs) lemon juice (30 ml)

1 oz (2 tbs) salt (30 g)

Mix pepper, mint, parsley, radishes, tomatoes, lettuce and onion.

Season with garlic, olive oil, lemon juice and salt.

Toss gently and serve.

Coconut-Spiced Vegetables

Hyatt Aryaduta Jakarta, Indonesia
Serves 4

1 ¾ pt (3.5 c) water (1 *l* or less)

salt to taste

2 ½ lb assorted vegetables—julienned (1 kg)

⅓ oz (1 ½ tbs) cumin pips (10 g)

1 ½ oz (3 cloves) garlic—peeled

2 fresh chillies

5 curry leaves

6 fl oz (¾ c) coconut milk (see glossary) (180 ml)

3 ½ oz (¾ c) coconut—grated (100 g)

Note: Curry leaves are an Indian seasoning usually sold fresh but sometimes also available dried in Asian markets. It is not related to curry powder.

Pour the water, with a little salt, into a saucepan and bring to a boil. Cook each vegetable separately until just tender. Remove vegetables, but reserve water.

Pour (13 fl oz) (1 ⅔ c) 400 ml of the vegetable water into a liquidiser. Add cumin, garlic and chilli. Purée until fine.

Transfer mixture to a saucepan and add curry leaves. Simmer for 5 minutes.

Add the vegetables and heat through.

At the last minute, add coconut milk. Season to taste.

Arrange on plates and sprinkle with grated coconut.

PA JEON

KOREAN PANCAKES WITH RED CHILLI AND GREEN ONION STRIPS

HYATT REGENCY SEOUL, KOREA

SERVES 4

3 oz (3 small) green onions (scallions) (85 g)

3 eggs

5 oz (1 c) flour (150 g)

¼ pt (½ c) water—to make pancake batter (120 ml)

1 ¾ oz (⅓ c) bean sprouts (50 g)

oriental sesame oil, salt and chilli powder to taste

3 red chillies—cut in half, pips removed and cut into thin strips

1 oz (¼ c) fresh parsley (30 g)

Slice green onions in half lengthwise, and flatten each strip with the handle of a knife.

To make pancake batter, mix eggs with flour and slowly whisk in water until the batter is of a cream consistency.

Dip the green onions and sprouts in batter.

Fry with a little sesame oil until golden brown.

Add the remaining batter and cook for another 2–4 minutes without turning.

Sprinkle on red chilli strips and parsley.

Serve hot.

PULSE AND VEGETABLE CASSEROLE
IN APPLE BROTH

○

HYATT REGENCY JERUSALEM, ISRAEL
SERVES 4

PULSE AND VEGETABLE CASSEROLE

2 ¾ oz (⅓ c) **dried red kidney beans (75 g)**

2 ¾ oz (⅓ c) **dried chickpeas (75 g)**

2 ¾ oz (⅓ c) **green lentils (75 g)**

2 ¾ oz (⅓ c) **dried white beans (75 g)**

1 stalk **celery—cut into ¾-inch (2 cm) diamonds, save trimmings (60 g)**

6 oz (2 large) **carrots—cut into ¾-inch (2 cm) long tournées; save trimmings (170 g)**

8 oz (1 small) **cucumber—cut and tournéed same size as carrots; discard trimmings (225 g)**

8 oz (2 large) **potatoes—peeled and tournéed same size as carrots; discard trimmings (225 g)**

4 oz (1 medium) **red bell pepper— peeled and cut into ¾-inch (2 cm) pieces (115 g)**

4 oz (1 medium) **green bell pepper— peeled and cut into ¾-inch (2 cm) pieces (115 g)**

A day in advance, soak the pulses (beans, chickpeas and lentils) separately in cold water, then boil separately till tender.

○

Drain and rinse under cold tap water.

○

Drain again and mix.

○

Separately cook the fresh vegetables in boiling water until just tender. Drain and rinse under cold tap water.

○

Mix with beans. Set aside.

APPLE BROTH

1 fl oz (2 tbs) **olive oil (30 ml)**

8 oz (2 medium) **red apples—peeled and finely chopped (225 g)**

2 oz (½ medium) **onion—finely chopped (55 g)**

1 oz (2 cloves) **garlic—peeled and cut in half (30 g)**

¼ pt (½ c) **apple or cider vinegar (100 ml)**

¼ pt (½ c) **sweet white wine (100 ml)**

1 ¼ pt (3 c) **cold water (700 ml)**

2 tsp **arrowroot or cornflour (cornstarch) (10 g) dissolved in 1 tbs water (15 ml)**

Heat oil in a large saucepan. Add the vegetables, trimmings from casserole, apples, and onions. Cook without browning for 5 minutes.

○

Add vinegar and reduce until vinegar is almost evaporated, then add wine and reduce by half.

○

Add the cold water and reduce by half.

○

Thicken liquid with dissolved arrowroot, then pour through a sieve. Set aside.

TO SERVE

salt and pepper to taste

1 oz (2 tbs) **chives—chopped (30 g)**

¼ oz (1 ½ tsp) **mixed fresh herbs (7 g)**

Bring the broth to a boil and add casserole beans and vegetables. Simmer for 2–3 minutes.

○

Season with salt and pepper and add chives.

○

Pour mixture equally into 4 soup plates, then garnish with fresh herbs.

Note: Tournée, from the French verb "tourner" that means "to turn," referring to cutting vegetables into a regular form for uniform cooking. The vegetable is turned as it is cut.

Tahu Sumbat
Stuffed Tofu

〇

Hyatt Saujana, Kuala Lumpur, Malaysia
Serves 4

6 soft tofu squares, about ½ lb (225 g) each

vegetable oil—for deep-frying

7 oz (1 large) cucumber—julienned (200 g)

7 oz (1 small) yam—julienned (200 g) (see glossary)

10 oz fresh red chillies—minced (300 g)

7 oz (1 ¾ c) bean sprouts(200 g)

2 oz (4 tbs) fresh ginger—peeled and grated (55 g)

2 oz (4 cloves) garlic—minced (55 g)

3 fl oz (6 tbs) vinegar (90 ml)

2 oz (4 tbs) sugar (55g)

½ oz (1 tbs) salt (20 g)

Deep-fry tofu in oil until golden brown, about 5 minutes.

〇

Cut each into 4 triangles, then cut a well in centre of each triangle.

〇

Mix cucumber, yam and sprouts, then stuff the mixture into tofu triangles.

〇

Place triangles on individual plates.

〇

Mix chilli, ginger, garlic, vinegar, sugar and salt in a bowl. Serve on the side.

Lumpia Basam Sauce Taoco
Steamed Spring Roll with Vegetable Filling and Red Miso Sauce

Hyatt Regency Surabaya, Indonesia
Serves 4

Lumpia

2 fl oz (4 tbs) peanut oil (60 ml)

2 oz (1 medium) carrot—julienned (55 g)

2 oz (1 stalk) celery—julienned (55 g)

2 oz (1 medium) leek—julienned (55 g)

2 oz (½ c) bamboo shoots—julienned (55 g)

2 oz wood ears—soaked in warm water, drained and julienned (55 g) (see glossary)

2 oz (½ c) green cabbage—shredded (55 g)

2 oz (½ c) bean sprouts (55 g)

2 oz (½ medium) onion—thinly sliced (55 g)

1 fresh red chilli—pips removed and chopped

1 fresh green chilli—pips removed and chopped

4 oz glass (cellophane) noodles—soaked in water until soft and then drained (115 g)

salt and pepper to taste

8 large lumpia or egg roll wrappers

20 celery leaves—for garnish

In a wok, heat oil and stir-fry vegetables and chillies until tender.

○

Add noodles and salt and pepper and stir-fry for another minute. Allow to cool.

○

Set aside ¼ of this mixture.

○

Divide remainder among lumpia wrappers and roll each like a cigar. Place 5 rolls on a steamer rack and steam for 4–5 minutes.

○

Arrange lumpia on plates (2 rolls per plate), and serve with reserved vegetable mixture. Garnish with celery leaves and serve sauce (recipe follows) on the side.

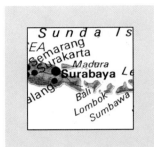

Red Miso Sauce

3 ½ oz (¾ c) red miso beans (100 g)

1 (1 lbs) fresh red chilli (30 g)

¾ oz (1 ½ tbs) brown sugar (20 g)

1 oz (1 large) shallot—peeled and diced (30 g)

⅓ oz (1 clove) garlic—peeled and diced (10 g)

4 oz (1 large) tomato—peeled and diced (115 g)

Place ingredients in a liquidiser and purée until smooth.

Note: Miso is soybean paste, used as a seasoning. It comes in varying shades, from cream to dark brown. It is available in Asian markets and health food stores. Lumpia or egg roll wrappers are available in Asian markets.

VEGETABLE TART IN BELL PEPPER SABAYON

HYATT REGENCY SINGAPORE, SINGAPORE

SERVES 4

TART

1 fl oz (2 tbs) olive oil (30 ml)

¾ oz (1 large clove) garlic—minced (20 g)

1 oz (¼ c) shallots—minced (30 g)

¼ oz (½ tsp) fresh basil—minced (7 g)

14 oz assorted garden vegetables— cubed, julienned or cut in rounds (400 g)

12 sheets phyllo dough

3 ½ oz (7 tbs) butter—melted (100 g)

2 dashes butter flakes

2 oz (½ c) grated Parmesan cheese (55 g) (optional)

Note: Butter flakes are dried, granular butter bits, used for flavouring.

Preheat oven to 375 °F (185 °C). Mix olive oil, garlic, shallots, and fresh basil. Set aside.

Blanch vegetables until al dente, drain and cool in ice water. Drain.

With a brush, butter the phyllo sheets, then cut into 6–8 inch (15–20 cm) rounds. Lay sheets into an 8-inch (20 cm) tart pan.

Brush top layer of phyllo pastry with the olive oil mixture.

Arrange vegetables on top and sprinkle with butter flakes.

Bake until pastry is crisp and golden brown, about 25 minutes.

Sprinkle vegetables with grated cheese if desired. Serve sauce separately (recipe follows).

3 egg yolks

1 ¾ fl oz (3 ½ tbs) dry white wine (50 ml)

1 ¾ fl oz (3 ½ tbs) vegetable stock (50 ml) (see glossary)

1 ¾ fl oz (3 ½ tbs) red pepper purée (50 ml)

1 ½ oz (½ small) red bell pepper—pips removed, finely diced (45 g)

salt and pepper to taste

¼ oz (1 ½ tsp) fresh basil—chopped (7 g)

In a bowl, whisk the yolks, wine and stock.

○

Place the bowl over barely simmering water and whisk vigorously until foamy and thickened.

○

Just before serving, add pepper purée and diced pepper.

○

Season with salt, pepper and basil.

Note: Red pepper purée is made by placing peeled roasted red bell peppers in a liquidiser and blending until smooth.

TAHU KERING BERSAYOR
DRIED BEAN CURD ROULADE

○

HYATT KUANTAN, MALAYSIA
SERVES 4

8 tofu sheets

4 oz spinach—trimmed, cleaned and cooked (115 g)

4 oz (2 medium) carrots—julienned (115 g)

1 oz sweet turnip—julienned (30 g)

6 oz celery—julienned (170 g)

6 oz bean sprouts (170 g)

½ fl oz (1 tbs) vegetable oil (15 ml)

1 oz (2 tbs) curry powder (10 g)

½ oz (1 tbs) salt (15 g)

8 fl oz (1 c) cream sauce of choice (240 ml)

Note: Tofu sheets are sold fresh, frozen or dried. They usually come in large folded rounds.

Blanch the tofu sheets in boiling water until soft.

○

Drain and lay out on flat surface.

○

Spread spinach on top.

○

Sauté the julienned vegetables and bean sprouts in oil until soft. Add the curry powder and salt; mix well.

○

Spread on sheets and roll up like spring rolls.

○

Slice rolls diagonally and serve with cream sauce of choice.

Vegetable Plate with Tofu

Hyatt Regency Saipan, Mariana Islands

Serves 4

Tofu and Vegetables

1 ½ lb tofu—sliced into 1-inch cubes (680 g)

2 ½ oz (½ c) flour (70 g)

2 eggs—beaten

4 oz (1 medium) red bell pepper—pips removed and sliced (115 g)

4 oz (1 medium) onion—sliced (115 g)

4 oz green beans—strings removed, sliced (115 g)

4 oz (2 stalks) celery—sliced (115 g)

4 oz (1 medium) yellow bell pepper—pips removed and sliced (115 g)

Garnish

4 cherry tomatoes

4 sprigs rosemary

4 sprigs thyme

4 sprigs basil

4 leaf red-leaf lettuce

1 green onion—cut in rings

Dip tofu cubes in flour, then in the beaten eggs.

Pan-fry in olive oil until golden brown, about 5 minutes. Set aside.

Heat pan and sauté onion and beans for about 30 seconds.

Add remaining vegetables and sauté 1 minute more.

Place vegetables on serving plate with tofu on top.

Garnish with cherry tomatoes and herb sprigs, lettuce and green onions.

GEFÜLLTE ARTISCHOCKE MIT TOFU
TOFU STUFFED ARTICHOKES

HYATT REGENCY COLOGNE, GERMANY

SERVES 4

ARTICHOKES

1 lb (4 large) artichokes (455 g)

1 ½ fl oz (3 tbs) olive oil (45 ml)

1 ¾ pt (4 ¼ c) vegetable stock (1 *l*) (see glossary)

¼ pt (½ c) dry white wine (120 ml)

salt to taste

Place olive oil, wine and stock in a pot. Add salt and bring to a boil.

Add artichokes; cook about 45 minutes.

Discard leaves, remove artichokes and set aside artichoke bottoms. Keep warm.

TOFU AND VEGETABLES

4 oz broccoli flowerettes (115 g)

4 oz cauliflower flowerettes (115 g)

4 oz (2 small) carrots—julienned (115 g)

4 oz snow peas (115 g)

4 oz asparagus—sliced 1-inch (2.5 cm) long (115 g)

1 ½ oz (3 tbs) butter (45 g)

4 oz tofu—sliced into strips, ⅓ x 2 ⅓-inches (1x6 cm) (115 g)

½ fl oz (1 tbs) vegetable oil (15 ml)

¾ pt (2 c) white wine sauce (480 ml) (see glossary)

2 fl oz (4 tbs) pesto (60 ml) (see glossary)

8 fl oz (1 c) double (heavy) cream—whipped (240 ml)

Blanch vegetables and drain well.

Sauté in butter until tender. Keep warm.

Sauté tofu strips in oil until lightly browned.

Heat white wine sauce with pesto in a saucepan. Cook until reduced and thickened.

Fold in whipped cream. Keep warm.

Place artichoke bottoms on individual plates.

Spoon vegetables over artichokes.

Spoon sauce alongside and arrange tofu on top.

Soufflé de Pimiento Morron
Sweet Pepper Vegetable Souffle

⌒

Hyatt Regency Acapulco, Mexico
Serves 4

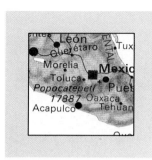

1 lb (4 large) red bell peppers (455 g)

vegetable oil for frying

7 oz (½ head) broccoli flowerettes (200 g)

5 ¼ oz (2 medium) carrots—peeled and cubed (145 g)

4 ½ oz (1 medium) turnip—peeled and cubed (130 g)

1 ¾ pt (4 ¼ c) double (heavy) cream (1 l)

¾ oz fresh coriander—chopped (20 g)

3 serrano or other hot chillies—diced

2 egg yolks

salt and pepper to taste

3 egg whites

3 ½ oz (¾ c) Parmesan cheese (100 g)

Lightly fry the peppers in oil until skins blister.

⌒

Remove skin, halve lengthwise, discard vein and pips and set aside.

⌒

Briefly blanch the vegetables in boiling water and drain.

⌒

Heat the cream and add the vegetables.

⌒

Cook until the vegetables are tender, about 5 minutes.

⌒

Preheat oven to 400° F (200° C).

⌒

Pour mixture into a liquidiser, add the coriander and chilli, blend until smooth.

⌒

Transfer to a large bowl and whisk in egg yolks, salt and pepper.

⌒

Beat egg whites until stiff; fold into vegetable mixture.

⌒

Arrange bell pepper halves in large baking dish and fill each with soufflé mixture until approximately ¾ full.

⌒

Sprinkle on cheese and bake for 15 minutes, or until set and lightly browned.

⌒

Serve with watercress sauce (receipe follows) and garnish with vegetables, if desired.

Watercress Sauce

10 ½ oz watercress (300 g)

1 ¾ pt (4 ¼ c) cream (1 l)

6 fl oz (¾ c) vegetable stock (180 ml) (see glossary)

½ oz (1 tbs) cornflour (cornstarch) (15 g)—dissolved in 1 tbs water (15 ml)

salt and pepper to taste

Blanch watercress briefly in boiling water and refresh in cold water.

⌒

Drain, put in a towel and squeeze well; place in a liquidiser and purée.

⌒

Heat the cream and stock and reduce by ⅓ over high heat.

⌒

Stir in the cornflour mixture to thicken and season with salt and pepper.

CABBAGE STUFFED
WITH STIR-FRIED VEGETABLES

○

HYATT ARYADUTA JAKARTA, INDONESIA

SERVES 4

2 fl oz (4 tbs) vegetable oil (60 ml)

1 oz (2 cloves) garlic—crushed (30 g)

⅓ oz (1 ½ tsp) ginger—fresh, peeled and grated (10 g)

14 oz (4-6 small) courgettes (zucchini)—sliced into rings or julienned (400 g)

14 oz (7 medium) carrots—sliced into rings or julienned (400 g)

14 oz bean sprouts (400 g)

14 oz broccoli flowerettes (400 g)

1 fl oz (2 tbs) oriental sesame oil (30 ml)

salt and pepper to taste

5 ½ oz red cabbage leaves (155 g)

5 ½ oz green cabbage leaves (155 g)

4 vine leaves

1 ⅓ lb (4 large) bell peppers—pips removed and cubed (605 g)

10 ½ oz (2 large) tomatoes—pips removed and cubed (300 g)

8 fl oz (1 c) vegetable stock (240 ml) (see glossary)

3 oz (¾ c) sweet corn kernels (85 g)

3 oz (1 large) leek—julienned (85 g)

In a wok, heat oil and stir-fry the garlic and ginger for 1 minute. Add the vegetables, stirring frequently. Add sesame oil, salt and pepper.

○

Blanch the cabbage leaves briefly in salted boiling water. Rinse under cold water. Dry slightly.

○

Lay each cabbage leaf and vine leaf out flat. Place equal amounts of stir-fried vegetables in the middle of each leaf and roll into different shapes as desired.

○

To make the sauce, purée the pepper and tomatoes in a liquidiser. Add a little stock until the desired consistency has been reached. Season to taste.

○

To serve, steam the stuffed leaves, corn and leek until tender; about 5 minutes.

○

Pour some on each plate. Arrange the different stuffed shapes over sauce and garnish with corn and leek.

CREAMED AUBERGINE WITH VEGETABLE STRUDEL

HYATT REGENCY JEDDAH, SAUDI ARABIA
SERVES 4

VEGETABLE STRUDEL

4 sheets phyllo dough, about 9x14 inches (22x35 cm)

¼ pt (½ c) olive oil (120 ml)

8 oz (3 c) cooked rice (200 g)

2 fl oz (4 tbs) soy sauce or tomato juice (60 ml)

6 oz (1 ½ c) blanched vegetables of your choice (170 g)

Preheat oven to 350° F (180° C).

With a pastry brush, brush some olive oil on phyllo sheets and stack.

Mix the cooked rice with soy sauce or tomato juice.

Spread rice mixture evenly on the phyllo, leaving a 1-inch (2.5 cm) margin on edges.

Spread vegetables over ⅔ of the rice and roll up tightly in a cylinder.

Brush phyllo with more oil and place in a lightly oiled tray. Bake for approximately 10–15 minutes, or until golden brown.

Cut the roll into pieces 1-inch (2.5 cm) thick, and serve with creamed aubergine.

2 lb (2 large) aubergines (egg plants) (900 g)

1 oz (2 cloves) garlic—peeled (30 g)

3 fl oz (6 tbs) tahina (90 ml) (see glossary)

3 fl oz (6 tbs) lemon juice (90 ml)

1 tsp salt (5 g)

Roast the aubergine in a very hot oven or over a charcoal grill until the skins darken and blister.

○

Peel off skin and put flesh in a colander to drain.

○

Cut up flesh and place in a food processor with remaining ingredients.

○

Blend to a smooth paste. If mixture is too thick, add a little water.

TAHU GORENG BERSUMBAT
STUFFED FRIED TOFU

○

HYATT KUANTAN, MALAYSIA
SERVES 4

STUFFED TOFU

1 oz (¼ c) carrots—julienned (15 g)

1 oz (¼ c) sweet turnips—julienned (15 g)

1 oz (¼ c) cucumbers—julienned (15 g)

1 oz (¼ c) bean sprouts—blanched (15 g)

4 tofu cakes, about 8 oz (225g) each—sliced

2 fl oz (4 tbs) vegetable oil (60 ml)

Combine vegetables in a bowl.

○

Fry the tofu slices in oil until golden brown. Drain.

○

Make "sandwiches" using vegetables as filling and serve with sauce (recipe follows).

SAUCE

1 ½ oz fresh red chilli (45 g)

⅓ oz (1 small clove) garlic—peeled (10 g)

½ oz (1 tbs) fresh ginger—peeled (15 g)

2 fl oz (4 tbs) distilled white vinegar (60 ml)

1 oz (2 tbs) sugar (30 g)

1 tsp salt (5 g)

Put chilli, garlic and ginger in a liquidiser and pulse lightly until minced.

○

Transfer to a bowl and add the vinegar, sugar and salt. Stir well.

Mousse de Coliflor y Poro Sombre Crema de Paprika
Leek and Cauliflower Mousse in Red Pepper Sauce

Hyatt Cancun Caribe Resort & Villas, Mexico

Serves 4

Mousse

1 lb cauliflower (500 g)

½ oz (1 tbs) butter (20 g)

3 fl oz (6 tbs) double (heavy) cream (118 ml)

salt, white pepper and nutmeg to taste

2 eggs

2 oz (1 large) leek (60 g)

vegetable oil—for deep-frying

Separate the cauliflower into flowerettes, then blanch for 1 minute in salted boiling water. Drain and cool in ice water. Drain again.

Melt butter in a pan and sauté the blanched cauliflower. Add cream, salt, pepper and nutmeg. Reduce by half.

Put cauliflower-cream mixture in liquidiser and purée.

Add eggs and purée until blended.

Pour mousse into a 1 ¾ pt (4 ¼ c; 1 *l*) dish and cover top with foil. Place dish in a pan of simmering water and poach for 40 minutes, or until firm.

Shred white part of leek and deep-fry in oil until crisp.

Unmould mousse and cut into wedges (as illustrated in photo). Place on a bed of red pepper sauce (recipe follows). Drizzle sauce on top to decorate as well. Garnish with leek and serve.

Red Pepper Sauce

½ oz (1 tbs) butter (15 g)

5 ¼ oz (1 large) red bell pepper—pips removed and chopped (145 g)

3 ½ oz (¾ c) shallots chopped (100 g)

6 fl oz (¾ c) dry white wine (180 ml)

2 fl oz (4 tbs) double (heavy) cream (60 ml)

salt and pepper to taste

Heat the butter and sauté the pepper and shallots until tender.

Add the wine and reduce by ⅔ over medium heat.

Put in a liquidiser and purée; strain through a fine sieve.

Add the cream and season with salt and pepper.

Pindaettok
Dried Pea Pancake

◯

Hyatt Regency Pusan, Korea
Serves 4

Pancake

8 oz (1 c) dried yellow peas—soaked in water for several hours (250 g)

4 oz (1 c) mustard sprouts (100 g)

4 oz (1 c) thin green beans (100 g)

2 oz (4 medium) spring onions (50 g)

1 oz (2 medium) carrots (20 g)

¾ oz (3 tbs) red bell pepper—pips removed and minced (20 g)

½ oz (1 clove) garlic—chopped (15 g)

½ tsp oriental sesame oil (2.5 ml)

1 ½ oz (3 tbs) butter (50 ml)

Drain and grind peas with some water in a liquidiser.

◯

Cut the vegetables into thin strips, then mix with garlic and sesame oil.

◯

Add to peas. Stir to make a batter.

◯

Heat butter in a nonstick pan and drop batter by ladle onto pan. Fry pancakes on both sides until golden. Serve with sauce (recipe follows).

Sauce

3 ½ fl oz (7 tbs) soy sauce (100 ml)

⅓ oz (1 ½ tsp) green onions—chopped (10 g)

¾ oz (1 large clove) garlic—chopped (20 g)

Mix ingredients until well blended.

AUBERGINE IN SOY BEAN PASTE

GRAND HYATT HONG KONG, HONG KONG

SERVES 4

1 ¼ lb (4 medium) aubergine (egg plants) (560 g)

salt and pepper to taste

vegetable oil—for deep-frying

4 fl oz (½ c) red soy bean paste (120 g)

6 oz (1 c) sugar (170 g)

2 fl oz (2 tbs) vegetable oil (60 ml)

8 fl oz (1 c) dry white wine (240 ml)

4 egg yolks

4 oz (½ c) yellow soybean paste (120 g)

¼ pt (½ c) sweet white wine (120 ml)

3 oz seaweed (85 g)

4 oz (1 medium) cucumber—sliced (115 g)

4 oz (1 c) sliced pickles (115 g)

Halve aubergine lengthwise, and then cut a slice from the bottom so they can lay flat on a plate.

Season with salt and pepper, then deep-fry the aubergine until crisp, about 5 minutes.

Meanwhile, place red bean paste in a small saucepan with half the sugar, the dry white wine and 2 egg yolks. Cook, whisking constantly, until thickened.

Cook the yellow soybean paste with remaining sugar, sweet wine and remaining yolks.

Arrange seaweed on a serving plate.

Place cooked aubergine over it. Top one half with the red bean paste; the other half with the yellow bean paste.

If desired, use a knife to make a design on top.

Garnish with sliced cucumbers and pickles. Chill until ready to serve.

Tofu Estofado com Rebentos de Soja
Sautéed Tofu with Bean Sprouts

Hyatt Regency Macau, Macau

Serves 4

4 ¼ fl oz (1 c) tofu (120 g)

1 ½ oz (3 tbs) vegetable oil (45 ml)

9 dried Chinese black mushrooms—soaked in warm water for 30 minutes

8 oz (2 c) bean sprouts (225 g)

4 oz (1 c) onions—diced (115 g)

2 lb (8–10 medium) tomatoes—peeled, pips removed and dried (910 g)

2 fl oz (4 tbs) chilli sauce (60 ml)

2 fl oz (4 tbs) tomato ketchup (60 ml)

salt and pepper to taste

2 oz (½ c) chives or green onions—chopped (55 g)

Cut tofu into 1x2 inch (2.5x5 cm) pieces.

Fry in 1 tbs (15 ml) oil until lightly browned.

Arrange on 4 plates and keep warm.

Remove stems from mushrooms and slice caps. Strain soaking liquid. Poach caps in liquid until soft, about 5 minutes.

Drain and garnish tofu with this and the bean sprouts.

For the sauce, sauté the onion in remaining vegetable oil; add tomatoes, chilli sauce and ketchup.

Season with salt and pepper.

Pour sauce over tofu and garnish with chives or green onion.

GUCCHI MUSSULUM
STUFFED MORELS

HYATT REGENCY DELHI, INDIA
SERVES 4

STUFFING

1 oz (¼ c) carrots—finely minced (30 g)

1 oz (¼ c) thin green beans—finely minced (30 g)

1 oz (¼ c) almonds—finely minced (30 g)

1 oz (¼ c) cashews—finely minced (30 g)

½ oz (1 tbs) fresh coriander—finely minced (15 g)

½ oz (1 tbs) green chillies—finely minced (15 g)

½ oz (1 tbs) fresh ginger—finely minced (15 g)

½ oz (1 tbs) raisins—chopped (15 g)

1 oz (¼ c) cottage cheese (30 g)

MORELS

6 oz dried morels—soaked in warm water for 30 minutes (170 g)

3 fl oz (6 tbs) vegetable oil (90 ml)

1 oz (¼ c) cumin pips (30 g)

8 oz (2 medium) onions—chopped (225 g)

1 oz (2 tbs) chilli powder (30 g)

1 oz (2 tbs) garam marsala (30 g) (see glossary)

10 oz (2 large) tomatoes—chopped (285 g)

8 fl oz (1 c) tomato concentate (paste) (240 ml)

1 oz (2 tbs) ginger garlic paste (30 g)

4 fresh chillies—slit in half

4 oz (½ c) cashew paste (115 g)

8 fl oz (1 c) plain yoghurt—whipped (240 ml)

2 fl oz (4 tbs) double (heavy) cream

turmeric and salt to taste

4 sprigs fresh coriander—for garnish

Mix ingredients for stuffing.

Drain morels, remove stems and fill caps with stuffing. Set aside.

Heat oil and add cumin pips. When they crackle, add onions and fry until golden brown.

Add chilli powder, garam marsala, ginger, garlic paste, tomato, tomato concentrate and chillies. Cook 5 minutes.

Add cashew paste and yoghurt; cook another 5 minutes.

Season mixture with turmeric and salt.

Add stuffed morels and cook for 2 minutes.

Stir in cream and serve; garnish with coriander.

SWEET POTATO VEGETABLE CURRY

○

HYATT KINABALU, MALAYSIA
SERVES 4

1 ¾ lb sweet potatoes—3 different varieties if possible (800 g)

4 oz (1 medium) onion—sliced (115 g)

½ oz (1 tbs) young fresh ginger—peeled and sliced (15 g)

½ oz (1 clove) garlic—minced (15 g)

1 oz (2 tbs) butter (30 g)

1 ½ oz (3 tbs) curry powder (45 g)

2 pt (5 c) coconut milk (1 ¼ l) (see glossary)

5 oz (2 medium) carrots—diced (140 g)

5 oz (½ head) cauliflower—cut into flowerettes (140 g)

4 oz (1 c) thin green beans—cut into 2-inch (5 cm) lengths (115 g)

½ fl oz (1 tbs) tamarind pulp—minced (15 ml) (see glossary)

5 oz snow peas—strings removed (140 g)

5 oz mustard greens—cut into 2-inch (5 cm) lengths (140 g)

5 oz (1 large) tomato—sliced into thin wedges (140 g)

Peel the sweet potatoes and grate separately, if using different varieties. Form into patties and set aside.

○

Sauté onion, ginger and garlic with half the butter until golden.

○

Add curry powder and coconut milk. Stir and bring to a boil.

○

Add carrots, cauliflower, beans, tamarind, snow peas, mustard greens and tomato. Simmer until vegetables are cooked.

○

Adjust seasoning with salt and keep warm.

○

Fry the sweet potatoes with remaining butter until crisp. Flatten as they cook.

Arrange sweet potato patties on a platter and top with the vegetable curry.

MUTABEL
AUBERGINE QUENELLES WITH TOMATO SAUCE

RABAT HYATT REGENCY, MOROCCO

SERVES 4

2 lb (8 small) aubergine (eggplants) (900 g)

¼ pt (½ c) vegetable oil (120 ml)

4 oz (1 medium) onion—finely chopped (115 g)

3 ½ fl oz (7 tbs) olive oil (100 ml)

3 ⅓ lb (9 medium) well-ripened tomatoes—peeled, pips removed and diced (1.5 kg)

1 oz (2 cloves) garlic—peeled and crushed (30 g)

juice of 3 lemons

½ oz (1 tbs) basil—stems removed; leaves chopped (15 g)

salt and pepper to taste

mixed green salad

Preheat oven to 375° F (190° C).

Slice aubergine in half lengthwise.

Coat both sides with oil and bake for 30–35 minutes, or until soft.

When cool enough to handle, scoop out the pulp with a spoon, leaving the peel intact.

Coarsely chop pulp and chill.

Sauté onion in 2 tbs (1 fl oz) olive oil (30 ml), then add half the tomatoes. Season and simmer until thickened. Chill.

Combine the chopped aubergine, garlic, lemon juice, basil, salt and pepper in a bowl.

Mix well, then add the remaining olive oil, followed by the uncooked tomatoes.

Arrange the mixed salad in the centre of each plate.

With the aid of 2 spoons, form the aubergine mixture into quenelles. Arrange them around the salad; spoon on onion-tomato purée and serve chilled.

Steamed Vegetables in Rice Paper

with Ginger Dressing

⌒

U.N. Plaza Hotel, A Park Hyatt Hotel, New York, U.S.A.

Serves 4

Rice Paper

10 round sheets rice paper 8–10 inches (20–25 cm) diameter

In a sheetpan or tray, put some water to a depth of ½-inch (1.25 cm) deep.

⌒

Dip each rice paper sheet in water, waiting a few seconds until each starts to soften.

Remove immediately and place on a clean towel.

⌒

Cut each sheet in half. Set aside.

Note: Vietnamese rice paper is brittle when dry but pliable when moistened. It is available in most Asian groceries.

Filling

1 oz ginger—fresh, peeled and lightly crushed (30 g)

1 bouquet garnie (thyme, leek greens, parsley stems, bay leaf)

4 oz (½ c) lentils—soaked in water for several hours and drained (115 g)

2 oz (1 medium) carrot—peeled and diced (55 g)

2 oz (1 stalk) celery—diced (55 g)

3 oz (1 small) turnip—peeled and diced (85 g)

2 oz angel hair pasta—cooked until al dente (55 g)

1 oz thin green beans—sliced into small rings (30 g)

1 ½ fl oz (3 tbs) olive oil (45 ml)

½ oz (1 medium) shallot—minced (15 g)

⅓ fl oz (3 tsp) soy sauce (10 ml) pepper to taste

20 fresh coriander leaves

10 fresh mint leaves

40 chives (optional)

salt and pepper to taste

Ginger Dressing

1 oz ginger—fresh, peeled and grated (30 g)

2 oz (4 cloves) garlic—finely minced (55 g)

½ fl oz (3 tsp) soy sauce (15 ml)

½ fl oz (3 tsp) honey (15 ml)

juice of 1 lemon

1 ½ fl oz (3 tbs) oriental sesame oil (45 ml)

¼ pt (½ c) olive oil (120 ml)

4 green onions (scallions)—diced

Mix ingredients until well blended.

In a saucepan, place ¾ pt (2 c; 480 ml) water, the bouquet garnie and pinch of salt. Bring to a boil.

⌒

Add ginger and boil for 5 minutes; then, add the lentils.

⌒

Cover and simmer for 30 minutes, or until lentils are soft.

⌒

Drain and discard ginger and bouquet garnie.

⌒

Blanch the carrot, celery, turnip and beans.

⌒

Heat olive oil in skillet and sauté shallot lightly.

⌒

Add pasta and blanched vegetables. Sauté 2 minutes.

⌒

Add lentils, soy sauce, salt and pepper to taste. Mix until well blended.

⌒

Put a teaspoon of stuffing on each half-moon rice paper and top stuffing with a coriander leaf and half a mint leaf.

⌒

Either wrap like a spring roll (fold edges like a rectangle, then roll up) or in a cylinder, tying the ends with a chive.

⌒

Place stuffed rice papers on a steamer rack above boiling water.

⌒

Steam, covered, for 10–15 minutes.

To Serve

Place steaming hot stuffed rice papers on a serving platter.

⌒

Either spoon the dressing over, or serve separately in a dish.

GATEAU D'AUBERGINES ET SON COULIS DE TOMATE
AUBERGINE CAKES WITH TOMATO COULIS

⌒

THE CARLTON TOWER, A PARK HYATT HOTEL, LONDON, UNITED KINGDOM
SERVES 4

3 ¾ oz (1 small) onion—sliced (105 g)

2 fl oz (4 tbs) olive oil (60 ml)

1 lb (4 medium) tomatoes—chopped (455 g)

1 oz (2 tbs) fresh parsley (30 g)

pinch sugar (optional)

4 lb (4 large) aubergine (eggplants) (3 ¾ kg)

juice of 1 lemon

3 eggs

2 egg yolks

Make tomato coulis by tossing onion in olive oil and adding tomatoes and parsley.

⌒

Cook for 20 minutes then purée in a liquidiser.

⌒

Return purée to heat until you have a light tomato coulis (if taste is too strong, add a little sugar). Set aside.

⌒

Preheat oven to 350° F (180° C).

⌒

Wrap aubergine in foil and bake until tender, about 1 hour.

⌒

Halve aubergine lengthwise and remove skin and pips.

⌒

Purée flesh in a liquidiser, then add lemon juice, eggs and yolks to form a smooth purée.

⌒

Season with salt and pepper.

⌒

Butter 4 moulds or ramekins that are ¾ pt (1.5 c; 355 ml) in volume.

⌒

Pour purée into moulds and put moulds into a larger pan fill halfway with water. Bake for about 20 minutes, or until set.

⌒

Unmould onto individual plates and serve coulis around the cakes.

BIBIM BAP
VEGETABLES ON RICE WITH SPICY PEPPER PASTE

HYATT REGENCY CHEJU, KOREA

SERVES 4

VEGETABLES AND RICE

10 ½ oz (1 ¼ c) rice (300 g)

pinch salt

3 oz spinach—trimmed, cleaned, blanched, drained and dried (85 g)

3 oz shiitake mushrooms—julienned (85 g)

3 oz (2 small) carrots—julienned (85 g)

3 oz (1 small) cucumber—julienned (85 g)

3 oz (1 small) turnip—julienned (85 g)

3 oz (1 small) courgette (zucchini)—julienned (85 g)

3 oz (1 small) potato—julienned (85 g)

3 oz (¾ c) bean sprouts (85 g)

salt and pepper to taste

1 ½ fl oz (3 tbs) oriental sesame oil (45 ml)

2 fl oz (4 tbs) vegetable oil (60 ml)

¾ oz (2 ½ tbs) sesame seed (20 g)

Cook rice with a little salt until tender, about 15 minutes. Set aside.

Season vegetables separately with salt and pepper.

Stir-fry vegetables separately in mixture of sesame and vegetable oil. Allow vegetables to cool.

Preheat oven to 450° F (230° C). Place rice in 4 large ovenproof dishes and heat for 5 minutes in oven.

Arrange vegetables attractively on rice and sprinkle with sesame seeds.

Serve with hot pepper paste (recipe follows).

SPICY PEPPER PASTE

¼ oz (1 ½ tsp) hot chilli paste or ground chillies (120 g)

1 oz (2 tbs) sugar (30 g)

¾ oz (1 large clove) garlic—chopped (20 g)

⅓ oz (1 ½ tbs) sesame seeds (10 g)

3 tbs lemon juice (45 ml)

5 fl oz (¾ c) water (150 ml)

¾ oz (2½ tbs) fresh ginger—chopped (20 g)

4 egg yolks

Place all ingredients in a bowl and mix well with a spoon.

VEGETABLE CREPES
WITH TOFU SAUCE, PINE KERNELS AND POMEGRANATE PIPS

HYATT REGENCY RIYADH, SAUDI ARABIA
SERVES 4

CREPES

5 oz (1 c) flour (150 g)

3 oz (6 tbs) powdered nondairy creamer (85 g)

pinch salt

1 fl oz (2 tbs) vegetable oil (20 ml)

2 ½ fl oz (5 tbs) water (75 ml)

vegetable oil—for pan

Put flour, nondairy creamer, salt and oil in a bowl.

Mix and add water gradually, whisking to form a smooth thin paste.

Lightly oil a 4 ½-inch (12 cm) round crepe pan and add a ladle of batter. Cook crepes on both sides until lightly browned. Make apporoximately 12 crepes.

Allow to cool.

TOFU SAUCE

7 oz tofu—cubed (200 g)

3 ½ fl oz (7 tbs) powdered nondairy creamer (100 g)

6 fl oz (¾ c) dry white wine or white grape juice (200 ml)

salt and pepper to taste

Push the tofu through a sieve, then add nondairy creamer and mix well.

Place mixture in a saucepan, slowly whisk in the wine or grape juice.

Bring to a boil, stirring constantly until thick; then, simmer for 10 minutes.

Season with salt and pepper.

Place in a liquidiser and purée.

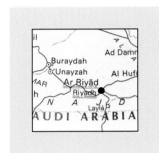

VEGETABLE FILLING

5 ½ oz (1 large) green bell pepper—pips removed (155 g)

5 ½ oz (1 large) yellow bell pepper—pips removed (155 g)

5 ½ oz (1 large) red bell pepper—pips removed (155 g)

5 ½ oz (1 small) aubergine (eggplant) (155 g)

5 ½ oz (1 small) vegetable marrow or large summer squash (155 g)

3 oz (1 small) onion—chopped (85 g)

5 oz (1 large) tomato—diced (140 g)

5 oz (½ c) tomato concentrate (paste) (160 ml)

⅓ fl oz (2 tsp) vegetable oil (10 ml)

salt and pepper to taste

Cut peppers, aubergine and marrow into ¼-inch (¾-cm) slices.

Sauté onion in oil until slightly brown.

Add the vegetables (not tomato) and cook until tender-crisp.

Transfer vegetables to bowl and set aside. Add the tomato, tomato concentrate, salt and pepper to the pan. Cook for an additional 5 minutes.

Add back the vegetables and stir well.

TO ASSEMBLE AND SERVE

2 oz (½ c) pine kernels (pignoli) (55 g)

4 oz (1 medium) pomegranate—cut in half, pips removed (115 g)

Preheat oven to 400° F (200° C).

Distribute filling among crepes and fold into pockets.

Put crepes in overproof baking dish, side by side.

Cover with tofu sauce and bake for approximately 15 minutes, or until heated through.

Sprinkle with pine kernels and pomegranate pips.

VEGETABLE TARTARE WITH SHIITAKE MUSHROOMS
WITH GARLIC AND CHIVE TOMATO COULIS

HYATT REGENCY HONG KONG, HONG KONG
SERVES 4

VEGETABLES

- **3 ½ oz (2 small) carrots (100 g)**
- **3 ½ oz thin green beans (100 g)**
- **3 ½ oz (¾ c) soybeans (100 g)**
- **3 ½ oz (¾ c) celery root (celeriac) (100 g)**
- **3 ½ oz shiitake mushrooms (100 g)**
- **3 oz (1 medium) tomato—peeled and pips removed (85 g)**
- **2 oz (4 cloves) garlic—roughly chopped (55 g)**
- **1 ½ oz (1 tbs) fresh basil—roughly chopped (50 g)**
- **1 oz (1 bunch) tarragon (30 g)**

TARTARE SAUCE

- **½ fl oz (1 tbs) Dijon mustard (15 ml)**
- **½ fl oz (1 tbs) Worcestershire sauce (15 ml)**
- **½ fl oz (1 tbs) Tabasco sauce (15 ml)**
- **1 ¾ fl oz (3 ½ tbs) olive oil (50 ml)**
- **1 oz (2 tbs) capers—chopped (30 g)**
- **1 oz (2 tbs) cornichons—chopped (20 g)**

Note: Cornichon are small pickles made from a unique variety of cucumber that is picked before maturity. Substitute another tiny, vinegary pickle if cornichons are unavailable.

Separately boil all vegetables and mushrooms in salted water till soft but not mushy.

Drain and dice vegetables.

In a liquidiser, purée tomatoes with garlic and basil. Strain mixture and then add chives and tarragon.

Grease a gelatine/custard mould.

Mix mustard, Worcestershire sauce and Tabasco sauce in a bowl. Drizzle in olive oil, whisking well. Then mix in capers and cornichons.

Mix the vegetables with the sauce until well blended.

Pour into mould and chill until firm.

Unmould onto a plate.

Spoon a little tomato coulis alongside, and serve remainder of sauce in a sauce boat.

Loh Han San Su

Braised Vegetables "Loh Han"

Hyatt Tianjin, People's Republic of China

Serves 4

6 dried black Chinese mushrooms

1 ¾ oz black fungus (tree ears) (50 g)

1 ¾ oz dried white fungus (50 g)

5 oz (2 large) carrots—peeled (140 g)

2 ¾ oz bamboo shoots (75 g)

2 ¾ oz water chestnuts (75 g)

4 ½ oz kale or other greens (125 g)

1 ¾ fl oz (3 ½ tbs) vegetable oil (50 ml)

1 ¾ oz tofu—chopped (50 g)

1 ¾ fl oz (3 ½ tbs) light soy sauce (50 ml)

⅓ fl oz (2 tsp) dark soy sauce (10 ml)

1 ¾ oz button mushrooms (50 g)

⅓ fl oz (2 tsp) oriental sesame oil (10 ml)

1 tsp sugar (5–7 g)

salt and pepper to taste

1 oz (2 tbs) cornflour (cornstarch) (30 g)—dissolved in 2 tsp water (30 ml)

Note: White fungus is similar to black fungus, or tree ears, but more rare. It is also known as white tree ears, silver fungus and trimella. Look for it in Chinese herbal shops.

Soak the black mushrooms in 8 fl oz (1 c; 240 ml) in warm water for 40 minutes; drain thoroughly and slice. Strain and reserve water.

Soak the black and white fungus separately in warm water for 15 minutes; drain and cut fungus into thin strips.

Slice carrots, bamboo shoots and water chestnuts into small cubes. Cut kale into shreds.

Heat vegetable oil in wok, then add black mushrooms and bean curd. Stir-fry for 3 minutes.

Add 1 ¾ fl oz (3 ½ tbs; 50 ml) the soy sauce and bring to a boil.

Lower heat and simmer for 10 minutes.

Add vegetables and black and button mushrooms.

Bring liquid to a boil, then add sesame oil, sugar, salt and pepper.

Lower heat and simmer 5 minutes; then, add fungus.

Stir in cornflour mixture and cook for an additional minute until thickened. Serve.

CREPES A LA MEXICANA
MEXICAN-STYLE CREPES

◯

HYATT REGENCY ACAPULCO, MEXICO

SERVES 4

CREPES	FILLING	TOPPING AND HOW TO SERVE

CREPES

5 ¼ oz (1 c) flour (150 g)

8 fl oz (1 c) milk (240 ml)

3 fl oz (6 tbs) light beer (90 ml)

2 oz (4 tbs) butter—melted (50 g)

3 eggs

¼ oz (1 ½ tsp) parsley—fresh, chopped (10 g)

salt to taste

Mix ingredients very well.

◯

Set aside, covered, for 30 minutes.

◯

Heat a nonstick crepe pan and cook crepes until lighly browned, about 3 minutes, turning once.

FILLING

2 oz (4 tbs) butter (60 g)

3 ½ oz (¾ c) onion—minced (100 g)

4 chillies—chopped

3 ½ oz pumpkin or squash flowers (105 g)

3 fl oz (6 tbs) milk (90 ml)

salt and pepper to taste

Melt butter in a pan and sauté onion until golden brown.

◯

Add remaining ingredients and cook until the milk is reduced and mixture is thickened.

TOPPING AND HOW TO SERVE

3 oz (6 tbs) double (heavy) cream (90 ml)

2 oz (4 tbs) butter—melted (60 g)

2 oz (½ c) grated Parmesan or shredded mozzarella cheese (55 g)

Preheat oven to 350° (180 ° C)

◯

Distribute filling evenly on the crepes and roll each up.

◯

Place crepes in a baking dish and cover with cream and cheese.

◯

Drizzle on butter.

◯

Bake for 15 minutes or until golden brown on top

◯

Serve warm.

PULUT PANGGANG
BAKED GLUTINOUS RICE CAKE

◯

HYATT SAUJANA, KUALA LUMPUR, MALAYSIA
SERVES 4

RICE CAKES

½ lb (1 c) glutinous rice (200 g)

4 banana leaves—for wrapping 5x4
  inches (13 cm x 10 cm)

vegetable oil—for brushing

Soak rice overnight.

◯

Drain, then steam for 20 minutes in a
colander above boiling water. Set aside
to cool.

◯

Spread a layer of rice on each banana
leaf.

◯

Place the filling (recipe follows) on top
of rice, close leaves and wrap securely
with string.

◯

Brush oil on top of the banana leaf
packages and lightly toast in broiler
until brown, about 3 minutes. Serve
hot.

FILLING

3 ½ oz (¾ c) coconut—grated (100 g)

¾ oz (1 ½ tbs) dried prawns—mashed
  (20 g)

½ oz (2 tbs) shallots—chopped (10 g)

pinch sugar

½ oz (2 tbs) onions—chopped (10 g)

¼ oz (1 tbs) lemongrass—chopped (5 g)

¼ oz (1 ½ tsp) turmeric (7 g)

pinch salt

In a skillet, cook all ingredients until
dry. Let cool.

POTATO STEAK WITH VEGETABLES

CENTURY HYATT TOKYO, JAPAN

SERVES 4

POTATO STEAK

2 lb (4 large) potatoes—peeled and cubed (90 g)

salt and pepper to taste

1 ½ oz (⅓ c) green peas—boiled (45 g)

1 lb (4 medium) turnips —peeled (455 g)

6 oz (1 medium) lotus root (170 g)

4 oz (3 medium) flap or other oriental mushrooms (115 g)

4 oz (1 medium) cucumber (115 g)

8 oz taro—chunked (225 g)

4 oz (1 medium) tomato (115 g)

1 green onion

vegetable oil—for frying

Note: Lotus root is a long brown rhizome sold fresh in season or in tins other times. Taro is a starchy tuber available throughout the year in Asian groceries.

Boil potato until tender. Drain and mash with salt and pepper.

Add peas, stir well and form 4 potato patties. Chill.

Cut vegetables attractively (see photo) and steam until tender. Keep warm.

Dredge potato patties in flour and fry in hot oil until crispy.

Place potato patties on plates and accompany with vegetables. Serve with sauce (recipe follows).

SAUCE

½ fl oz (1 tbs) vegetable oil (15 ml)

½ oz (1 tbs) flour (15 g)

1 tsp curry powder (5 g)

8 fl oz (1 c) plain yoghurt (240 ml)

salt and pepper to taste

In a saucepan, heat oil and add flour. Stir to blend well.

Add curry powder and yoghurt. Stir rapidly, then season with salt and pepper.

Mi Tsi Tsei Shan Yee

Crisp Lettuce with Fried Tofu on Honey Dressing

Hyatt Tianjin, People's Republic of China

Serves 4

7 oz (½ head) iceberg lettuce (200 g)

4 oz red leaf lettuce (115 g)

4 oz curly endive lettuce (chicory) (100 g)

7 oz tofu (200 g)

1 egg

1 ¾ oz (½ c) white bread crumbs (50 g)

½ fl oz (1 tbs) vegetable oil (15 ml)

¼ pt (½ c) peanut oil (100 ml)

¾ fl oz (1 ½ tsp) tarragon vinegar (25 ml)

¾ fl oz (1 ½ tbs) honey (25 ml)

1 tsp mustard

salt and pepper to taste

½ fl oz (1 tbs) lemon juice (15 ml)

Wash and dry lettuce.

Tear leaves and place in a salad bowl.

Cut tofu into 1-inch x 2-inch (2.5 cm x 5 cm) rectangles.

Whisk egg in a bowl; sprinkle bread crumbs on a plate.

Dip tofu first in egg, then in bread crumbs.

Carefully fry tofu in vegetable oil over low heat until browned.

Drain on absorbent paper. Keep warm.

Place peanut oil, vinegar and honey in a bowl. Whisk until well blended.

Fold in mustard, salt, pepper and lemon juice.

Add dressing to greens and toss.

Arrange salad neatly on plates and place warm tofu on top.

DESSERTS

SPICED FRUIT SOUP
WITH MANGO ICE CREAM

HYATT REGENCY SINGAPORE, SINGAPORE
SERVES 4

SPICED FRUIT "SOUP"

2.2 lb assorted fresh fruit in season—washed and cut into bite-size pieces (1 kg)

5 ½ fl oz (¾ c) orange juice (150 ml)

¾ oz (1 ½ tbs) sugar (20 g)

1 star anise

½ vanilla bean or 1 tsp vanilla essence (extract) (5 ml)

½ cinnamon stick

3 cardamom seeds

2 whole cloves

3 lemon leaves

juice and zest of 1 lemon

zest of 2 oranges

1 ½ fl oz (3 tbs) honey (45 ml)

Place assorted fruit in a nice bowl and chill.

Make sauce by combining all remaining ingredients except the honey.

Bring to a boil and simmer 10 minutes.

Remove from heat and add honey. Remove vanilla bean or add vanilla essence.

Allow to cool, then pour onto fruit.

Serve with mango ice cream. (recipe follows).

3 eggs yolks

3 ½ oz (½ c) sugar (100 g)

½ vanilla bean or 1 tsp (5 ml) vanilla essence (extract)

8 fl oz (1 c) milk (240 ml)

12 oz (1 ½ c) fresh mango purée (350 g)

juice of ½ lemon

¼ pt (½ c) double (heavy) cream (120 ml)

Beat egg yolks and sugar until light in colour.

○

Scrape vanilla bean seeds into milk, then bring to a boil.

○

Slowly whisk hot milk into yolk-sugar mixture.

○

Return to saucepan over very low heat (do not allow to boil), stirring with a wooden spoon until thick enough to lightly coat spoon.

○

Strain mixture, add vanilla essence if using and allow to cool.

○

Stir in cream, then whisk in mango purée and lemon juice.

○

Freeze in ice cream maker according to manufacturer's directions.

STUFFED PRUNES WITH BRANDY CREAM
ON STRAWBERRY COULIS

○

HYATT REGENCY MANILA, PHILIPPINES
SERVES 4

15 pcs dried prunes

4 ½ fl oz (½ c) double (heavy) cream whipped

2 tsp icing (confectioners) sugar (10 g)

dash brandy

7 oz fresh strawberries—wash and hulled (200 g)

1 ½ oz caster sugar (40 g)

whipped cream and chocolate curls for garnish

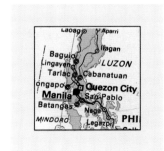

Remove seeds from prunes.

○

Whip cream vigorously with icing sugar and brandy for flavour.

○

Place whipped cream in a pastry bag with a small tip.

○

Pipe into the prunes. Set aside to chill.

○

Cook strawberries in caster sugar. Purée in a liquidizer and chill.

○

To serve, pour some strawberry sauce on plate.

○

Arrange prunes neatly on top, and garnish with chocolate curls and whipped cream.

PINEAPPLE SOUFFLÉ
WITH TROPICAL FRUIT SAUCE

⌒

HYATT REGENCY HONG KONG, HONG KONG
SERVES 4

SOUFFLÉ

1 vanilla bean or ½ tsp vanilla essence (extract) (1 ml)

8 fl oz (1 c) milk (240 ml)

3 ½ oz (7 tbs) butter—softened (100 g)

1 ¾ oz (⅓ c) flour (50 g)

½ oz (1 tbs) cornflour (cornstarch) (15 g)

4 eggs—separated

4 oz (1 c) crushed pineapple (save shells; see photo)

2 oz (¼ c) caster sugar (granulated) (55 g)

1 ½ oz (⅓ c) coconut—grated (40 g)

¾ oz (1 ½ tbs) icing (confectioners') sugar (15 g)

Preheat oven to 425° F (220° C).

⌒

Mix vanilla with milk in a saucepan and bring to a boil. Remove vanilla bean. Set aside.

⌒

Soften 2 oz (4 tbs; 55 g) butter and mix with flour and cornflour until it forms a paste.

⌒

Slowly add this paste to hot milk, mixing vigorously.

⌒

Return mixture to medium heat, stirring continuously until it has a custard consistency (thick and smooth).

⌒

Whip yolks into custard, add crushed pineapple, and set aside.

⌒

Brush insides of pineapple shells with remaining butter (melted), then sprinkle with grated coconut. Set aside.

⌒

Beat egg whites till soft peaks form. Gradually add sugar and beat until very stiff.

⌒

Fold beaten whites into custard.

⌒

Immediately pour mixture into hollowed out pineappled, filling only ¾ high.

⌒

Bake until soufflé has risen, about 15 minutes.

⌒

Serve immediately with icing sugar sprinkled on the soufflés. Serve with sauce (recipe follows) on the side.

SAUCE

¾ pt (2 c) orange juice (500 ml)

2 oz (⅓ c) sugar (100 g)

¾ oz (1 ½ tbs) cornflour (cornstarch) (15 g)

1 fl oz (2 tbs) Grand Marnier (30 ml)

10 ½ oz (1 ½ c) assorted tropical fruits—cut up (200 g)

7 oz (1 c) fresh berries (200 g)

Boil orange juice and sugar in a saucepan until syrupy.

⌒

Dissolve cornflour in Grand Marnier and add to juice; boil until thickened.

⌒

Add tropical fruits and berries.

Pots de Creme
with Ragout of Oranges with Ginger

Hyatt Regency Adelaide, Australia

Serves 4

Marjolaine Basket

½ oz (1 tbs) butter—melted (10 g)

8 oz (½ c) sugar (85 g)

¾ oz (2 ½ tbs) orange zest—grated (20 g)

¾ oz (1 ½ tbs) flour (20 g)

2 egg whites

3 oz (¾ c) slivered almond (100 g)

Mix ingredients and allow to rest for 12 hours.

Preheat oven to 400° F (200° C).

Cut a sheet of greaseproof paper into rounds (5-inches; 12-cm in diameter).

Spread mixture on rounds and bake until golden brown, about 15 minutes.

While still hot, drape rounds over cups to form baskets. Let cool until firm.

Orange Ragout

3 lb (8 medium) oranges (1 ⅓ kg)

8 oz (1 c) sugar (240 g)

1 tsp fresh ginger—grated (5 g)

1 fl oz (2 tbs) Cointreau (30 ml)

Grate the peel of 1 orange.

Squeeze all but 2 oranges until you have 1 pt (2 ½ c ; 600 ml) juice.

For the 2 remaining oranges, peel and separate into segments.

Place sugar in heavy saucepan and heat until melted. Continue to cook, stirring until a light amber colour is obtained.

Add the orange zest and juice, and reduce by ¾.

Remove from stove and add ginger, Cointreau and orange segments. Allow to cool.

Pots and Serving

¾ pt (2 c) milk (500 ml)

3 ½ oz semisweet chocolate—chopped (100 g)

2 ½ oz (⅓ c) sugar (75 g)

1 vanilla bean or 1 tsp vanilla essence (extract) (5 ml)

6 egg yolks

Preheat oven to 350° F (180° C).

Over low heat, simmer the milk, chocolate, sugar and vanilla bean for 1 minute.

Whisk yolks in a bowl and stir into the chocolate mixture, whisking continuously.

Strain mixture through a sieve and pour into four 8 oz (1 c; 240 ml) ramekins or pots de creme moulds.

Put on a baking tray in a water bath.

Bake until firm, about 15–25 minutes.

Pour some orange ragout in the marjolaine baskets.

Place pots de creme on a square plate and arrange baskets on the side.

Kuih Onde-Onde
Brown Sugar Ball

Hyatt Saujana, Kuala Lumpur, Malaysia

Serves 4

5 ¼ oz (1¼ c) rice flour (150 g)

1 ¾ oz (½ c) plain (all-purpose) flour

¼ pt (½ c) pandan juice (118 ml)

¼ pt (½ c) water (120 ml)

½ tsp baking powder (2 g)

¼ tsp salt (1 g)

1 drop green food colouring

8 oz (2 c) white grated coconut (225 g)

1 ¾ oz (3 ½ tbs) gula meleka or brown sugar (50 g)

Mix flours, pandan juice, water, baking powder, salt and food colouring.

○

Shape into rounds, then roll in gula meleka or brown sugar.

○

Boil the water and poach the balls until they rise to surface.

○

Drain and roll in coconut. Serve.

Note : Pandan is a plant with long spike-like green leaves. The flavouring is sold in liquid form, in jars. Dried leaves can be substituted, reconstituted in hot water.

BRANDY-FLAVOURED CHOCOLATE MOUSSE
WITH HOT CHERRIES

HYATT REGENCY SINGAPORE, SINGAPORE

SERVES 4

MOUSSE

4 ½ oz (1 c) semisweet chocolate— chopped (125 g)

1 egg

⅓ fl oz (2 tsp) brandy (10 ml)

½ pt (1 c) double (heavy) cream— whipped (300 ml)

Melt chocolate in double boiler.

Beat the egg in a bowl over hot water until thick and frothy.

Immediately add the chocolate and brandy, then fold in whipped cream.

Pour into buttered 4-oz (½-c or 120-ml) moulds, cups or glasses, and chill for at least 3 hours.

CHERRIES

1 ¾ fl oz (3 ½ tbs) cherry juice (50 ml)

1 ¾ fl oz (3 ½ tbs) dry red wine (50 ml)

¾ oz (1 ½ tbs) sugar (40 g)

1 stick (small) cinnamon

zest of ¼ orange

5 cloves—whole

½ tsp cornflour (cornstarch) (2 g)—dissolved in 1 tbs water (15 ml)

7 oz (1 ¾ c) brandied cherries (200 g)

Bring the cherry juice, wine, sugar, cinnamon, orange zest and cloves to a boil; simmer for 2 minutes.

○

Add the cornflour mixture and cook until thickened.

○

Add the cherries and keep warm.

TO SERVE

3 ½ oz (1 c) semisweet chocolate—chopped (100 g)

3 ½ oz (1 c) white chocolate—chopped (100 g)

icing (confectioners') sugar—for dusting

Melt the chocolates separately in 2 double boilers.

○

Spread both mixtures (separately) on greaseproof paper, using a metal spatula. Allow to set in refrigerator.

○

Break up chocolate into pieces.

○

Unmould mousses and set in centre of individual plates.

○

Arrange the chocolate pieces around mousse.

○

Dust with sugar and serve separately with hot cherry sauce.

BENGKA ULI KELEDEK
SWEET POTATO CAKE

○

HYATT KUANTAN, MALAYSIA
SERVES 4

8 ¾ oz sweet potato—cleaned (250 g)

5 ¼ oz palm sugar (150 g)

5 ¼ oz grated coconut (150 g)

1 egg—beaten

3 oz glutinous flour (85 g)

3 ½ oz water (100 g)

Boil the sweet potato until soft. Mash and set aside.

○

In a saucepan, melt palm sugar till it becomes liquid.

○

Add in remaining ingredients and stir until they stay together.

○

Pour in a baking pan and bake in a preheated 350° F (177 ° C) oven until it turns dark brown.

○

To serve, slice into squares and serve on plates.

HIPPENBLUTE GEFÜLLT MIT BAYERISCHER CREME
BAVARIAN CREAM

HYATT REGENCY COLOGNE, GERMANY

SERVES 4

BAVAROISE

8 fl oz (1 c) milk (250 ml)

½ tsp vanilla essence (extract)—(2 ml)

2 oz (¼ c) sugar (60 g)

2 egg yolks

⅔ oz (4 leaves) gelatine (20 g)

¾ pt (2 c) double (heavy) cream—
  whipped (500 ml)

sugar for sprinkling cups

Scald milk and vanilla.

Whisk sugar, yolks and gelatine
together.

Slowly pour into the hot milk mixture, then allow to cool.

Fold in whipped cream and chill until
half-set.

Butter 4 individual coffee cups or
ramekins and sprinkle with sugar.

Fill cups with the bavaroise and chill
for several hours, or until set.

Unmould Bavarian creams and set
into pastry "blossoms" (recipe
follows).

Serve with fresh fruits and a fruit
purée.

BLOSSOMS

3 oz (1 c) icing (confectioners') sugar
  (75 g)

¾ fl oz (5 ½ tbs) double (heavy) cream
  (75 ml)

3 oz (½ c) flour (75 g)

2 drops each vanilla and lemon
  essence (extract)

Preheat oven to 350° F (180° C).

Mix sugar and cream, then whisk in
flour and essences.

Spread batter on a parchment lined
baking sheet, making 4 squares.

Bake until golden, about 10 minutes.

While still very hot, shape squares by
draping over glasses to resemble
blossoms as illustrated.

GLAZED MANGO STRUDEL
WITH GRAND MARNIER SABAYON

HYATT REGENCY HONG KONG, HONG KONG

SERVES 4

CINNAMON ICE CREAM

2 fl oz (4 tbs) honey (60 ml)

¾ oz (1 ½ tbs) butter (20 g)

3 drops vanilla essence (extract)

½ tsp ground cinnamon (2 g)

1 egg

1 oz (2 tbs) sugar (30 g)

5 fl oz (⅔ c) double (heavy) cream (150 ml)

Combine honey, butter, vanilla and cinnamon in a saucepan and bring to a boil.

Beat egg and sugar until frothy, then add to honey mixture. Thoroughly whip cream and fold into chilled mixture.

Freeze in ice-cream freezer according to manufacturer's directions.

STRUDEL

½ lb phyllo dough (240 g)

3 oz (6 tbs) butter—melted (80 g)

1 ¾ oz (½ c) hazelnuts—ground (50 g)

1 ½ lb (3 medium) mangoes—halved, peeled and sliced ⅓-inch (1 cm) thick (680 g)

Preheat oven to 450° F (230° C).

Cut phyllo sheets into rectangles 6x2-inches (15x5 cm).

Brush phyllo sheets with melted butter and stack them in sets of 4.

○

Brush topmost sheet again with butter and sprinkle nuts on top.

○

Divide mango slices among rectangles.

○

Roll each into a small strudel, and brush again with butter.

○

Bake strudels for about 10 minutes, or until pastry is golden.

1 oz (2 tbs) sugar (30 g)

3 egg yolks

1 ¾ fl oz (3 ½ tbs) Grand Marnier (50 ml)

¾ fl oz (1 ½ tbs) sweet white wine (20 ml)

Put sauce ingredients in a small bowl and set into water bath.

○

Whisk vigorously until mixture thickens and becomes frothy. Keep warm.

Place strudels on individual broiler-proof plates.

○

Cover neatly with sabayon, then glaze lightly under broiler.

○

Serve with a small scoop of cinnamon ice cream or other flavour of ice cream.

○

Decorate with fresh raspberry or mango slices.

TULIP FRUIT TART

○

HYATT REGENCY SAIPAN, MARIANA ISLANDS

SERVES 4–6

CRISP CONES

1 oz (2 tbs) butter—melted (30 g)

¾ oz (¼ c) icing (confectioners') sugar (30 g)

1 ¼ oz (¼ c) flour (35 g)

1 egg white

Preheat oven to 350° F (180° C).

○

Mix above ingredients into a smooth paste.

○

Draw 4–6 jagged circles on a piece of parchment paper resembling a tulip flower opened flat.

○

Using a cake spatula, spread the paste onto parchment paper, using the pattern as a guide.

○

Bake until golden brown, then immediately remove "tulips" from paper and drape overturned glasses to cool. Tulip cones will harden in flower shape.

CUSTARD CREAM FILLING

8 fl oz (1 c) milk (240 ml)

6 oz assorted fresh seasonal fruits— sliced (170 g)

2 tsp sugar (10 g)

1 oz (2 tbs) cornflour (cornstarch) (30 g)

1 egg yolk

¼ tsp vanilla essence (extract) (1 ml)

Place milk and half the sugar in a saucepan and scald milk.

○

Dissolve cornflour in a little water, then mix with the yolk, remaining sugar and vanilla extract.

○

Pour cornflour mixture into boiling milk, stirring constantly over low heat, until thickened.

○

Let cool, then put into a pastry bag.

○

Pipe custard into tulips and top with fruits.

FROZEN WALNUT MOUSSE
WITH PASSION FRUIT PURÉE AND TUILES

HYATT REGENCY ADELAIDE, AUSTRALIA

SERVES 4

FROZEN WALNUT MOUSSE

3 ½ oz (¾ c) walnuts—chopped (100 g)

8 fl oz (1 c) milk (240 ml)

12 oz (1 ½ c) sugar (350 g)

3 ½ oz (¾ c) walnut halves (100 g)

4 eggs

2 egg yolks

¾ pt (2 c) double (heavy) cream—whipped (480 ml)

Soak chopped walnuts in milk overnight.

○

Put chopped walnuts and milk in a liquidiser and purée. Pour mixture through muslin or cheesecloth and reserve walnut milk. Discard walnut paste.

○

Put 3 ½ oz (½ c ; 100 g) sugar in a saucepan and cook until golden brown. Add walnut halves and stir to coat with caramel.

○

Spread caramel-covered nuts on greased surface and let cool.

○

Chop finely and set aside.

○

Beat eggs, yolk, and remaining sugar until pale in color.

○

Whisk in walnut milk and add all but 3 ½ oz (½ c; 100 g) of the chopped caramel-covered walnuts.

○

Gradually fold in the whipped cream, then pour mixture into greased individual moulds or custard cups. Freeze.

TUILES

2 oz (4 tbs) butter (50 g)

2 oz (⅔ c) icing (confectioners) sugar (50 g)

2 egg whites

1 ½ oz (2 tbs) flour (40 g)

pinch lemon zest

Cream the butter and sugar, then add remaining ingredients.

○

Cover and refrigerate until well chilled.

○

Preheat oven to 400° F (200° C).

○

Trace several small circles on parchment-lined baking sheet; circles should be about 2–3 inches (5–7 cm) in diameter. Spread batter thinly inside circles and bake until golden, about 10 minutes.

○

Immediately drape circles over a rolling pin to shape into graceful curves.

TO GARNISH AND SERVE

14 oz (1 ¾ c) passion fruit purée (400 ml)

mint leaves

icing (confectioners') sugar—for dusting

Unmould frozen mousses and slice, if desired. Arrange slices on individual plates.

○

Surround slices with passion fruit purée and tuiles. Scatter the reserved caramel-covered nuts over, and top with a few mint leaves. Dust plates with icing sugar.

Chilled Sago Cream
with Melon and Strawberries

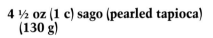

Hyatt Regency Hong Kong, Hong Kong

Serves 4

4 ½ oz (1 c) sago (pearled tapioca) (130 g)

1 oz (2 tbs) sugar (30 g)

8 fl oz (1 c) warm water (240 ml)

2 fl oz (4 tbs) coconut milk (60 ml) (see glossary)

2 fl oz (4 tbs) milk (60 ml)

1 ½ oz (⅓ c) diced cantaloupe (45 g)

1 ½ oz (⅓ c) diced strawberry (45 g)

Soak sago in cold water to cover for 1 hour. Bring to a boil and simmer approximately 10 minutes, or until soft.

○

Drain and rinse well under cold running water.

○

Dissolve sugar in warm water. Add coconut milk, milk and sago.

○

Stir in fruit and chill.

○

Serve chilled.

Queensland "Pickled" Pineapple Meringue
with Raspberry Sauce

Hyatt On Collins, Melbourne, Australia
Serves 4

"Pickled" Pineapple

7 oz (1½ c) pineapple—cubed (200 g)

1 ¾ pt (4 ¼ c) water (1 *l*)

10 ½ oz (2 c) sugar (300 g)

4 ¼ oz (1 c) pink peppercorns (120 g)

Place ingredients in a saucepan and bring to a boil.

When mixture boils, remove from heat and cool at room temperature. Repeat procedure 4 times.

Drain and chop the pineapple; set aside for meringue. Discard cooking liquid.

Meringue

3 ½ oz (¾ c) slivered almonds—lightly toasted and chopped (100 g)

1 ¾ oz (5 tbs) candied orange peel (50 g)

1 fl oz (2 tbs) Kirsch (30 ml)

5 egg whites

3 ½ oz (½ c) sugar (100 g)

8 fl oz (1 c) double (heavy) cream—whipped (240 ml)

Mix the chopped pineapple, almonds, orange peel and kirsch in a bowl.

Beat egg whites until soft peaks form; gradually add sugar and continue beating until very stiff.

Fold whipped cream into beaten egg whites, then fold in the pineapple mixture.

Spread mixture on a tray 8 x 13 inches (20x35 cm) and freeze overnight.

RASPBERRY SAUCE

8 oz (2 c) raspberries—fresh or frozen (230 g)

3 ½ oz (½ c) sugar (100 g)

Place raspberries and sugar in a saucepan and bring to a boil.

○

Lower heat and simmer 12 minutes.

○

Strain through a fine sieve.

CHOCOLATE SPIRES

7 oz (1¾ c) semisweet chocolate (200 g)

Melt chocolate in a double boiler.

○

Thinly spread melted chocolate on greased surface, such as a cookie sheet.

○

Chill chocolate until hard.

○

Carefully cut out spire shapes, using a hot knife. Set aside.

TO ASSEMBLE AND SERVE

Cut the frozen meringue into 3-inch (7.5 cm) circles, using a biscuit cutter.

○

Place on individual plates and arrange 3 chocolate spires on top, as shown in photo.

○

Spoon raspberry sauce around meringue and serve.

GULAB JAMUN

○

HYATT REGENCY DELHI, INDIA

SERVES 4

1 lb (2 ½ c) sugar (500 g)
12 fl oz (1 ⅔ c) water (400 ml)
4 ¼ oz (1 ¼ c) nonfat dry milk (150 g)
1 oz (1 c) flour (30 g)
¼ tsp baking soda (bicarbonate) (1 g)
1 ¾ oz (3 ½ tbs) butter (50 g)
2 fl oz (4 tbs) water (60 ml)

vegetable oil—for frying
4 oz (1 c) pistachios—sliced or chopped, for garnish (115 g)

In a saucepan, combine sugar and water. Boil until a slightly thickened syrup forms; set aside.

○

Mix the remaining ingredients except pistachios together to form a dough.

○

Make small balls from dough and fry in oil over low heat until golden brown, about 5 minutes.

○

Dip balls in syrup and serve with pistachios.

Mille-Feuille of Tamarillo
with Mango Sorbet

Hyatt Regency Adelaide, Australia

Serves 4

Mille-Feuille

1 lb puff pastry (450 g)

icing (confectioners') sugar—for top

Preheat oven to 450° F (220° C).

◦

Roll out puff pastry to ⅛ inch (3 mm) thick and cut out 2-inch (5 cm) discs.

◦

Sprinkle with some confectioners' sugar and bake on ungreased sheet until golden brown, about 15 minutes.

Note : Puff Pastry is available, usually frozen in gourmet food shops.

Tamarillo and Raspberry Sauce

¾ oz (1½ tbs) butter (20 g)

1 ¼ lb (10 large) tamarillos—peeled and sliced with 4 slices still with stems on (560 g)

3 oz (½ c) sugar (caster) (85 g)

14 fl oz (1 ¾ c) raspberry purée (400 ml)

additional caster sugar to taste

In a saucepan, melt the butter; add tamarillos, sprinkle sugar on top and sauté until caramelized.

◦

Pour in raspberry purée and bring to a boil.

◦

Take out the tamarillos and set aside.

◦

Strain the sauce and sweeten to taste.

To Assemble and Serve

icing (confectioners' sugar)

mint leaves

1 pt mango sorbet (450 ml)

5 fl oz (⅔ c) mango coulis (150 ml)

Place a puff pastry circle on each plate.

◦

Add some tamarillo slices, then top with another pastry circle.

◦

Top stacks with stemmed tamarillo slices.

◦

Sprinkle with confectioners' sugar and decorate with mint leaves.

◦

Surround pastry with raspberry sauce. Arrange mango sorbet alongside, with mango coulis.

Note : A fruit coulis is a slightly sweetened purée of fruit, without additional flavours to complicate taste. For mango coulis, purée fresh mango with sugar to taste until very smooth.

Chocolate Pudding
with Coffee and Rum Sauce

The Hotel Canberra, A Park Hyatt Hotel, Australia

Serves 4

Pudding

1 oz (2 tbs) butter (30 g)

2 eggs—separated

1 oz semisweet chocolate—melted and kept lukewarm (30 g)

½ oz (2 tbs) sugar (15 g)

⅓ oz (2 tsp) flour (10 g)

1 oz (¼ c) ground almonds (30 g)

Preheat oven to 400° F (200° C)

Cream butter, yolks and half the sugar until smooth. Add melted chocolate and stir until well mixed.

Beat egg whites until soft peaks form.

Add remaining sugar and continue beating until stiff peaks form.

Fold whites into chocolate mixture.

Sift flour and ground almonds over mixture and gently fold in.

Pour mixture into 4 floured and buttered 4-inch(10 cm) pudding moulds (ramekins)

Place moulds in a water bath and bake for 30 minutes. Unmould and serve with coffee-rum sauce (recipe follows)

Coffee-Rum Sauce

3 egg yolks

¾ oz (1 ½ tbs) sugar (20 g)

8 fl oz (1 c) milk (240 ml)

⅓ oz (2 tbs) powdered instant coffee (10 g)

½ fl oz (1 tbs) dark rum (10 ml)

Beat yolks and sugar together.

Scald milk, then whisk into yolk mixture.

Pour back into saucepan and simmer over extremely low heat until slightly thickened.

Remove from heat and add coffee while mixture is still hot.

Let cool. Then add rum.

Strain through a sieve.

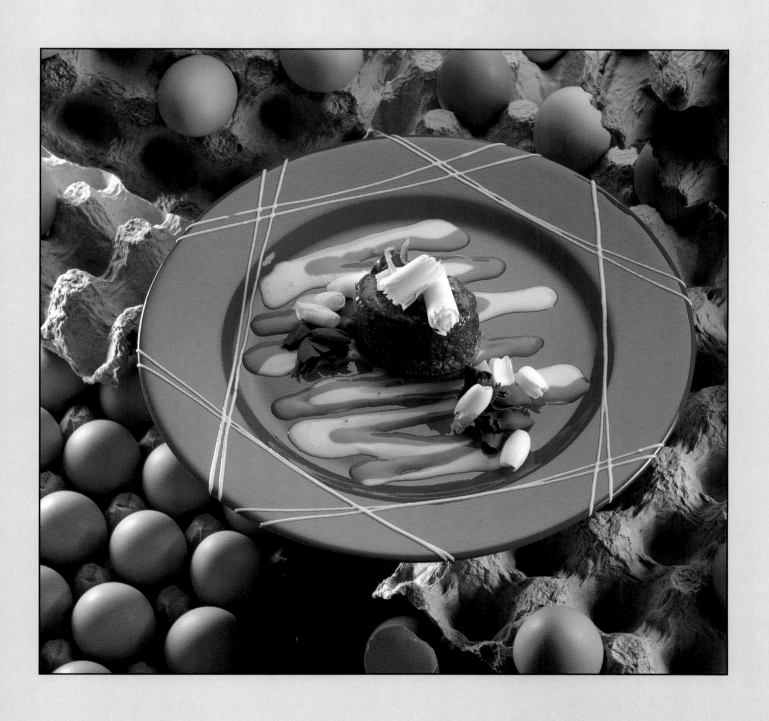

APPLE AND PEAR TARTLETS

WITH CALVADOS SABAYON AND VANILLA ICE CREAM

HYATT ON COLLINS, MELBOURNE, AUSTRALIA

SERVES 4

tart pastry for a 9-inch crust (23 cm)

12 oz (2 large) Granny Smith apples (340 g)

12 oz (2 large) pears—halved (340 g)

2 oz (4 tbs) butter—melted (55 g)

2 sheet phyllo pastry (see glossary)

icing (confectioners') sugar—for dusting

4 scoops vanilla ice cream

4 springs mint

1 vanilla bean—cut in 4 pieces

Preheat oven to 375° F (190° C).

Roll out pastry until ⅛-inch (2.5-mm) thick and cut into 4 circles of 4-inches (10-cm) in diameter.

Bake until three-quarters cooked, about 7 minutes. Set aside. Increase oven temperature to 400° F (200° C).

Peel and quarter apples, then thinly slice crossways.

Place apple slices close together in a circle on pastries, just in from edge.

Place another layer inside the first.

Repeat to have 3 layers of apples.

Poach and purée the pear.

Place a small spoonful of the purée in the centre of each tartlet.

Cut phyllo sheets into small ovals and brush with melted butter.

Form into small carnation petals by punching at the base, then arrange the flowers on top of the pear purée.

Bake for 12–15 minutes, or until tartlets are lightly browned.

Dust tartlets with icing sugar.

Place the sabayon (recipe below) alongside.

If desired, serve with scoops of ice cream topped with a sprig of mint and piece of vanilla.

CALVADOS SABAYON

3 egg yolks

1 oz (2 tbs) Calvados (30 ml)

1 oz (2 tbs) sugar (30 g)

Put in a double boiler and whisk vigorously until thick and frothy.

Red Wine Cherry Soup

U.N. Plaza Hotel, A Park Hyatt Hotel, New York, U.S.A.

Serves 4

Soup and Cherries

¾ pt (½ c) red wine (1.2 *l*)

9 oz (1 c) sugar (255 g)

4 sticks cinnamon

36 cherries—pips removed

Bring wine, sugar and cinnamon to a boil, then reduce by ½.

Add cherries and cook over very low heat for 1 minute. Remove cinnamon.

Chill in refrigerator.

Cinnamon Ice Cream

5 egg yolks

7 oz (1 c) sugar (200 g)

1 ⅓ pt (3 ¾ c) milk (900 ml)

1 ¾ pt (4 ¼ c) double (heavy) cream (1 *l*)

1 tsp ground cinnamon

Beat yolks and sugar until light in colour.

Scald milk, then add cream and cinnamon.

Pour milk mixture into yolk mixture and return to saucepan.

Place over low heat and stir with a wooden spoon until mixture lightly coats back of spoon.

Chill in refrigerator.

Pour mixture into ice-cream machine and follow manufacturer's directions.

To Serve

Divide soup among 4 bowls.

Place a scoop of ice cream in the centre of each bowl.

BAKED FIGS
WITH HOT CHERRY SAUCE

HYATT REGENCY RIYADH, SAUDI ARABIA

SERVES 4

BAKED FIGS

12 fresh figs

1 lb (3 ¾ c) flour (450 g)

8 fl oz (1 c) lukewarm beer (240 ml)

¼ oz (1 tbs) yeast (7 g)

1 ½ fl oz (3 tbs) olive oil (45 ml)

pinch salt

2 egg whites

Dissolve yeast in beer.

In another bowl, place flour and make well in centre. Add beer mixture, oil and salt. Mix quickly by hand, gradually incorporating the flour until batter becomes smooth and just coats the fingers. (Do not overmix batter or it might become elastic.)

Cover bowl with a plate and allow to stand in a warm place 45 minutes. The mixture will rise and bubble.

Preheat oven to 350° F (180° C).

Just before using, gently fold in stiffly beaten egg whites.

Dip the figs in batter and bake on greased tray for 20—30 minutes. Serve with sauce (recipe follows).

SAUCE

6 oz (1 c) sugar (170 g)

1 tbs lemon zest (7 g)

8 fl oz (1 c) dry red wine (240 ml)

1 small vanilla bean or 1 tsp (5 ml) vanilla essence (extract)

1 small cinnamon stick

½ lb sweet cherries—stems and pips removed (225 g)

1 tsp cornflour (cornstarch) (7 g) dissolved in 1 tbs water to thicken (15 ml) (optional)

In a saucepan, bring sugar, lemon zest, wine, vanilla bean (if using) and cinnamon to a boil.

Add cherries and simmer 15 minutes.

Place mixture in a liquidiser to purée. Add vanilla essence, if using. Remove vanilla bean.

If sauce seems too thin, place back in saucepan, and add a little dissolved cornstarch. Cook until the right consistency.

GREEN APPLE CRUNCH

HYATT KINGSGATE SYDNEY, AUSTRALIA

SERVES 4

1 ½ lb (6 large) green apples (680 g)

5 oz (10 tbs) butter (140 g)

3 ½ oz (½ c) sugar (100 g)

1 ½ fl oz (3 tbs) golden syrup or light table syrup (45 ml)

½ tbs ground cinnamon (7 g)

4 oz (2 c) corn flakes (115 g) vanilla ice cream

mint leaves—fresh, for garnish

Preheat oven to 350° F (180° C).

Peel, core and slice apples.

Melt half the butter in pan and sauté apple slices for 3 minutes.

Add sugar while constantly stirring apples.

When sugar has glazed apples, remove from heat; sprinkle on cinnamon and mix well. Place apples in a baking dish.

Melt remaining butter with syrup.

Stir in corn flakes, then spread over apples and bake for 20 minutes or until crunchy.

Serve with vanilla ice cream and garnish with mint leaves.

PASHKA WITH DATE SABAYON

⌒

HYATT REGENCY JEDDAH, SAUDI ARABIA
SERVES 4

¼ pt (½ c) double (heavy) cream (125 ml)

½ vanilla bean

2 egg yolks

3 ½ oz (½ c) sugar (100 g)

3 ½ oz (7 tbs) butter (100 g)

17 oz ricotta cheese (½ kg)

3 ½ oz (¾ c) almonds—blanched, chopped (100 g)

½ tbs lemon juice (7 ml)

1 oz (¼ c) sultanas (golden raisins)— soaked in warm water to soften (25 g)

½ oz (1 tbs each) glazed pineapple, apricot, peach and fig—chopped (15 g)

1 oz semisweet chocolate—chopped (30 g)

cinnamon—ground, for dusting tops

Scald cream with vanilla bean. Remove vanilla bean.

⌒

Beat yolks and sugar in a bowl until pale yellow.

⌒

Add hot cream slowly to egg yolk mixture, whisking constantly, then return mixture to saucepan and simmer over moderate heat until mixture coats the back of a wooden spoon. Cool.

⌒

Beat butter with ricotta and add to cooled custard.

⌒

Stir in the remaining ingredients except cinnamon.

⌒

Spoon mixture into 4 small cylindrical moulds lined with dampened muslin or cheesecloth that overhangs by about 2 ¼-inches (6-cm). Fold over cloth and cover the mixture. Weight the tops.

⌒

Leave overnight to chill in refrigerator.

⌒

To serve, unmould and peel off cloth. Place on serving plates and spoon warm sabayon (recipe follows) around. Sprinkle with cinnamon.

SABAYON

4 egg yolks

8 pitted dates—puréed

½ fl oz (1 tbs) water (15 ml)

Place ingredients in a bowl and set over a water bath.

⌒

Whisk mixture continuously until very frothy.

Ma Twan

Sesame Cakes

Hyatt Tianjin, People's Republic of China

SERVES 4

Dough 1

5 ¼ oz (1 c) flour (150 g)

½ tsp baking powder (2.5 g)

3 fl oz (6 tbs) cold water (90 ml)

Place flour in a bowl; add baking powder and water and mix by hand until dough is smooth.

Let rest for 20 minutes.

Dough 2

1 ¾ oz (2 tbs) flour (50 g)

1 ½ fl oz (3 tbs) peanut oil—heated (50 ml)

Place flour in a bowl; make a well in centre and add hot oil. Mix well with a spoon.

Final Assembly

salt

flour

1 egg yolk—beaten

1 ¾ oz (⅓ c) sesame seeds (50 g)

Preheat oven to 250° F (120° C).

Roll out Dough 1 until 12-inches (30-cm) long and 5-inches (12-cm) wide.

Spread Dough 2 evenly over Dough 1 with a spatula.

Sprinkle some salt and flour over top and roll up like a sausage. Cut into 1 ½-inch (4-cm) pieces.

Roll dough pieces around by hand until all openings or cracks are closed.

Flatten dough balls slightly and brush with beaten egg yolk.

Sprinkle sesame seeds on a table or tray and press the flattened dough balls upside down on the sesame seeds.

Arrange cakes on a baking sheet and bake for 10 minutes or until golden brown.

Serve warm.

PINEAPPLE SPRING ROLL
WITH FROZEN RUM MOUSSE AND SABAYON SAUCE

HYATT REGENCY SINGAPORE, SINGAPORE

SERVES 4

FROZEN RUM MOUSSE

1 egg yolk

½ pt (1 ½ c) double (heavy) cream (350 ml)

3 oz (½ c) sugar (85 g)

½ fl oz (1 tbs) dark rum (15 ml)

Whisk ingredients in a bowl. Chill at least 2 hours.

Whip like cream, then pour into individual moulds or ramekins. Freeze overnight.

PINEAPPLE SPRING ROLL

8 oz (2 c) crushed pineapple (250 g)

1 oz (2 tbs) sugar (30 g)

pinch ground cinnamon

⅓ oz (2 tsp) raisins (10 g)

4 spring roll wrappers

½ oz (1 tbs) custard powder (15 g)— dissolved in 1 tbs rum or water (15 ml)

1 egg white—beaten

vegetable oil—for deep-frying

Bring pineapple, sugar, cinnamon and raisins to a boil.

○

Blend with custard powder mixture and set aside.

○

Divide filling among wrappers. Brush edges of wrappers with egg white and roll up like spring roll.

○

Deep-fry spring rolls in hot oil until crisp. Drain on towels. Keep warm.

2 egg yolks

2 oz (4 tbs) sugar (60 g)

¼ pt (½ c) sweet white wine (125 ml)

In a bowl, place all ingredients and whisk vigorously.

○

Set bowl over hot water and continue to whisk vigorously until mixture foams, thickens and doubles in volume.

1 oz (¼ c) grated coconut (30 g)

½ oz (1 tbs) cocoa (15 g)

Unmould mousses and sprinkle with coconut, then dust with cocoa.

○

Dust spring rolls with icing sugar and place on plate.

○

Serve with sauce. If desired, garnish with a piece of tropical fruit, such as rambutan or lychee.

SWEETENED SNOW FUNGUS
WITH MANDARIN ORANGE

○

HYATT REGENCY XIAN, PEOPLE'S REPUBLIC OF CHINA

SERVES 4

½ oz dried snow fungus (10 g)

1 mandarin orange—peeled and separated into segments

1 ½ lb (1 ⅓ c) sugar (225 g)

8 fl oz water (240 ml)

Soak fungus in hot water for 5 minutes until softened. Drain.

○

Place fungus, mandarin orange segments and sugar in a bowl and add water.

○

Place this bowl in a water bath over medium heat and heat for 20 minutes until sugar is dissolved. Serve hot, or chill for 3–4 hours and serve cold.

Note : Snow fungus is also known as white fungus or silver fungus. It is dried cultivated fungus, which are bland and has a crunchy texture. When soaked in water, it expands dramatically. Available at most Asian foodstores.

FRUIT SUSHI
WITH MANGO AND RASPBERRY SAUCES

HYATT REGENCY SINGAPORE, SINGAPORE

SERVES 4

FRUIT SUSHI

13 ¼ oz (1 ¾ c) white rice (375 g)

12 fl oz (1 ⅔ c) cold water (395 ml)

1 ½ fl oz (3 tbs) coconut milk (45 ml) (see glossary)

1 oz (2 tbs) sugar (30 g)

½ fl oz (1 tbs) coconut liqueur (15 ml)

6 oz assorted fruit—fresh in season, sliced (175g)

pinch salt

Rinse rice several times in cold water. Drain.

Put rice in a pan with cold water.

Quickly bring to a boil, then cover and turn heat down to very low and steam for 15 minutes.

Remove from heat, leaving cover on, and let stand for 10 minutes.

Transfer rice to a large bowl and add coconut milk, sugar, salt and coconut liqueur.

Mix gently and thoroughly until cool.

Moisten your hands with water and form the rice into oval shapes.

Arrange the fresh fruit on top of the rice and serve the mango and raspberry sauces (recipes follow).

MANGO SAUCE

1 mango—halved, pulp scooped out

1 oz (2 tbs) sugar (30 g)

Purée mango with the sugar and strain.

RASPBERRY SAUCE

4 oz raspberries (135 g)

1 oz (2 tbs) sugar (30 g)

Purée raspberries with sugar and strain.

STRAWBERRY TEMPURA

⌒

HYATT REGENCY SINGAPORE, SINGAPORE
SERVES 4

STRAWBERRIES

vegetable oil for frying

2 pt (16 large) strawberries—hulled and diced

4 sesame leaves

4 oz (¾ c) flour (100 g)

Heat vegetable oil in a wok or deep sauté pan.

⌒

Near work area, have a pair of chopsticks (or tongs) and a draining rack over a drip tray. Have ready the sesame leaves and strawberries.

BATTER

2 egg yolks

¾ pt (2 ⅛ c) ice water (500 ml)

pinch baking soda

½ lb (1 ½ c) tempura flour (250 g)

3 ½ oz (¾ c) plain (all-purpose) flour (100 g)

With a whisk, briskly beat yolks with ice water.

⌒

Add baking soda and the 2 flours until the flour is incorporated.

⌒

Do not overbeat. Batter should be thin. If it seems too thick, add a few drops of ice water.

Note: Tempura flour is a pre-mixed blend of flour. It is often sold in Asian Markets.
The secret of good tempura is undermixing the batter; if overworked, it becomes flat and hard.

TO ASSEMBLE AND SERVE

icing (confectioners') sugar—for dusting

strawberry frozen yoghurt

Lightly coat strawberries with flour.

⌒

Shake excess flour off, then dip strawberries in batter.

⌒

Slide strawberries into the hot oil and fry until batter is crisp, turning occasionally—about 1 minute. Drain on towels.

⌒

Dip and fry the sesame leaves, and drain on towels.

⌒

Dust strawberry tempura with icing sugar, then serve with frozen yoghurt.

Pisang Rai
Bananas in Coconut

Bali Hyatt, Indonesia
Serves 4

Bananas

1 ⅓ lb (4 small) bananas (600 g)

1 ½ fl oz (3 tbs) Bali liqueur or Kahlua
(45 ml)

4 ½ oz (¾ c) rice flour (125 g)

4 ½ oz (¾ c) flour (125 g)

pinch salt

1 tsp vanilla essence (extract) (5 ml)

10 fl oz (1 ¼ c) water (300 ml)

3 pandan leaves

9 oz (2 c) coconut—freshly grated
(255 g)

Peel the bananas and halve lengthwise.

○

Place on a plate and sprinkle on
liqueur. Set aside for 5 minutes, then
cut into 1-inch (2.5-cm) slices.

Sift the flours and salt into a bowl.

○

Make a well in the centre, add vanilla
and water and whisk until smooth.

○

Simmer pandan leaves in a large pot of
water.

○

Dip banana slices in the batter, then
poach in pandan water until they rise
to the surface.

○

Roll bananas in grated coconut.

○

Arrange bananas in a circle on a plate
and put a bowl of orange sauce (recipe
follows) in the centre.

Orange Sauce

3 ½ oz (½ c) sugar (100 g)

1 fl oz (2 tbs) water (30 ml)

8 fl oz (1 c) orange juice (237 ml)

1 tsp orange zest—grated (5 g)

2 oz (4 tbs) butter-chilled, cubed (55 g)

In a saucepan, combine sugar and
water; cook until lightly browned,
about 15 minutes.

○

Add the orange juice and zest. Stir
over high heat for 5 minutes.

○

Remove from heat, cool slightly, then
swirl in butter cubes.

Fruit Tacos

Hyatt Regency Manila, Philippines
Serves 4

Sweetened Tacos

1 ½ oz (3 tbs) butter (45 g)

2 ¾ oz (1 c) icing (confectioners') sugar (75 g)

2 egg whites

3 oz (½ c) cake flour (85 g)

1 ½ oz semisweet chocolate—melted and kept warm (40 g)

Preheat oven to 350° F (180° C).
○

Cream the butter, sugar and egg whites together.
○

Stir in flour and mix until smooth. Allow to rest for 1 hour.
○

Trace 3-inch (7.5 cm) circles on a sheet of parchment paper.
○

With a spatula, spread the taco batter inside circles.
○

Bake until taco shells are golden brown and gently curled, about 15 minutes.
○

With a pastry brush, brush inside of shells with melted chocolate. Let harden.

Strawberry Cream

¼ pt (½ c) strawberries—fresh, puréed (120 ml)

½ fl oz (1 tbs) orange juice (15 ml)

¾ oz (1 ½ tbs) caster (granulated) sugar (20 g)

¼ oz (1 tbs) gelatine (5 g)

¼ fl oz (1 tsp) Grand Marnier (5 ml)

4 fl oz (½ c) double (heavy) cream—whipped (120 ml)

Simmer puréed strawberries, orange juice, sugar and gelatine in a saucepan until gelatine is dissolved.
○

Remove from heat and let cool.
○

Add Grand Marnier, mix, then fold in whipped cream.

Fruit Filling

3 oz (1 medium) kiwifruit—peeled and sliced (85 g)

6 oz (1 medium) mango—peeled and sliced (170 g)

6 oz (1 medium) orange—peeled and sliced (170 g)

1 ½ oz (⅓ c) seedless grapes (40 g)

1 ½ oz (⅓ c) pineapple—crushed (40 g)

1 ½ oz (⅓ c) strawberries—sliced (40 g)

Mango Sauce

6 oz (1 medium) mango—halved, peeled and pips removed (170 g)

juice of ½ lime

1 tsp honey (5 ml)

Purée ingredients in a liquidiser.

To Assemble and Serve

icing (confectioners') sugar—for dusting

Half-fill taco shells with strawberry cream.
○

Nicely arrange some of the fruit over strawberry cream.
○

Arrange tacos on plates and decorate with extra fruit slices.
○

Dust icing sugar, and serve mango sauce alongside.

Two-Layer Cake
with Orange-Yoghurt Cream

Hyatt Regency Hong Kong, Hong Kong
Serves 4

Chocolate Meringue Cake Batter

5 egg whites

6 oz (1 c) sugar (175 g)

4 ¾ oz (1 ¼ c) almonds—finely diced (135 g)

1 oz (2 tbs) cocoa (30 g)

Beat egg whites with half the sugar until stiff.

Mix remaining sugar with the almonds and cocoa.

Carefully fold cocoa mixture into beaten egg whites.

Butter Cake Batter

8 oz almond paste (225 g)

3 ½ oz (7 tbs) butter—cubed (90 g)

3 eggs—beaten

2 ½ oz sifted cake flour (75 g)

⅛ oz (¼ tsp) baking powder (3 g)

Cream almond paste and butter until fluffy and light.

Blend in eggs.

Sift together flour and baking powder.

Carefully fold flour mixture into creamed mixture.

To Assemble and Bake the Cake

1 oz (2 tbs) almonds—sliced (30 g)

Preheat oven to 350° F (180° C).

Sprinkle almond slices on the sides of a well-buttered 8-inch (20 cm) round baking pan.

Carefully spread the Butter Cake batter in tin to ¹⁄₁₆ inch (1 mm) height (covering all the almonds).

Fill tin with Chocolate Meringue Cake batter. Tap tin to settle batters.

Bake for approximately 30 minutes, or until centre springs back when pressed and top is firm. Let cool, then remove from tin.

Orange-Yoghurt Cream

½ fl oz (1 tbs) orange juice (15 ml)

¼ fl oz (1 tsp) lemon juice (5 ml)

grated peel ½ orange

⅔ oz (1 ½ tbs) butter (20 g)

1 ½ oz (3 tbs) sugar (45 g)

1 egg—separated

1 oz (¼ c) pineapple—crushed (30 g)

2 ½ fl oz (5 tbs) plain yoghurt (75 ml)

¼ oz (1 tsp) gelatine (7 g)— dissolved in 2 tbs (30 ml) warm water

4 fl oz (½ c) double (heavy) cream— whipped (120 ml)

Bring orange and lemon juices, orange peel, butter and 1 oz sugar (2 tbs; 30 g) to a boil.

○

Whisk egg yolk carefully, then slowly add to juice mixture while whisking vigorously. Boil approximately 2 minutes.

○

Add pineapple and let mixture cool. Beat egg white and remaining sugar until light and fluffy.

○

Add yoghurt and gelatine, then carefully blend with the cold orange mixture.

○

Fold in the whipped cream.

12 oz (3 medium) oranges—cut into sections or sliced (340 g)

Wrap a long strip of greaseproof paper or foil around the cake, letting it come up to the top by 2 inches (5 cm), like forming a "collar" for a soufflé.

○

Cut a thin cone-shaped incision in cake.

○

Fill cavity, up to ¾–1 inch (3 cm), with orange-yoghurt cream.

○

Chill for 2 hours.

○

Remove collar and decorate with orange segments or slices.

○

Keep cake refrigerated until you are ready to serve.

Jajan Uli

Three-Layer Rice Cake

Bali Hyatt, Indonesia

Serves 10

Syrups

½ pt (1 ¼ c) coconut milk (280 ml)
(see glossary)

3 ½ oz (½ c) caster (granulated) sugar
(100 ml)

7 oz (1 c) palm or brown sugar (200 g)

Place 3 ½ fl oz (7 tbs; 100 ml) coconut milk and caster sugar in pan. Bring to a boil and boil vigorously.

Combine remaining coconut milk with palm sugar and boil for 1 minute.

Strain through a fine sieve. Set aside.

Glutinous Rice

1 lb (2 c) white glutinous rice (500 g)

2 ¾ pt (6 ½ c) lukewarm water (1 ⅓ l)

1 lb (2 c) black glutinous rice (500 g)

Wash each type of rice separately in several changes of cold water.

Put each kind of rice in a saucepan with half the warm water.

Cover and cook white glutinous rice for 25–35 minutes or until tender. Cook black glutinous rice for 40 minutes or until tender.

Note: Black glutinous rice has the bean still attached to the rice kernel. It has a nuttier taste than refined white rice.

Cake

¼ fl oz (1 ½ tsp) vanilla essence
(extract) (7 ml)

salt

fresh fruit or fruit sauce—for garnish

Mix half the white rice with the sugar syrup. Add ½ tsp (2 ml) vanilla essence and a pinch of salt. Cook for approximately 5 minutes, stirring continuously, until mixture sticks to a spoon.

Spread evenly in a deep oiled baking pan, 8-inches (20-cm) in diameter.

Mix remaining half of white rice with half the palm sugar ½ tsp (2 ml) syrup, vanilla essence and a pinch of salt. Cook for 5 minutes, stirring until it coats the spoon.

Spread evenly on top of bottom layer in pan.

Mix all the black rice with the remaining half of the palm syrup. Add remaining sugar, vanilla essence and a pinch of salt. Cook for 5 minutes, or until mixture coats the spoon.

Spread evenly over middle layer.

Chill the cake, then cut into 10 slices.

Decorate with fresh fruit or a fruit sauce.

Epres Gombóc Vanilia Mártással
Strawberry Dumpling with Cream

Atrium Hyatt Budapest, Hungary

Serves 4

DUMPLINGS

1 ¼ pt (3 c) milk (700 ml)

1 ½ oz (3 tbs) butter (45 g)

¼ oz (1 ½ tsp) salt (5–7 g)

10 oz (2 c) flour (300 g)

4 eggs

16 strawberries—fresh, hulled

7 oz (1 ¾ c) bread crumbs—lightly
    browned in oven (200 g)

Bring milk, butter and salt to a boil.

Add flour and stir well until mixture
starts to leave sides of pan.

Remove from heat and add eggs, one
at a time.

Mix thoroughly. Let cool at room
temperature.

Roll out dough until ⅓ inch (1 cm)
thick.

Cut into 4-inch (10-cm) squares, then
place a strawberry in the centre of
each square and fold dough around
strawberry.

Put dumplins in boiling water and
wait for them to rise, about 2 minutes.

Drain and roll dumplings on bread
crumbs.

Serve with cream sauce (recipe
follows)

CREAM SAUCE

5 oz (¾ c) sugar (150 g)

8 oz (2 c) strawberries—hulled (225 g)

¾ pt (2 c) double (heavy) cream
    (480 ml)

1 fl oz (2 tbs) Triple Sec (30 ml)

Mix ingredients in a liquidiser and
purée.

Apple Paté
with Caramel Sauce

Hyatt Regency Coolum, Queensland, Australia
Serves 4

Crepes

5 ¼ oz (1 c) flour (150 g)

pinch salt

3 eggs

¾ oz (1 ½ tbs) vegetable oil (20 ml)

grated zest of ¼ lemon

8 fl oz (1 c) milk (240 ml)

Mix flour and salt in a bowl; make a well in the centre.

Add the eggs, oil and zest.

Whisk until smooth while pouring in milk. Strain batter if lumpy.

Heat a nonstick crepe pan and cook crepes on both sides until done, about 3 minutes.

Apple Paté

1 ⅔ lb (4 large) apples (750 g)

¼ pt (½ c) dry white wine (120 ml)

¼ pt (½ c) water (120 ml)

2 oz (¼ c) sugar (55 g)

zest of ½ lemon

juice of 2 lemons

12 cloves—whole

½ cinnamon stick

1 tbs Calvados (15 ml)

¾ oz (1 ½ tbs) cornflour (cornstarch) (20 g)—dissolved in 1 tbs water (15 ml)

Peel the apples and slice ½-inch (1.25 cm) thick.

Bring the wine, water, sugar, zest, lemon juice, cloves, cinnamon and Calvados to a boil.

Add apple slices and poach for 3 minutes.

Remove apples and strain juice.

Thicken apple juice with cornflour mixture, then fold in apple slices.

Line a 9-inch (23-cm) pie pan with half the crepes.

Cover with the apple mixture and cover with remaining crepes. Chill for 2 hours.

Cut into slices and serve with caramel sauce (recipe follows).

Caramel Sauce

5 ¼ oz (1 c) sugar (150 g)

¼ pt (½ c) water (120 ml)

8 fl oz (1 c) milk (240 ml)

¾ oz (1 ½ tbs) cornflour (cornstarch) (40 g)

Place sugar in a pan and cook until caramelized. Add water and stir until caramel is completely dissolved.

Mix the cornflour with a little of the milk.

Add to the syrup, stir and boil for 2 minutes until thickened.

Remove from heat and allow to cool.

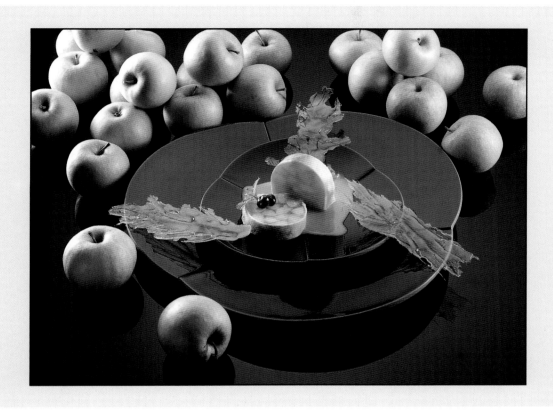

FLAN DE COCO
COCONUT FLAN

○

HYATT REGENCY ACAPULCO, MEXICO

SERVES 4

8 oz (1 large) coconut (225 g)

14 fl oz (1 ¾ c) evaporated milk (420 ml)

1 fl oz (2 tbs) vanilla essence (extract) (30 ml)

8 oz (1 c) sugar (240 g)

5 eggs

Poke 2 holes in coconut at the "eyes" and drain the coconut water. Crack with hammer and pry meat from shell. Put coconut meat in a liquidiser with the evaporated milk and blend until smooth.

○

In a saucepan, combine coconut purée with half the sugar and the vanilla essence.

○

Heat over medium heat and stir continuously with a wire whisk while adding eggs, until the mixture comes almost to a boil. Remove from heat and cool in refrigerator.

○

Prepare the caramel topping by melting the remaining sugar with about 2–3 tbs water.

○

Stir continuously until the sugar melts and turns golden brown.

○

Immediately pour hot caramel into the bottom of 4 custard cups. Allow to cool and harden.

○

Once the custard mixture has cooled, fill cups almost to the brim.

○

Preheat oven to 300° F (150° C).

○

Place custard cups in water bath and bake for approximately 1 hour, or until set.

○

Allow flans to cool, then loosen sides with a knife and invert onto plates.

Tartlet of Fromage Blanc
with a Lime Compote

<hr>

Hyatt Regnecy Adelaide, Australia

Serves 4

Lime Compote

2 lb (8 medium) limes—zest grated and flesh cut into segments (900 g)

10 oz (2 ½ c) sugar (250 g)

1 pt (2 ½ c) lime juice (600 ml)

Caramelize 3 oz (¼ c; 50 g) of sugar lightly. Add ¾ of zest, then deglaze with 3 ½ tbs (50 ml) of lime juice.

Carmelize remainder of sugar. Add remainder of juice and reduce by one-third.

Cool and add lime segments.

Place praline circle in the centre of a dessert plate and unmould fromage blanc cream on top of it.

Arrange lime segments on top of fromage blanc, and garnish with remaining zest.

Praline

3 ½ oz (½ c) sugar (100 g)

3 oz (¾ c) roasted almonds—sliced thinly (85 g)

In a saucepan, melt sugar gently. Do not stir until it begins to melt.

When sugar has turned golden brown, quickly add almonds and mix well.

Turn the sugar-almond mixture (praline) onto an oiled marble slab, spreading thinly with an oiled spatula.

Cut out 2 ¾-inch (7-cm) rounds before the praline cools.

Fromage Blanc Cream

2 egg yolks

3 oz (½ c) sugar (85 g)

1 ¾ fl oz (3 ½ tbs) water (50 ml)

8 fl oz (1 c) double (heavy) cream (200 ml)

⅓ fl oz (2 tsp) sugar syrup (10 ml)

8 ¾ oz (1 c) fromage blanc (250 g)

½ fl oz (1 tbs) unflavoured gelatine (15 g)

4 fl oz (½ c) single (light) cream (100 ml)

Whisk yolks until thickened and light in colour.

Boil sugar and water together until a thin syrup forms.

Slowly pour syrup into beaten yolks, whisking constantly until egg mixture cools.

Whip the 2 creams together with the gelatine until soft peaks form.

Stir the cheese into the yolk mixture, then gently fold in the cream.

Fill four 2 ¾- inch (7-cm) removable-bottom moulds up to the rim with cream mixture. Chill at least 2 hours or until set.

WARM SAGO PUDDING
WITH CANTALOUPE

HYATT REGENCY HONG KONG, HONG KONG

SERVES 4

3 ½ oz sago (pearled tapioca)—soaked in water for 1 hour (100 g)

14 fl oz (1 ¾ c) milk (400 ml)

½ vanilla bean, or ¼ tsp vanilla essence (extract) (1 ml)

1 egg—separated

1 ¾ oz (¼ c) sugar (50 g)

2 fl oz (4 tbs) whipped cream (60 ml)

3 ½ oz (1 c) raspberries—puréed (100 g)

icing (confectioners') sugar

1 cantaloupe—cut with melon baller into small balls

Preheat oven to 400° F (200° C). Boil sago in water to cover for 8 minutes. Drain.

Bring milk and vanilla to a boil over medium heat.

Add sago and simmer for another 2 minutes, then set aside to cool at room temperature.

Whisk in egg yolk.

Beat egg whites till soft peaks form, then add sugar, and beat until stiff.

Fold sago mixture into beaten egg whites.

Lightly fold in whipped cream.

Pour mixture into buttered custard cups or ramekins, then arrange cups in a deep pan set in a water bath.

Bake until firm, about 30 minutes.

Serve warm with puréed raspberries, icing sugar and small balls of cantaloupe.

Li Zhi Bu Ding

Rice Pudding with Lychees

Hyatt Tianjin, People's Republic of China

Serves 4

PUDDING

7 oz (¼ c) glutinous rice (200 g)

¼ pt (½ c) coconut milk (120 ml) (see glossary)

3 ½ oz (¾ c) palm or brown sugar (100 g)

1 tsp salt (5 g)

3 ½ oz (¾ c) lychees—finely chopped (100 g)

Wash rice under cold running water, then soak overnight.

Drain and steam in a colander over boiling water.

In a saucepan, bring coconut milk to a boil.

Add sugar and salt and continue to cook, stirring frequently, until mixture is thick.

Add rice and blend well.

Add chopped lychees, then simmer over medium heat until very thick.

Pour into a buttered mould or cup and allow to cool.

Unmould pudding onto serving plate and surround with sauce (recipe follows).

SAUCE

3 ½ oz (½ c) sugar (100 g)

1 pt (2 ⅛ c) milk or cream (500 ml)

2 egg yolks—lightly beaten

Pour sugar into a large pan over high heat and stir frequently until sugar dissolves and is golden in colour.

Take pan off heat and immediately whisk in cream or milk, stirring constantly.

Return to heat and whisk for 3–4 minutes.

Remove from heat again and stir in egg yolks.

Pass custard sauce through a sieve and allow to cool.

SANGRILA WITH FRUITS AND ICE CREAM

HYATT REGENCY DUBAI, UNITED ARAB EMIRATES

SERVES 4

1 fl oz (2 tbs) gelatine (2 packets) (30 ml)

2 fl oz (4 tbs) water (60 g)

½ pt (1 ¼ c) rosé wine (300 ml)

juice of ½ lemon

6 fl oz (¾ c) champagne or other sparkling wine (100 ml)

6 oz (2 medium) kiwifruit—peeled and sliced crosswise (175 g)

1 ¼ lb (6 medium) apricots—fresh, halved and stones removed (560 g)

3 oz (¾ c) pineapple chunks (85 g)

6 oz (1 medium) mango—halved, peeled and sliced diagonally (170 g)

1 lb (4 medium) plums—halved with stones removed (455 g)

4 oz (8 large) strawberries—washed, hulled and sliced in halves or quarters (115 g)

4 scoops ice cream—any flavor

1 carambola (star fruit)—for garnish

mint sprigs—for garnish

Dissolve gelatine in water and place over gentle heat. Stir in wine, then add lemon juice and stir. Let cool, but do not allow to set completely.

Stir champagne or sparkling wine into the gelatine mixture; chill again until softly gelled.

Arrange fruits on 4 individual plates.

Spoon gellied sauce on the plates and over fruit.

Neatly arrange ice cream over the fruit, then garnish with carambola and mint leaves.

Lychee Dumplings

with Pineapple Sauce

⌒

Hyatt Regency Hong Kong, Hong Kong

Serves 4

Dumplings

1 lb (2 large) potatoes—baked (500 g)

4 oz (8 tbs) butter—softened (125 g)

1 ¾ oz (¼ c) semolina (50 g)

¼ oz (1½ tsp) salt (7 g)

1 egg—separated

3 ½ oz (¾ c) flour (100 g)

3 ½ oz (½ c) palm or brown sugar (100 g)

12 fresh lychees—peeled

3 ½ oz (¾ c) grated coconut (100 g)

red food colouring

icing (confectioners') sugar

mint leaves—fresh for garnish

Peel baked potatoes and mash to a fine purée.

⌒

Place mashed potatoes in a bowl making a well in the centre.

⌒

Add half the softened butter, the semolina, salt, half the egg white and the yolk to the well.

⌒

Work together with your hands, then sift flour over the mixture. Knead well to a smooth dough and chill 15 minutes.

⌒

Mix palm sugar with a little water until a paste is formed.

⌒

Remove pips from lychees and fill seed cavities with the palm sugar paste.

⌒

Roll out chilled dough until ⅛-inch (3-mm) thick on a floured board.

⌒

Cut into 12 equal squares and wrap a lychee in each.

⌒

Lower dumplings into salted boiling water and poach until they rise to the surface, approximately 15 minutes.

⌒

Remove with a slotted spoon and refresh in cold water.

⌒

Heat remaining butter in a pan; add grated coconut and a few drops of red food colouring.

⌒

Toast coconut until crisp, then dry with a paper towel.

⌒

Roll dumplings in coconut and sprinkle icing sugar over them.

⌒

Serve with sauce (recipe follows). Garnish with mint.

Sauce

¾ oz (1 ½ tbs) cornflour (cornstarch) (15 g)

1 fl oz (2 tbs) Kirsch (20 ml)

1 ¾ oz (¼ c) sugar (50 g)

¾ pt (2 c) pineapple juice (400 ml)

3 ½ oz (¾ c) crushed pineapple (100 g)

Dissolve cornflour in Kirsch.

⌒

Bring pineapple juice, sugar and cornflour mixture to a boil and cook until thickened, about 5 minutes.

⌒

Add crushed pineapple tidbits.

Pere Rellena con Salsa de Frutas
Stuffed Pears with Fruit Coulis

◯

Hyatt Regency Cancun, Mexico
Serves 4

Pears

4 pears—firm, any variety

1 ¾ pt (4 ¼ c) red burgundy wine (1 𝑙)

10 oz (1 ¾ c) sugar (300 g)

4 ¼ oz marzipan or almond paste (120 g)

Core the pears, keeping the skins and stems intact.

◯

In a deep pot, poach pear in wine and sugar over low heat until soft.

◯

Remove and allow to cool. Reduce cooking liquid to a syrup.

◯

Stuff pear hollows with marzipan.

◯

Place pears on individual plates, glaze with the wine syrup and serve with coulis (recipe follows).

Fruit Coulis

3 ½ oz (1 large) kiwi-fruit—peeled and puréed (100 g)

3 ½ oz strawberries—puréed (100 g)

3 ½ oz (½ medium) mango—puréed (100 g)

3 ½ oz quayaba (guava)—fresh, puréed (100 g)

3 ½ oz mamey sapote—puréed (100 g)

Mix fruit purées, adding water if necessary to have sauce with light consistency.

Note: Guaveas and mamey sapote are semitropical fruits. They are sold fresh in Hispanic groceries in season, or in tins, usually as sweetened purées.

TARTE AU CITRON
LEMON TART

⌒

THE CARLTON TOWER, A PARK HYATT HOTEL, LONDON, UNITED KINGDOM
SERVES 4

SWEET CRUST PASTRY

5 oz (1 ¼ c) softened butter (300 g)

5 ¼ oz (2 c) icing sugar (confectioners) (150 g)

2 eggs

10 oz (2 c) flour (300 g)

Cream the butter and sugar together.

⌒

Add eggs and mix well.

⌒

Add flour and mix again. Form into a ball.

⌒

Wrap ball of dough and let rest in refrigerator for a few hours.

⌒

Preheat oven to 350° F (180° C)

⌒

Roll out dough and fit into 9-inch (23-cm) tart pan.

⌒

Bake for 15 minutes or until crust is lightly browned. Let cool.

FILLING

grated zest of 3 lemons

5 ¼ oz (¾ c) caster sugar (granulated) (150 g)

5 fl oz (⅔ c) double (heavy) cream (150 g)

2 eggs

2 tsp light rum (10 ml)

Mix ingredients until foamy and pour into preheated tart shell.

⌒

Bake for 20 minutes or until filling is set.

⌒

Let cool.

TOPPING

lemon segments or slices from 3–5 lemons

icing (confectioners' sugar)—for garnish

Top baked tart with lemon segments or slices.

⌒

Dust icing with sugar.

⌒

Put under broiler for a few seconds to glaze top.

SUMMER PUDDING

WITH BERRIES

⬭

THE CARLTON TOWER, A PARK HYATT HOTEL, LONDON, UNITED KINGDOM

SERVES 4

4–8 slices white bread

6 oz strawberries—fresh, hulled (170 g)

6 oz raspberries—fresh (170 g)

6 oz blueberries—fresh (170 g)

6 oz blackberries—fresh (170 g)

berries—fresh for garnish

whipped cream or fruit sauce (optional)

Line a 2-pint (945 ml) pudding or soufflé mould with the bread slices, covering bottom, then sides.

⬭

Bring fruit to a boil in a saucepan with very little water, then remove from heat.

⬭

Pour fruit into mould, then cover with more slices of bread.

⬭

Press down with a small weighted saucer and leave to soak overnight in the refrigerator.

⬭

Unmould pudding onto a plate. Decorate with fresh berries and serve with whipped cream, if desired, or fruit sauce.

GRANDMOTHER'S VICTORIAN PICKLED FRUIT

─── ◯ ───

HYATT ON COLLINS, MELBOURNE, AUSTRALIA

SERVES 4

FRUITS

3 ½ oz (¾ c) strawberries—washed, dried and hulled (100 g)

7 oz (1 ½ c) pineapple chunks (200 g)

7 oz (2 medium) kiwifruit—peeled and sliced crosswise (200 g)

3 ½ oz (¾ c) prunes (100 g)

3 ½ oz (¾ c) blackberries (100 g)

vanilla ice cream

Layer fruit neatly in a large container with lid.

◯

Pour sugar syrup over fruit.

◯

Close top and refrigerate 4 days.

◯

To serve, scoop out fruit with slotted spoon and place in dessert bowls.

◯

Serve with vanilla ice cream.

SYRUP

2 lb (5 c) sugar (1 kg)

1 ¾ pt (4 ¼ c) water (1 l)

juice of 4 lemons

3 ½ oz (¾ c) pink peppercorns (100 g)

In a saucepan, bring sugar, water, lemon juice and pink peppercorns to a boil.

◯

Simmer 10 more minutes, then allow to cool.

COCKTAILS

SWISS WHITE WINE PUNCH

⬭

HYATT CONTINENTAL MONTREUX, SWITZERLAND

SERVES 8

½ pt (1 c) fresh strawberries—halved lengthwise (100 g)

½ pt (1 c) fresh raspberries (100 g)

½ pt (1 c) fresh red currants (100 g)

5 ¼ oz (¾ c) sugar (150 g)

5 fl oz (⅔ c) maraschino liqueur (150 ml)

5 fl oz (⅔ c) cognac (150 ml)

3 fl oz (7 tbs) Chambord (raspberry) liqueur (100 ml)

2 bottles dry white wine (1.5 *l*)

In a punch bowl, place strawberries, raspberries and currants.

⬭

Add sugar, maraschino liqueur and cognac.

⬭

Toss carefully and refrigerate to chill for 2 hours.

⬭

Mix in the Chambord and white wine and refrigerate another 2 hours before serving.

SCHEHERAZADE

HYATT REGENCY DUBAI, UNITED ARAB EMIRATES
SERVES 1

2 fl oz (4 tbs) apricot nectar (60 ml)

2 fl oz (4 tbs) mango juice (60 ml)

2 fl oz (4 tbs) pineapple juice (60 ml)

5 tbs (⅓ c) plain yoghurt (75 ml)

dash grenadine

dash sugar syrup (see glossary)

2 pineapple leaves—for garnish

1 pineapple wedge—for garnish

1 fresh strawberry—for garnish

4—5 ice cubes

Pour all ingredients, except grenadine, in a liquidiser and blend for 12–15 seconds.

○

Strain into a large goblet or stemmed white wine glass.

○

Add grenadine on top and garnish with pineapple leaves, pineapple wedge, and strawberry.

GINSENG COCKTAIL

HYATT REGENCY CHEJU, KOREA
SERVES 1

14 fl oz (1 ¾ c) water (415 ml)

½ oz (1 tbs) freeze-dried ginseng tea extract (15 g)

¾ oz (1 ½ tbs) fresh ginseng—chopped (20 g)

1 tsp dried jujubes—sliced (5 g)

½ tsp pine kernels (pignoli) (3 g)

3 fl oz (6 tbs) whiskey (90 ml)

small pc fresh ginseng—for garnish (40 g)

1 ½ fl oz (3 tbs) honey (45 ml)

Note: Freeze-dried ginseng tea extract has no substitute. It may be available in Chinese groceries or herb shops or in natural foods stores. Jujubes are Chinese red dates, sold in Asian markets.

Boil water and add ginseng tea extract. Stir well.

○

In a tall glass, place fresh ginseng, jujubes and pine kernels.

○

Pour in whiskey and hot ginseng. Stir well.

○

Garnish glass with fresh ginseng root.

○

Put honey in a separate bowl and serve as accompaniment.

MELONIE

Hyatt Aryaduta Jakarta, Indonesia

Serves 1

1 sm slice honeydew melon or about
4 tbs of diced honeydew (115 g)

¾ fl oz (1 ½ tbs) maraschino liqueur
(25 ml)

½ fl oz (1 tbs) fresh pineapple juice
(15 ml)

½ fl oz (1 tbs) lemon juice (15 ml)

¼ fl oz (½ tbs) sugar syrup
(see glossary)

½ crushed ice

half-moon slice of honeydew melon—
for garnish

Place all drink ingredients in a
liquidiser with crushed ice.

Blend 8–10 seconds then pour
unstrained into stemmed wine glass or
highball glass.

Garnish with honeydew slice and
serve with a long straw.

DESERT ROYAL

HYATT REGENCY RIYADH, SAUDI ARABIA

SERVES 1

3 fl oz (6 tbs) fresh apple juice (90 ml)

2 oz (½ c) pineapple slices (55 g)

⅓ fl oz (2 tsp) sugar syrup (10 ml)
(see glossary)

5 fl oz (½ c) fresh red grape juice
(140 ml)

1 lemon slice—for garnish (optional)

1 mint leaf—for garnish (optional)

Mix apple juice, pineapple slice
and sugar syrup in a liquidiser for
1 minute. Pour into a glass.

Add red grape juice over the mixture.
It will drop to the bottom of the glass
and the apple-pineapple mixture will
float to the top.

Garnish with lemon slice and mint
leaf, if desired.

Jo Jo Ivory

Hyatt Regency Perth, Australia

Serves 1

½ c crushed ice

1 fl oz (2 tbs) Kahlua (coffee liqueur) (30 ml)

1 fl oz (2 tbs) Bailey's Irish Cream (30 ml)

½ fl oz (1 tbs) creme de banana (15 ml)

2 fl oz (4 tbs) double (heavy) cream (60 ml)

4 oz (½ medium) banana—sliced (115 g)

powdered chocolate—for garnish

Fill liquidiser halfway with crushed ice and pour in remaining ingredients.

Blend well.

Pour into glass and sprinkle with powdered chocolate.

RHINEGOLD

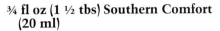

HYATT REGENCY MANILA, PHILIPPINES

SERVES 1

¾ fl oz (1 ½ tbs) Southern Comfort (20 ml)

1 ½ fl oz (3 tbs) vodka (45 ml)

3 fl oz (7 tbs) pineapple juice (100 ml)

⅓ fl oz (2 tsp) simple syrup (10 ml) (see glossary)

⅓ fl oz (2 tsp) yellow Chartreuse (10 ml)

⅓ fl oz (2 tsp) white creme de menthe (10 ml)

½ c crushed ice

1 pineapple slice—for garnish

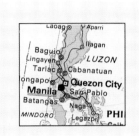

Shake all drink ingredients in a shaker, strain and pour into a stemmed glass.

Garnish with a slice of pineapple and serve with a straw.

DRUNKEN PINEAPPLE

HYATT KUANTAN, MALAYSIA
SERVES 1

4 ½ fl oz (½ c) fresh orange juice (130 ml)

4 ½ fl oz (½ c) fresh pineapple juice (130 ml)

¾ fl oz (1 ½ tbs) grenadine (20 ml)

⅓ fl oz (2 tbs) sugar syrup (10 ml) (see glossary)

½ c crushed ice

Pour drink ingredients in a shaker with crushed ice and shake well.

Pour into a 12-oz (360 ml) glass or scooped out pineapple.

PINK SQUIRREL

HYATT ON COLLINS, MELBOURNE, AUSTRALIA
SERVES 1

1 fl oz (2 tbs) Amaretto (30 ml)

1 fl oz (2 tbs) white creme de cacao (30 ml)

1 tsp grenadine (5 ml)

1 fl oz (2 tbs) double (heavy) cream (30 ml)

½ c crushed ice

1 pineapple wedge—for garnish

1 strawberry—cut in half, for garnish

Place ingredients in a shaker and shake well.

Strain and pour into a glass.

Garnish with a wedge of pineapple and half a strawberry on each side.

NATHAN 67

1 ¼ fl oz (2 tbs) melon liqueur (35 ml)

½ fl oz (1 tbs) blue Curaçao (15 ml)

½ fl oz (1 tbs) creme de banana (15 ml)

2 fl oz (4 tbs) orange juice (60 ml)

1 fl oz (2 tbs) pineapple juice (30 ml)

⅓ fl oz (2 tsp) fresh lime juice (10 ml)

2-3 ice cubes

1 pineapple wedge—for garnish

½ fresh strawberry—for garnish

Mix all ingredients in a shaker with a few cubes of ice and shake well.

Strain into a tall glass and serve immediately.

Garnish with pineapple slice and strawberry half, and serve immediately.

MERRY MIX-UP

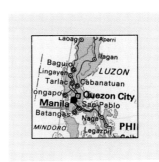

⅓ cantaloupe—cut in balls

1 ½ fl oz (3 tbs) Peachtree liqueur (45 ml)

4 ½ fl oz (½ c) fresh orange juice (130 ml)

¾ fl oz (1 ½ tbs) milk (20 ml)

1 tsp Galliano (5 ml)

1 cucumber slice—for garnish

1 maraschino cherry—for garnish

Peel cantaloupe and slice in half. Scoop out the pulp of one half and purée in a liquidiser.

Use melon baller to form balls with the other half.

Combine all remaining ingredients except Galliano in a shaker with 3–4 ice cubes.

Shake vigorously and pour into stemmed wine glass. Float Galliano on top.

Garnish with cantaloupe balls and cucumber slice and cherry.

Serve with straw.

THE BROMO COCKTAIL

○

HYATT REGENCY SURABAYA, INDONESIA

SERVES 1

*Bromo is a volcano. It is a spectacular
sight (especially at sunrise), and is one
of the main attractions in East Java.*

**3 fl oz (6 tbs) coconut water
(see glossary) (90 ml)**

½ fl oz (1 tbs) vodka (15 ml)

½ fl oz (1 tbs) Cointreau (15 ml)

1 fl oz (2 tbs) orange juice (30 ml)

½ c crushed ice

1 fl oz (2 tbs) pineapple juice (30 ml)

1 bamboo drink holder (optional)

1 half-slice orange—for garnish

Place all ingredients in a shaker with
crushed ice and shake well.

○

Strain and pour into a highball glass
and, if desired, place glass inside a
bamboo drink holder.

○

Decorate with half a slice of orange.

*Note: Photo shows the dramatic
effects achieved when some dry
ice is placed on top of drink
holder. Use caution when
handling dry ice. Do not place
in cocktail.*

WHITE LILY

HYATT REGENCY SINGAPORE, SINGAPORE

SERVES 1

1 ½ fl oz (3 tbs) gin (45 ml)

1 fl oz (2 tbs) Cointreau (30 ml)

1 ½ fl oz (3 tbs) coconut milk
(see glossary) (45 ml)

1 ½ fl oz (3 tbs) lime juice (45 ml)

3 fl oz (6 tbs) pineapple juice (90 ml)

½ c crushed ice

Combine all in a shaker with some crushed ice.

Shake well and pour into glass.

SNOW COUNTRY (YUKIGUNI)

1 lime wedge

sugar (to coat glass rim)

1 ⅓ fl oz (3 tbs) vodka (40 ml)

⅓ fl oz (2 tsp) Cointreau (10 ml)

⅓ fl oz (2 tsp) lime cordial (10 ml)

½ c crushed ice

**1 green maraschino cherry—
   for garnish**

Place all ingredients in a shaker and shake well.

Strain and pour into a glass.

To make the drink more festive you may garnish with a green maraschino cherry.

Note: Before pouring the cocktail into the glass, rub rim of cocktail glass with lime wedge. Dip glass edge in sugar to coat rim.

TEQUILA SUNRISE

HYATT ON COLLINS, MELBOURNE, AUSTRALIA
SERVES 1

1 ⅔ fl oz (3 tbs) tequila (45 ml)

6–8 ice cubes

orange juice (17 ml)

1 tsp grenadine (5 ml)

1 lemon wedge—for garnish

1 lemon leaf —for garnish

1 slice kiwifruit —for garnish

Pour tequila in a highball glass filled with ice cubes.

Top with orange juice, place a swizzle stick in it, and drip grenadine down the stick.

Garnish with lemon wedge, lemon leaf and slice of kiwi.

Note: The grenadine will gradually rise to top, mimicking a "sunrise."

Chamolinian

Hyatt Regency Saipan, Mariana Islands
Serves 1

1 fl oz (2 tbs) gin (30 ml)

1 fl oz (2 tbs) brandy (30 ml)

2 fl oz (4 tbs) lime juice (60 ml)

2½ fl oz (5 tbs) pineapple juice (75 ml)

½ fl oz (1 tbs) crushed ice

2 fl oz (4 tbs) orgeat syrup (60 ml)

1 pineapple wedge—for garnish

1 coconut leaf—for garnish

1 palm leaf—for garnish

Place all ingredients except pineapple wedge and coconut leaf in a liquidiser with ice and blend.

Pour into a small glass and garnish with pineapple wedge and coconut leaf.

Note: Orgeat is a sweet flavouring of orange and almond used in cocktails and food.

Frozen Ginseng Daiquiri

Hyatt Regency Seoul, Korea
Serves 1

1 fl oz (2 tbs) ginseng wine (30 ml)

1 fl oz (2 tbs) light rum (30 ml)

½ fl oz (1 tbs) sugar syrup (15 ml)

1 fl oz (2 tbs) lemon juice (30 ml)

5 fl oz (½ c) crushed ice (150 ml)

1 fresh ginseng root—for garnish

Blend all drink ingredients in a shaker with crushed ice.

Pour into cocktail glass. Cut a small slit in bottom of ginseng root and place on edge of glass. Serve.

JERUSALEM SKYLIGHT

HYATT REGENCY JERUSALEM, ISRAEL
SERVES 1

6 fl oz (¾ c) orange juice (200 ml)

⅓ fl oz (2 tsp) grenadine (10 ml)

2 fl oz (¼ c) grapefruit juice (60 ml)

1 ½ fl oz (3 tbs) white tequila (45 ml)

1 fl oz (2 tbs) blue Curaçao (30 ml)

4–6 ice cubes

Pack a tall 15-oz glass (highball or similar), with ice cubes.

Pour in orange juice, then grenadine.

Float grapefruit juice on top by gently pouring in without letting it blend with lower liquids.

In a separate glass, mix tequila and Curaçao.

Float the mixture on top of grapefruit juice layer, pouring in gently for a multilayered pousse-cafe look.

SUN-KISSED COOLER

HYATT REGENCY MANILA, PHILIPPINES
SERVES 1

3 fl oz (6 tbs) rum (90 ml)

¾ fl oz (1 ½ tbs) vodka (25 ml)

4 ½ fl oz (½ c) pineapple juice (120 ml)

1 ½ fl oz (3 tbs) orange juice (45 ml)

1 tsp Galliano (5 ml)

1 ½ fl oz (3 tbs) triple sec (45 ml)

1 ½ fl oz (3 tbs) simple syrup (45 ml) (see glossary)

½ c crushed ice

1 lemon slice—for garnish

mint leaves —for garnish

palm leaf—for garnish

Place all ingredients except granish in a shaker and shake.

Pour into a stemmed glass and serve, garnished with lemon, mint and palm.

CHAMPAGNE CONCOCTIONS

HYATT REGENCY SEOUL, KOREA
SERVES 1

CHAMPAGNE CURAÇAO

½ fl oz (1 tbs) blue Curaçao (15 ml)

5 fl oz (⅔ c) champagne—well chilled
  (150 ml)

Place Curaçao in tall glass.

Gently pour in champagne.

CHAMPAGNE GALLIANO

3 fl oz (6 tbs) champagne (90 ml)

½ fl oz (1 tbs) Galliano (15 ml)

2 fl oz (4 tbs) orange juice (60 ml)

Place Galliano and orange juice in tall
glass.

Gently pour in champagne.

CHAMPAGNE CHERRY BRANDY

½ fl oz (1 tbs) cherry brandy (15 ml)

5 fl oz (⅔ c) champagne (150 ml)

Place cherry brandy in tall glass.

Gently pour in champagne.

CHAMPAGNE BENEDICTINE

3 fl oz (6 tbs) champagne (90 ml)

2 fl oz (4 tbs) dry white wine (60 ml)

½ fl oz (1 tbs) D.O.M. Benedictine
  (15 ml)

Mix wine and Benedictine in a tall
glass.

Gently pour in champagne.

PINEAPPLE GIN COCKTAIL

HYATT REGENCY SINGAPORE, SINGAPORE
SERVES 1

1 ½ fl oz (3 tbs) gin (45 ml)

4 fl oz (½ c) pineapple juice (130 ml)

¾ fl oz (1½ tbs) Galliano (20 ml)

¾ fl oz (1½ tbs) Coco Lopez (20 ml)

⅓ fl oz (2 tsp) grenadine (10 ml)

½ c crushed ice

Put all ingredients in a shaker with crushed ice.

Shake well, then serve.

BLUE DANUBE COCKTAIL

ATRIUM HYATT BUDAPEST, HUNGARY
SERVES 1

¾ fl oz (1 ½ tbs) light rum (20 ml)

¾ fl oz (1 ½ tbs) blue Curaçao (20 ml)

¾ fl oz (1 ½ tbs) lemon juice (20 ml)

1 ½ fl oz (3 tbs) pineapple juice (45 ml)

½ c crushed ice

1 strawberry—for garnish

1 orange slice—for garnish

Mix all ingredients and pour into a tall glass with crushed ice.

Garnish with a strawberry and an orange slice.

HERMANA MAYOR

1 ½ fl oz (3 tbs) vodka (45 ml)

¾ fl oz (1 ½ tbs) rum (25 ml)

4 ½ fl oz (⅔ c) pineapple juice (150 ml)

3 fl oz (6 tbs) orange juice (90 ml)

3 dashes grenadine

2 dashes Anis del Mono or Pernod

¾ fl oz (1 ½ tbs) milk (20 ml)

¾ fl oz (1 ½ tbs) simple syrup (20 ml)
(see glossary)

1 lemon slice—for garnish

Shake drink ingredients in a shaker
and pour into a tall stemmed glass.

Garnish with a slice of lemon.

Serve with a straw.

THE BOROBUDUR COCKTAIL

HYATT REGENCY SURABAYA, INDONESIA

SERVES 1

Borobudur is an old
Buddhist Temple located
in Central Java. It was
constructed around 750
A.D. by a powerful and
wealthy ruler of the
Cailendra Dynasty. The
meaning of "Borobudur"
remains unexplained, but
might be a modification
of something from
Sanskrit meaning, "Com-
plex of Temples on the
Hill."

A second explanation is
offered by an inscription
dating back to the year
842 A.D., according to
which the word
"Borobudur" means
"Accumulation of Virtue
in the Ten Stages of the
Bodhisattvas.'

1 ¼ fl oz (3 tbs) coconut milk (35 ml)

1 fl oz (2 tbs) light rum (30 ml)

½ fl oz (1 tbs) Galliano (15 ml)

3 fl oz (6 tbs) orange juice (90 ml)

¼ fl oz (1 tsp) lime juice (5 ml)

3 fl oz (6 tbs) pineapple juice (90 ml)

⅓ fl oz (2 tsp) sugar syrup (10 ml)
(see glossary)

½ c crushed ice

½ slice orange—for decoration

Place all ingredients in a shaker with
crushed ice and shake well.

Strain and pour into a decorative glass.
Garnish with a half-slice of orange and
an orchid.

Moroccan Mint Tea

⌒

Casablanca Hyatt Regency, Morocco

Serves 1

½ fl oz (1 tsp) green tea (15 ml)
10 fresh mint sprigs—washed
5 tsp sugar (30 g)
1 ¼ pt (3 ⅓ c) boiling water (750 ml)

*Japanese green tea or Gunpowder tea
from Twinings may be substituted.*

Put tea, mint sprigs and sugar in a metal heatproof teapot.

⌒

Pour in boiling water and place over high heat for 3–5 minutes (until mint sprigs rise to top).

⌒

Remove from stove and mix tea well.

⌒

Pour hot liquid into tea glass until half-filled. Serve while still very warm.

Note: In Morocco, this is usually drunk before or after a meal, especially when the weather is very warm.

The Blossom

⌒

Hyatt Kingsgate Sydney, Australia

Serves 1

1 fl oz (2 tbs) tequila (30 ml)
1 fl oz (2 tbs) peach schnapps (30 ml)
1 fl oz (2 tbs) triple sec (30 ml)
1 fl oz (2 tbs) lemon juice (30 ml)
½ c crushed ice
3 drops grenadine
1 fresh strawberry—for garnish
1 lime twist—for garnish

Place all ingredients except grenadine and garnishes in a liquidiser and blend until smooth.

⌒

Put 3 drops of grenadine in a glass. Pour contents of liquidiser into glass.

⌒

Garnish with fresh strawberry and lime twist.

THE MEXICAN GALLEON

HYATT REGENCY CANCUN, MEXICO

SERVES 1

1 ½ fl oz (3 tbs) white rum (45 ml)

1 ½ fl oz (3 tbs) vodka (45 ml)

3 fl oz (6 tbs) orange juice (90 ml)

1 fl oz (2 tbs) grenadine (30 ml)

1 fl oz (2 tbs) Kahlua (30 ml)

½ c crushed ice (150ml)

5 tbs crushed pineapple (55 g)

1 small melon

pineapple slices, orange half-slices, and cherries—for serving (optional)

Mix ingredients in a shaker and shake for 10 seconds.

If desired, serve in a scooped out melon (see photo), decorated with sails of sliced pineapple on bamboo-skewer masts and orange half-slices along the hull. Secure with cherries held on by toothpicks.

Note: Drink can also be served in a very large glass.

GLOSSARY AND BASICS

Basic Beef or Lamb Stock

Makes 3 quarts (2.8 *l*)

Prepare like Basic Chicken Stock, but substitute 4–5 lb (2 kg) beef bones and 3 lb (1 ⅓ kg) beef shin meat.

Basic Chicken Stock

Makes 3 quarts (2.8 *l*)

6 lb chicken, cut up (2 ¾ kg)

3 lb chicken bones (necks, wings, and backs) (1 ⅓ kg)

3 oz (3 tbs) coarse salt (90 g)

6 oz (3 medium) carrots (180 g)

12 oz (6 small) leeks (340 g)

4 oz (1 large) onion (115 g)

2 oz (1 stalk) celery (55 g)

½ oz (1 tbs) salt (15 g)

5 qts water (4.7 *l*)

In a heavy-bottomed stockpot, place all ingredients and bring to a boil. Simmer, uncovered, for 3 hours, skimming foam from surface. Strain through a sieve and discard bones and vegetables. Cool, then chill and remove the solid fat on surface. Can be used immediately, stored in refrigerator for about 1 week, or up to 3 months.

Basic Fish Stock

Makes 2 quarts (1.9 *l*)

½ oz (1 tbs) butter (15 g)

4 oz (1 medium) onion (115 g)

2 oz (½ c) diced carrot (55 g)

2 oz (½ c) diced mushrooms (55 g)

4 lb fish bones and parts (heads, backbones, etc.) (1 ¾ kg)

2 qt water (1.9 *l*)

¼ oz (1 tsp) salt (7 g)

Fresh herbs of choice—bay leaf, dill, parsley, celery leaves

6 black peppercorns

In a heavy saucepan, melt butter and add onion, carrot and mushrooms. Stir to coat with butter, then add fish bones and remaining ingredients. Bring to a boil, then reduce heat and simmer, uncovered, for 1 hour. Strain through a sieve and discard solids.May be used immediately, stored in refrigerator for about 1 week, or frozen for 3 months.

Basic Vegetable Stock

Makes 2 quarts (1.9 *l*)

Prepare like fish stock, but substitute a selection of firm green and yellow vegetables in place of fish bones. Cook for about 45 minutes, or until vegetables are tender. Strain and use or store for future use.

Note: You can also assemble a mild vegetable stock by saving the cooking liquid from boiling beans, etc. After you cook the vegetables, save cooking liquid in freezer until you have about 1 quart. Bring to a boil in a wide saucepan and boil until slightly reduced and the flavour is intensified.

Brown Sauce

Makes 12 fl oz (1 ½ c; 360 ml)

There are many brown sauces in the classic French repertoire, but for the purposed of this book, use the following general recipe.

½ oz (1 tbs) butter (15 g)

½ oz (1 tbs) chopped onion (15 g)

¾ pt (1 ½ c) dry red wine (360 ml)

1 bay leaf

salt and black pepper to taste

bouquet of fresh herbs (parsley, thyme)

12 fl oz (1 ½ c) rich beef stock (360 ml)

Heat butter in a heavy saucepan and sauté onion until soft. Add wine and herb. Stir in the stock and reduce by two-thirds. Strain sauce through a sieve. Use immediately or store for 2–3 days.

Brown Veal Stock

Makes 2 quarts (1.9 *l*)

4 lb veal bones with some meat (1 ¾ kg)

vegetable oil for browning

5 qts water (4.7 *l*)

4 oz (2 medium) carrots (115 g)

1 lb (4 medium) onions (455 g)

4 oz (2 stalks) celery (115 g)

12 oz (3 medium) tomatoes (340 g)

½ oz (1 tbs) salt (15 g)

Place bones in heavy-bottomed pot and add oil. Stir to coat with oil, and brown bones until encrusted. Add water and bring to a boil. Skim off foam, then add vegetables and salt. Bring back to a boil and then reduce heat, cover pot and simmer stock for 4 hours. Strain through a sieve and discard solids. Cool, then chill and remove any solid fat on surface. May be used immediately or stored in refrigerator for 1 week, or frozen for up to 6 months.

COULIS (TOMATO)

A coulis is a purée of fruit or vegetables uncomplicated by the addition of herbs and spices. To make a tomato coulis, peel, remove pips and chop desired number of tomatoes, then place in a saucepan with a little melted butter. Sauté tomato bits until softened, then purée in liquidiser until smooth. Season to taste with salt and pepper.

DUXELLES

Makes about 4 oz (1 c; 115 g)

2 lb button mushrooms (900 g)
1 oz (2 tbs) butter (30 g)
2 shallots—minced
salt and pepper to taste

Chop mushrooms into tiny pieces and place in a muslin bag. Squeeze to eliminate as much liquid as possible. Melt butter in a wide skillet, then add shallots and mushrooms. Sauté mushrooms until they give up remaining liquid, shrink in volume, and pan becomes dry. Season with salt and pepper and store for future use.

GUACAMOLE

Makes about 12 fl oz (½ c; 360 ml)

1 oz (2 tbs) chopped onion (30 g)
1 small chilli—minced
2 sprigs fresh coriander
¼ tbs salt
6 oz (1 large) avocado (170 g)
5 oz (1 large) tomato (110 g)

Mash together the onion, chilli, coriander and salt. Peel avocado, remove stone and mash flesh. Mix with onion paste and stir well. Peel, remove pips and chop the tomato, then add tomato pieces to the avocado paste. Mix well and serve immediately, otherwise avocado will darken (To help prevent darkening, sprinkle guacamole with lemon or lime juice.)

LEMON BUTTER SAUCE

Melt desired amount of butter in a heavy saucepan over low heat. Add lemon juice to taste and stir to mix well. Sauce is ready to serve.

MEXICAN SAUCE

2 oz (½ c) fresh cilantro—finely minced (55 g)
3 chilli serrano
2 oz (1 small) white onion—chopped (55 g)
1 lb (4 medium) tomatoes—peeled and pips removed (455 g)
Juice of 1 lime
⅓ fl oz (2 tbs) olive oil (10 ml)

Combine all ingredients. Stir and refrigerate for one hour before using.

PASTA DOUGH

Makes about 1 lb (455 g)

8 oz (2 c) flour (240 g)
3 eggs
½ tbs salt
1 tbs olive (15 ml)

Place flour in a bowl and make a well in center. Break eggs into well and add salt and oil. Gradually incorporate flour into well, blending until you have a smooth dough. Incorporate only as much flour as the dough will absorb. Knead dough for a few minutes, then wrap and let rest in refrigerator for 30 minutes. Using a pasta machine, run dough through the series of opening widths until you have several thin sheets of dough. Then cut pasta dough into desired shapes and set aside to dry.

Note: To make flavoured pasta dough such as saffron pasta, soak a pinch of saffron in 1 tbs (15 ml) milk until softened. Add to well along with eggs and salt, then proceed.

PESTO SAUCE

Makes about 8 fl oz (1 c; 240 ml)

8 oz (2 c) fresh basil leaves (225 g)
8 fl oz (1 c) olive oil (240 ml)
2 oz (½ c) pine kernels (pignoli) (55 g)
2 oz (½ c) grated Parmesan cheese (55 g)

Place basil and oil in a liquidiser and purée until smooth. Add pine kernels and continue to process until smooth. Stir in the cheese and mix well. Use pesto immediately, or wrap tight and keep refrigerated until ready to use.

Port Wine Sauce
(Sauce Au Porto)

4 fl oz (½ c) port wine (118 ml)

½ tbs shallots—chopped (7 g)

sprig thyme

1 bay leaf

juice of 1 orange

juice of ½ lemon

pinch grated orange peel

7 fl oz (¾ c+2 tbs) veal stock—thickened

Mix all ingredients, heat over high flame and bring to a boil. Allow mixture to boil for a few minutes. Strain through muslin (cheesecloth).

Refried Beans

Mexicans prepare refried beans simply by putting cooked red beans in saucepan and heating, stirring to break up beans somewhat, so mixture is a blend of purée and bean pieces. The beans are cooked until paste-like, with little liquid remaining in pan. Refried beans can be made from tinned kidney beans or pinto beans.

Sugar Syrup
(for Drinks)

Combine equal parts water and sugar in saucepan and place over medium heat. Sugar will melt, but continue to cook until mixture becomes syrupy, about 5 minutes more. Let cool, then store for future use.

Tart Pastry

Makes enough dough
for 1, 9 inch (23 cm) tart

4 oz (8 tbs) butter

1 oz (2 tbs) sugar (30 g)

6 oz (1 ½ c) flour (170 g)

3-4 tbs cold water (45-60 ml)

Place butter, sugar and flour in large bowl. With 2 knives or a pastry blend, mix until it resembles coarse meal. Add water and mix until dough cleans the sides of the bowl and comes together in a ball. Wrap ball and refrigerate for about 30 minutes. Roll out dough into a circle about 10 inches (25 cm) in diameter and place in tart pan, fitting it loosely into pan and up sides. Roll a rolling pin over top of pan to cut off excess pastry. Let rest about 30 minutes. *To bake blind*: Grease a piece of foil and fit it into the crust. Line tart shell with baking weights or dried bean and bake crust in 375°F (190°C) over for 15 minutes. Remove weights and foil, prick bottom if it has bubbled up, and bake for an additional 10 minutes, or until the crust is lightly browned. *To fill and bake*: Follow recipe directions for filling and baking tart.

White Sauce

Makes 12 fl oz (1 ½ c; 360 ml)

2 oz (4 tbs) butter (55 g)

1 oz (¼ c) flour (30 g)

1 ¾ pt (3 ½ c) hot milk (1 *l*)

salt and white pepper to taste

freshly grated nutmeg

Melt butter in heavy saucepan. Add flour and stir, cooking flour for about 5 minutes. Gradually stir in the milk, turning the paste into a smooth sauce. Season with salt and pepper, and sprinkle on nutmeg. Use at once, or store for 1–2 days.

White Wine Sauce
(Sauce Au Vin Blanc)

¼ pt (½ c) fish fumet (reduced fish stock made with white wine)

2 egg yolks

5 oz (½ c) clarified butter (150 g)

salt and pepper to taste

½ tbs lemon juice (3 ml)

2 mushrooms—chopped

Boil the fish fumet until reduced by two-thirds. Allow to cool slightly and add 2 egg yolks. Whisk over a gentle heat, as for hollandaise sauce. As soon as the yolks thicken to a cream consistency, whisk in the clarified butter, a little at a time. Season with salt and pepper. Add the lemon juice and mushrooms. Rub through a fine sieve and reheat, but do not boil. Serve warm.

A

Achiote: This is the pip of the annatto tree. It is sometimes sold in a paste form, but most often only the hard pips are available, usually in Mexican groceries. Soak the pips in warm water to soften before using.

Al Dente: An Italian expression meaning "to the teeth" indicating the correct degree of cooking for pasta. The stage is reached when the pasta is still a bit resistant to the bite and it is firm, slightly chewy, and has no taste of raw flour. When the al dente stage is reached, the pasta is drained, tossed with butter and seved in heated dishes. If the pasta is not to be served immediately, it may be cooked and rinsed with cold water, heated, and seasoned with butter later.

B

Bell Pepper (Capsicum): Though known by different names in different parts of the world, both names refer to the bell-shaped fruit of the pepper plant, *capsicum frutescens grossum*. It is available in red, yellow, purple, orange, ivory and green colours, each having a slightly different taste, ranging from the sweetest (red), to slightly bitter (green). It can be eaten raw or cooked, and is used in all the great cuisines of the world.

C

Cactus Leaves (Nopales): These are the leaves of the prickly pear cactus. The spines are removed and the leaves are steamed or pickled. Fresh leaves are available in Mexican markets; if unavailable, substitute jarred leaves.

Candlenuts: These are raw macadamia nuts, often used crushed. If unavailable, substitute roasted macadamia nuts, but rinse off salt if nuts have been salted for snacking.

Cardamom: Cardamom pods are white or light green and have a husk that encloses a cluster of small, round black seeds. Some recipes call for pips themselves, while others used the pod with husk.

Chayote: Also called the vegetable pear (and, in Asian cooking, the chaya), the chayote is a squash-like vegetable. Peel and steam for best flavour.

Chillies: Mexican cuisine make heavy use of chillies of varying hotness and flavour. In addition, both dried and fresh chillies are used for stuffings, sauces and flavourings. There are several varieties of fresh chillies. *Serrano chillies* are small and smooth, mostly rounded, averaging about 1 ½ inches long. They are fleshy and spicy. *Jalapeño chillies* are about 3 inches long and moderately hot. *Poblano chillies* vary in shape and size but are usually large, about 5 inches long. They are roasted and peeled before being used. Of the dried chillies, *ancho* is the ripened version of the poblano. After soaking, it becomes a rich dark red. *Pasilla chillies* are long and slender, most black in colour and about 6 inches long. They are very sharp and rich tasting. *Guajillo chillies* are smooth, with a brownish-red skin, and about 4 ½ inches long. They are very hot. *Chipotle chillies* are light brown, with a wrinkled skin and smokey taste. They are the basis for the adobo sauce. *Cascabel chillies* are similar to guajillos, with a pleasant nutty flavour.

Chilli Sauce: There are a multitude of sauces made from chillies, but the common chilli sauce sold in supermarkets is a basic red or green chilli sauce used mostly for quick flavouring and as dipping sauce.

Chinese/Oriental Ingredients (Miscellaneous): *Jellyfish* is frequently used in Asian cooking. It is usually sold dried and must be reconstituted before use. Cover pieces with cold water and soak overnight, changing water at least once. Parboil the jellyfish the next day before using. *Seaweed* consists primarily of kelp and laver (nori). Kelp is sold fresh or dried; laver is available as a dried sheet. The Asian form of gelatine, agar-agar, is from a seaweed, too. *Lotus root* is actually a rhizome which, when cut crosswise, reveals a pattern of holes. When shopping for lotus root, look for firm pieces. Once you cut it, keep it in water to prevent discolouration. *Taro* is a starchy tuber. In the market, look for tubers that are firm and unblemished, with hairy skin and sharp rings. *Gingko nuts* are sold fresh in season, abundant in Chinese and Japanese markets. They are oval, with a buff exterior. *Jujubes* are also known as Chinese red dates. They should be soaked overnight before use, and are used mostly in sweet dishes.

Chinese/Oriental Sauces: There are many sauces and pastes used in Chinese cooking. *Soy sauce* is well known, but watch for the difference between dark and light soy sauce. Dark soy sauce is aged longer and mixed with molasses. *Oyster sauce* is a mixture of oysters, water, salt and cornflour; it is an all-purpose seasoning. *Plum sauce* is a sweet dipping sauce. *Fermented black beans* and *salted black beans* are readily available in Asian markets. They are usually crushed or puréed, and added for flavouring. There are several types of soybean paste, with a variety of names: *yellow bean paste, brown bean sauce, bean paste*. They are sold in tins and available at Asian markets. When chillies are added, they are usually sold as *hot bean paste. Sweet bean paste* is a mixture of azuki beans and sugar, used mostly in sweet dishes. *Miso* is a paste made from fermented soybeans; it comes in a variety of colours, packed in tins, packets, and bottles. *Shrimp paste* is a firm reddish mixture of dried shrimp and salt; when the mixture is more liquid, it is called *shrimp sauce*. Either way, it is extremely strong in taste. *Chilli paste, chilli sauce,* and *chilli oil* are condiments whose primary ingredient is chilli. They are very hot, so use with care.

Cilantro (Also called Fresh Coriander, Chinese Parsley-"Fragrant Green," or Mexican Parsley): This variety of names refers to one and the same herb; (Latin, *Coriandrum*; Greek, *Koriandron*). It is medium green in colour and has a willowy stem supporting broad, flat, serrated leaves. Strong, distinctly flavoured and highly aromatic, this herb differs greatly from curly-leafed parsley

(Latin, *Petroselinum*). When a recipe calls for ground coriander, it refers to a spice made from the dried seeds of the same plant. Its sweet pungent flavour, reminiscent of sage and lemon peel, is extremely different from that of the fresh leaves, thus ground coriander can never be substituted for fresh coriander. This herb, known by many different names, is used in cooking all over the world. It is sold fresh by weight. To use, wash, remove stems and use the leaves whole or chopped.

Coconut Milk: Several recipes call for coconut milk. The liquid inside a coconut is considered its " water," whereas coconut milk is the pressed juice of the pulp. To make fresh coconut milk, break coconut in a liquidiser with about ¾ pint (1 ½ cups or 355 ml) water, then purée. Strain the mixture through cheese-cloth or muslin; the resulting milky liquid is coconut milk, the first pressing is the thickest, sometimes referred to as "coconut cream." Coconut milk is also sold in tins, available in Asian groceries.

Coriander Pips: These are small round pips that are used either whole or in ground form. Do not use dried coriander or coriander pips as a substitute for fresh coriander (Chinese parsley or cilantro).

Couscous: This is a cereal steamed and served with meats. Couscous grains must be sifted to eliminate lumps. Quick-cooking couscous is available in many groceries.

Cream: Recipes call for *double (heavy) cream*, which has a butterfat content of about 38 percent. This cream will increase in volume when whipped. *Half and half* is a 50-50 mixture of double (heavy) cream and whole milk. *Créme fraîche* is lightly fermented cream, make by mixing 1 tablespoon (15 ml) of buttermilk with 8 fluid ounces (1 cup or 240 ml) cream. Cover and let sit at room temperature for about 12 hours; the resulting cream will have thickened slightly and have a mild tartness. *Créme fraîche* can be whipped.

Curry Leaves: These are from the curry plant, and the leaves are used as an aromatic seasoning. There is no relationship to curry powder.

D

Deglaze: When foods are sautéed in a skillet, the browned particles that stick to the pan can be used to enhance a simple sauce. Deglazing is the technique of adding some liquid to the pan (usually wine, vinegar, or water), bringing it to boil and scraping up the particles to make a flavourful liquid.

F

Fish and Shellfish: Different species of fish and shellfish inhabit different regions of the world, so it is not always possible to duplicate a recipe that includes these ingredients. Whenever possible, we have offered a substitute or provided a description of the original so that you can find a suitable substitute from your region. Bear in mind also that same term may be used for different species in varying parts of the world. For example, the Australian term "crayfish" is the same crustacean that Europeans call a " spiny lobster." The recipes have been made as universal as possible by giving alternative names when applicable.

Fish Sauce: A dark, clear liquid made from fermented fish or shrimp, and used as a seasoning. It is called *patis* in the Philippines and *nuoc mam* in Vietnam.

Flavoured Vinegars: Recipes sometimes use fruit-flavoured vinegars such as raspberry vinegar. These are available in gourmet groceries, or you can make your own by steeping 4 ounces (1 cup) fresh raspberries in 2 pints (4 ¼ cups or liter) distilled white vinegar for two weeks. Balsamic vinegar is wine vinegar that has been aged to acquire a robust flavour. It is available in gourmet food stores.

Fresh Herbs (Chinese/Oriental): The most common fresh herb is fresh coriander, or Chinese parsley. Since it plays such a big role in many other cuisines as well, fresh coriander is readily available. Dried coriander is not a suitable substitute.

Fruits: Although modern-day shipping methods bring fresh fruits to markets all over the world, it is still not possible to ship especially tender or perishable fruits. Consequently, tropical fruits rarely reach local markets in other parts of the world. These recipes frequently use exotic fruits; our suggestion is to use the fresh ingredient when possible or, substitute the tinned variety, if available.

G

Garam Masala: An aromatic mix of spices, including cardamom, cinnamon, cumin, cloves, pepper and nutmeg. You can make your own version or buy a prepared mix in any Indian grocery.

Ghee: This is the Indian word for clarified butter. Indian cooks prefer to use clarified butter when sautéeing foods and seasonings. To make clarified butter, melt butter in a saucepan over low heat until liquid separates into a foamy top, a clear liquid center, and a milky residue on the bottom. Spoon off the foam and use the clear liquid, discarding the milky solids on the bottom.

Ginger: Fresh root ginger is a rhizome, or underground stem, that Asians use to flavour foods and lend a clean spiciness. It is commonly available. To use, peel and grate or slice, as recipe directs. Do not substitute dried ginger. Young ginger is softer and more delicate; it is less common and is not a substitute for ginger. Instead, it is usually sold as pickled ginger.

Green Tomatoes (Tomatillos): These husk-covered green vegetables appear similar to tomatoes, but taste sharper. They are available fresh in Mexican markets or tinned at specialty shops.

H

Hoisin Sauce: A thick, sweet, mahogany-coloured sauce made from soybeans, flour, vegetables, chilli, red beans and red colour, available in cans or jars. It has a sweet, pungent, slightly garlicky taste and is used as a seasoning or condiment.

K

Kaffir lime: The leaves of the Kaffir lime tree are used as a flavouring agent because they have a strong flavour and fragrance. They are available dried.

L

Lemongrass: The stems of this plant are used for their lemon flavour. Lemongrass is sold both fresh and dried, although the fresh is preferred for most recipes.

M

Masa Harina: This is a finely ground meal made from husked corn kernels. It is the basis for corn tortillas. If unavailable, substitute a fine white cornmeal.

Mushrooms (Chinese/Oriental): Asian cuisine encompasses a vast array of fresh and dried mushrooms and fungi. The most common is the *Chinese dried black mushroom*, which is a large, fleshy mushroom (when fresh, these are also called shiitake); soak them in hot water for 30 minutes, then drain and discard the woody stems. *Tree ears*, *cloud ears*, *white tree fungus* and the like are delicate fungi used sparingly in Chinese cooking. They are available dried in most Asian groceries and must be soaked before use. *Enoki* are fresh, pencil-thin mushrooms, now sold in many supermarkets.

O

Oils (Chinese/Oriental): The *sesame oil* used in Asian cooking is an oil made from roasted sesame seeds. It is not the same as the lighter cooking oil also called sesame oil. When a recipe specifies "oriental sesame oil", it is a reference to roasted sesame oil and is used as a seasoning, not as a frying oil. *Chilli oil* is cooking oil flavoured with chillies. It is available in most Asian markets.

Oils (Western/European): Most recipes use vegetable oil, whether for sautéeing or deep-frying. Occasionally, recipes use peanut oil for deep-frying, since it has a greater resistance to smoking at high temperatures. Walnut or hazelnut oil is mostly used for flavouring salad dressings and when the taste of the nut should come through. Grape seed oil, which is more readily available in Europe and Australia, can be substituted by vegetable oil.

P

Palm Sugar: This is the sugar made from the palmyra palm. It is grainy and sticky, often sold in a brick that must be softened with hot water before use. If unavailable, substitute brown sugar.

Pandan: The long, spikelike leaves of this plant are used as a flavouring and for colour, sometimes also called pandanus leaf or screw pine. Dried leaves are sold in Asian markets, and the flavour is also bottled , in concentrated form.

Pastry: Several recipes call for phyllo pastry, or phyllo sheets. This is a Greek pastry dough that is sold in paper-thin sheets which can be used as a wrapper, especially when brushed with melted butter and stacked. Phyllo (or filo) dough is sold in supermarkets and gourmet food stores. Puff pastry is used in a few dessert recipes; this French pastry dough can be made at home using your favourite recipe, or be purchased as frozen puff pastry at gourmet food shops.

Pork Cutlet: A chop cut from the best end of neck of pork.

Prove: To increase in volume the dough using a raising agent. To make the dough rise it should be placed away from draughts in a warm temperature (25-30°C, 75-80°F). While it is proving the dough should be covered with a cloth to prevent the formation of a crust.

R

Rice, Noodles and Wrappers: Recipes in the book call either steamed *white rice* or *glutinous (or sticky or sweet) rice*. The latter is short-grain rice whose starchiness in employed to bind ingredients in certain dishes. It is available as a refined white rice and also with the bran, when it is called black glutinous rice. The noodles in these recipes are either *fresh egg noodles*, or mein, or else mung beam noodles (also called *cellophane noodles* or *bean threads*). The egg noodles should be cooked until al dente; cellophane noodles need to be soaked in hot water for about 30 minutes before use in a recipe. *Wonton skins* or *wrappers* are thin squares or circles of wheat pastry, ideal for stuffing. *Spring roll wrappers* are thinner and more delicate, also good for stuffing. Both are sold fresh or frozen in Asian markets. *Tofu sheets* are wrappers made of soybean milk. They are sold fresh or dried; dried sheets must be soaked before use.

Roux: A roux is a flour and butter paste used to thicken sauces. Usually, the butter is melted in a sauce pan, then flour is added and the mixture is stirred until smooth and tight. The roux is cooked for a few minutes to cook the flour, then liquid is usually added to make the sauce.

S

Saffron: a spice consisting of the dried stigmas of the saffron crocus, a plant originating in the East and cultivated in Spain and other Mediterranean regions. It is also cultivated in Greece, Iran, and South America. The best saffron comes from Valencia in Spain and takes the form of dried brownish filaments or an orange-yellow powder with a pungent smell and bitter flavour. As it is very expensive, safflower or turmeric may be substituted—as paraphrased from *Larousse Gastronomique* edited by Jenifer Harvey Lang, 1988.

Salad Green: Crisp green salads call for local greens, and you should substitute whatever lettuces and other salad ingredients are available locally. We've offered suggestions in the recipes, but feel free to make your own substitutions.

Sambal Ulek: This is a hot Indonesian seasoning consisting mainly of ground chillies. It can be made from scratch or purchased in a jar.

Sambal Tomat: This is a spicy Javanese tomato stew; substitute a spicy tomato sauce if unavailable.

Scallions: Scallions, shallots, leeks and chives belong to the onion family. Scallions, or spring onions are marketed in bunches and both the white part and green tops may be eaten raw or cooked. Shallots have bulbs that may be divided, like garlic.

Sealegs: Any firm white fish can be substituted.

Seasoning: Some recipes call for Worcestershire Sauce, which is a patented blend of flavourings that is dark and spicy. Tabasco is a proprietary blend of hot pepper and vinegar. Both are commonly available in Western markets and groceries.

Shrimp Paste: The Southeast Asian version of this condiment/seasoning is also known as belacan, blachen or terasi. Bagoong is fermented shrimp paste.

Simple Syrup: Sugar dissolved in water and used to sweeten cold drinks. Same as sugar syrup.

Soy Sauce (Indonesian): Also called sweet soy sauce or kecap manis, this is a dark, richer tasting soy sauce.

Sumak: This is the crushed berry of a species of the sumak tree. It has a sour, lemony taste. Use only commercially packaged sumak, available in Middle Eastern groceries as Armenian sumak.

T

Tahina: An oily paste of ground raw white sesame seeds popular throughout the Middle East. Available in many supermarkets, health food stores and Middle Eastern groceries.

Tamarind Pulp: This flesh of the tamarind pod is available in tins. Lemon juice can be substituted to duplicate the sharp taste.

Toasting Nuts, Pips or Chillies: Toasted nuts and pips enhance flavour to recipes: when a recipe calls for toasted nuts or pips, place them in a dry skillet and toast over medium heat until light brown; do not allow to burn or scorch.

Tofu: Tofu, or soybean curd, is a staple of Asian cooking. Both soft and firm cakes are sold widely, in Asian markets and also in supermarkets. Look for fresh cakes with no off aroma, and keep covered with cold water until used.

Tortillas: This round, flat pancake-like bread is made from either flour or cornmeal (masa harina). Tortillas are often filled with cheese or meat, or served alongside a meat dish as a bread.

Turmeric: The root of a plant in the ginger family, turmeric is used in ground form as a colouring agent and seasoning. It turns most foods a bright yellow-orange, and therefore is often used as a poor substitute for saffron.

U

Unmoulding Puddings: When a recipe instructs you to unmould a pudding or mousse, you can make the process easier by gently warming the mould before flipping it upside down. Gently lower the mould into a pan of hot water and immediately lift it up again. This warms the contact area between mousse and mould, and allows the mousse to slip out of the mould without breaking or sticking.

V

Vietnamese Rice Papers: These are brittle sheets of rice paper, used as a wrapper for spring rolls. Soften before use by moistening.

W

Water Bath: Often, to bake a delicate custard, or to melt chocolate without scorching, or to cook a soufflé, the dish is placed in a larger pan of hot water and baked or cooked according to directions. The cushion of hot water makes for uniform heat and more even cooking.

Y

Yams: These round or elongated edible tubers come from tropical climbing plants cultivated in Africa, Asia and America. The flesh is white, yellow or pink, while the skin may be rough or smooth, with a white, pink, yellow or blackish-brown colour (depending on the variety). Yielding 102 calories per 100 grams, a yam has a very high starch content and is a basic food in many tropical countries. Very small yams can be cooked in their skins. Larger ones, weighing up to 20 kg (45 lbs), are peeled, washed in cold water, and blanched for 10–20 minutes in boiling salted water. They can then be used the same way as potatoes or sweet potatoes (in soups, ragouts. purées, soufflés, croquettes, fritters, gratins, chips, etc., as well as various sweet dishes). A starch extract from yams called "Guiana arrowroot" is widly used in cookery and confectionery. Yams can be substituted by potatoes or sweet potatoes.

Correction:

P. 76 -
"Japanese" should read "Javanese."

INDEX

APPETIZERS

Carpaccio of Fallow Deer with Paua 56

Ceviche caracol
Sea Conch Cocktail 56

Chicken Kelaguin 37

Chicken Quenelles with Gippsland
Blue Cheese Sauce 40

Camarones Con Coco y Cerveza Batida
Coconut Beer-Batter Shrimp 34

*Currys Rizzsel Toltott Paprika
Nemzeti Szinekben*
Stuffed Bell Peppers with Curry Sauce 28

Deep-Fried Mushrooms Stuffed with Kosher
Seafood on a Saffron-Basil Sauce 50

Deep-Fried Squid Balls 41

Fried Feta on Assorted Lettuce with Mint
Vinaigrette 29

Gado-gado
Vegetable Skewers with Coconut and
Peanut Sauce 46

Hummus
Chickpeas with Sesame Seed Paste 63

Lamb-Stuffed Mushroom Caps with
Wild Rice 53

Lobster-Stuffed Squid in Carrot Sauce 58

Marinated Tasmanian Salmon with Fresh
Herbs 55

Marron in Papaya and Chilli Sauce 48

Masala Lassi
Herbed Yoghurt Drink 47

*Mini Pastilla Bil Halazoun oua
Salsat Charmoula*
Escargot Wonton with Moroccan
Charmoula Sauce 45

Pinoy Enchiladas
Pork-Stuffed Tortillas 36

Poisson Cru a la Tahitienne
Marinated Tuna Tahitian Style 38

Prawn Taboulet 37

Rillettes aux Deux Saumons
Potted Salmon with Fresh Coriander 52

Shredded Roast Duck and Jellyfish 33

Smoked Salmon and Potato Terrine 35

Smoked Salmon Egg Rolls on
Mixed Greens 61

Smoked Tasmanian Salmon and Shiitake
Mushroom Salad 42

Smoked Venison in a Passion Fruit Vinaigrette
with Mandarin Oranges and Grapes 51

Spatchcock Breast with Squash Blossoms and
Mustard Sprouts 47

Stuffed Choy Sum with Wild Mushrooms and
Rice on a Tomato-Basil Coulis 62

Stuffed Clam Shell 60

Sweet and Sour Snail Wonton 54

Tacos de Camarones
Prawn Tacos 32

Warm Pacific Prawn Salad with Avocado,
Mango and Curried Dill Sauce 39

Water Buffalo Terrine with Kakadu Plums in
Port Wine Glaze 30

Yabbies in Leek Papillotes with Mushroom
Ravioli 43

SOUPS

Artichoke Cream with Hazelnuts 83

Baby Papaya with Crabmeat 98

Caldo de Pulpo con Mezcal
Octopus Soup with Mexican Liqueur 88

Chilled Corn Chowder with Avocado and
Crabmeat 94

Chilled Mango and Cucumber Soup 92

Chilled Papaya Soup with Crabmeat 79

Chilled Strawberry and Mango Soup 78

Chilled Watercress and Avocado Soup 68

Chorba Bil Kamh
Ground Wheat Germ Soup 79

Cold Green Asparagus Soup 97

Deritett Gulyasleves
Clear Goulash Soup 69

Fish Dumpling Soup with Herbs 72

Hot and Sour Soup 93

Hot and Sour Tofu Soup 70

Max's Seafood Soup 73

Mee Sup Pedas
Spicy Seafood Mee Soup 84

Melon Soup with Pink Shrimp 96

Mushroom Essence with
Pistachio Quenelles 71

Onion and Herb Soup with Lamb Shanks 87

Prawn Mee Soup 80

Seafood Chowder Served in an Pumpkin 74

Sinigang Na Hipon
Filipino Shrimp Soup 86

Sopa de Medula
Marrow Soup 99

*Sopa de Tomate e Brocus con
Chourico Chines*
Broccoli and Tomato Soup Garnished with
Chinese Sausage 90

Soup Buntut
Nutmeg-Flavoured Dark Oxtail Soup 76

Spring Vegetable and Coconut Milk Soup
with Frogs' Legs 89

Tomato Soup with Coconut 91

Tom Yam Kung
Prawn Soup 85

Wontons with Salmon Mousse in a Fennel
Chicken Consomée 82

SALADS

Avacado Salad with Tomato and Egg 114

Avocado and Smoked Salmon Salad 106

Cham Chi Salad with Gul Sauce
Red Leaf Lettuce and Marinated Tuna
and Honey Dressing 136

Crispy Ratatouille in Phyllo Pastry on Diced
Tomatoes Flavoured with Herbs 108

*Ensalada de Calamares con Alcachofas
y una Vinagreta de Chile Dulce*
Calamari and Artichoke Salad with a
Sweet Pepper Vinaigrette 134

Ensalada de Chaya y Duraznillos
Chaya and Chanterelle Salad 130

*Ensalada de Endibias, Aguacate, y Elote
con Salsa de Olivo*
Witloof, Avocado and Corn Salad with
Olive Oil Dressing 139

*Ensalada de Los Chiles Pimiento
Morron con Crepas de Elote*
Three Pepper Salad with Corn Crepes 104

Ensalada de Nopalitos
Cactus Salad 121

*Ensalada de Palmitos con
Majillones Marinados*
Avocado-Palm Hearts Salad with
Marinated Mussels 126

Ensaladang Talong
Warm Filipino Eggplant Salad 119

Fatoush Salad in a Crisp Basket 138

Fresh Lobster Salad with Saffron Mango
Dressing and Stuffed Lychees 109

Glass Noodle Salad with Seafood and
Crabmeat 112

Lobster and Tropical Fruit Salad 127

Noodle Salad with Fresh Orange 141

Poulet au Curry et Salade de Riz
Curried Chicken and Rice Salad 130

Prawn Salad in Chilli Lime Dressing 132

Red Emperor Fish on Garden Salad with
a Toasted Pine Kernel Vinaigrette 120

Roast Quail Salad with Grilled Courgettes
and Spinach with a Balsamic Olive-Oil
Dressing 124

Rojak Betik Muda
Young Papaya Salad 110

*Salada de Espinafres, Abacate Azeitonas e
Laranja Com Molho de Mel e Gekigibre*
Spinich, Avocado, Olives and Orange Salad,
Honey and Ginger Dressing 111

Salad of Belgian Endive with Pears and
Roquefort Cheese 140

Salata Bil Fatayer
Crispy Salad on Pitta Bread 107

Shredded Carrot and Radish Salad
with Smoked Salmon 118

Smoked Lamb and Goat Cheese Salad
with Tomato Chutney 128

Spinach Salad with Chicken Livers and
Raspberry Vinaigrette 137

Spring Salad with Warm Lamb Loin 125

Tender Scallops Sauteed in
Café de Paris Butter served with Chilled Apples
and Cheese Salad 122

Tropical King Prawn Salad 115

Warm Salad of Rabbit with a
Macadamia Nut Dressing 131

Yam Nua
Thai Beef Salad 116

POULTRY

MEAT

FISH AND SEAFOOD

PASTA AND NOODLES

PERFECT BALANCE

This project disproves the old adage that "too many cooks spoil the broth." Over fifty talented and technically proficient chefs in 30 countries are responsible for this book.

Andreas Stalder, corporate culinary authority for Hyatt International Hotels, was instrumental in the massive job of collecting and editing the recipes. His special interest in today's marriage of cuisines flavours the final product.

Mr. Stalder assists in the development of new food concepts for Hyatt International Hotels, is actively involved in establishing Hyatt's culinary approach worldwide, and is a member of numerous international culinary associations.

Without the specific input of the following chefs, there would be no book. We are deeply appreciative to all of them and their local kitchen teams.

Christian Alunno	Hyatt Regency Rabat
Gunther Angermann	Hyatt Regency Hong Kong
Rainer Becker	Park Hyatt Sydney
Roland Becker	Hyatt Continental Montreux
Dieter Bender	Hyatt Regency Macau
	Hyatt Regency Belgrade
Cristobal Blanco	Hotel Villa Magna,
	A Park Hyatt Hotel
Gunther Bohuslav	Hyatt Regency Coolum
Stefan Bollhalder	Hyatt Regency Cologne
Josef Budde	Grand Hyatt Hong Kong
Francis Drillien	U.N. Plaza, A Park Hyatt Hotel
Bruno Christen	Hyatt On Collins Melbourne
Peter Cole	Hyatt Aryaduta Jakarta
Marc Cosyns	Hyatt Regency Jerusalem
Rene Fernandez	Hyatt Regency Cancun
Hans Fillistorf	Hyatt Regency Guadalajara
Robert Fischer	Hyatt Regency Riyadh
Bernard Gaume	The Carlton Tower,
	A Park Hyatt Hotel
Roger Gustavson	Grand Hyatt Erawan Bangkok
Atilano Guzman	Hyatt Hotel Villahermosa
Peter Haefeli	Hyatt Coral Grand, Puerto Vallarta
Rainer Holzmann	Hyatt Regency Acapulco
Mak Hung	Grand Hyatt Taipei
Urs Inauen	Hyatt Regency Adelaide
Hartmut Kehm	Hyatt Regency Xian
Stephen King	Hyatt Auckland

Christopher Koehler	Hyatt Regency Manila
Roger Lienhard	Hyatt Regency Perth
Hubert Lorenz	Bali Hyatt
Istvan Lukacs	Atrium Hyatt Budapest
William Marshall	Hyatt Regency Jeddah
	Hyatt Regency Birmingham
Karl Moser	Hyatt Saujana
Harmohinder Oberoi	Hyatt Regency Delhi
Koreyoshi Okamura	Centry Hyatt Tokyo
Anthony Owen	Hyatt Tianjin
Lalit Pandit	Hyatt Kingsgate Sydney
Gerard Percheron	Hyatt Cancun Caribe
Andre Perez	Hyatt Regency Tahiti
Walter Raeber	The Hotel Canberra,
	A Park Hyatt Hotel
Mokhtar Ramdani	Hyatt Regency Casablanca
Gerd Sankowski	Hyatt Regency Cheju
Peter Schatzmann	Hyatt Regency Sanctuary Cove
Roger Seitz	Hyatt Regency Pusan
Heinz von Holzen	Hyatt Regency Singapore
	Grand Hyatt Bali
August Wehrle	Hyatt Kuantan
Klaus Wiemeyer	Hyatt Regency Dubai
Anton Wuersch	Hyatt Regency Surabaya
Jean-Claude Weibel	Hyatt Regency Seoul
	Grand Hyatt Jakarta
Ralf Wiedman	Hyatt Kinabalu
Hans Peter Zindel	Hyatt Regency Saipan